Architect
of Reformation

Architect
of Reformation

An Introduction to Heinrich Bullinger,
1504–1575

Edited by
Bruce Gordon and Emidio Campi

WIPF & STOCK · Eugene, Oregon

Wipf and Stock Publishers
199 W 8th Ave, Suite 3
Eugene, OR 97401

Architect of Reformation
An Introduction to Heinrich Bullinger, 1504-1575
By Gordon, Bruce and Campi, Emidio
Copyright©2004 Baker Publishing Group
ISBN 13: 978-1-5326-7916-2
Publication date 1/16/2019
Previously published by Baker, 2004

Table of Contents

Part II: Humanism, Politics and Family

Notes on Contributors

Daniel Bolliger works in the Institute for Swiss Reformation History in Zurich. His book *Infiniti contemplatio. Grundzüge der Scotus- und Scotismusrezeption im Werk Huldrych Zwinglis* (2003) received the 2001 J.F.G. Goeters Prize.

Emidio Campi is professor of Church History in the Theological Faculty of the University of Zurich and Director of the Institute for Swiss Reformation History. His publications include (ed) *Peter Martyr Vermigli. Humanism, Republicanism, Reformation* (2002) and *Zwingli und Maria. Eine reformationsgeschichtliche Studie* (1997).

Roland Diethelm is *Assistent* in the Institute for Swiss Reformation History in Zurich and is writing a doctoral dissertation on Heinrich Bullinger and Reformed Worship.

Edward A. Dowey was professor of the History of Christian Doctrine at Princeton Theological Seminary. He was the author of *The Knowledge of God in Calvin's Theology* (1952) and of numerous works on Reformed theology.

Carrie E. Euler is a graduate student at Johns Hopkins University finishing a dissertation entitled "Religious and Cultural Exchange during the Reformation: Zurich and England, 1531-1558." From 2005 she will be a postdoctoral fellow at the Folger Shakespeare Library in Washington, DC.

Bruce Gordon is Reader in Modern History and Deputy Director of the Reformation Studies Institute in the University of St Andrews. His recent publications include *The Swiss Reformation* (2002) and (with Peter Marshall) *The Place of the Dead. Death and Remembrance in Late Medieval and Early Modern Europe* (2000).

Rainer Henrich is senior editor of the Heinrich Bullinger Correspondence (*Bullinger Briefwechsel Edition*) in Zurich. He has written numerous articles on aspects of Zurich Reformation history.

Elsie Mckee is Archibald Alexander Professor of Reformation Studies and the History of Worship at Princeton Theological Seminary. Her *The Writings of Katharina Schutz Zell* (2 vols) appeared in 1998.

Christian Moser is a doctoral student in the theological faculty of the University of Zurich working on Heinrich Bullinger as historian. His principal publication is (with Martin Graf) *Strenarum lanx. Beiträge zur Philogie und Geschichte des Mittelalters und der Frühen Neuzeit* (2003).

Andreas Mühling is *Privatdozent* for Church History at the University of Lucerne. He is the author of *Karl Ludwig Schmidt* (1997) and *Heinrich Bullingers europäische Kirchenpolitik* (2001).

Peter Opitz is *Oberassistent* in the Institute for Swiss Reformation History in Zurich and editor of *Zwingliana*. He is producing a critical edition of Bullinger's *Decades* and is editor of the six-volume translation of Bullinger's works into German. His publications include *Calvins theologische Hermeneutik* (1994) and a study of the theology of Bullinger's *Decades* (forthcoming).

Kurt Jakob Rüetschi is an editor of the Bullinger Correspondence in Zurich and a specialist on the life and work of Rudolf Gwalther, on whom he has published extensively. He has also written widely on aspects of the Zurich Reformation in their European context.

Mark Taplin works for the Scottish Parliament in Edinburgh. He is the author of *The Italian Reformers and the Zurich Church, c. 1540-1620* (2003).

Series Preface

The heritage of the Reformation is of profound importance to the church in the present day. Yet there remain many significant gaps in our knowledge of the intellectual development of Protestantism in the sixteenth century, and there are not a few myths about the theology of the Protestant orthodox writers of the late sixteenth and seventeenth centuries. These gaps and myths, frequently caused by ignorance of the scope of a particular thinker's work, by negative theological judgments passed on the theology of the Reformers or their successors by later generations, or by an intellectual imperialism of the present that singles out some thinkers and ignores others regardless of their relative significance to their own times, stand in the way of a substantive encounter with this important period in our history. Understanding and appropriation of that heritage can occur only through the publication of significant works—monographs and sound, scholarly translations—that present the breadth and detail of the thought of the Reformers and their successors.

Texts and Studies in Reformation and Post-Reformation Thought proposes to make available such works as Caspar Olevianus's *Firm Foundation,* Theodore Beza's *Table of Predestination,* and Jerome Zanchi's *Confession of Faith,* together with significant monographs on traditional Reformed theology, under the guidance of an editorial board of recognized scholars in the field. Major older work's, like Heppe's *Reformed Dogmatics,* will be reprinted or reissued with new introductions. These works, moreover, are intended to address two groups: an academic and a confessional or chruchly audience. The series recognizes the need for careful, scholarly treatment of the Reformation and of the era of Protestant orthodoxy, given the continuing presence of misunderstandings particularly of the later era in both the scholarly and the popular literature as well as the recent interest in reappraising the relationship of the Reformation to Protestant orthodoxy. In addition, however, the series hopes to provide the church at large with worthy documents from its rich heritage and thereby to support and to stimulate interest in the roots of the Protestant tradition.

Richard A. Muller

Preface

This collection of essays on Heinrich Bullinger has been prepared for the 500th anniversary of the reformer's birth. The purposes of the book are to attempt to draw together recent scholarship on Bullinger and to stimulate further research. The volume is the first fruit of a formal agreement of co-operation, signed in 2001, between the St Andrews Reformation Studies Institute and the Institut für Schweizerische Reformationsgeschichte in Zurich. It is envisaged that this arrangement will lead to a range of shared activities in the future, including study exchanges, conference sessions, books, and informal colloquia. To inaugurate our collaboration, members of the Zurich Institute came to St Andrews in September 2002 for a three-day workshop on Bullinger at which it was decided to prepare this volume. This book also presents an opportunity to publish an important essay by the late Ed Dowey, who passed away last spring. It was Professor Dowey's intention to write a book on Bullinger, but that, sadly, could not come to pass. We are delighted to be able to make available *in extenso* his expansive treatment of Bullinger's theological vision. For this we thank Elsie McKee.

The editors are grateful to a number of people for their assistance. Rona Johnston Gordon once again threw herself into the world of Heinrich Bullinger with characteristic willingness and humour and assisted greatly with the translation and proof reading of the papers. Above all, we are indebted to her Herculean, and often late-night, battles with the computer in formatting the text. Christian Moser, who was in St Andrews as a visiting scholar during 2003-4, gave generously of his time and textual expertise and we are particularly grateful for his preparation of the bibliography. In Zurich, Rainer Henrich helped with the translations as well as with innumerable other needs, all with indefatigable good cheer. In St Andrews Bridget Heal read part of the text and offered helpful advice. Mark Taplin likewise offered useful criticism and corrected the manuscript. Andrew Pettegree, Director of the St Andrews Reformation Studies Institute, has supported this endeavour from the start and the workshop in September 2002 also marked the 10th anniversary of the Institute. It was a pleasure to reflect back on ten years of productive collaboration. We also thank Professor John Hudson, Head of the School of History in St Andrews, for his unstinting support of our collaborative venture. Richard Muller generously backed the project and we are delighted that he has included the volume in his series. Brian Bolger at Baker steered the manuscript through the press with a firm hand and we thank him for his advice and guidance. At the time of writing my colleague and friend Emidio Campi has just undergone surgery. It is a great pleasure to work with him and he has been a tremendous partner in our endeavours. The current revival in Bullinger studies owes much to his energy, scholarship, and enthusiasm. We wish him a speedy recovery.

Abbreviations

CC.SL	*Corpus Christianorum. Series Latina.* Turnhout: Brepols 1953ff.
CO	*Ioannis Calvini opera quae supersunt omnia.* G. Baum et al. eds. Braunschweig: 1834-60.
Correspondance	*Correspondance de Théodore de Bèze.* F. Aubert et al. eds. Geneva: 1960-.
CR	*Corpus Reformatorum.* Brunswick: 1834-1900.
HBBibl	*Heinrich Bullinger, Bibliographie.* Joachim Staedtke and Erland Herkenrath eds. 2 vols. Heinrich Bullinger. *Werke.* part 1; Zurich 1972/7.
HBBW	*Heinrich Bullinger, Briefwechsel.* Ulrich Gäbler et al. eds. Heinrich Bullinger. *Werke* part 2; Zurich: 1973-.
HBD	*Heinrich Bullingers Diarium (Annales vitae) der Jahre 1504-1574.* Emil Egli ed. Quellen zur Schweizerischen Reformationsgeschichte II; Basle: 1904; rpt. Zurich: 1985.
HBRG	*Heinrich Bullingers Reformationsgeschichte,* J[ohann] J[akob] Hottinger and H[ans] H[einrich] Vögeli eds. 3 vols. Frauenfeld: 1838-40; rpt Zurich: 1985.
HBTS	*Heinrich Bullinger. Theologische Schriften.* Joachim Staedtke et al. eds, in association with the Zwingliverein Heinrich Bullinger. *Werke.* part 3; Zurich: 1983-.
PL	*Patrologiae cursus completus [Series Latina].* Jacques Paul Migne ed. Paris: 1844-55.
StA	Staatsarchiv Zurich
TRE	*Theologische Realenzyklopädie.* Gerhard Krause and Gerhard Müller eds, in association with Horst Robert Balz et al. Berlin/New York: Walter de Gruyter, 1977ff..
TVZ	Theologischer Verlag Zürich
Z	*Huldreich Zwinglis sämtliche Werke* Emil Egli et al. eds. vol. I., Berlin: 1905, vols IIff., Leipzig: 1908ff., vols XIIIff., Zurich: 1956ff. (*CR* 88-101).
ZB	Zurich Zentralbibliothek
ZBRG	Zürcher Beiträge zur Reformationsgeschichte

Edward A. Dowey, Jr. (1918-2003)

Heinrich Bullinger is not a familiar household name in all circles, but for Professor Edward Dowey and those who knew him, the theologian who led Zurich and many other Reformed communities through nearly half a tumultuous century was a significant key to the sixteenth-century Reformation.

Edward A. Dowey, Jr. was born on 18 February 1918, in Philadelphia, Pennsylvania, the first son of a minister in the United Presbyterian Church in North America. Edward Dowey, Sr. was of Scotch-Irish heritage, his wife Margaret Turner from a German Reformed family who had come to the United States from Frankfurt. Young Edward and his brother William grew up in churches of Covenanter and Presbyterian background which had a rather strict Reformed theology and a strong sense of social justice. Both of these traits marked Edward, Jr. for life; with the former he wrestled fruitfully, while the latter propelled him into action. At university Dowey became fascinated with philosophy and hesitant about continuing his plans to become a minister, until he heard President John Mackay of Princeton Theological Seminary lecture on Kierkegaard, Unamuno, and Dostoyevsky.

Having completed the B.A. at Lafayette College in 1940, Dowey went to study theology at Princeton Seminary. When he graduated in 1943, he became a chaplain in the United States Navy and served in the Pacific theatre for two years and then a third year in a military hospital. After the war Dowey went to Columbia University to work with Paul Tillich and especially Reinhold Niebuhr, earning the M.A. in 1947. The following two years Dowey spent in Zurich, writing his Th.D. dissertation under Emil Brunner. This thesis became an impressive book, *The Knowledge of God in Calvin's Theology*, published in 1952 by Columbia Press, and since then reprinted twice, once in 1965 and again in 1994. Dowey's exploration and explanation of Calvin's view of faith as an existential knowledge, and the two-fold character of the knowledge of God which offers a very persuasive way of understanding the structure of *The Institutes of the Christian Religion*, caused quite a stir. Over the years since it appeared, *The Knowledge of God in Calvin's Theology* has continued to serve as one of the best introductions to Calvin's theology more generally.

The young teacher Dowey first worked at Lafayette College (1949-51), next as a pastor to university students at Columbia University for a year, and then as Assistant Professor at Columbia (1952-4). The following three years he taught at McCormick Theological Seminary in Chicago, until he moved to Princeton Seminary where he was Professor in both theology and (ecclesiastical) history departments until his retirement in 1988. As a professor who was still an ordained pastor of the Presbyterian Church (USA), Dowey trained future ministers and doctoral students. He also continued his service to the church in various ways. One of these ways–following in the reformers' steps–was to take an active role in the confessional work of the church. He acted as chairperson and one of the main authors of the *Confession* of 1967, a contemporary statement of faith, and also as an important advocate for the introduction of a *Book of Confessions* for the PC (USA).

In the course of his teaching, Professor Dowey shifted the primary focus of his research from John Calvin to Heinrich Bullinger. This scholarly work involved spending several sabbatical years in his favorite city of Zurich, where his family also enjoyed the experience and Professor Dowey extended his circle of acquaintances, both early modern and twentieth-century. He was especially happy to visit in the Institute for Swiss Reformation History, and to recommend it to his students. Through these years, Professor Dowey was reading, analysing, and reflecting on Bullinger's many writings. At one point, he arranged for a German colleague to transcribe one of Bullinger's manuscript texts so that he could study it more carefully. He took copious notes both on Bullinger's own writings and on all the relevant secondary literature.

Professor Dowey was pursuing the goal of grasping Bullinger's theology comprehensively. At times he spent months working on a single article, or trying to organise his reading and notes into a larger form. A sabbatical never seemed to be enough time, and when he was able to return to concentrated work three or four years later, he usually began to re-read and re-think. Dowey was a perfectionist, and set extremely high standards for himself as well as others. Never was he convinced that he had set out the whole picture of Bullinger's theology in a really satisfactory way.

Thus, although he knew a great deal about Heinrich Bullinger, Edward Dowey did not complete his book-length study of the reformer's theology before his death on 5 February 2003 in Princeton, N.J. Nonetheless, over the years Dowey published a number of thoughtful articles, both in German and in English, which provided glimpses of his delving into the thought of the remarkable theologian who corresponded with and influenced so many in the sixteenth century through his writings as well as his hospitality in Zurich. While digging at his research, Dowey also lectured on Bullinger, both to students and at various professional conferences.

The chapter presented in this collection was among the pieces which Professor Dowey wrote in the 1990s, with later editing only a couple of years before his death. The chapter offers some suggestions—or provocation!?—for Bullinger experts, as they continue the dialogue with the Zurich reformer, a dialogue which was such a rich and stimulating part of Professor Dowey's own scholarly, theological life. We acknowledge with gratitude what we have learned from this gifted interpreter of Bullinger, and—as he would want—challenge each new interpreter of the reformer to carry the exciting project further.

Elsie McKee
November 2003

Introduction

Architect of Reformation

Bruce Gordon

Heinrich Bullinger has been called *the* forgotten reformer of the sixteenth century. Naturally, such claims are regularly made to justify research into obscure, unmemorable figures, but in the case of the man who led the Zurich church for almost fifty years after the death of Huldrych Zwingli, the assertion is not without grounds.[1] The five hundredth anniversary of his birth in 2004 has focused attention on this rather self-effacing figure who, despite voluminous correspondence, sermons, and theological writings, left few vestiges of the inner life of the man above all responsible for the construction of the Reformed church in the sixteenth century. The visual images we have of him reveal little more than standard sixteenth-century portraits of the bearded patriarch. Yet this was a man who was married for forty years to Anna, whom he described on her death as "his staff," and who outlived most of his children, including his beloved daughter Margaretha, who (along with her newborn child) died of the plague. He was musical, and the household, about which he wrote so passionately, was the centre of his world, filled with numerous children, servants, students, and refugees.[2] Bullinger rarely travelled, except to take the waters at local springs, and his physical world was Zurich, a city of which he was not a native. As a young man he had journeyed through German lands, but from his election as Zwingli's successor, it was exceptional for him even to make his way to neighbouring Basle. Yet his name was known across Europe, from the court of Elizabeth I to the nascent Reformed church communities in Hungary, making him one of the most widely consulted figures of the age.

Why then did he disappear into the trough of the wave? The answer to this question lies in a concatenation of circumstances that have much to do with the nature and character of Bullinger himself, the historical and theological fabric of the Zurich reformation, and the subsequent course of Reformation scholarship. Let us turn to the man.

---

1. Useful overviews of Bullinger's life and work are found in Fritz Büsser, "Heinrich Bullinger," *TRE* 7:375-87, and Bruce Gordon, "Heinrich Bullinger," in Carter Lindberg ed., *The Reformation Theologians* (Oxford: Blackwell, 2002), 170-83.
2. See the essay by Carrie Euler in this volume.

Biography

Like many of the Protestant Reformers of southwest German and Swiss lands, Heinrich Bullinger was born into a clerical family, on 18 July 1504.[3] His father, Heinrich, was a priest in Bremgarten, and his mother Anna Widerkehr lived with him and bore him children in a manner that although officially condemned by the church was largely tolerated. Children could be made legitimate through the payment of the "cradle tax," a not insignificant source of revenue for the bishop.[4] Education was a central part of the Bullinger household and the young boy began school at age five before being packed off at the age of twelve to the Latin school in Emmerich. Although the school was not officially run by the Brethren of the Common Life, many of its masters, including those most influential on the young Bullinger, were heavily influenced by the *Devotio moderna* tradition.[5] At the age of fourteen Bullinger arrived at the University of Cologne, a bastion of the *via antiqua*. This was to prove a decisive period in his life as he was in the great city during the time of Luther's major publications and the subsequent drama at the Diet of Worms. By 1522 Bullinger had completed his *Magister artium*. Although he did not officially study theology, his time in Cologne brought him a strong familiarity with the Dominican tradition of Thomas Aquinas and other scholastic writers. Another impulse was provided by two of his teachers, Johannes Pfrissemius and Arnold von Wesel, both humanists devoted to the new educational ideals. As a centre of new theological and intellectual developments Cologne also afforded the young Bullinger the opportunity to read the new editions of the Latin and Greek church fathers, particularly those of Erasmus, which flowed from presses in the Empire. It was, as Bullinger was later to record in his diary, the reading of Erasmus, Luther, and Melanchthon that led him to break with the Roman church and by 1522 he had ceased receiving the sacrament of the Eucharist.

Bullinger returned to Swiss lands in 1523, when he was invited by the young Abbot Wolfgang Joner of a new Cistercian monastery at Kappel, south of Zurich, to take up the position of teacher. It was at Kappel that Bullinger was able to put his humanist principles into practice. During the six years that he worked at the monastery he began a reform of the traditional medieval curriculum of the *Trivium* in a humanist direction. He introduced the works of Erasmus, Agricola, and Melanchthon, and he began a series of public lectures on the Pauline epistles that would, in part, form a model for the *Prophezei* in Zurich.[6] During this period he came to know Huldrych Zwingli, who was to be his mentor and friend and whose memory and reputation Bullinger robustly defended for the rest of his life. Bullinger was ordained as a parish minister in the new Reformed church of Zurich and he served in the rural churches at Kappel and Hausen. It was also at this

---

3. The essential information on Bullinger's life is found in his diary. The original text was known to have survived till the nineteenth century, but is now lost. Abbreviated as *HBD*.

4. Bruce Gordon, *The Swiss Reformation* (Manchester: Manchester University Press, 2002), 29-30.

5. See the essay by Kurt Rüetschi in this volume.

6. On the *Prophezei*, see the essays by Roland Diethelm and Kurt Rüetschi.

time that he married Anna Adlischweiler, who would remain at his side until her death from plague in the early 1560s.

From 1529 Bullinger was preacher in his native town of Bremgarten until he was forced to flee by the Catholic forces following their victory at Kappel and the death of Huldrych Zwingli on 11 October 1531. When the twenty-seven year old Bullinger arrived in Zurich the city was in chaos after the defeat, and the leaders of the Reformation feared a public lynching. The young Thomas Platter described hiding under his bed in the house of Oswald Myconius, while Leo Jud's friends wanted him to wear women's clothing in public to disguise his identity.[7] Those who had been associated with Zwingli feared for their lives, as many in Zurich believed that their bellicose preaching had brought the disaster upon the city.

Bullinger was one of three candidates for the post of principal preacher in the Grossmünster (essentially, head of the Zurich church) whose names were put to the council. There was little doubt that he would be chosen; indeed, both Berne and Basle similarly sought to attract him to lead their churches. Bullinger's learning was greatly respected and he benefitted, as minister in Bremgarten, from not being seen to have been too close to Zwingli. The Zurich church, however, faced a crisis. The magistrates were determined that never again would the ministers interfere in political matters, by which they meant no more explicitly political preaching.[8] Bullinger acceded to this in principle but he was not prepared to surrender what he regarded as the freedom of the minister to preach the Word of God.

During the 1530s Bullinger was faced by the daunting task of rebuilding the Zurich church after Zwingli's death, repairing relations with Basle and Berne, and entering the maelstrom of the international Reformation. The first stage was to draw together the Swiss churches in a common statement of faith, and to this end Bullinger co-wrote the *First Helvetic Confession* of 1536. The background to these first steps towards restoring some sense of unity to the Swiss Reformed churches was the complex set of negotiations that would lead to the *Wittenberg Accord* of the same year.[9] Martin Bucer took a leading role in attempting to bring the Zwinglian and Lutheran parties together, but Bullinger's distrust of the Strasbourg reformer was so intense that there was little chance of success, and by 1538 the negotiations between the two sides had collapsed.[10] At the same time Bullinger was attempting to face down the continuing challenge posed by the

---

7. Platter's account has been recently retold in Emmanuel Le Roy LaDurie, *The Beggar and the Professor. A Sixteenth-Century Family Saga* (Chicago/London: University of Chicago Press, 1997), 56-57. The other story is found in the biography of Leo Jud written by his son: "Historische Beschreibung von dem Leben und Tod, Haus und Geschlecht, Kinder und Kindskinderen des fürtrefflichen manns hrn. Leonis Jud...," *Miscellanea Tigurina* 3 (Zurich ZB 1-138): 55-56.

8. See the essay by Andreas Mühling in this volume; Hans Ulrich Bächtold, *Bullinger vor dem Rat. Zur Gestaltung und Verwaltung des Zürcher Staatswesens in den Jahren 1531 bis 1575* (ZBRG 12; Berne/Frankfurt a. Main: Peter Lang, 1982), 11-58; Gordon, *Swiss Reformation*, 140-2.

9. Martin Friedrich, "Heinrich Bullinger und die Wittenberg Konkordie. Ein Ökumeniker im Streit um das Abendmahl," *Zwingliana* 24 (1997): 59-79.

10. Mark U. Edwards, *Luther and the False Brethren* (Stanford: Stanford University Press, 1975), 147-55.

Anabaptists.[11] From 1525 he had been involved in debates with the radicals and just after his appointment as Zwingli's successor he travelled to Berne for another confrontation. His work of 1531, *Four Books to Warn the Faithful of the Shameless Disturbance, Offensive Confusion, and False Teachings of the Anabaptists*, formed the core of his rejection of radical thought. To this he would add *On the Origins of Anabaptism* in 1560.

While Luther still lived there was continuing warfare between Wittenberg and Zurich. Perhaps the ugliest event was Luther's damning rejection of the Zurich Bible sent to him by Christoff Froschauer in 1543.[12] This was followed by a final and categorical denunciation of the Zwinglians in his *Short Confession of the Lord's Supper*. It was in response to this that Bullinger wrote his *True Confession (Wahrhaftes Bekenntnis der Diener der Kirche zu Zürich)* of 1545.

There were other events occupying Bullinger's mind in the 1540s. By the middle of the decade the Schmalkaldic War, the defeat of the Protestant league, and the summoning of the Council of Trent threatened to roll back the Protestant Reformation.[13] With no agreement with the Lutherans, Bullinger was keenly aware of the precarious position of the Swiss Reformed churches. This drew him into closer contact with John Calvin, and their first piece of cooperation was a jointly penned response to the Council of Trent.[14] Both men understood the need for unity, but they also understood how deep the divisions within the Protestant world ran, and it is a measure of their desire for mutual support that they could put their names to a document on the Lord's Supper, the *Consensus Tigurinus* of 1549.[15] Too much has been made of this agreement, which was, for the most part, a practical arrangement which suited both men. It was a partnership which worked well: Bullinger supported Calvin both openly and tacitly, agreeing not to disagree in public, and together they formed a common front against Lutheran opponents, such as Joachim Westphal, who wrote against the Swiss in the mid-1550s.

The 1550s marked a transitionary period in Bullinger's tenure as head of the Zurich church. Following the publication of his *Decades*, his treatment of the tenets of the Christian faith in fifty sermons which appeared between 1548 and 1551, Bullinger had become a major international figure, but at home there was little to celebrate. These years were marked by bitter strife with the Zurich council over a range of practical matters. In addition, many of his close circle, men such as Konrad Pellikan and Theodor Bibliander, were now old and close to death. There was a generational change with only the aging patriarch still in

11. On Bullinger's relationship with the Anabaptists, see Heinold Fast, *Heinrich Bullinger und die Täufer* (Weierhof: 1959); Gordon, *Swiss Reformation*, 210-2.

12. Edwards, *Luther and the False Brethren*, 185-7.

13. On Bullinger's involvement in these events, see Andreas Mühling, *Heinrich Bullingers europäische Kirchenpolitik* (Berne: Peter Lang, 2001).

14. Bruce Gordon, "Calvin and the Swiss Reformed Churches" in Andrew Pettegree, Alastair Duke and Gillian Lewis eds, *Calvinism in Europe 1540-1620* (Cambridge: CUP, 1994), 64-81.

15. Paul Rorem, "Calvin and Bullinger on the Lord's Supper. Part I: Impasse," *Lutheran Quarterly* 2 (1988): 155-84, and his "Calvin and Bullinger on the Lord's Supper. Part II: The Agreement," *Lutheran Quarterly* 2 (1988): 357-89.

place. Zurich was ravaged by bad weather, poor harvests, and plague. Bullinger himself nearly died in the early 1560s when plague took away his wife and daughter. Within the Swiss Confederation there were innumerable confessional conflicts, such as in Glarus (1560-4)–a stark reminder that 1531 had brought only a cessation of hostilities and no agreement. This was also a fertile period for Bullinger's writing, but his thoughts, as he preached and published on the books of Daniel and Revelation, were increasingly disappointed, world weary, and even angry.[16] As Christian Moser writes in his essay, Bullinger was already preparing to leave the world and was thinking about his legacy. The tone is very much caught in his 1573 work for the persecuted French Huguenots (*Von der schweren Verfolgung der christlichen Kirchen*) in which he counselled patience in the face of persecution, promising that deliverance would be in the next world. There was, however, to be one final major theological achievement. Bullinger's *Second Helvetic Confession* of 1566 was his most systematic and mature theological statement. Bullinger wanted this to be a confession of the whole Swiss church, though Basle would refuse to sign until much later. Nevertheless, it was, and remains, one of the principal achievements of Reformed thought. It is the mature expression of theology that Bullinger had championed from the late 1520s.[17]

Bullinger continued to preach and write until his death in 1575. By the time of his passing he was one of the best-known reformers in Europe. The extent of his international network of contacts is indicated by the 12,000 letters that have survived and are being edited in Zurich. Rainer Henrich argues in his essay that Bullinger functioned as a one-man communication system. Bullinger corresponded with the leading reformers of England, France, the Empire, Eastern Europe, the Netherlands, and Scandinavia. Many of his correspondents, such as those in England, had stayed in his house as religious refugees whilst others simply knew him as the wise patriarch of the Reformed church. He taught and gave refuge to innumerable students and co-religionists fleeing persecution. Bullinger may have shied away from revealing much of himself, but in their letters these men have left behind a portrait of a kindly, warm man, full of hospitality and always prepared to use his dinner table to further the cause of Christ's church.

The Reformer

One thing can be asserted unequivocally about Heinrich Bullinger: he was extraordinarily consistent. He devoted his life to the service of God and saw himself above all as a preacher of God's Word. As Peter Opitz shows, the communication of the gospel lay at the heart of Bullinger's theological and pastoral work. He was consumed by the transforming power of the biblical message, which he thought to be irresistibly clear to those who believed. Preaching was the foundation of the Christian ministry and nothing would move him to greater righteous anger than any perceived threat to the freedom of the minister to proclaim the Word of God.

---

16. Emdio Campi, "Über das Ende des Weltzeitalters. Aspekte der Rezeption des Danielbuches bei Heinrich Bullinger" in Mariano Delgado, Klaus Koch and Edgar Marsch eds, *Europa, Tausendjähriges Reich und Neue Welt* (Stuttgart: Universitätsverlag Freiburg, 2003), 225-38.

17. See the essay by Edward Dowey in this volume.

This issue haunted the post-Zwingli church and continued to dog Bullinger's relations with the Zurich magistrates who were determined to control the pulpit in order to silence criticism and ward off clerical intervention in contentious political and social matters.[18] Bullinger, however, was adamant that a church denuded of its ability to preach unfettered the Gospel of Christ was not a true church. He constructed his leadership in Zurich around this principle, but the manner in which he did so tells us much about how he operated. To preserve the "freedom" of the church against the hegemonic interests of the magistrates Bullinger struck a tacit deal by which he assumed personal control over the clergy. Through the principal institutions of the Zurich church, the *Examinatorenkonvent* (committee of examiners) and the synod, Bullinger exercised his will upon the ministers. He kept himself keenly informed of every event in the urban and rural parishes (approximately 120 in total); he was involved in the examination and appointment of every minister; when there was trouble Bullinger personally interviewed the ministers and determined the course of action. This extraordinary level of activity reflected Bullinger's essential approach to church affairs: he made a strict division between the private and visible spheres of church life. For Bullinger this meant that he did not probe too deeply into what those around him actually believed; it was not his style to make them write confessions of faith. As long as ministers and lay people publicly adhered to the teaching and worship of the Zurich church Bullinger did not make trouble. This was a decision he would live to regret.[19] Nevertheless, he took the same view on the wider church. Although his approach was heavily didactic, Bullinger argued that outward conformity was all that the church could demand; it could not know the thoughts of the heart.

The terms of the agreement with the Zurich council were intended to prevent public scandal or disruption. The role of the preachers in leading Zurich into the disastrous Kappel War of 1531 with their incendiary sermons had led to a backlash against the clergy that had almost overturned the Reformation. Bullinger knew that he had to prevent church affairs from being discussed publicly; all relations with the council were conducted behind closed doors. Likewise, all internal issues of the church were kept away from the public gaze through the use of the synod, a meeting of the whole clerical body twice a year. Through his control of the synod and close relations with the council, Bullinger mediated all potentially troublesome issues. This meant, naturally, that the whole polity of the Zurich church was dependent on the activity of Heinrich Bullinger.

In addition to running the synod, Bullinger (as *Schulherr*) was also responsible for education in Zurich. This meant the running of Latin schools in the city and rural areas and the provision of theological education for young men preparing to be ministers. Bullinger did not hold a professorship and he left most of the teaching to the highly-talented cast of scholars in Zurich: Theodor Bibliander, Konrad Pellikan, Konrad Gesner, and Peter Martyr Vermigli. Together these men turned Zwingli's *Prophezei* into the *Lectorium*, a higher education institution of the Reformed church, but not a university.

---

18. On this see Pamela Biel, *Doorkeepers at the House of Righteousness. Heinrich Bullinger and the Zurich Clergy 1535-1575* (Berne: Peter Lang, 1991), 44-71.

19. See the essay by Mark Taplin in this volume.

One of the reasons Bullinger did not teach was on account of his extensive preaching commitments. He was the chief minister in the Grossmünster in Zurich and with this came the obligation to preach at least three times a week. There have been various estimates, but it would seem that he preached around 7500 times in Zurich during his tenure. Roughly 600 of these sermons were printed. The preaching was closely linked to his lifelong commitment to biblical exegesis. From the large amount of surviving material, it is possible to gain a clear idea of how Bullinger worked. The regular preaching in the Grossmünster formed the backbone of his activities in Zurich and he believed it to be his primary duty. It is likely that Bullinger never wrote out his sermons but rather chose to take notes into the pulpit. A large number of these notes, or sermon outlines, have survived and they enable us to observe the close connection between his exegesis and the sermons. At the same time, particularly from the 1540s onwards, Bullinger produced a large number of vernacular pastoral tracts for his clergy and educated laity. Once again we can see that these tracts are closely aligned with the subjects of the sermons and the commentaries. He was an extremely economical worker.

The tradition of Zwingli, through which the Reformation had been brought about by the charismatic leadership of one person, remained central to the Reformed church, which, during Bullinger's tenure, continued to have a weak institutional basis. This meant that when personal relations between Bullinger and the council faltered the shaky foundations of the institutional church in Zurich threatened to give way. During the 1550s, it seemed possible that a series of issues, most prominently poor relief, might tear apart the agreement struck in 1531. Bullinger's anger at the unwillingness of the magistrates to play their role as guardians of the Word of God spilled from the pulpit into the print shop. He came very close to abandoning his arrangement with the council, a sign that he took very seriously his role as prophet of the Zurich church, as Nathan rebuking David. The 1550s, which await proper examination, saw a significant change in Bullinger's position as head of the Zurich church: he was developing a different understanding of the Christian ministry; his relations with the council were deeply troubled; there was to be a serious farrago in the circle of colleagues which he built around himself. The distinction between private and public was to undergo a change in Bullinger's close circle of friends when, as Mark Taplin has shown, he discovered that men such as Lelio Sozzini and Bernardino Ochino, to whom he had offered protection and whom he had never examined too closely on their private beliefs, were using his name as protection whilst writing heterodox texts.[20]

The shock and bitterness following the expulsion of Bernardino Ochino had much to do with the fact that Bullinger had devoted himself to defending the Zurich church against accusations of heresy. Ochino, the celebrated Italian preacher and former head of the Capuchins, had been pastor to the Italian community in Zurich. He was dismissed and banished by the council following the unauthorised publication of a work that Zurich ministers judged heretical. Martin Luther, in the wake of the polemical warfare over the Lord's Supper, had accused

---

20. Mark Taplin, *The Italian Reformers and the Zurich Church, c.1540-1620* (Aldershot: Ashgate, 2003).

Zwingli of holding a Nestorian position on the nature of Christ. In addition, the rise of radicalism in Zurich had in the eyes of many contemporaries much to do with the neo-platonic dualism of Zwingli's thought. The Zurich church, until well into the seventeenth century, struggled to exonerate itself from claims that it had fostered false religion. For Bullinger, deeply aware of the accusations, the greatest threat came not from the Catholics, but from the Anabaptists, against whom he wrote with uncharacteristic vehemence.

The issue of Martin Luther and the German Lutherans was for Heinrich Bullinger a profoundly complex matter on psychological and theological grounds.[21] Luther's damnation of Zwingli, his cold response to the reformer's death in 1531, and his vitriolic attacks on the Zurichers during the 1530s and 1540s scarred Bullinger. Almost all of Bullinger's writings, regardless of subject, have as a subtext a defence of Zurich theology against the attacks of the Lutherans. The issues of the sacraments and the presence of Christ are repeatedly discussed and explained in a rather defensive manner. For Bullinger himself, theological questions could not be separated from the person of Huldrych Zwingli, his one-time friend, mentor, and predecessor. The memory of Zwingli was sacred for Bullinger, and he saw himself as the protector of Zwingli's legacy in a world that had misunderstood the Zurich reformer. He considered Zwingli to be a latter-day patriarch of the church and included his name in a list of church fathers to be studied. Yet, at the same time Bullinger was fully aware of the danger of speaking about the man; Bullinger's history of the Reformation could not be published because its subject, Huldrych Zwingli, was too controversial. Likewise, he felt it prudent not to write a biography of Zwingli, as every mention of the dead reformer's name only led to another excoriation from the Lutherans.[22] By the 1530s there was little chance that the Lutheran/Zwinglian divide over the Eucharist could be repaired as it had taken on so many other aspects of identity and pride. This is perhaps most evident in the Swiss responses to Martin Bucer, whose repeated attempts to find unity between the two camps brought only suspicion. For Bullinger the prolix Bucer lost all credibility because he regarded the debate as a misunderstanding over a few words. Bullinger's own theological position was probably not so very far from Bucer's, but the reduction of the dispute to a quibble over words lost sight of the fundamental fact that Luther had damned Zwingli and his followers. That was the point which Bullinger could not forget and the curse of that damnation darkened the whole of his life as head of the Zurich church. Calvin was probably correct when he commented that the Zurichers were so sensitive to the memory of Zwingli that they construed everything as an insult.[23]

In the end Bullinger realised that he had to come to some sort of accommodation with the Lutherans, though he rightly saw this as impossible while Luther

---

21. Stephen Strehle, "Fides aut Foedus. Wittenberg and Zurich in Conflict over the Gospel," *Sixteenth Century Journal* 23 (1992): 3-20.

22. Ernst Rüsch, "Vadians Gutachten für eine Zwingli-Vita, 1544," *Zwingliana* 15 (1979): 40-49.

23. Gordon, "Calvin and the Swiss Reformed Churches," 66.

lived.[24] His most important relationship was with Philip Melanchthon, whose theological influence on the Zurich church awaits proper investigation.[25] Apart from Zwingli, the most significant contemporary figures in the formation of Bullinger's thought were Melanchthon and Johannes Oecolampadius, Zwingli's friend in Basle. Bullinger almost never cited any author from his own day with the exception of Zwingli, Erasmus, and John Calvin. His relationship to the Frenchman was complex, built on necessity and respect more than friendship. It could be argued that through their mutual efforts, which began in the mid 1540s with their polemical attack on the Council of Trent, they successfully integrated the Zwinglian tradition into a broader Reformed culture. Certainly, their working relationship was crucial to securing Calvin's position in Geneva, as Bullinger used his good name to vouch for the Frenchman. Likewise, Calvin relied on Bullinger's support during the disputes with Berne and the Servetus crisis. Yet the two men were fundamentally different. Their positions on predestination, despite an agreement not to argue in public, cannot be easily reconciled, while the much vaunted *Consensus Tigurinus* of 1549 was, as Amy Nelson Burnett has argued, designed to sink Martin Bucer, and by no means knitted together their views on the Lord's Supper.[26] There were also fundamental differences of mentality: the Swiss Republican and the Frenchman who believed in an essentially aristocratic structure of the church did not share a common view of the world. For Bullinger, the world was a dark place and he ultimately looked to the next world for relief. He had little of Calvin's humanist optimism.

For Bullinger, humanism was an essential tool of the church because it enabled the proper interpretation of scripture. As for many of his generation, and in particular for the reformers of the south-western German and Swiss lands, the influence of Erasmus was enormous. Yet we need to think more critically about the place of learning and scholarship in Bullinger's building of the Reformed church. In particular, the manner in which he read and appropriated ancient texts is something to which historians and theologians have not yet turned their attention. The recent discovery by Urs Leu of two volumes of Bullinger's notes in the Zurich Zentralbibliothek is of great importance.[27] Briefly, these notes, which are likely to be from the mid-1530s, are organised according to a system of loci that Bullinger would use for most of his life. Under each locus Bullinger would provide an extensive list of citations and notes from his reading of the church fathers as well as numerous biblical references. It is striking that when one looks, for example, at his *Decades* one finds these exact references deployed in the precise

24. On Bullinger's willingness to work with Lutheran princes, see Andreas Mühling's contribution to this volume.

25. An outline of Melanchthon's Swiss relations is found in Bruce Gordon, "Wary allies: Melanchthon and the Swiss Reformers" in Karin Maag ed., *Melanchthon in Europe. His Work and Influence Beyond Wittenberg* (Grand Rapids: Baker Books, 1999), 45-67.

26. The remark was made during a session on Martin Bucer at the Sixteenth Century Studies Conference in Pittsburgh in November 2003. On predestination, see Cornelius Venema, "Heinrich Bullinger's correspondence on Calvin's doctrine of predestination," *Sixteenth Century Studies* 17 (1986): 435-50.

27. ZB, Ms. Car 152 and 153. I am grateful to Dr Leu of the ZB for bringing these volumes to my attention.

order laid out in the notes. Further, in almost every passage on particular topics Bullinger used the same biblical and patristic references. This, of course, was not unusual in the sixteenth century, but it throws light on how he worked. First, it meant that Bullinger very early on in his career had the essential schema of his theology which he used as a filter in reading through the church fathers. He took from those patristic texts quotations and references which were congenial to his position, or, as he often did, excerpted passages with which he was not in agreement to demonstrate that even the church fathers could err. Bullinger was an assiduous student of the tradition of church theology, and he studied both the early church and medieval sources with close attention, but we must not imagine that he was reading them with what we would call an "open mind." He knew what he was looking for before he opened the volumes. Humanism was certainly a pedagogical tool, but it was also a weapon in the battle over the church fathers in the sixteenth century.

Second, this also explains how he was able to write so much alongside his innumerable duties as head of the Zurich church. A systematic study of Bullinger's work will, no doubt, demonstrate the extent to which he recycled his writings. If one compares the sermonic, pastoral, and Latinate theological works it is striking how passages are repeated verbatim. The same references and quotations are used to make the same points. This should not surprise–most of his contemporaries, notably Erasmus and Calvin, did exactly the same thing. It reflected a belief that once a position had been worked out there was no reason to reformulate one's argument. This helps us to recognise that the source and theological bases for Bullinger's work were indeed much smaller than one might initially believe. Bullinger had a clear system for his labours. He was not an isolated figure, but worked closely with a small group of churchmen who were friends, dedicated to the memory of Zwingli, and who shared a similar theological disposition. Perhaps most crucially, Bullinger attended daily the lectures by Theodor Bibliander in the Zurich *Lectorium* (his notes from these lectures have survived). The core of Bullinger's intellectual endeavour was his preaching activity in the Grossmünster; as Roland Diethelm demonstrates, these sermons were drawn from the exegesis of Bullinger and his close circle (Bibliander, Pellikan, Gwalther). The series of *lectio continua* sermons would be followed by the publication of a commentary on the biblical book. In addition, Bullinger would then publish many of the sermons as pastoral aids for the clergy and literate laity. As for all his contemporaries, the language of theology was Latin and Bullinger's main works were generally written in response to external developments of the European Reformation, such as in England or the Empire. Throughout the Latin and vernacular works, however, one finds a high degree of consistency in both argumentation and sources.

Through his preaching and writing, Bullinger sought to convey the message of the Bible. The whole enterprise of the Zurich reformation was based around the interpretation of scripture. The *Prophezei* founded in the Grossmünster in 1525 had two crucial aspects. It was, as Roland Diethelm remarks, a confraternity of a semi-monastic nature of men bound together by friendship and a commitment to the interpretation of the Bible by the humanist tools of languages and textual criticism. The southern German, Alsatian, and Swiss reformers were distinguished by their love of the Hebrew Bible and the Hebrew language, and by their view that the New Testament was a commentary on the Old Testament. This was at the root of the prophetic model of ministry articulated by Zwingli and others. The role of the ministers was to interpret scripture through the leadership of the Holy Spirit, and there was a striking confidence in the clarity of God's Word. In Zurich, the chair of Old Testament remained the senior academic appointment. A further characteristic of this "exegetical community," as Daniel Bolliger refers to it, was its focus on the practical Christian life in which each person sought to emulate the way of Christ. This orientation saw as its first fruit the Zurich Bible of 1531 with Zwingli's lucid articulation of his attitude towards scripture in the preface. The Zurich Bible began a tradition that Bullinger maintained and developed, with the help of Leo Jud, Bibliander, and Pellikan. Under the rubric of making scripture comprehensible to the minister and layperson, subsequent editions of the whole Bible and individual Testaments were increasingly framed by chapter outlines, marginal notes, and cross references, all intended to provide a guided reading of the text. Each person was to be educated in how to read scripture, and this included instruction in the meaning of passages. Bullinger presided over the shaping of the Reformed Bible in Zurich in which the text was presented in such a manner as to make it indispensable for instruction in the Zwinglian tradition. Again, this was certainly not uncommon in the sixteenth century, but the manner in which the Bible was confessionally framed in Zurich needs to be studied more carefully.

The appropriation of the church fathers and of the Bible was matched by Bullinger's work as a historian. Christian Moser's groundbreaking work on the sources of the *Reformation History* has thrown light on Bullinger's historical understanding. As with his approach to theological tradition, Bullinger went to the historical sources with a clear idea of what he wanted to find. Following in the tradition of Vadianus, the lay reformer of St Gall, Bullinger made extensive use of documents and his search for sources marked a crucial stage of development in the writing of history in the Protestant Reformation, but again this was done within a mental framework shaped by his theological convictions.[28] History was to be brought into the service of the church because, as with the Reformation, it revealed both God's hand in human affairs and the nature of humanity. Bullinger's increasingly confident sense of his place in God's church, discussed by Bolliger, Moser and Henrich, is demonstrated by the manner in which he saw his historical work as his testament to the Reformed church. His account of the Reformation in Zurich was to be treated as authoritative by future generations. It was to remind people of what God had done, and Bullinger's "accurate" and "authentic" account was to ensure that the correct interpretations were drawn from events. Thus the interplay between tradition and authority in Bullinger's work, so important in his biblical and theological writings, is strongly echoed in his approach to and writing of history.

---

28. On Vadianus's historical writing, see Hans Conrad Peyer, "Der St. Galler Reformator Vadian als Geschichtsschreiber. Programatische und mythische Geschichtsauffassung in der Schweiz des 16. Jahrhunderts," *Schweizer Monatshefte* 65 (1985): 315-28.

Bullinger believed in the peaceful outward ordering of religion. This meant, in true Zwinglian fashion, proper worship and obedience to the Christian laws of the state. He preached and wrote continually that what fundamentally divided humanity was whether or not a person believed in God's gracious gift of salvation in Christ. Faith was everything for Bullinger and he viewed God as a willing partner who extended the hand of friendship to humanity, and who sought the salvation of all. This he contrasted with the mendacity of men and women, whose rejection of God was unpardonable. Despite preaching the necessity of faith, however, Bullinger rejected all attempts by men to judge the souls of others; he was adamant that the authority of the magistrates had to be upheld, and that both believers and non-believers had to be punished when they transgressed the laws of the state, but his attitude towards the sacraments and church discipline revealed the depth of his abhorrence of the arrogance of human presumption. For Bullinger, this meant that excommunication could have no role in the life of the church. Unlike Calvin, Bullinger did not believe that the Lord's Table was to be protected from unbelievers, because it was not up to humans to discern the identity of the elect. This was at the heart of his distinction between the private and the public.

Bullinger and Historians

It is conventionally argued that by the time of Bullinger's death in 1575 the Zurich church, once predominant in the Reformed world, had given way to Calvinist Geneva under the leadership of Theodor Beza. This thesis is difficult to sustain or deny given the paucity of research on the Swiss Reformed church in the period of the so-called orthodoxy. When one reads general histories, such as Rudolf Pfister's church history of Switzerland, the same arguments tend to be repeated uncritically, but the case is not proved.[29] There is a desperate need for work on late-sixteenth, early seventeenth-century Reformed Protestantism in order that we might be able to speak with greater clarity about its theological and ecclesiological topography. This work should not confine itself to theology: we need to know about scholarly networks, patterns of reading, preaching, lay education, and personal libraries. Until this is undertaken we shall be compelled to continue to rehearse the same pieties about late-sixteenth and early-seventeenth century Reformed religious cultures.

Nevertheless, as research currently stands, it does seem that Bullinger performed a vanishing act in the seventeenth century. To some extent, Bullinger was responsible for his own fate. In his account of the Reformation in Zurich he ends the story at 1531 and says nothing about his own role.[30] In so doing, therefore, he set the norm of seeing 1531 as the decisive endpoint of the Zurich Reformation–a pattern that would be repeated until the late twentieth century. There are other reasons for his demise: the theological climate changed and the Reformed churches were increasingly led by a generation of reformers who had had virtu-

---

29. Rudolf Pfister, *Kirchengeschichte der Schweiz*, vol. 2 (Zurich: TVZ, 1974). Still the standard work of Swiss church history.
30. *HBRG*. On the *History*, see the essay in this volume by Christian Moser.

ally nothing to do with the Swiss churches of the sixteenth century. Trained in Herborn, Heidelburg, Leiden and other centres of higher education, their theological orientation owed little explicitly to the work of Zwingli and Bullinger. The influence of Herborn on the Swiss churches during the seventeenth century was particularly strong, as Gerhard Menk has established.[31] Further, as Karin Maag has clearly demonstrated, the Swiss institutions of higher education, such as in Zurich, Berne, and Geneva, became extremely provincial, wishing only to appoint professors from their own communities and primarily concerned with the training of clergy.[32] The position of the Swiss churches at the Synod of Dordrecht was rather marginal; they no longer held authority in the same manner. Yet, against this theory of isolation and decline there is evidence that in the seventeenth century the Swiss churches still occupied a place of esteem and importance in the Reformed international community. The Scottish covenanters, invoking the name Heinrich Bullinger, consulted the Swiss churches on a range of theological points at the time of the Westminster Assembly.[33] Similarly, during the Protectorate Cromwell himself took an interest in Swiss affairs and sought an alliance with the Reformed churches; his representative, the Scot John Dury, travelled to the Confederation to hold talks on theological unity.[34]

When Johann Jakob Breitinger addressed the Synod of Dordrecht in December 1618 he offered an apology for Heinrich Bullinger.[35] In particular it was Bullinger's doctrine of predestination that was being debated, for the Remonstrants had sought to prove that the chief minister in Zurich had differed from Calvin just as they did from the Counter-Remonstrants. Breitinger knew that once again Zurich was in danger of being seen as the centre of heresy. This had been the stigma that Luther had so effectively inflicted on the Zwinglians, but this time the accusation had arisen from within the Reformed camp. To persuade the Synod of Bullinger's theological reliability, Breitinger invoked the name of Peter Martyr Vermigli as a witness, a telling example of the changing fortunes of reputations. Breitinger succeeded in defending Bullinger to the extent that the Remonstrants abandoned him as a source, but the damage was more far reaching; essentially, Bullinger was no longer cited in the canon of Reformed writers. The Reformed orthodoxy had little place for Bullinger because his theology lacked the structural rigour favoured by later generations. Although he worked with a set order of *loci*, Bullinger's theology was not overtly systematic; he preferred the dynamic relationship between the individual and the Word. Bullinger did not, however, vanish

31. Gerhard Menk, *Die Hohe Schule Herborn in ihrer Frühzeit (1584-1660). Ein Beitrag zum Hochschulwesen des deutschen Kalvinismus der Gegenreformation* (Wiesbaden: Historische Kommission für Nassau, 1981), 302-5.

32. Karin Maag, *Seminar or University? The Genevan Academy and Reformed Higher Education, 1560-1620* (Aldershot: Ashgate, 1995).

33. J.K. Cameron, "The Swiss and the Covenant," in G.W.S. Barrow ed., *The Scottish Tradition. Essays in Honour of Ronald Gordon Cant* (Edinburgh: 1974), 155-63.

34. Bruce Gordon, "'The Second Bucer': John Dury's Mission to the Swiss Reformed Churches in 1654-55 and the Search for Confessional Unity" in John Headley and Hans Hillerbrand eds, *Confessionalization in Europe 1555-1725. Essays in Memory of Bodo Nischan* (Aldershot: Ashgate, 2004), 191-210.

35. Breitinger's speech is found in *Historicae Ecclesiasticae novi testamenti tomus VIII, Saeculi XVI. Pars IV.* Tiguri, 1666, 958-77.

entirely from the scene in Zurich. During the seventeenth and eighteenth centuries two important collections of his manuscripts were assembled, the first by Johann Heinrich Hottinger and the second by Johann Jakob Simler.[36]

In the English-speaking world Bullinger came back into view with a Victorian reprinting with notes of the Elizabethan "translation" (1587) of his *Loci Sermonum quinque ...*, the *Decades*.[37] In the preface to the edition of 1849 knowledge of Bullinger is by no means taken for granted and the reader is reminded of two salient points: that Bullinger had harboured English refugees under Mary, and that the *Decades* had enjoyed such a high reputation in the English church that Archbishop Whitgift had declared that each of the lower clergy should possess a copy.[38]

In Switzerland the manner in which the Reformation was remembered had much to do with the contested world of nineteenth-century theology and church politics. By the middle of the century there were three identifiable groups in the Zurich church: the liberals (*Speculativen*), who rejected the verbal inspiration of the Bible, the orthodox, and those who sought a middle way.[39] The liberals were focused in the theological faculty around the Professor of Dogmatics, Aloys Emanuel Biedermann, while the orthodox party consisted mostly of rural ministers. The mediating party stood, above all, for the continuing link between the church and state and the avoidance of controversies that would destroy the bond forged at the Reformation. This split became entangled in the constitutional reforms of the 1860s, when a majority of the people voted for the introduction of direct democracy in the canton of Zurich. This movement put the position of the established church in question as many now called for the separation of the secular and sacred. It was largely due to the work of the *Antistes*, or head of the Zurich church, Georg Diethelm Finsler, that the position of the church was secured, although opposition from the liberal parties remained.

In order to protect the delicate relationship between the church and the government Finsler was persuaded that the people of Zurich needed to be reminded of the past great leaders of the church. With an eye to the 400th anniversary of Zwingli's birth in 1884, he and other leading ministers in the city of Zurich began in 1872 to petition for an appropriate monument for the reformer.[40] The Luther monument in Worms was very much in mind. It took until 1882 to choose the plan, which had been put forward by the Viennese sculptor Heinrich Natter. During 1884 the anniversary of Zwingli's birth was celebrated: the reformer was interpreted variously as a hero of Protestantism and Zurich, an opponent of liberal theology, and a symbol of the new church-state relations in the canton. The

---

36. Both collections are now available on microfiche from IDC publishers in the Netherlands.

37. *The Decades of Henry Bullinger*, translated by H.I. (first printing London, 1587), Th. Harding ed., (Cambridge: 1849).

38. Walter Phillips, "Henry Bullinger and the Elizabethan Vestiarian Controversy: An analysis of influence," *Journal of Religious History* 11 (1981): 363-84.

39. On the nineteenth-century Zurich church, see Theodor M Vial, *Ritual Theory and Protestant Reform in Nineteenth-Century Zurich* (London: Routledge, 2003).

40. Hedy Tschumi-Häfliger, "Reformatoren-Denkmäler in der Schweiz: Historischer Hintergrund und Anlässe ihrer Entstehung," *Zwingliana* (1987): 195-262.

money for the hugely expensive statue of Zwingli, which stands by the Wasserkirche in Zurich, was raised by public subscription. Shortly after the Zwingli jubilee in 1884 work began on a critical edition of the reformer's works. Zwingli had been reclaimed by those parts of the Zurich church that feared the twin demons of liberalism and secularism. He was presented as the Zurich alternative to the Martin Luther of Bismarck's German Empire. As a consequence the whole of the nineteenth century crisis in church-state relations was telescoped onto to Zwingli to the exclusion of virtually all other figures. Bullinger had been conjured up by the Parker Society in defence of evangelical religion in nineteenth-century England, but in Zurich it was Zwingli alone who mattered.

With the founding of the Zwingliverein in Zurich in 1897 and its journal, *Zwingliana*, a few years later, it was clear that Zwingli was to be the symbol of a fiercely Reformed, anti-Catholic confessionalism.[41] He had been drawn into the Swiss Kulturkampf of the late nineteenth century. If one looks at the early issues of *Zwingliana* one hardly finds a note critical of the eponymous reformer. In 1904, Emil Egli, the first editor of *Zwingliana*, made a speech in which he argued that although Zwingli was now recognised, it was Heinrich Bullinger who had arguably made the greater contribution to the Reformed church.[42] Egli was putting the case for a critical edition of Bullinger's works, but the redoubtable Georg Finsler and Hermann Eescher put the counter case that an edition of Zwingli's works was a greater need. Finsler carried the day and the Zwingliverein devoted its financial resources to the production of Zwingli's works, an edition that continues to this day. The consequence was the skewing of research in the direction of Zwingli, who put his successor in the shade, where he would remain for much of the twentieth century.

Along the way there have been fairly isolated attempts to deal with Heinrich Bullinger. In the nineteenth century the most significant came from the pedagogue Carl Pestalozzi, who produced his *Heinrich Bullinger. Leben und ausgewählte Schriften* (1858). During the Second World War an extremely important work appeared which has never been given due attention: André Bouvier's *Heinrich Bullinger. Réformateur et conseiller oecuménique, le successeur de Zwingli, d'après sa correspondance avec les réformés et les humanistes de langue française* (Paris 1940). Its failure to make an impact on Reformation scholarship had much to do with its unfortunate timing. Another work which appeared during the War did, however, prove much more influential, and this was Fritz Blanke's slightly pious and pietistical study of Bullinger's youth, *Der junge Bullinger 1504-1531* (1942). The 1950s brought two significant studies, the first on the Europe-wide influence of Bullinger's *Decades* and the second on Bullinger's relationship with the Anabaptists: Walter Hollweg, *Heinrich Bullingers Hausbuch. Eine Untersuchung über die Anfänge der reformierten Predigtliteratur* (1956); and Heinold Fast, *Heinrich Bullinger und die Täufer* (1957). In the following decade there appeared three more influential works: Ernst Koch, *Die*

---

41. Bernd Moeller, "Der Zwingli Verein und die reformationsgeschichtliche Forschung," *Zwingliana* 25 (1998): 5-20.

42. Fritz Büsser, "Zürich-'Die Stadt auf dem Berg.' Bullingers reformatorisches Vermächtnis an der Wende zum 21. Jahrhundert," *Zwingliana* 25 (1998): 21-42.

Theologie der Confessio Helvetica posterior (1962); Joachim Staedtke, *Die Theologie des jungen Bullinger* (1962); and Susi Hausammann, *Römerbriefauslegung zwischen Humanismus und Reformation. Eine Studie zu Heinrich Bullingers Römerbriefvorlesungen von 1525* (1970).

It was not until the 1970s, with the approach of the 400th anniversary of Bullinger's death, that scholarship on Bullinger began to take flight. Here one must note above all the 1972 bibliography of Bullinger's works by Joachim Staedtke.[43] This was to form the prelude to an edition of the reformer's works that would include the letters, theological writings, and historical works. This has remained the blueprint and now under new leadership it has been revived by the John à Lasco Library in Emden. The conference marking the anniversary in 1975 proved to be a watershed in Bullinger research.[44] Under the leadership of Fritz Büsser the Institute for Swiss Reformation History in Zurich became dedicated to work on Bullinger. Over the past thirty years there has been a proliferation of work on Bullinger by British, North American, German and Swiss scholars such as Wayne Baker, Hans Ulrich Bächtold, Pamela Biel, Andrew Pettegree, Bruce Gordon, Diarmaid MacCulloch, Andreas Mühling, Peter Opitz, and Mark Taplin.[45]

The 500th anniversary of Heinrich Bullinger's birth in Bremgarten has brought the opportunity to continue our study of this remarkable and enigmatic figure and, perhaps more importantly, to test our assumptions about the Protestant Reformation. Bullinger lived through a remarkable span of the sixteenth-century Reformation. In the 1570s he stood alone among the leaders of Protestant Europe as one who had lived through the heady days of the 1520s: Zwingli, Luther, Melanchthon, and Calvin were all gone. Heinrich Bullinger constructed the Reformed church through his understanding of theology, the Bible, history, and politics. The many dimensions of his life remind us of how complex and contradictory the Reformation could be, and above all that it was a profoundly human event.

---

43. *HBBibl.*

44 Ulrich Gäbler/Erland Herkenrath eds., *Heinrich Bullinger 1504-1575. Gesammelte Aufsätze zum 400. Todestag*, vol. 1: *Leben und Werk* (ZBRG 7; Zurich: TVZ, 1975).

45. J. Wayne Baker, *Heinrich Bullinger and the Covenant. The Other Reformed Tradition* (Athens, Ohio: Ohio University Press, 1980); Hans Ulrich Bächtold, *Bullinger vor dem Rat;* Pamela Biel, *Doorkeepers at the House of Righteousness.* Andrew Pettegree, *Foreign Protestant Communities in Sixteenth-Century London* (Oxford: OUP, 1986); Bruce Gordon, *Clerical Discipline and the Rural Reformation. The Synod in Zurich 1532-1580* (Berne: Peter Lang, 1992); Diarmaid MacCulloch, *Thomas Cranmer. A Life* (New Haven, CT: Yale UP, 1996); Andreas Mühling, *Heinrich Bullingers europäische Kirchenpolitik;* Mark Taplin, *The Italian Reformers and the Zurich Church;* Peter Opitz's habilitation on Bullinger's *Decades* will appear in 2004.

Part I: Theology, Spirituality and Ecclesiology

1

Heinrich Bullinger as Theologian:
Thematic, Comprehensive, and Schematic

Edward Dowey

Our title is not Heinrich Bullinger's theology, but Heinrich Bullinger *as theologian.*[1] It is not primarily the what or content of his thought, but the how of it, his method or methods. The two are inseparable, but our chief concern in this essay is with the latter. What *kind* of thinker was Bullinger?

Despite the vast increase of research in recent years, which has issued in numerous splendid articles, monographs, an increased availability of sources, and quite naturally, a growth in common knowledge of many kinds concerning Bullinger, there has not yet emerged a consensus on how to understand the baffling variety of ways in which he did his work or the multiple forms in which he published and republished his theological ideas.[2] Our present task is to study this widely recognised problem and to proffer a way of understanding Bullinger that may advance the discussion, possibly by means of the terms offered in our title: thematic, comprehensive, and schematic. Part I is an informal survey of some commonly received results of twentieth-century research. Part II is a debate with several specific recent characterisations of Bullinger as theologian. Part III offers an alternative approach, based on brief analysis of selected Bullinger titles, both thematic and comprehensive. Part IV endeavours to characterise Bullinger as theologian, evincing a preference for the *Decades* in the process.[3] Part V offers a suggested outline for a conspectus of his theological thought. This outline is not

---

1. This essay is largely as it was left by the author. In places the footnotes have been completed or updated. The text itself has only been altered in order to have consistency of spelling and titles.

2. The secondary literature about Heinrich Bullinger from the sixteenth century onward, surveyed by E. Herkenrath in 1977 (*HBBibl* II) lists about 2,000 items, 40% of which date from the 1940s and after. Where appropriate, subsequent references to secondary literature will generally include the serial number assigned by Herkenrath. Bullinger's own work will carry the serial number assigned in *HBBibl* I. More recent bibliographies of work on Bullinger are found in Bruce Gordon, "Heinrich Bullinger" in Carter Lindberg ed., *The Reformation Theologians* (Oxford: Blackwell, 2002), 170-83. A list of recent publications is to be found in the "Neue Literatur zur zwinglischen Reformation" in *Zwingliana.*

3. *The Decades of Henry Bullinger* (Cambridge: CUP, 1851), *HBBibl* I, no. 223f. Generally, reference to the *Decades* will be to this English version. Where necessary, the Latin text, *Sermonum Decades quinque* (Zurich: Froschauer, 1552), *HBBibl* I, no. 184, will be used.

drawn from any one of Bullinger's works, but through analysis of all of his major works.

I. Characteristics of Bullinger as Theologian Generally Recognised

In both the older and the more recent Bullinger interpretation, four common conceptions are generally recognised. Always he has borne the sobriquet "Zwingli's successor," and this has frequently been the point of departure for study of his work. In addition there is a long-standing, increasing awareness of the genuine independence and originality with which he marked the Reformed tradition in Eastern Europe, in Germany and Holland, and in Anglo-Saxon Puritanism. Secondly, Bullinger has been long designated as an important source of the covenant or federal theology that was powerful in the following centuries for the Reformed church and theology, and in political federalism. Thirdly, he is increasingly recognised as important for biblical interpretation, both in the 1520s and throughout the century through his widely distributed biblical commentaries and sermons. Finally, Bullinger's contributions to the doctrine of the sacraments have long been seen to be formative and unifying for the Reformed tradition; and formidable in polemic, especially against Lutheranism. His joint work with Calvin on the Lord's Supper in the *Consensus Tigurinus*[4] was a major contribution toward holding together the Reformed branch of the Reformation.

In the course of the foregoing common opinions, there has also been more or less general agreement that Bullinger's theology may be characterised as (1) biblical in root, (2) orthodox and catholic in intent, (3) dominated by practical, churchly motifs in expression, (4) historical in its conceptuality, and (5) comprehensive in scope. Somewhat more fully: (1) Bullinger's doctrine of the Word shows strong preference for the *viva vox* as passed along by the patriarchs before finally being written down, by inspiration of the Spirit. This written word served to guide the preaching in the "living voice" in the church where "the preaching of the Word of God is the Word of God." Bullinger was also, throughout his career as interpreter of the scriptures, a thorough humanist in grammatico-historical and rhetorical analysis and representation of the text. (2) Bullinger's intent to be orthodox and catholic is evident in his assurance that he speaks with and for the whole history of the true church, against the eight hundred years of canonised novelties that Rome had imposed. Bullinger prefixes twelve ancient documents to the *Decades* in the conviction that anyone who looks will understand that the Protestant faith is not new, but is the doctrine of all, derived from the Word of God, supported by the fathers and councils. (3) The practicality of Bullinger's teaching is twofold: negatively it is wholly non-speculative in intent; and positively his thought lives wholly within and on behalf of the historical and daily life of the church. There is no private virtuoso theology in Bullinger, and no theological or spiritual or other soliloquy. This feature is of special significance to the *ad hoc* character of most of his writing, and the rhetorical determination of appropriate writing style and organisation of his material. (4) History seems to be the most natural *metier* of Bullinger's mind. Sequence, comparative chronology,

4. *HBBibl* I, no. 624.

facts of background, the movement from origins to the present play a large role in his apologetic, his polemic, and his conception of what is "orthodox and catholic." At the same time he has been said to have a platonically tinted apprehension of history in which no real development takes place. The substance of faith and of the covenant are the same from the "first basic gospel" of Genesis 3:15 to the end of time. (5) Throughout his theological life work, Bullinger saw the biblical revelation and the teaching and practice that arose therefrom in the various circumstances of history as a comprehensive whole. While he developed many individual themes in various ways, his thought was never, from the earliest times, piecemeal, but conceived as a part or aspect of the whole. In this matter several questions must be raised as the present essay proceeds.

II. Critique of Several Characterisations of Bullinger as Theologian

Implicit in the foregoing is the question of what kind of theologian Bullinger was. Several writings of the last twenty-five years have offered significant comment on this matter. The weightiest of these is the very detailed and heavily documented study of the *Second Helvetic Confession* by Ernst Koch, *Die Theologie der Confessio Helvetica Posterior,*[5] which has been called by Wilhelm Neuser "a veritable textbook of Bullinger's theology."[6] And so it is. Not only is every aspect of the *Confession* meticulously analyzed, but through wide reading in about seventy other Bullinger titles, each element of the *Confession* is seen as dealt with in others of Bullinger's published works. All this is founded on careful textual work, noting Bullinger's own emendations in his original manuscript and their significance.[7]

While professing not to characterise Bullinger's theology as a whole, but to produce only what is called for by the theology of this one document,[8] Koch nonetheless argues, against certain other Bullinger specialists, "that Heinrich Bullinger was a really systematic thinker, and that the *Confessio Helvetica Posterior* is a really systematic writing."[9] Koch warns that some others who see Bullinger as a "mediating theologian and a man of praxis," run the danger "of overlooking the fact that Bullinger's theology is a systematic whole, and as such offers a thoroughly self-contained, independent achievement."[10] He holds that the *Confessio* "as a systematic writing may rightly be taken as a summary recapitulation of Bullinger's theology."[11] And "the *Confessio Helvetica Posterior* takes its place as a dogmatic work of magnificent completeness and impressive theological consistency."[12] At the same time Koch insists that he is not making an effort

---

5. *HBBibl* II, no. 1854.
6. v. *infra*, note 35.
7. This part of Koch's work is published in J. Staedtke/E. Herkenrath eds, *Glauben und Bekennen: 400 Jahre Confessio Helvetica Posterior* (Zurich: Zwingli Verlag, 1966), 13-40.
8. Koch, *Theologie*, 16.
9. Ibid., 16.
10. Ibid.
11. Ibid., 18, note 7.
12. Ibid., 415.

"to present the individual chapters of the *Confession* as systematically deducible elements of a higher concept."[13]

Koch does, however, despite his own disavowals, characterise Bullinger's theology as a whole: "Bullinger's theology is Federal theology."[14] He insists upon "the constitutive significance" of the covenant concept for Bullinger's theological thought structure. "The covenant conception in the entire fullness of its possibilities for expression and ramifications is...the symbol of the inclusive conception of Bullinger's entire theology." Koch thus forms a judgement that goes beyond his stated purpose, and crosses the limits of his professed method. Here, he resembles certain other Bullinger specialists (Gooszen, Van t'Hooft, and to a degree Staedtke), who find in the covenant the "golden thread" that can be traced through his thought. But Koch is first in insisting that the complete systematic coherence of the *Confessio* has its key in the covenant concept, although that concept is all but totally absent from the document.[15] The term *foedus* appears once as a synonym for *testamentum*, and it appears four more times within the brief compass of the doctrine concerning baptism, the sign of the covenant. That is all.[16] Koch does not derive the doctrine from the *Confession* itself. That would be a total impossibility. Rather, he writes a long excursus on the "Concept of the Covenant according to Heinrich Bullinger."[17] Here he ranges widely through Bullinger's teaching, none of which comes from the *Second Helvetic Confession*. "It is not of decisive significance that the *concept* of the covenant is relatively seldom used(!). The analysis of the theology of the *Confession* itself, both in single parts and in its entire conception, has led by a compelling inner logic to this concept and its structure."[18]

It would seem that the alleged "inner logic" has compelled only Koch–not Bullinger himself–and has led to serious over-interpretation. It causes Koch to rearrange the chapters into his own original sequence to expose the covenant structure. Thus the chapter sequence in his soteriology was originally xi, xvi, vi, x. After criticism of his dissertation,[19] for publication, he removed vi and x (providence and predestination) from soteriology to the doctrine of God with the following sequence: iii, vi, vii, viii, x, xi, xii. The argument, however, did not change.[20] The "inner logic" also leads Koch to engage in a tortuous process of finding covenant elements and structure throughout. The proper procedure here should not be to fit the parts of the confession into a structure that is plainly not there–however impressive it may be elsewhere in Bullinger's thought–but to ex-

13. Ibid., 415f.
14. Ibid., 416.
15. "This conception (covenant), which is never uttered *expressis verbis*, is nonetheless the hidden law of the theological thought development." Ibid., 415 *et passim*.
16. Ibid., 416, text and note 6. N.B. Schrenk's terminology.
17. Ibid., 388-99.
18. Ibid., 417.
19. Leipzig Dissertation (1960) of Koch shows this sequence. The criticism is from Dowey, *Glauben und Bekennen* (*HBBibl* II, no. 1811), 211.
20. Koch continues to defend altering the sequence in *Theologie* (*HBBibl* II, no. 1854), 19f. Strange, that this condition should arise in the theological masterpiece of such a strenuously systematic theologian as Koch claims Bullinger to be.

pose the actual contents of the document and appreciate the structure that is actually present. What Koch's method proves at most is that the teaching of the *Confession* does not contradict Bullinger's covenant scheme as elsewhere presented—which in any case, one would not expect.

The problem remains: why did Bullinger *not* use a covenant scheme in the *Second Helvetic Confession*, if he is a truly systematic theologian and the key to his thought is the covenant and the *Second Helvetic Confession* is his crowning theological masterpiece? To interpret a Bullinger writing in this way, as if, since he is allegedly a systematician, his work must be a tightly constructed whole and dominated by a single principle, may be to miss his character as a thinker. At best, it reads implications drawn by the researcher back into the work of Bullinger, where he, himself, did not do so.

Two more objections to Koch's presentation remain. Despite close attention to an immense amount of primary material and secondary interpretation, Koch has made one or two mistakes in reading Bullinger that are important for his thesis. (1) One is that he speaks of an "Adamic"[21] covenant in Bullinger that lays the groundwork for a "supralapsarian covenant of creation."[22] There is no such thing. The "Adamic" covenant of Bullinger is based on his reading of Genesis 3:15, the so-called Protoevangelion, whereby the announcement of salvation to Adam *after* the fall is read as the first announcement of the covenant. This is, in any case, a covenant of *salvation*, not creation. (2) Koch wrenches the matter further when he speaks of the "original relation of God and humanity" as the "true reflection of the relationship of covenant God and covenant partner"[23] consisting of command and obedience. This procedure gives a "legalistic-ethical" tone to his whole theology.[24] Bullinger, however, never extrapolates the covenant concept into the order of creation, any more than did Calvin. This came later and constituted probably the decisive element of what may properly be called the Federal theology. When that step was made, a covenant *system* was underway that could embrace all aspects of the God-man relationship, including finally with Cocceius, the reading of predestination as a covenant of redemption. Bullinger was certainly a fore-runner of these important streams of thought, but he himself did not go so far—most especially not in the *Second Helvetic Confession*. The continuing question is why he did not.

Koch's thesis that the covenant doctrine is the systematic key to the *Second Helvetic Confession* is, surprisingly, taken up by an old master of Swiss Reformed theology, Gottfried Locher. In his contribution to the jubilee book for the 400th anniversary of the *Second Helvetic*, his assignment is to treat "the doctrine of the Holy Spirit." Locher writes, "E. Koch shows convincingly that the eternal covenant belongs to the basic concepts of Bullinger's *Confession*, even though

---

21. Ibid., 395ff. (*Adambund*).

22. Ibid., 397, note 59, *et passim*. Koch registers his disagreement with von Korf, Schrenk, and Staedtke.

23. Ibid., 425, 429, *et passim*.

24. Ibid., 427. cf. David Weir, *The Origins of Federal Theology in Sixteenth Century Reformation Thought* (New York: OUP, 1990), 34.

the expression is seldom mentioned."[25] Then Locher proceeds so as to identify the doctrine of the Spirit with that of the covenant.

> It appears more and more that "Covenant" and "Spirit" not only balance one another or merely supplement one another, but that we must recognise a certain identity of the two...Both lines of expression are numerous enough to present and explain one another. The Spirit lives in the covenant, or the covenant lives in the Spirit.[26]

This means that covenant, though practically absent from the *Second Helvetic Confession*, is present under the code-word "Spirit"! All must agree that Locher's motive is certainly correct: that is, to read the Spirit's work in the community which is the church, and through Christ–and not privately in individual souls. The *Second Helvetic* is not a document of pietism: agreed. But Bullinger himself makes this vividly clear from beginning to end–and he does so *without* using the term or the idea of covenant to explain what he means by Spirit! We should not do it for him.

Endre Zindely's analysis of the *Second Helvetic* in the *Theologische Realenzyklopaedie* adopts as unproblematic Koch's view that the key concept of the Confession is the covenant but, predictably, mentions it only in connection with baptism.[27] Walter E. Meyer, while admiring the treatment of the Spirit in the above named work of Gottfried Locher rejects Koch's view of the centrality of the covenant.[28]

Again, our solution should not be to smuggle the covenant into the *Second Helvetic Confession*. Our very real problem is to find out what it means that after about forty years of reflection, of preaching, of teaching, and of writing–which included about a dozen full, formal, comprehensive presentations of his theological thought–Bullinger's masterpiece, the *Confessio Helvetica Posterior*, does not contain the doctrine that he from time to time elsewhere calls the *scopus Scripturae*, and *scopus legis, prophetarum, et apostolorum*.

J. Wayne Baker, in *Heinrich Bullinger and the Covenant*, begins by focusing narrowly on covenant material in Bullinger's earliest period and finds that "Bullinger's *De Scripturae negotio* of 30 November 1523, contains important background for his later covenant idea, although it does not treat of the covenant per se."[29] But in *Von dem Touff,* of 10 November 1525,[30] "Bullinger had expressed all the elements of his fully developed covenant theology." Although this may be "perhaps ... too early to call Bullinger a covenant theologian, unquestionably the covenant became the first principle of his theology in the next two years."[31] And

25. *Glauben und Bekennen*, 311.
26. Ibid., 335.
27. *TRE* VIII:169-73.
28. Walter E. Meyer, "Soteriologie, Eschatologie und Christologie in der Confessio Helvetica Posterior," *Zwingliana* 12/6 (1966): 402, notes 58f.
29. J. Wayne Baker, *Heinrich Bullinger and the Covenant: The Other Reformed Tradition* (Athens, Ohio: Ohio Univ. Press, 1980), 4.
30. J. Staedtke, *Die Theologie des jungen Bullinger* (Zurich: Zwingli Verlag, 1962), doc. no. 32, 273f.
31. Ibid., 9f.

finally his *Answer to Burchard* demonstrates that by early 1527 the covenant had become the interpretive motif of Bullinger's theology, the principal formative and organising factor in his thought."[32] Although the mosaic of Bullinger materials thus assembled seems to make Baker's point, a broader survey of Bullinger's thought demonstrates not only that this judgement is premature, but possibly that Bullinger in his entire theological lifework never had a single "principal formative and organising factor." Certainly neither Staedtke nor Hausammann, working with these same early writings, reaches Baker's conclusion. And Ernst Koch, who holds that at a later period the covenant is such a key for Bullinger, cannot go all the way with Baker. In an admiring review of Baker's book, he suggests gently that "the author presents his view single mindedly, clearly, and almost simplistically, and draws unbroken lines in theological history. On this issue the question arises if it is not *too* unbroken."[33] My own suggestion is that it may be Baker's consuming interest in both theological and political federalism that leads him to be less concerned with the problems of Bullinger's thought as a whole, and overly concentrated on a single theme of subsequent great influence.[34] The problem remains: given these grounds for a covenant program, early and late, why did Bullinger *not* develop such a theology in his principal comprehensive writings?

Professor Wilhelm Neuser in the *Handbuch der Dogmen- und Theologiegeschichte*, takes another tack.[35] He, too, regards the *Second Helvetic Confession* as a "comprehensive summary of Bullinger's theology," and uses the *Confession* as an outline for presenting Bullinger's thought, even though its "systematic structure is a matter of controversy," and even though "the covenant theology, which is typical of Bullinger's other writings, is here missing."[36] Accepting the warning not to reorganise the *Second Helvetic* as Koch did, or to reduce everything to a single systematic method, he offers a different type of clue. Bullinger's systematic method is easy to demonstrate when one compares the sequence of chapter titles of the dogmatic writings that Koch presents in his diagrammatic overview. The special character of the systematic method, and beyond this, of the theology of Bullinger, becomes clear: the God concept and the Christology are interchangeable (*austauschbar*).[37] That means the doctrine of God already contains the soteriology, and the Christology merely extends the general doctrine of God. On this basis in the *Decades* (1549-51) he can begin the first part with faith, justification, Apostles' Creed, love, law, magistracy, and good works, and then follow in the second part with creation, providence, predestination, and Christology. Also in the *Catechesis pro Adultioribus* of 1559, creation is handled first in Christology. In other writings, Christology and justification/salvation are found at the beginning in the doctrine of creation and

32. Ibid., 14, cf. 48.

33. *Theologische Literaturzeitung*, 1984, col. 44.

34. Charles S. McCoy/J. Wayne Baker, *Fountainhead of Federalism: Heinrich Bullinger and the Covenantal Tradition. With a Translation of De testamento seu foedere Dei unico et aeterno (1534)* (Louisville, Kentucky: Westminster/John Knox Press, 1991) which contains the first English translation of Bullinger's *De Testamento*.

35. (Göttingen: Vandenhoeck & Ruprecht, 1980), II:203ff., 207ff., 224-38.

36. Ibid., 225.

37. Ibid., 226, 229, 230.

providence. The confusing variety finds its solution in the continuing situation that Christology and soteriology are only extensions of the God concept. So he can conclude:

The *Second Helvetic Confession* is thus a typical production of the Bullingerian theology, even though the covenant theology is not presented and worked out here. It bears the distinguishing marks of Bullinger's systematic work: (1) At the beginning stands a detailed hermeneutic reflection concerning Holy Scripture. (2) The general doctrine of God is completed by special Christological and pneumatological statements. (3) God's activity in Holy History is always the same and good; Old and New Covenant have the same content.[38]

The observations–with the exception concerning *Catechesis*–are externally correct, but very serious problems remain, as follows. This analysis simply leaves the covenant concept stranded. It becomes marginal to Bullinger's systematic work, and in fact plays no further role in Neuser's presentation. Having criticised Koch for an exaggerated effort to make the covenant a systematic key to unlock the *Second Helvetic* and Bullinger's theology in general, Neuser must now be criticised for dropping it altogether.

Neuser takes Koch's diagrammatic overview too much at face value, as if all these writings were sufficiently analyzed by a comparative survey of their chapter titles. Just one example: there is no way to tell from Koch's display that the doctrinal *Wahrhafftes Bekenntnis* of 1545 is organised throughout, not by Bullinger's personal method, but by the traditional twelve articles of the Apostles' Creed.

Neuser's approach fails to deal with the special character of the various writings. Particularly he ignores the purpose and the audience to which each was directed, and the effects this may have had on the "systematic" method as revealed in the sequence of topics.

Neuser's most original suggestion–repeated several times, as we have just seen–is that the God concept and the Christology are "exchangeable" or "interchangeable." If this means merely a matter of the external sequence of subject matter, it is certainly a right observation in a comparison of the *Decades* and the *Second Helvetic Confession*. But is this more than a matter of what the later scholastic orthodox thinkers referred to as the *ordo essendi* and the *ordo cognoscendi*–always posing viable alternatives to any Christian theologian? I suspect the formal problem here represented was not decided by Bullinger on formal, systematic grounds, but was based on several other considerations out of which he evolved a scheme (for want of a better word, and avoiding the term system) for each of the writings. These other considerations might be polemic, didactic, confessional, traditional, historical, even homiletic, and require close analysis of all his comprehensive presentations of doctrine.

The article by Fritz Büsser in the *Theologische Realenzyklopaedie* divides Bullinger's theological lifework into three successive phases, the third of which begins with the *Decades* (1549-51) and includes both the *Summa* (1556) and the

---

38. Ibid., 226.

Confessio Helvetica Posterior (1561-66).[39] Büsser characterises the latter period with Koch and Locher as a "systematic unfolding of the covenant concept ensconced in the *Second Helvetic Confession,*" then notes objections that have been offered "on good grounds"[40] (Dowey) to this way of understanding. He concludes "all in all this survey shows clearly that a comprehensive overview of Bullinger's theology in its historical development, now as formerly, is lacking." And he predicts that many more monographs on the most important *loci* must be written before such a comprehensive whole will be possible.

Certainly the latter evaluation is correct. Nonetheless, the matter may not be quite so indecisive if Bullinger's *ad hoc* rhetorically accommodated schemata are taken more seriously than heretofore.

III. An Alternative Approach to Understanding Bullinger's Theological Method

Among Bullinger's numerous theological works there are, broadly speaking, three major types especially relevant to our investigation: biblical commentary; thematic and polemic treatises; comprehensive presentations spanning the whole territory of Christian theology. The latter, for specific reasons that will emerge, one must refrain from calling "systematic" works.

As to the first, biblical works, these consist chiefly of commentaries and sermons. Bullinger had commented both on the Gospels of Matthew, John and Luke, and the Acts and epistles (especially Romans and Hebrews) in publicly delivered lectures in German (1525-7) while still a young schoolmaster in Kappel.[41] In the 1530s he brought out singly, then altogether in a folio that was to go through twelve editions, Latin commentaries on the epistles. Then in the 1540s he published expanded folio size Latin commentaries on each of the Gospels. Also included here are several hundred of Bullinger's published sermons, e.g. on Jeremiah (1557), Revelation (1537), Daniel (1565), and Isaiah (1567), as biblical commentary, because he always worked from exegesis of a text, and characteristically in sequence, *lectio continua.* These biblical works, while indubitably basic in revealing the mind and method of Bullinger, will not be discussed here. Bullinger's profile as a constructive thinker does not emerge so clearly in these writings because he necessarily follows the sequence and disposition of the biblical material. He must be found working on projects of his own devising.

Thematic and Polemic Treatises of the 1530s

In this brief presentation, one may get a more advanced picture of how Bullinger constructed his theology if one looks at the second and third categories mentioned above: thematic and comprehensive theological works. It is difficult to know which to place first, because Bullinger was concerned with the whole as

---

39. *TRE* VII:375-87.
40. Ibid., 384.
41. Susi Hausammann, *Römerbriefauslegung zwischen Humanismus und Reformation: Eine Studie zu Heinrich Bullingers Römerbriefauslegung von 1525* (Zurich: TVZ, 1970*), HBBibl* II, no. 1880.

well as the parts from the very beginning. Arbitrarily, then, we turn first to a selection of five thematic and polemic treatises of the 1530s–all written after he had
become head of the Zurich church, although foreshadowed in the Kappel years.

The treatises mentioned here with thumbnail descriptions show the biblical,
catholic and orthodox, and historical elements of Bullinger's thought in his own
idiom and plan. These writings can be characterised as thematic in two senses:
they carry through biblical historical themes, and also life-long motifs of Bullinger's thought.

1. *On the One Eternal Covenant...*(1534).[42] This is one of Bullinger's most
famous and influential works, called by Gottlob Schrenk the first use in theological history of the covenant idea as a "constitutive dogmatic principle." The thesis
is in the title: that there is in essence *one* covenant between God and the human
race and that the twoness of "old" and "new" covenants concerns only accidental
and historical variety; that various abrogations of ceremonial, civic, or political
elements do not affect the fundamental definition, conditions, or eternal duration
of the covenant. This covenant is the summary and scope of all scripture. The
polemic point is chiefly against the Anabaptists' denigration of the value of the
Old Testament in the Christian era. By contrast Bullinger holds that the true
Christian faith is not merely a few hundred years old, but 6,733 years! Formally,
this orderly, careful treatise shows that Bullinger knows how to build an argument from philologically based definitions through the gathering and ordering of
biblical and other material to a summary epilogue.

Bullinger reprinted this treatise in all the large folio editions of the commentaries on the epistles, together with number three below. The Latin text is basic.
Translations were made into German and Dutch.

2. *The Old Faith ("Der alte Glaube")* (1537).[43] The same basic theme that
makes up the epilogue of *De Testamento* now appears developed with scant mention of the covenant as such under the rubric of "faith"–this time with pointed
polemic against the Roman church's argument that the Protestant Reformation
was introducing a novel and heretical faith. Against it Bullinger argues that "our
first Christian parents," Adam and Eve, "from the beginning of the world" (more
precisely, from the announcement of the "blessed seed" in Genesis 3:15) knew
Christ and held the same faith as all patriarchs, prophets, "pious kings," and
apostles–and of course the sixteenth century reformers. Translated into English
by Miles Coverdale and published without mention of Bullinger,[44] this German
treatise is even more single-minded than *De Testamento*, although less technical
and more eloquent. The stated purpose was to comfort and strengthen people
troubled by the alleged novelty of the Reformation faith, a strongly pastoral concern.

---

42. Bullinger works are here cited by short title and the number assigned in Joachim Staedtke's *Beschreibendes Verzeichnis der gedruckten Werke von Heinrich Bullinger (HBBibl I)*. In
this case, as follows: *De Testamento (HBBibl I, no. 54)*.

43. *HBBibl* I, no. 99, cf. E. A. Dowey, "The Old Faith: Comments on One of Heinrich Bullinger's Most Distinctive Treatises" in Willem van 't Spijker ed., *Calvin: Erbe und Auftrag. Festschrift für Wilhelm Neuser zu seinem 65. Geburtstag* (Kampen: Kok Pharos, 1991), 270-8.

44. *Writings and Translations of Miles Coverdale* (Cambridge: CUP, 1844), *HBBibl* I, no.
108.

Bullinger in the *Decades* specifically links these two treatises as dealing with a common theme.[45]

3. *An Orthodox Assertion of the two natures of Christ* (1534).[46] Bullinger's first detailed presentation of Christology, written in Latin and never translated, was published, after the first edition, with the folio volumes of Pauline and "canonical" epistles.[47] This is a distinction it shares with *De Testamento*, written the same year. Its chief feature is the defence of the catholic and orthodox Christology of the early councils and fathers, solely from the Bible, and not on the basis of any intrinsic or ecclesiastical authority. He holds throughout for the simplicity of the doctrine itself, and attributes to various human vices the attacks from the beginning of heretical distortions and perversions. Delivered as an address on the holiday of Zurich's early martyrs, Felix and Regula, the subject matter was chosen to fight the errors of Claudius of Savoy, who confused the two natures. There is much presentation of creedal and patristic texts, then errors, respectively on the deity, the humanity, and the unity of the natures. While Bullinger's constructive arguments are rigorously biblical, he defends the use of non-biblical terms (*vocabula nova in religionis negotia*) to protect scripture from heretics, as Calvin did also at a later date.

4. *On the Authority of Scripture...*(1538)[48] was dedicated to Henry VIII. It is a long treatise in two books, and yet Bullinger's classic statement (later built into the *Decades*) on the sole authority of the Word over all traditions does not appear in it. Whether in oral form (the patriarchs) or written form (scripture), or subsequently as preached in the living voice, the Word is one and the same Word. Bullinger's biblical, patristic and classical learning are displayed in a fulsome way to show that pagan philosophy is all more recent than scripture, that the Word found in scripture created the church, and not vice versa, that scripture is perfect in fulfilling all needs for the worship of God and living the Christian life. It is "the oldest and most perfect philosophy," adequate against the superstitions and tyranny of the Roman "antistes." There is no mention of the New Covenant in this long and many-sided defence, even at several places, such as Bullinger's dealing with the law and aspects of the law that are passing in contrast to those that are eternal, where his usual covenant arguments would seem to be called for.

5. *On the Origin of Errors...*(1539).[49] After two much shorter works of this title (1526, 1529), Bullinger greatly lengthened this material to a large volume that was to appear in translation in French, German, and Dutch. In Book I (36 chapters), he occupies himself largely with errors of worship, after six chapters on a true doctrine of God, which include covenant teaching in chapters 4 and 6. First come the superstition and errors of the pagans (chapters 7-10), then errors of Jews (chapters 10-11), then the errors of Christians (to the end of the book) in matters of idolatry, invocation of the saints, and so on. Book II is devoted wholly

---

45. Bullinger, *Sermonum Decades quinque*, (*HBBibl* I, no. 184), *Tomus Secundus*, f. 149ᵛ, v. *infra*. III. viii.
46. *HBBibl* I, no. 62.
47. Ibid., no. 84-8, 91-5.
48. Ibid., no. 111.
49. Ibid., no. 12.

to errors of the papal mass. Polytheism, following Lactantius, is the root of all these errors, and its equivalent, the corruptions of true worship whether outside of Christianity or within it.

These treatises, just quickly sketched, could be supplemented by others from the same period. In each Bullinger was defending the same thing: the single, simple, perfect Word of God, known from the beginning of human history, and sufficient for salvation, for worship, and holy living. Each was called forth by some polemic situation. Differences in depth, style, form, language, and learned elaboration are accounted for primarily by accommodation to intended recipients. Along with the fundamental *sola scriptura* are themes that constantly appear in the more comprehensive works, especially in the *Decades*, sometimes almost verbatim. Chief among these are (1) the antiquity of the Christian faith, (2) the one eternal covenant, and (3) catholic orthodoxy. These closely related themes in Bullinger's theology create not so much a formal presupposition, or even a body of unquestioned assumptions or systematic principles, but rather the theological atmosphere within which he works.

The suggestion here is to designate these themes as *pervasive convictions* with which his thought is imbued. Together they lend a kind of moderate triumphalism to Bullinger's outlook on life. The data of historical awareness with which he reinforces the divine word and divine providence are always in the service of the unchanging truth, present from the beginning to the consummation of human history. Despite the alacrity with which Bullinger rises to defend truth and combat error, as the true church has always done even at the cost of persecution, there is a historico-theological calm in his basic apprehension (*Grundanschauung*) of reality which this invented term "pervasive conviction" is meant to express. If these observations are authentic, this reveals a prominent quality of Bullinger as theologian.

Comprehensive Works

This third category of Bullinger titles may be considered "programmatic and theologically comprehensive," that is, writings that treat all or nearly all theological topics within a single work. All who study Bullinger have profited from Ernst Koch's diagrammatic and comparative overview of these *Gesamtdarstellungen*, which is printed as a large fold-out page in his volume discussed above. His helpful diagrammatic and comparative table of Bullinger's comprehensive writings, presents in parallel columns the chapter headings of nine Bullinger titles, spaced where possible to expose the likeness and dissimilarity of their structure. The titles chosen are as follows: *Loci Communes, Wahrhaffte Bekanntnuss, Sermonum Decades quinque, Antithesis et compendium evangelicae, Ecclesias evangelicas, Summa Catechesis pro adultioribus, Vester Grund, Confessio Helvetica posterior.*

In the present work, we exclude two of these works. The *Antithesis et Compendium* (1551) is too incomplete to be considered theologically comprehensive. Similarly, the *Ecclesias Evangelicas...* (1552) contains no doctrines of the Trinity, Christology, Man, Sin, Fall, Church, Providence or Predestination, and is thus set aside for the purposes of this chapter.

However, a document not seen by Koch, the manuscript *Institutionum* (1531), which qualifies in every way as a carefully worked out series of topics in outline form, has been added. The dates of these presentations are both earlier and later than the thematic treatises discussed above, which manifests Bullinger's awareness of the whole of theology from early to late in his career; they are not a late development.

The thesis of the following survey–stated in advance to put the reader on guard–is that Bullinger's thought does not lend itself to a single "systematic" method or structure. No one of his own comprehensive theological works can serve as an adequate structure on which to arrange a synoptic presentation of his thought. Further, that the program or sequence of treatment of the *themes*, which in content remain fairly constant across the years, is determined more by the particular purpose of a given writing (broadly, a rhetorical accommodation) than by working out from within the interrelation of biblical themes throughout a life-long systematic interest, as is the case with Calvin.

The following selection deals with two sketches from his early years as Kappel schoolmaster and Bremgarten pastor, one full-bodied confession which was written for the defence of the Zurich theology, following the treatises presented above and embodying or ignoring variously their content. And finally, three works that are unquestionably on any list of his masterpieces of theology are presented.

1. *Loci Communes Sacri...*(1527).[50] This first comprehensive sketch of the whole field of theology by Heinrich Bullinger appears as part of his conception of a program for the education of theological students, in his *Ratio Studiorum* (1527), while he was still schoolmaster in Kappel. Part II of the *Ratio* on biblical and theological studies (following a first part containing detailed classical propaedeutic) contains chapters on biblical interpretation, the main work of the preacher. To this is attached the *Loci Communes Sacri*, which is an undifferentiated list of the titles, one to six words each, of well over 250 theological topics. Bullinger says he had composed the list three years earlier–that would be at the age of nineteen! Although sometimes unclear in detail, these topics can readily be seen to be made up of about fifteen major groups of subjects, opening dramatically with ten items on the "one and eternal covenant" (*testamentum*), already called the *scopus* or main theme of scripture, in the preceding chapters. We must forego detailed analysis of this fascinating mélange edited in two volumes by Peter Stotz, opting only for some conclusions related to the interests of our present subject.[51]

Bullinger himself did not see fit to publish this early and somewhat inchoate but influential work, which was nonetheless significant in showing (1) the breadth and comprehensiveness of Bullinger's theological grasp from the beginning, (2) the early prominence of the covenant idea in both biblical interpretation and theological construction, and (3) a general sequence of topics that (apart from opening with the covenant, which he was not to do again for thirty years) charac-

50. *HBBibl* I, no. 712, published after his death by Ulrich Zwingli, Jr.

51. Bullinger, *Studiorum Ratio - Studienanleitung*, published as a *Sonderband* to Peter Stotz ed., *Heinrich Bullinger Werke*, in two half volumes (Zurich: TVZ, 1987).

terises his later work. For example: the priority of scripture; the close relation of the doctrine of God with the theme of true and false worship; elaborate concern for Old Testament law; a limited law/gospel scheme carefully differentiated from Luther; the gospel of Christian liberty; and a broad practical concern for all aspects of the Christian life and its perils. At the same time certain anomalies of placement (sin and anthropology separated, an odd intermixture of positive and negative elements), some tendency to miscellaneousness, and difficult or non-existent transitions all show this to be far from a carefully articulated systematic effort.

2. *Institutionum* (1531).[52] Among the unpublished Bullinger papers in the Zentralbibliothek Zurich is a handwritten outline sketch of a complete "*philosophia Christiana*," dated 1531. It was prepared most likely in the months before the pastor in Bremgarten fled to Zurich and became Zwingli's successor. This is seven years after the *Loci Communes Sacri*, and is a much more carefully articulated list than that. In this case Bullinger was evidently projecting a comprehensive theological work of his own, with no indication of any particular educational or polemic function. Since fulfillment was to wait until the *Decades*, 1549-51, it is highly significant to have a sketch of his early interest in such a project. The whole is divided into twelve books, each with a title, and each book divided into ten to eighteen chapters. Since the document is unknown, it might be well to list at least the titles of the twelve books.[53]

I	On the Absolute Necessity of Scripture
II	On the Nature of God and his Majesty
III	On Law, Sin, and Grace
IV	On Jesus Christ our Lord
V	On the Holy Church of God
VI	On True Religion and the True Worship of God
VII	On the Sacraments
VIII	On the Discipline of Christians
IX	On the Righteousness of Faith and Christian Virtue
X	On the Resurrection and Eternal Life
XI	On the Kingdom and Errors of Antichrist
XII	On Heretics and Heresies

Notably this disposition, by contrast with the *Loci*, gives no programmatic or systematic role to the doctrine of the covenant, just three years before the writing of *De Testamento*. The covenant appears only once in the entire outline as the title of Book I, chapter 10 on scripture. Except for this very important matter of both content and form, and the heaping of polemic elements in Books XI and XII, the *Institutionum* bears some resemblance to the grouping and sequence of materials in the *Summa*, more than to other comprehensive writings, but with no such covenant doctrine as we will find there.

52. ZB, Ms. Car III 206d.
53. Thanks is hereby expressed to Riccarda Froehlich of Princeton, NJ for transcribing the very difficult handwriting of this document.

3. *Wahrhafftes Bekenntnis* (1545).[54] This document is a reply from the Zurich ministers collectively (written entirely, however, by Bullinger) to Luther's vitriolic attack on the Zurich church as heretical, chiefly aimed at the Zurich teaching about the sacraments. The reply also deals with the sacraments, but the opening unit of Part II is a complete Confession of Faith meant to demonstrate that Zurich follows the "true, old, indubitable" faith, and is "not Zwinglian, nor Oecolampadian, much less Lutheran," but merely Christian, depending wholly on scripture, "in which we find no straw," and the "true, plain apostolic teaching."

The Confession begins with scripture in Bullinger's manner as to authority, interpretation, and rejection of human traditions: inspired (*yngeben*) by the Holy Spirit and "has of and in itself authority, respect, trust, strength, truth, esteem, and perfection enough," and needs no authentication by men or church. From scripture arises the apostolic teaching of the creed. For our present purposes, two remarks seem apposite: the claim of antiquity and orthodoxy here is biblical and patristic, not Adamic, as in *Der alte Glaube* with its exaggerated treatment of Genesis 3:15; and the covenant teaching of *De Testamento* is totally absent! Faith is briefly mentioned. After this one subject–scripture–the entire remainder of the confession of faith is an exposition of the traditionally designated twelve articles of the Apostles Creed. Although Bullinger includes analysis of the Creed in the *Decades*, the *Summa*, and the *Catechesis pro Adultioribus*, and showered upon it unmeasured praise, this treatment is notable because it is the only instance in which he followed the twelve-article scheme for a general presentation of the entire Christian faith. A detailed analysis shows fascinating idiosyncratic treatment of these points, including a full Nicene-Chalcedonian orthodoxy, a doctrine of original sin, an attack on Purgatory and monasticism, defence of the perpetual virginity of Mary, a recital of some deeds from Christ's ministry, and an ethic of faithful good works–the last of these remarkably placed under the Last Judgement. Notable also is the comparative lengths of certain sections. Some doctrines, such as the triune God, are only half an octavo page in length, and others, such as the Ascension to the Right Hand of the Father and the Return to Judgement, receive three pages each. The swelling of the latter two represents the elaboration of his polemic point against Luther's doctrine of ubiquity. The ingenuous freedom by which Bullinger does almost whatever he wants within and in addition to the Creed structure makes it all the more remarkable that the author of the *Loci* of 1524 (from the *Ratio* of 1527) and the famous *De Testamento* (1534, and repeatedly published with his commentary on the Epistles), in both of which the covenant is the chief theme of scripture, here makes no mention of the covenant at all. What kind of systematician is this? Although the data cannot be presented within this present sketch, it is demonstrable that this document is primarily a polemic program to which the covenant does not contribute. The creedal sequence is not "systematic" but "schematic" arranged for purposes other than to display how various doctrines hold together cogently.

4. *Sermonum Decades* (1549-1551).[55] Bullinger's *Decades*, a major Reformation classic, is unchallengeable as his most full-bodied and comprehensive

---

54. *HBBibl* I, no. 161.
55. Ibid., no. 184.

theological work, containing the richness of his scholarship, gathering together themes of all his major writings up to that time, and exhibiting the churchly purpose of being a theological source book for pastors to aid them in the preparation of sermons. This material is presented in the form of fifty Latin "sermons to clergy"[56] or lecture sermons in a style quite different from Bullinger's regular vernacular preaching, and was most probably delivered at the Zurich *Prophezei*[57] to the teachers and pastors of the city. The *Decades* was probably the chief avenue of Bullinger's influence until the time of the Synod of Dordrecht. The title comes from the classification of the work into five groups of ten sermons each, hence "decades." This plan is curiously irrelevant to the actual disposition of the subject matter. German and Dutch translators simply abandoned Bullinger's own title for the work, and called it *Hausbuch*, printing the sermons, each with its own title, in a sequence numbered one to fifty.[58]

"Hausbuch" implies a lay dogmatic for home use, and Hollweg shows that it was widely disseminated and read as such. The individual sermons were also sometimes read on Sunday at public worship–against Bullinger's expressed wish–when no ordained preacher was present; for example, on ship board, or served as sermons for those unable to attend church.

We offer here an analysis based on the actual disposition of the subject matter, but retaining Bullinger's enumeration into decades (capital Roman numerals) and sermons (lower case Roman numerals). After the dedicatory epistle, there appear to be four major divisions: Ancient Catholic Doctrine (12 documents from the early church); Soteriology (I.i-IV.ii); God and Creation (IV.iii-x); Church and Sacraments (V.i-x)

The twelve ancient documents of Part One and the accompanying explanations for their choice represent Bullinger's unrelenting claim to be "ancient and orthodox" and are essential to the *Decades*, not merely introductory matter. Part Two is an impressive development of the major themes of Reformation theology, no less catholic (that is, biblical) than the former for Bullinger: the Word of God as scripture; Faith; Justification; Love, which is the fulfilling of the Law (a long Decalogue analysis); the Law's uses, culminating in the Gospel as Christian Liberty; and the Doctrine of Sin and Evangelical Repentance. The sequence Faith and Love reflects Bullinger's two Augustinian principles of biblical interpretation.

Part Three is marked with an inserted dedicatory epistle to Edward VI and a review of what has preceded. Then, instead of a methodological remark concerning the transition he is making, Bullinger writes merely: "since we are now come to the end of these former parts,"[59] and proceeds to give a preview of what is to follow. Here he presents almost a new beginning to the work: the doctrine of the knowledge of God and true worship; the Trinity; and the Father's Creation,

56. Walter Hollweg, *Heinrich Bullingers Hausbuch. Eine Untersuchung über die Anfänge der reformierten Predigtliteratur* (Neukirchen: 1956), *HBBibl* II, no. 1679.

57. Ibid., 58.

58. Ibid., 71f.

59. Bullinger provides no methodological statement explaining his remarkable transition or how he relates the two elements methodologically. *Supra*, 42 where Neuser offers his suggestion on this subject.

Providence, Predestination; the Son; and the Spirit; followed by Good and Evil Spirits and a doctrine of Man. Part Four is the Church, including Ministry, Prayer, the Sacraments, and miscellaneous church practices.

Embedded in this four-part sequence are the familiar catechetical elements: the Apostles' Creed, three sermons under Faith (I.vii-ix); the Decalogue, thirteen sermons under Love and Law (II.ii-III.viii); the Lord's Prayer, one sermon under Church (V.v.); and the Sacraments, four sermons under Church (V.vi-ix). These elements are the cause of some repetition in the general disposition; for example, Christology. Although it may be materially irrelevant, the reader is struck that the sermons increase considerably in bulk with each succeeding decade, from the first, which covers seventy pages in a Latin folio edition, to the fifth, which occupies two hundred and thirty-four of these pages.

Decades - Structure

Main Parts

Part one Preface of Ancient Documents

Part two I.i - VI.ii Special Reformation Concerns (law and gospel, *sola scriptura, sola fidei, etc.*): Doctrine of Salvation

Part three IV.iii - x Doctrine of God, Creator: Trinity, Christology, Spirit, and evil spirits, doctrine of man

Part four V.i - x Doctrine of the Church

Main Parts – Expanded Description

Dedication to Gwalther

Part one ANCIENT CREEDS

Part two 1. WORD - I.i-iii. Word & Scripture. Central principles of interpretation, faith and love, from which he proceeds to the Apostles' Creed, and Love and Law.
2. FAITH - I.iv-vi. and justification.
3. Articles of Faith (Apostles' Creed) - I.vii-ix.
4. Love of God and Neighbour - I.x.
5. Law of Nature and Men - II.i
6. *Decalogue* - II.ii - III.iv
   Excursus: 6th commandment - II.vi-ix
   The State
   9th commandment - IV.i-iii
   Possessions and Calamities - 13 sermons
7. OT ceremonial & judicial law - III.v-vii
8. Use of law - III.vii
9. Christian Liberty - III.ix
10. Doctrine of Sin - III.x
11. The Gospel of Repentance - VI.i-ii

Dedicatory Epistle to Edward VI inserted here.

Part three 12. OF GOD ["...we are now come to the end of these former parts..."]
13. Knowledge of God - IV.iii and worship

14. Trinity - IV.iii
Father: Creation, Providence, Predestination - IV.iv
True Worship - IV.v
15. Son - IV.vi-vii
16. Spirit - IV.viii (end Summary on Trinity)
17. Good and Evil Spirits - IV.ix
18. Man - IV.x - reasonable soul, eternal life
Part four 19. CHURCH - V.i-ii
20. The Ministry - V.iii-iv
21. Prayer - V.v - including the Lord's Prayer
22. Signs, sacraments - V.vi-vii
23. Baptism - V.viii
24. Lord's Supper - V.ix
25. Miscellaneous Christian Practices - V.x

With this overview, it is possible to compare and contrast the *Decades* with Bullinger's other, smaller comprehensive works in our chosen series. But first we should observe the kind of problems that arise within the *Decades* itself concerning the systematic interrelation of the elements. A ready example is the treatment of revelation in two places, at the beginning of Part Two, Soteriology, I.i-iii, and at the beginning of Part Three, On God, IV.iii.

"Word of God," rather than scripture, stands in the title of the first two sermons of the *Decades* (I.i-ii). Although Bullinger commonly called the Bible directly God's Word, or indicated that it "is" God's Word, the distinction is here particularly significant because Bullinger pointedly begins with the *eloquium Dei, revelationemque voluntatis divinae*, the utterance of God and the revelation of the divine will[60] which was "first pronounced in the living voice" and afterward set down in writings. As a word discloses the mind from which it comes, so the Divine Word discloses God, adjusted to human capability and weakness. Bullinger uses his chronological learning to establish a mere seven witnesses that passed along the Word, *viva vox*, as it were "from hand to hand," between Adam to whom salvation was first announced, and Moses, the first inspired writer. After proceeding from oral Word to Word written down, Bullinger deals with the canon of scripture, exegetical techniques such as languages and historical setting, and the principles of faith and love for the interpretation of scripture (I.iii). Noteworthy for our present inquiry is that much the same subject matter is handled all over again, in a different manner, at the start of what we are calling Part III of the *Decades*, beginning at Sermon IV.iii, "Of God: of the True Knowledge of God and of the Diverse Ways of Knowing Him." Here Bullinger introduces five "forms" or "modes" by which God accommodates his revelation of himself to human capacities. This broad, inclusive set of categories embracing all ways of knowing God is not a wholly consistent arrangement. Bullinger lists God's ways of revelation as (1) "His Word," (2) "the making of the world," (3) scripture, (4) the oracles of prophets and apostles, and (5) in the soul or conscience of man. Farther along in the same chapter, he lists and discusses fives "modes" of know-

---

60. *Decades*, 1:37.

ing God as the divine names, visions and appearances, "as it were in parables,"[61] the incarnation, from the contemplation of His works, and the sayings of prophets and apostles.

It would seem that in I.i-iii there is an empirical-historical account of how revelation came and comes, after the pattern of *Der alte Glaube*. On the other hand, IV.iii offers a more formal epistemological analysis, making much use of materials from *De Origine Erroris*. These two approaches to the same subject matter are not contradictory, but neither are they easily integrated, and Bullinger does not attempt to integrate them for us either in the *Decades* or elsewhere.

Bullinger's paragraph at the beginning of IV.iii is a simple listing of topics already covered and those yet to come. It does not appear to bear out the systematic rationale attributed to Bullinger by Professor Neuser.[62] This is a retention of an older scholastic mode; for example, the divine names, along with a Reformation mode; *sola scriptura, sola gratia*, without a decision or resolution as to alternate methods.

In this same Problematic, we must note that the covenant, which plays a role particularly in Bullinger's doctrine of scripture in the *Decades* as well as in the whole law-gospel scheme, does not function as the major formative principle or systematic program in the *Decades*, as one might expect if Bullinger is to be classified as a systematic covenant or federal theologian. It will be seen to play a much larger role in the *Summa* which he intended as a popularised version of the *Decades* for laypersons.

Our summary observation is that in single sermons or short sequences of sermons on the *Decades*, we meet again the thematic Bullinger, but that the general architectonic of this large work is less than exemplary. Further comments on this issue will follow in Part IV, *infra*.

5. Summa Christlicher Religion (1556).[63] Bullinger's *Summa* was published five years after the completion of the *Decades*. He called it an "epitome" of the former work, following persistent requests that he provide a briefer, more accessible instruction for the adult layperson. *"Summa"* (sometimes *Summe*) is here a German, not a Latin, term, fully naturalised on all levels of German by the year 1500, and means a brief summation of essential material. So we are not to expect an extended medieval *summa theologiae*. When this vigorous German work was translated into Latin, it was titled *Compendium*. Bullinger has one goal here: "A summary of the Christian religion in which we present briefly and correctly, without wrangling and scolding, such matters drawn from Holy Scriptures as are necessary for every single Christian to know, believe, do and allow, and also to suffer and to die in blessedness." It advertises also on the same title page that this material includes short explanations for the Decalogue, Creed, Lord's Prayer, and Sacraments. This was an opportunity for the adult to recall catechism instruction and advance to necessary and appropriate maturity. The book was to be studied, Bible in hand, for which reason Bullinger gives many biblical references but few completely quoted texts.

61. Ibid., 138 (altered English translation).
62. *supra* 42.
63. *HBBibl* I, no. 283.

The title page, the sharply stated index, the dedicatory epistle including instructions on "How one should read this book," and a summary of the summary in bold type at the beginning of each of the ten articles, shows this book wholly dominated by a pastoral and practical didactic purpose of which the chief virtue would be simplicity. It would stay away from the disputes among the learned which so often confuse good people. The point of departure in the opening chapters illustrates admirably how Bullinger's practical purpose controls the material.

The first subject matter is the vernacular Bible in one's hand. Now forty years after Luther's 95 Theses, the readiest point of contact with the Protestant lay believer is the Book and the names commonly used to describe it. Reversing the order of the *Decades*, which begins with God's Word, or revelation, and proceeds through a described historical process to Moses, who first wrote it down, Bullinger now begins with what is at hand, a written document. First comes the common term, writing (*Schrifft*), in this case distinguished by two adjectives: "Holy" because this writing is inspired by the Holy Spirit, intended for a holy people, leads toward a Holy God, and contains only Holiness, no impurity; and "biblical" (*biblische*) from the Greek word for "books" which reminds us of the imperial and royal books that give us laws and constitutions of various lands–so also our Lord and God has given us His books which we commonly call "Holy Bible." And just as "testament" means not only a will by which heirs are chosen, but also an alliance, pact, treaty, understanding, or covenant, so God's book contains His will to His chosen heirs to come with the death of His Son, and also His covenant with them. And as the "heirs" and "covenanted people" are "old" and "new," so is the covenant "old" as to the time of Christ and "new" from then on to the end of the world.

After this amazingly compact introduction of a few sentences, Bullinger names biblical and apocryphal books, strung skillfully on a historical sequence with indications of content and brief evaluations. He has completed this on the fourth small octavo page, to conclude with the same idea with which he started: these described books of the Old and New Testament are the true holy, biblical (also called canonical) testament or covenant books–indeed the Bible is the true, authentic, infallible, "land" or church book of God.

The analogy with secular, national constitutions and the church is then carried on into a second chapter of popular apologia.

"That the holy, biblical writing of the Old and New Testaments shall incontestably be believed" (title of Chapter II) is a surprisingly thin essay. Bullinger argues that many lesser books and more recent ones–the law books and constitutions, wills, letters, and seals of many lands and places are highly regarded and thoroughly believed ("indeed to doubt them is unlawful")–although they have a thousand-fold less authority than the Bible. Then how much more shall *God's* Word be believed! This Word has been truly, rightly, and genuinely read, preached, heard, held, and defended for so many centuries before and after Christ, in so many kingdoms, lands, tongues, and peoples, throughout the world– orient and occident, midday and midnight, and is recommended by Josephus, Jesus, John, and Augustine. Therefore, writes Bullinger, scriptures shall be believed without any contradiction.

In the entire Chapter II, Bullinger presents primarily the public reputation of the Bible. It seems to be an argument–or is it merely an appeal?–from *consensus populi*, and *a fortiori*. It is an argument from prestige. We have already seen above in the *Decades* that Bullinger presents an argument from famous men, the patriarchs. But this is supportive in the *Decades*, not foundational. When we contrast the *Summa*, we find that a popular point of contact, a tactic of communication, determines the sequence. The philological and historical point of departure in the *Decades* is more determined by subject matter, and is certainly Bullinger's actual theological point of departure, as many of his writings demonstrate, not least the *Second Helvetic Confession*, to which we turn later.

More broadly, and not to be demonstrated here, it is impossible to reduce in a convincing and coherent manner the structure of the *Decades* to that of its epitome, the *Summa*. The difference is not systematic, but schematic and programmatic. Bullinger is not solving theological problems, but presenting forcefully the simple essentials that need to be known by all without learned philology or refined theology; although both are necessary in the life of the church, as he insists so emphatically in the *Vester Grund* of 1563,[64] defending Vermigli against the Strasbourgers. To ordinary believers, however, sophisticated philology and theology may seem confusing and overly complex.

It must be noted also that the two publications in which Bullinger most nearly approximated making his covenant teaching the dominant key and organising principle are works intended for popular use: the *Summa*, and three years later, the student catechism *Catechesis pro adultioribus*; both of which lack the technical basis for the covenant teaching such as appears in *De Testamento* and the *Decades*. It is the *Summa* and not the *Decades* that forms his "lay dogmatic." Through twenty-seven editions in various languages, it functioned as such.

6. *Catechesis pro Adultioribus*...(1559). Bullinger's lifelong zeal for simplicity and directness, especially in the education of the laity, is carried out brilliantly in his *Catechesis pro Adultioribus* of 1559[65] that he prepared at the behest of the Zurich Synod for use in upper school classes. It was never so popular as the *Summa*, having been published only three times in Latin (1559, 1561, and 1562) and much later twice in German translation (1597, 1598) as an appendix to a German translation of the *Decades*. Like every catechism, it included sections on the Decalogue, the Creed, the Lord's Prayer, and the Sacraments,[66] expounded in question and answer form. Bullinger divides the whole course of instruction into nine sections of uneven length, of which the Law and the Creed are the longest by far.[67] Together with the *Summa*, this catechism gives a very prominent place to the doctrine of the covenant.

---

64. Ibid., no. 426.

65. Ibid., no. 377; *HBD*, 60, 9; Carl Pestalozzi, *Heinrich Bullinger: Leben und ausgewählte Schriften. Nach handschriftlichen und gleichzeitigen Quellen* (Leben und ausgewählte Schriften der Väter und Begründer der reformierten Kirche V; Elberfeld: Friderichs, 1858), 414.

66. Following Luther, who first brought together catechetical material with explanations as a separate book. See Surkau, "Katechismus" in Kurt Galling ed., *Religion in Geschichte und Gegenwart: Handwörterbuch für Theologie und Religionswissenschaft* 7 vols (3rd ed., Tübingen: Mohr, 1957-65), III:1182f.

67. These major sections are all listed in the lengthy subtitle to the whole.

I. Beginning with scripture in a way very like that of the *Summa*, explaining the words Holy, Bible, etc., Bullinger fastens on the term "testament" or "covenant" as the subject matter of scripture, for which the two chief parts are named. Scripture is the sole authority in the church, to the exclusion of all human traditions. Covenant, however, will receive fuller treatment in the section so named,– the only time in Bullinger's general disposition of theological material that the covenant is so prominently treated.

II. On the Living and Eternal God is a very compact and simple account of the "orthodox and catholic" doctrine of God. The Oneness and Threeness of the Trinity are given biblical basis as found, respectively, in passages from the Old and New Testaments. Although beyond "human parables" and to be believed from the Word rather than exactly described, the mystery of the Trinity is taught by Bullinger's analogy to the Sun. We observe the body of the Sun itself, out of which flows light and splendour, and from both together emanates heat. One is not confused with the other, nor do they make three, but only one Sun. In the same manner, the Son is eternally generated from the Father, and from both proceeds the Holy Spirit. Bullinger promises to return to the subject of his Creed analysis, and does so without repetition.

III. On the Covenant (*foedus*) of God and True Worship, Bullinger first explains that God's benevolence toward humanity is declared by his "promise," apart from all human merit, but moved by His natural and sheer goodness and grace. "But how does Holy Scripture otherwise explain to us this matter of benevolence and friendly alliance?" "Through the likeness to a contract or covenant. For just as men are bound together closely in other ways by contracts, so God joins himself to humanity by an eternal covenant."[68] This covenant was concluded with Adam, Noah, Abraham and his seed, and the faithful of all nations. Thus we are covenanters (*confoedatores, genossen*) with God, mutually bound by two "conditions" or "articles": (1) God's promise of what we can expect of him, and (2) what he requires of us. God wills to be uniquely our fulfillment and sufficient for all needs from whom alone we expect everything and to whom alone we make petition. God requires of us true worship, by which we are the "religious" or covenanted ones, friends and partners of God,–not the so-called "religious," the monks.

IV-VI. These three sections deal with the Law as the Decalogue and the two tables as explaining what the covenant demands, setting forth "true worship and true religion." These commands apply, not only in former times to Israel, but to Christians and to all humanity. Through his explanation of adoration as "bowing down" internally and externally, involving faith (Creed), love (Law), and invocation of God (Lord's Prayer), Bullinger implicitly includes the whole of the Christian faith and life under the First Commandment.[69] He then explains the

---

68. "Per similitudinem pacti vel foederis. Sicut enim homines foedere aliquo archtissimo connectatus inter sese: ita deus foedere sempiterno coaluit cum hominimbus." f. 6ᵛ.

69. Luther's treatment of the Decalogue in his catechism begins not with the prologue passage, "I am the LORD..." but with the first commandment itself, from which in a remarkable tour de force, he extracts the doctrine of justification by faith alone. Calvin uses the prologue to identify the speaker, namely God, and to cite the saving activity of God in the Prologue before he

commandments with remarkable inclusiveness and economy: uncharacteristic brevity on the "name" of God, delicate analysis of the Sabbath for Christians, plus a finely nuanced exposition of the second table, concluding with an Augustine-like exposition of avarice and concupiscence. After distinguishing the ceremonial and judicial law from the moral, Bullinger presents two uses of the law (to convict of sin and to guide the Christian life), and the Great Commandment of Mark 12. This treatment includes seventy-one questions and answers in all, from the total of two hundred eighty-nine. Only the Creed analysis is larger, with one hundred and one questions. Other sections run from three to twelve questions each.

The Apostles' Creed, called a symbol because it functions as does a banner for an army, distinguishing between friend and foe, is treated in two ways: (1) as "the faith," Christian doctrines, rites, and mores in distinction from Jewish and Muslim faiths, and (2) as the means by which salvation is freely given to the believer. This latter faith is defined (1) as related to scripture, to apostolic doctrine, and to Christ "who is the *scopus* of the law, the prophets and the apostles." (2) Bullinger sees the creed as divided into the traditional twelve articles, falling into four major headings: belief in God the father, and concerning the creation of the universe; what we believe concerning Jesus Christ and our own salvation; comprehends Holy Spirit and our sanctification; more fully explains and illustrates that sanctification itself is a fruit and effect of faith.[70] Although the church is not used as a major title, the treatment is proportionally extensive with other major topics in the Creed.

Part I of the Creed analysis is brief: the omnipotent God is the creator and providential governor of all that is. Notable is here more extensive treatment of man's creation, made of soul and body, but from Adam's fall, fails to do the good, and a concluding portion on the New Man, through the gospel and the Holy Spirit.

Part II, the Second Person, articles 2 through 7, begins with stress upon the identity of Jesus as the son, deity incarnate, whose indubitable reality is the heart of the gospel, and the only way of eternal life. Jesus is the Christ, the true Son of God, and our Lord. In the Virgin conception, he was made man, truly, having two natures, consubstantial in one Person, free of sin and thus able to redeem fallen humanity. He suffered under Pontius Pilate for the expiation of sin and our justification, which takes place solely by grace and faith. The Descent to Hell (*Höllenfahrt*) in a few words–frees all saints from the beginning of the world. By rising again in the *same* body (not spiritual or divinised) but a glorious human body, he wounded the head of the "old serpent." The Right Hand, to which he ascended, signifies majesty and divine power, and "seated" signifies an actually reigning Lord. The Return to judgement here (unlike the *Wahrhaffte Bekenntnis*) is unrelated to good works of the faithful, but concerns solely the dramatic scene

---

comes to the first commandment. Bullinger, while not making use of the Prologue in this connection, includes the whole of the Christian faith and life under the first commandment.

70. Ibid., "Quartum caput plerius absolvit et illustrate sanctificationem illam et fidei effectum vel fructum." f. 31ᵛ.

of a general resurrection with the faithful meeting Christ "in the air," and the eternal fate of the lost.

Part III, the single article on the Holy Spirit, makes up the third main heading of the Creed, and here the Spirit is treated in only one aspect, sanctification. This is the work of the Spirit alone, including the sanctifying effects of the Word, Prayer and the Sacraments. This was true also under the Old Testament.

Part IV, the remainder of the Creed, articles 9-12, Bullinger designates as "Fourth Part," more fully explaining and illustrating that sanctification section and the effects or fruits of faith. This is the longest section of the Creed, dealing rather fully with the Holy, Catholic Church as the communion of saints. These saints are not absolutely holy, bearing infirmities and imperfections of the flesh, but are sanctified by the Spirit. The Church, thus constituted, is One and Catholic throughout the world. Both militant and triumphant, visible and invisible, the Church is One only. It bears four marks: (1) the preaching of the sincere Word of God, or evangelical doctrine; (2) public prayer or supplication, the invocation of God through the intercession of Christ; (3) legitimate use of the sacraments; and (4) beneficence or the community of goods for charitable purposes. Can this church err? Yes, if not united in the Word–Paul calls Galatians and Corinthians the church. Is the Roman church, church? Here Bullinger gives a long list of ills, referring to Revelation 19, and Romans 16, and the predictions of Anti-Christ in the last days. Rome appears heretical and schismatic.

In Article 10, sins are forgiven in the church where Christ promises life and "outside the Church, there is no remission of sin but eternal condemnation."[71] Here Bullinger presents his doctrine of sin, defined as opposition to God's law, originating in the corrupt human will and the impulse of Satan, punished by death. He presents sin as Original, Actual, Mortal and Venial (infirmities of the faithful requiring daily repentance). God only remits sins by the Word of Truth. Remission, a metaphor implying debtors and creditors, follows the satisfaction for the debt of the human race by Christ's cross alone,–not indulgences and the like. Article 11, Resurrection of the flesh, is brief. All flesh arises, good and evil, in the same body in which they died, but the faithful are glorified in this body as Christ was, and enter into eternal life, Art. 12. Here Bullinger's interrogator asks about purgatory, allowing him to turn, "after expounding the Creed," to the subject of non-meritorious good works, and the works that flow from faith, a constant theme in all his writings and preaching. Our works do not justify, for all merit comes from Christ. But the Christian faith is *maxime actuosa*, and includes both justification and vivification. The good works that flow from faith are the Spirit's work, not ours. James 2 does not refer to this living Pauline faith, hence is no critique of Pauline teaching. The last word is from I Cor. 4, "What do you have that you did not receive?"

The Apostles' Creed, thus expounded, bears nearly all the main themes of the Reformatory theology of Bullinger, and many of his characteristic emphases.

VIII. On Calling upon God, and the Lord's Prayer, present prayer as petition and praise, necessary, useful, and required of believers, offered to God alone (not the saints) through Christ, the only Intercessor. The preface and seven petitions

---

71. "Extra ecclesiam non esse ullam remissionem, sed interitum perpetuum."

of the Lord's Prayer from Matthew are all expounded so as to engage the sanctification of the believer. The plural "our" Father is appropriate for prayer from the church.

IX. Quickly listing what has already been covered in the Catechism, Bullinger's interrogator asks, what more? The sacraments: sacred symbols, rites, or actions, constituted of signs and things drawn from the Word of God, of highest benefit in the church, because they retain in memory and renew those things which they represent, which are presented to us, and at the same time show what is required of us. There are two sacraments only, given by God, in elements representing their substance (*res*). The sign and thing are joined sacramentally–there is no mutation of one into the other,–so that regeneration and the body and blood of the Lord "which they represent are spiritually received by the faithful through faith. The sacraments do not justify or confer grace, rather the thing itself, which the signs represent, if perceived by faith, both justify and confer grace."

There are separate treatments, then, of baptism with reference to the eternal covenant of God, and the Supper, which contains a critique of the Mass as being not according to the original institution of the Lord.

In summary, the architectonics of this work, and the disposition of material here is largely controlled by the standard catechetical elements. But Bullinger both introduces (I-III) and infuses (IV-IX) with Reformed teaching. Although the main components are in the same sequence as in Luther's catechism, the framework of presentation is the prior authority of scripture and God's eternal covenant, which is the *scopus* of scripture. Covenant is the context in which the Decalogue, the Creeds, the Lord's Prayer, and Sacraments, are to be understood. More than ever in the *Summa*, the covenant is the *Leitmotif* of this document. The two together show the groundwork of a genuine covenant theology, while not yet achieving what one might have expected from Bullinger's program in *De Testamento*, twenty-five years earlier.

7. Vester Grund...(1563).[72] *Vester Grund Uff den ein yetlicher glouben sicher buwen und sich verlassen magj* [*Fundamentum firmum...*] of 1563 is a lengthy defence of Peter Martyr Vermigli, who died in 1562 after some years as professor of theology in Zurich, against an attack by Johannes Brenz on the persistent issue of the presence of Christ's body in the Lord's Supper.[73] Bullinger first takes up the subject of divisions in the church–OT, NT, and church history–as a condition continuing from the first. This treatment does not concentrate on blaming the devil or bemoaning the condition of the church, nor is it a defence or justification of partisan strife as Bullinger points out to Brenz in chapter IV. Rather, to avoid scandalising the faithful or jeopardising their faith, he points out that it has existed in the earliest and most orthodox days of the church, not only between the church and the church of Satan, but among the soundest Catholic teachers. Therefore, no one may dismiss the Reformation as unorthodox merely because it is divisive. Even differences on chief articles of faith may be only a misunderstanding that time will heal.[74] Not all tension comes from sects and heretics, even the or-

72. *HBBibl* I, no. 425.
73. *HBD*, 72, 5-8.
74. f. 6' and 42'.

thodox experienced tension themselves, witness Peter and Paul in Galatians 2. Just as in marriage there are tensions and misunderstandings that nonetheless do not break up the marriage.[75]

He distinguishes between those matters in which sectarian/heretical ideas and practices are to be excluded from the church, and lesser differences of opinion or misunderstandings among those who hold to the same chief articles of faith, the "orthodox." These chapters I-III might be considered the *locus classicus* in Bullinger's writings for this familiar theme of his. The *Vester Grund* among the tensions and divisions in the church, whether ancient or contemporary, is Christ the Rock on which Peter's confession was founded, who *alone* is the salvation offered by God, and on whom *alone* the believer trusts, all works being set aside. Against this background of tensions, Bullinger sets out in ch. VIII-XIII to give the Reformed position on all the chief doctrines. As Koch has noted that these chapters constitute a *Gesamtdarstellung* of the *chief* heads of Christian doctrine.

The sequence and structure of this section is closer than in any other of Bullinger's *Gesamtdarstellungen* to the *Second Helvetic Confession*, which had already been completed in its first form by this time–and approved by P.M. Vermigli before he died. The sequence in Koch's *Übersicht* is easily paralleled with the *Confession*, and yet some differences can be noted, e.g. the location of the Christology and the reverse positions of Sin and Election, although they are still close together in the disposition. Especially noteworthy is the complete absence of covenant teaching in this document.

8. *Confessio ex expositio simplex...*(1566).[76] In 1561 Bullinger wrote this "Simple Confession and Exposition of Orthodox Faith and Catholic Doctrine....," first published in 1566 to aid the cause of the Reformed tradition in the Empire, and known in English generally as the *Second Helvetic Confession*. Bullinger intended it originally as his legacy to the Zurich church, attached to his will, but it became the confession most widely adopted internationally, and was the organising document of the *Harmonia Confessionum* of 1581,[77] which showed the catholicity of the Reformed wing over against the canons and decrees of Trent and against the Lutheran *Book of Concord*. Translated through the years into fifteen languages and published in more than 115 editions, the *Second Helvetic Confession* proved to be the most widely disseminated and the most influential of Bullinger's writings to the present time. Against the reverie of E.F.K. Mueller, supported by Koch and most others, that this was intended first as a private expression of his own personal faith, I have held in a chapter of Staedtke's *Glauben und Bekennen*–with strong support from Leonhard von Muralt's review in *Zwingliana*[78]–that this document, patterned after the *First Helvetic Confession* of 1536, was from the first intention meant for the whole church.[79] This is not an independent constructive effort as an aid to preachers as the *Decades*, nor primarily a popular lay dogmatic as the *Summa*, nor an *ad hoc* polemic as the

75. f. 6ʳ.
76. *HBBibl* I, no. 433.
77. *HBBibl* I, no. 436, 659.
78. von Muralt, *op cit.*, 377ff. esp. 382-6.
79. *Glauben und Bekennen*, 206f.

Wahrhaffte Bekenntnis. Rather this work is Bullinger's major, formal effort to speak to and for the one church catholic, orthodox, and reformed. Thus it is not surprising that in general disposition and format it follows the *First Helvetic.* Surprising is that none of the works Bullinger prepared in the twenty-five year span between the confessions follows the same structure and sequence, or anything significantly close to it. Even more surprising is that the covenant doctrine is missing except in connection with the sacrament of baptism.

General characteristics of the *Confession* express outstanding characteristics of Bullinger's thought, already observed in other writings:[80] a theology that is totally non-speculative, but throughout oriented to the existing, practical life of the believer in the church before God and in the context of world history; a broad churchly consciousness by which the whole history of creedal and confessional response, including major controversies, is always in play; and a grouping, as in the *Decades*, of patristic, early creedal materials separate from the main soteriological themes of the Reformation; with the whole based upon and held together by the most catholic of all doctrines for Bullinger, namely, scripture alone as the source of the Christian faith.

One device for citing large divisions of the document is as follows. Part I: Ancient Catholic/orthodox teachings, creedal documents; chapters I-XI, closing with reaffirmations of the first four ecumenical Councils and the Athanasian Creed. Part II: Soteriological themes recovered in the Reformation; chapters XII-XVII on Law and Gospel, Spirit and Letter, Justification by Faith, and Good Works of the Faithful. Part III: The One Holy Catholic Church; chapters XVIII-XXX, its Ministry, Sacraments, and various institutions. It is interesting to note that by contrast with the *Decades*, the old orthodoxy is dealt with at the beginning of the Bullinger text, rather than afterwards, and by contrast with the *Summa* and *Catechesis*, there is no appearance of the covenant as an organising scheme for the whole.

Since this is the easiest available still in print of all Bullinger's writings, and has been elaborately analyzed by many already mentioned, I shall leave the matter here and turn to the question again of Bullinger as theologian.

IV. Bullinger as Theologian: A Preference for the *Decades*

Taken together, the foregoing comments on selected writings of Heinrich Bullinger and the summary generalisations of Part I are meant to contribute to a more adequate characterisation of his way of writing theology than heretofore achieved by application of terms such as systematic, practical, mediating, scholastic, and the like. A first result, given at the end of Part II. A was the introduction of three pervasive convictions among which all his life as a theologian seems to have been lived. Along the way, it was repeatedly pointed out that his thematic writings have an *ad hoc* character by which he met the needs of the polemic situation, or threatened faith, of those for whom he wrote. The latter was seen in Part II. B to apply also to the comprehensive works, a genre that he practiced through the entire forty-some years of public life.

---

80. *supra*, 36.

Among these, increasingly, through some years of reading Bullinger, I have been moved to the conclusion that the Bullinger of the *Decades* is Bullinger himself, more truly than in any other major writing. Produced at a mature age, 45 to 47 years old, in good health and at the height of his powers, having recently contended with Luther in print and with Calvin in person on the mode of Christ's presence in the Lord's Supper, Bullinger undertook the exhausting labour of presenting the whole spectrum of Christian doctrine in a single work. He struck out on his own, not patterning on any model, classic or Reformation, with the goal closest to his own highest purpose: a contribution to preaching in the church. Here we find the prematurely venerable preacher-teacher addressing his colleagues in Zurich and throughout the world in a source book of doctrine and learning, composed of lecture-sermons designed to help other preachers in the preparation of sermons for the church.

He published it in three fascicles, 1549-51, then all together in a folio of 418 pages in 1552. All this was accomplished in about three years' time, and never revised. Most of the subject matter of the *Decades* is also found elsewhere in Bullinger, for he is exceedingly repetitious and occasionally tedious.

Here, in one work, we find Bullinger the exegete, and the Bullinger of the treatises pursuing major biblical themes in his chosen and variable idiom. Also in the *Decades*, he is free to indulge in displays of classical learning and philology that would stand aside from the purposes of either the *Summa*, meant for lay consumption, or the *Confessio Helvetica Posterior*, meant as a standard for the church. Much of the use of philology and classical and even Cabbalistic lore is highly idiosyncratic and questionable. He is free to be brief or verbose, technical or popular, to review and summarise and preview and illustrate, to spread out his biblical and historical and humanist learning as the subject suits him.

Bullinger arranges and rearranges his ideas frequently and painlessly to suit the purposes at hand. There appears to be no such theological agony as when Calvin revises, rearranges, and expands his *Institutio* for twenty-five years, or struggles with himself about how to say two things at once, then puts the "second" before the "first" in order that no reader can think the first–justification– may be stated without the second–regeneration–in III.vi.1.[81] One does not find in Bullinger personally or theologically either the *Anfechtungen* that terrified Luther, or anxiety such as Calvin expressed as a concomitant of faith.[82]

But Bullinger is not careless, hit or miss, or unpredictable. And we have seen that he has given the impression to many that he is quite systematic. He appears to be a massively conservative intellect, inwardly at peace with Christian truth, able to move about freely in his biblical-orthodox world of thought, and largely without tension. His problems of ordering his thought stem neither from an inner tension, nor from questions of structure among the doctrines he holds. Rather the

81. This is no minor problem for Calvin. It concerns both the make-up and sequence of Book III in the *Institutes* of 1559, and the polemic situation with Lutheranism and with Tridentine Catholicism. One would be hard pressed to find any comparable wrestling with such a problem in Bullinger's works. Hence, our reluctance to call him "systematic."

82. Bullinger's hypersensitivity shown in his polemic on Christology and the problem of free will related to his doctrine of Predestination may seem to be an exception to this general characterisation.

problems are didactic, homiletical, and pastoral. Hence I would describe his comprehensive works as "schematic" or programmatic rather than systematic.

V. Concluding Problem and Suggestion

Suppose one were to present a conspectus of Bullinger's thought and found difficulty in using any of his own writings to represent it adequately, even the commodious *Decades*. Would it be possible to develop a Bullingerian schema, not one of Bullinger's own, that would be both adequate to the task and more able to show him in depth and variety? The impasse might be overcome by such a scheme as is given below, which by the way, lists only major topics, not the full outline. For such a disposition to be useful, it should be introduced by a detailed descriptive analysis after the manner of my "Theologischer Aufbau der Confessio Helvetica Posterior," published in Staedtke's *Glauben und Bekennen*, of all the comprehensive presentations found in Bullinger's writings. Thus the individual schemata would be preserved, and the wider purpose served.

Risking arrogance and also the kind of criticism aimed at Ernst Koch in Part II *supra*, but hoping at least that discussion will be ignited, I offer the following suggestion.

Heinrich Bullinger as Theologian

A presentation of the main motifs of Bullinger's thought in a form derived chiefly from his several comprehensive "systematic" presentations, with attention throughout to the present state of Bullinger studies.

I. Pervasive Convictions of Bullinger's Theological Lifework
    1. The Antiquity of the Christian Faith (*Der alte Glaube*)
      a. Origins and Authority
      b. Historical Apologetics
      c. Reform as Repeated Recovery of the Original
    2. The One Eternal Covenant (*De Testamento...*)
      a. El Shaddai and the Seed of Abraham
      b. Grace and Obedience
      c. The excellence of Law
      d. Covenant and History
    3. Catholic Orthodoxy (early church materials, *passim*)
      a. The Fathers
      b. The Creeds
      c. Christendom

II. Revelation and Faith
    4. The Word of God
      a. *Viva Vox*, Scripture, Preaching from Scripture
      b. The Various Modes of Revelation
      c. The Interpretation of Scripture
    5. Christ and the Gospel

a. The Work of Christ
b. Justification
6. The Source and Content of Faith
   a. Faith defined
   b. The Problems of Faith and Knowledge
   c. Faith and Love
7. Human Nature and Sin
   a. The Fall (*instinctu serpentis, et sua culpa*)
   b. Inherited Sin and Freedom of the Will
   c. Actual Sin and Punishment
8. Predestination or Election
   a. Grace Alone, from All Eternity
   b. Means and Instruments
   c. Curiosity Forbidden

III. Law, Repentance, and Good Works
9. Love and the Forms of Virtue
   a. God's love
   b. Love of God and Neighbour
   c. The Decalogue and Other Forms of Old Covenant Law
   d. Uses of the Law
10. Repentance and Conversion
11. The Christian Life
    a. Good Works of the Believer
    b. Hope and Consolation
    c. Death and Resurrection
    d. The Last Judgement and Eternal Life

IV. God and the World
12. The Trinity and Classic Christology
    a. The Highest Good
    b. Received Doctrine
    c. The Understanding of Christ's Two Natures
    d. God's Right Hand and Christ's rule
    e. The Spirit
13. Providence and Historical Life
14. True and False Worship, with further discussion of the Covenant

V. The Church and Its Ministry
15. One, Holy, Catholic
16. The Ministers
17. Sacraments
    a. Definition and Function of a Sacrament
    b. Baptism
    c. The Supper
    d. *Consensus Tigurinus*

2

Bullinger on the Trinity:
"Religionis Nostrae Caput et Fundamentum"

Mark Taplin

Since the quatercentenary of his death in 1975, Heinrich Bullinger has again become a focus of scholarly interest. Monographs, articles and, above all, the on-going publication of Bullinger's correspondence have revealed the multifaceted nature of his achievement: domestically, as the chief architect of the institutions of the reformed Zurich church following Zwingli's premature demise; interna-tionally, as a source of advice, encouragement and leadership to Protestants throughout Europe; and intellectually, as a humanist, educator and historian. At the same time, Bullinger the theologian has begun to emerge from the shadow of his younger and more brilliant contemporary, John Calvin. J. Wayne Baker has identified Bullinger as the principal source for the Reformed idea of the cove-nant–what he terms "the other Reformed tradition," alongside the tradition that took its inspiration from Geneva.[1] Bullinger's doctrines of predestination and sanctification, his understanding of the Eucharist and his exegetical method have all been the subject of dedicated studies.[2]

Less well researched is Bullinger's contribution to Reformed thinking on the Trinity. The failure of scholars to give much attention to this aspect of his theol-ogy is to some extent understandable, in that it reflects Bullinger's own practice. Like other mainstream reformers, Bullinger had no wish to reopen the triadologi-cal and Christological controversies that had dominated the history of the early church, as he believed those to have been resolved definitively by the first four

1.   J. Wayne Baker, *Heinrich Bullinger and the Covenant: The Other Reformed Tradition* (Athens, Ohio: Ohio Univ. Press, 1980); idem, "Heinrich Bullinger, the Covenant, and the Re-formed Tradition in Retrospect," *Sixteenth Century Journal* 29 (1998), 259-76.

2.   Peter Walser, *Die Prädestination bei Heinrich Bullinger im Zusammenhang mit seiner Gotteslehre* (Zurich: 1957); Mark S. Burrows, " Christus intra nos Vivens': The Peculiar Genius of Bullinger's Doctrine of Sanctification," *Zeitschrift für Kirchengeschichte* 98 (1987), 48-69; P. Rorem, *Bullinger and Calvin on the Lord's Supper* (Nottingham: Grove Books, 1989); Paul Sanders, "Heinrich Bullinger et le 'zwinglianisme tardif' aux lendemains du 'Consensus Tiguri-nus'," in H. Oberman et al. eds, *Das Reformierte Erbe. Festschrift für Gottfried W. Locher*, 2 vols (Zurich: TVZ, 1992), I:307-23; Joel E. Kok, "Heinrich Bullinger's Exegetical Method: The Model for Calvin?," in Richard A. Muller/J. L. Thompson eds, *Biblical Interpretation in the Era of the Reformation* (Grand Rapids, Mich.: William B. Eerdmans Publishing Company, 1996), 241-54.

ecumenical councils. Where possible, he limited himself to formulaic restatements of the orthodox position, usually supported by proof-texts from scripture and citations from the fathers. However, it would be a mistake to conclude from the brevity of Bullinger's discussions of the Trinity that the subject is marginal to his theology. As will become clear, Bullinger regarded God's self-revelation as Father, Son and Holy Spirit as the cornerstone of the Christian faith, with each of the three persons of the Trinity playing a distinct and clearly designated role in the economy of salvation. Just as important, he believed that the maintenance of trinitarian orthodoxy by the Reformed vindicated their claim to represent the true church; it served as their bridge back to the Fathers and the pristine catholic tradition of the early Christian centuries, which Bullinger saw as having been interrupted and submerged by the corruptions of the papacy. When that tradition was again imperilled–this time by criticism of the received doctrine of the Trinity from radical elements within the Reformed churches, who had come to believe that it lacked biblical foundation–Bullinger argued vigorously in its defence. In the process, he redefined the relationship between scripture and the ancient creeds, now incorporated within the Protestants' own confessions. Although dependent on the authority of scripture, the creeds showed how the Bible's teaching on the nature of God and Christ was to be harmonised and consolidated, setting the bounds for acceptable exegesis and providing a necessary safeguard against heresy.

I. Bullinger's Doctrine of the Trinity

During the early years of the Zurich Reformation, Zwingli and his followers took care to indicate that their assault on medieval doctrine and piety did not extend to the orthodox Christian teaching that the one God subsists in three persons.[3] In his sermon *On the clarity and certainty of the Word of God*, published in September 1522, Zwingli cites the conjunction of plural and singular forms in Genesis 1:26 ("Let us make man in our own image and likeness") as evidence for the existence of a Trinity of persons within the divine substance.[4] Similar brief professions of faith in the Trinity are to be found in Zwingli's major theological works: the *Commentary on true and false religion* (1525), *An account of the faith* (1530) and *An exposition of the faith* (1531).[5] In the *First Berne sermon*, given on 19 January 1528, Zwingli sketches out his theology of the Trinity in greater detail. Echoing the language of the so-called Athanasian Creed (also known as the "Quicunque vult") he affirms that God is one in substance, but subsists in three distinct persons as the Father, Son and Holy Spirit. Like Augustine, Zwingli sees the Trinity reflected in the human soul, with its three interrelated faculties of mind, memory and will. For those who find this image difficult to grasp ("the simple folk"), he provides a more concrete analogy that harks back to his child-

---

3.   Gottfried W. Locher, *Die Theologie Huldrych Zwinglis im Lichte seiner Christologie. Erster Teil: Die Gotteslehre* (Studien zur Dogmengeschichte und systematischen Theologie, 1; Zurich: Zwingli Verlag, 1952), 99-133 is the best and most detailed analysis to date.

4.   *Z* I., 342.

5.   *Z* III., 675; *Z* VI.2., 792; *Z* VI.5., 61-2.

hood in rural Toggenburg. The Trinity, he proclaims, may be compared to a three-cornered spring from which water is drawn off by three runnels: each of the corners is distinct, but together they form "one spring, one source of water, one revitalising and thirst-quenching force."[6] As one might expect, given his belief in the utter separateness of the divine and the creaturely, the spirit and the flesh, Zwingli habitually emphasises the unity of God's substance over the distinction of persons, to the extent that he finds fault with Luther's description of God as "of three sorts" ("dreyerley") rather than merely triune.[7] According to Zwingli, the scripture writers' tendency to associate particular qualities with the Father (omnipotence, creation), the Son (wisdom, grace, goodness) and the Holy Spirit (comfort, love, truth) is to be understood as a figure of speech; in truth, those attributes are common to all three persons.[8] However, he avoids full-blooded modalism by at the same time acknowledging the existence of real distinctions within the Godhead. Again following the Athanasian Creed, Zwingli argues that each person has a unique characteristic that defines both his origin and his relationship with the other two members of the Trinity. Thus the Father is unbegotten, the Son is begotten, and the Holy Spirit is neither begotten nor unbegotten, but proceeds from the Father and the Son.[9]

Although the eighty or so works that survive from the formative phase of Bullinger's career (his student years in Cologne and his time in charge of the Cistercian school at Kappel) do not include a systematic consideration of the Trinity, the doctrine is nonetheless fundamental to his theology during this period.[10] In an unpublished commentary on the letter to Titus, Bullinger suggested that there was no need for him to expound the finer points of the church's teaching on the Trinity, as that task had already been performed adequately by Athanasius, Augustine, and Tertullian in his work *Against Praxeas*. Like Zwingli, Bullinger may have been reluctant to stress the existence of a plurality of persons within the Godhead for fear of diluting his principal message: that God alone is to be worshipped, and that the cult of saints constitutes idolatry. In those passages where he does discuss the Trinity, Bullinger tends towards the Augustinian understanding of the Father, Son and Holy Spirit as "relations," distinguished only by their peculiar origins; as we have seen, this is the case also for Zwingli. Rejecting all forms of subordinationism, he repeatedly affirms the consubstantiality of the Son (and, though less frequently, of the Holy Spirit) with the Father. Joachim Staedtke suggests that in his concern to uphold the full divinity of all three persons Bullinger sometimes comes close to modalism.[11] However, on other occasions he insists on their distinctiveness–for example, when making

---

6. *Z* VI.1, 456-7.
7. *Z* VI.2, 295; cited in Locher, *Theologie Zwinglis*, 104.
8. *Z* VI.1, 462; *Z* VI.3., 77-8. According to Locher, here Zwingli draws on the scholastic notion of *appropriatio* (*Theologie Zwinglis*, 131).
9. *Z* VI.1, 461.
10. See the comments of Joachim Staedtke, *Die Theologie des jungen Bullinger* (Zurich: Zwingli Verlag, 1962), 88; 103.
11. Ibid., 104-5.

clear that God became incarnate in Christ "in a different person" from the Father.[12]

Bullinger's appointment in December 1531 to the post of first minister (*Antistes*) in Zurich heralded his emergence as a Reformed theologian of international stature. Although never comfortable with the more "speculative" aspects of traditional triadology, Bullinger took the opportunity both in his New Testament commentaries (1532-46) and in his later dogmatic works to demonstrate his orthodoxy with regard to the Trinity. His most extensive treatment of the issue is to be found in the *Decades* (1549-51), a cycle of 50 sermons in which Bullinger attempted to systematise the teachings of the Zurich church. Here the Trinity is discussed in two places: in sermons 7 and 8 of the first decade, as part of an exposition of articles 1 and 2 of the Apostles' Creed; and in sermon 3 of the fourth decade, entitled "Of God, and the true knowledge of God."[13] Sermon 6 of the fourth decade, which deals with the person of Christ, is also relevant in this context, given the close connections between Bullinger's trinitarianism and his Christology, as is sermon 8, on the Holy Spirit.[14]

In the *Decades*, Bullinger aligns himself firmly with the received teaching of the western church on the nature of God and the interrelationship between the Father, Son and Holy Spirit. God, he declares, is both one in substance and three in persons. The Son is not merely pre-existent, but eternally begotten from the Father: indeed, God is termed "Father" in the first instance because he has always been the Father of the Son–described in Hebrews 1:3 as "the exact imprint of [God's] substance"–rather than simply the Father of humanity.[15] Whereas the faithful are sons of God merely by adoption, Christ is God's Son by nature, so it is appropriate to refer to him as consubstantial or co-essential with God. In stressing the equality of the Son with the Father, Bullinger repudiates the Platonic understanding of the Logos as the mediator between God and his creation; the pre-existent Christ is instead to be identified with the creator himself.[16] But at the same time, he is careful to repudiate the contrasting errors of Noetus and Sabellius, who by confusing the persons gave birth to "the gross heresy of the Patripassians." Although for Bullinger there is no inequality, division or separation within the Trinity, there is order and distinction, based on each person's unique

12.   Ibid., 149-50.

13.   *Sermonum Decades quinque, de potissimis Christianae religionis capitibus, in tres tomos digestae, authore Heinrycho Bullingero, ecclesiae Tigurinae ministro* (Zurich: Christoph Froschauer, 1577), *HBBibl* I, no. 188, f. 20^r-7^v; 204^r-14^v. See the discussion in Walser, *Prädestination*, 66-9.

14.   Ibid., f. 228^v-36^r; 241^v-8^r.

15.   Ibid., f. 20^v. Compare ibid., f. 228^v-9^r: "Vniuersa enim scriptura concorditer Deum appellat patrem, & patrem quidem aeternum. Nullus autem pater sui ipsius, sed filij pater est: & quia pater hic aeternus est, necessariò filium aeternum habeat oportet, aequalem sibi per omnia, coaeternum & consubstantialem."

16.   Compare Staedtke, *Theologie*, 153. Here Bullinger's approach differs subtly from that of Calvin, for whom the office of mediator has cosmological as well as soteriological significance. By some, Calvin's position was seen as implying a degree of subordinationism. See George H. Williams, "Strains in the Christology of the Emerging Polish Brethren" in Samuel Fiszman ed., *The Polish Reformation in its European Context* (Bloomington: Indiana UP, 1984), 61-95.

characteristics (*proprietates*).[17] He underlines this point by identifying the divine person who appeared to the patriarchs and prophets of the Old Testament (for example, to Moses in Exodus 33-4) as the Son, in a prefiguration of his incarnation.[18] So central is the orthodox doctrine of the Trinity to Bullinger's vision of Christianity that he does not hesitate to denounce its critics as Antichrist. According to Bullinger, it is impossible to deny God's properties without denying his very nature.[19]

The arguments set out by Bullinger in the *Decades* are recapitulated in his systematic works of the late 1550s and 1560s: the *Compendium of the Christian religion* (1556), the *Catechism* (1559), and the *Second Helvetic confession* (written in 1561, but published in 1566). The *Compendium* provides a comprehensive overview of the Reformed faith organised under ten doctrinal headings: scripture, God, sin, the law, grace and justification, faith and repentance, prayer, the sacraments and the church, good works and death. The work is essentially pastoral in tone; in his preface, addressed to the future Landgrave Wilhelm IV of Hesse-Kassel, Bullinger describes it as his response to demands for a summary of the cardinal teachings of Christianity from those confused by the quarrels of the theologians, expressing the hope that it will put an end to "strange questions" about the faith.[20] In line with those sentiments, Bullinger's treatment of the Trinity in the *Compendium* is brief and impeccably orthodox in tone. Characteristically, he emphasises the unity of God and explains the distinction between the divine persons in terms of their particular "properties," as manifested in the history of salvation. Thus the Father sends the Son into the world, the Son becomes incarnate as man, while the Spirit, proceeding from them both, sanctifies the faithful.[21]

In his *Catechism*, Bullinger again affirms the proposition that God is both one and triune. The Father, Son and Holy Spirit are of a single essence and nature, and together they constitute one true, living and eternal God. However, they are distinct "in their persons and properties": the Father generated the Son by "an eternal and ineffable generation"; the Son is begotten and was sent into the world by the Father; and the Spirit proceeds from the other two persons. Responding, perhaps, to popular misconceptions of the Trinity, and mindful of the *Catechism*'s target readership–pupils at the Zurich Latin schools–Bullinger stresses

17. *Sermonum Decades quinque*, f. 211^r; 242^v.

18. Ibid., f. 207^v-8^v.

19. Ibid., f. 212^v: "Imo quisquis negat hanc Trinitatem, Antichristus esse pronunciatur [in 1 John 2:22-3]. Deum enim, qui vnus est in Trinitate, et trinus in unitate, negat, adeoque proprietates Dei confundens aut auferens, ipsum Deum talem qualis est negat."

20. *Summa Christenlicher Religion. Darinn vß dem wort Gottes / one alles zancken vnd schälten / richtig vnd kurtz anzeigt wirt / was einem yetlichen Christen notwendig sye zů wüssen / zů glouben / zů thůn / vnd zů lassen / ouch zů leyden / vnd säligklich abzůsterben: in X. Artickel gestelt / durch Heinrychen Bullingern* (Zurich: 1556), *HBBibl* I, no. 283 f. ai^v- aii^v.

21. Ibid., f. 24^v-5^r. Here and elsewhere Bullinger endorses the doctrine of the dual procession of the Holy Spirit ("filioque"), added to the Nicene Creed by the western church but rejected by the Greeks as tending towards modalism. Compare *Sermonum Decades quinque*, f. 243^v-44^v; *In Apocalypsim Iesu Christi, reuelatam quidem per angelum Domini, uisam uero uel exceptam atque conscriptam a Ioanne apostolo & euangelista, Conciones centum: authore Heinrycho Bullingero* (Basle: Johannes Oporinus, 1557), *HBBibl* I, no. 327, 65-6.

the compatibility of the doctrine with monotheism. When asked whether the teaching that the Father, Son and Holy Spirit are distinct from one another is not equivalent to saying that they are three gods, the respondent in the *Catechism* replies that, although scripture does not confuse the three persons, neither does it divide or separate them. Rather, it attributes to all of them a single and co-equal nature and divinity.[22]

Perhaps the definitive summary of Bullinger's teaching on the Trinity is to be found in chapter three of the Second Helvetic confession, entitled "On God, his unity and Trinity."[23] To emphasise the orthodox credentials of the Reformed, Bullinger constructs his treatment of the Trinity around formulations derived from the ancient creeds. In declaring that God exists in three persons "inseparably" but "without confusion," Bullinger finds a triadological application for terms used originally by the Council of Chalcedon (451) to describe the relationship between the two natures of Christ.[24] These persons are distinguished from one another by their origins: the Father begets the Son, the Son is begotten from the Father "by an ineffable generation," and the Holy Spirit "truly proceeds from them both." Echoing the "Quicunque vult," Bullinger declares that "there are not three gods, but three persons, consubstantial, coeternal, and coequal," sharing a single divine nature. Jews, Muslims, blasphemers against the Trinity, and the heretics of the early church, who taught variously "that the Son and Holy Spirit are God in name only, and also that there is something created and subservient, or subordinate to another in the Trinity, and that there is something unequal in it, a greater or a less, something corporeal or corporeally conceived, something different with respect to character or will, something mixed or solitary, as if the Son and Holy Spirit were the affections and properties of one God the Father," are all to be condemned.

Bullinger's support for the orthodox doctrine of the Trinity is rooted in his conviction that it is the teaching of scripture: indeed, he regards trinitarianism as the only way of reconciling those biblical passages that assert the oneness of God with those that attribute divinity to the Son and the Holy Spirit as well as the Father. Like the early church fathers, Bullinger finds numerous allusions to the Trinity in the Old Testament as well as the New, in accordance with his belief "that the mystery of the Trinity was very well known to the patriarchs and the prophets."[25] In particular, the Hebrew writers' use of a plural noun for God ("Elohim") in conjunction with both singular and plural verb forms is interpreted

---

22.   *Catechesis pro adultioribus scripta [...] authore Heinrycho Bullingero* (Zurich: Christoph Froschauer, 1559), *HBBibl* I, no. 2377, f. 5ʳ⁻ᵛ: "Nam scriptura apertè distinguit, non confundit patrem, filium & spiritum sanctum, & tamen eosdem nec diuidit, neque discindit aut discerpit, sed ijsdem unam & coaequalem tribuit naturam uel diuinitatem."

23.   Wilhelm Niesel ed., *Bekenntnisschriften und Kirchenordnungen der nach Gottes Wort reformierten Kirchen* (Zollikon-Zurich: Theologische Buchhandlung, 1985), 225-6. English translation in Arthur C. Cochrane ed., *Reformed Confessions of the 16th Century* (Philadelphia: The Westminster Press, 1966), 228-9.

24.   Ernst Koch, *Die Theologie der Confessio Helvetica Posterior* (Neukirchen: Neukirchener Verlag des Erziehungsvereins GMBH, 1968), 57.

25.   *Sermonum Decades quinque*, f. 213ᵛ.

as signalling their belief that the one God subsists in three distinct hypostases.[26] Confirmation of this doctrine is supplied by Genesis 1:26, Genesis 18:1-15 (the appearance of Yahweh to Abraham by the terebinths of Mamre under the appearance of three men), Genesis 19:24 ("the Lord rained down on Sodom and Gomorrah burning sulphur–from the Lord out of the heavens") and Yahweh's use of a triune formula to describe himself ("the God of Abraham, the God of Isaac and the God of Jacob"). In his early work *The old faith*, written specifically to demonstrate the unchanging character of true religion from the age of the patriarchs down to the Reformation, Bullinger cites Psalms 110:1 ("The Lord says to my Lord: 'Sit at my right hand until I make your enemies a footstool for your feet'") and 33:6 ("By the word of the Lord were the heavens made, their starry host by the breath of his mouth") in support of his contention that King David recognised both the divinity of the Messiah–like the apostle Thomas in John's gospel–and the existence of a plurality of persons within the Godhead.[27] Here Bullinger is more respectful of tradition (and less sensitive to Hebrew rhetorical conventions) than Calvin, who rejects the patristic use of Psalm 33:6 as a proof-text for the Trinity on the grounds that "it is common practice in the Psalms to repeat the same thing twice."[28] Elsewhere Bullinger, too, shows himself alert to the dangers of reading the Trinity into Old Testament texts, such as the threefold "sanctus" of Isaiah 6:3, which are capable of bearing a number of interpretations. In his view, there is no need to engage in such tortuous exegesis when scripture contains other, more explicit passages that confirm the church's teaching.[29]

In the *Compendium of the Christian religion* Bullinger concedes that, although the Trinity was taught by the Hebrew prophets "very clearly everywhere," the strongest support for it is provided by the works of the evangelists and apostles.[30] Of particular significance for him are Matthew 3:16-17, with its description of the descent of the Holy Spirit on Christ at his baptism while a voice from heaven (the Father) proclaims his divine sonship, and the "great commission" of Matthew 28:19.[31] Bullinger also sees the Trinity made manifest in Luke's ac-

---

26. *Sermonum Decades quinque*, f. 206[r-v]; 213[v]. Compare Isaias excellentissimus Dei propheta ... expositus Homilijs CXC [...] authore Heinrycho Bullingero (Zurich: Christoph Froschauer, 1567), *HBBibl* I, no. 558, f. 34[v] (on Isaiah 6:8).

27. Der alt gloub. Das der Christen gloub von anfang der wält gewart habe / der recht waar alt vnnd vngezwyfelt gloub sye / klare bewysung Heinrychen Bullingers (Zurich: Christoph Froshauer, 1539), *HBBibl* I 100, f. F[r-v]: "Denn die heilige Dryfaltigkeit in einiger Gottheit bekennt er [David] nit nun hie [Psalm 110] / sunder ouch im xxxiij Psalmen / sprechend / Durch das wort Gottes sind die himmel gmachet / vnd durch den geist sines munds all jre macht vnd heer. Denn es ist ye gewüß / daß nun ein einiger Gott / schöpffer himmels vnd der erden / ist / der wirt aber hie Herr oder Gott / Wort vnd geist / die Dryfaltigkeit gnennt." Compare *Sermonum Decades quinque*, f. 21[r]; 214[r].

28. John Calvin, *Institutes of the Christian Religion*, John T. McNeill ed. 2 vols (The Library of Christian Classics 20-1; Philadelphia: The Westminster, 1960), I:140.

29. *Isaias*, f. 32[v]: "Referunt alij triplicatum illud, Sanctus, ad tres personas in adoranda Trinitate, ut sanctus dicatur pater, sanctus filius, sanctus spiritus sanctus. Quod ut apprimè placet, ita euidentioribus testimonijs potest approbari distinctio personarum in adoranda Trinitate."

30. *Summa*, f. 25[v].

31. *Sermonum Decades quinque*, f. 20[v], 211[v]; *Summa*, f. 25[v].

count of the annunciation (Luke 1:26-38). Commenting on this passage in the *Decades*, he exclaims:

What, I ask, could be clearer or more evident than these words? Here you have the person of the Most High, that is to say the Father. For just before this the angel says, "He will be great and will be called the Son of the Most High." But the son is the Son of the Father. The persons of the Son and the Holy Spirit are also represented, with their characteristics, which are neither mingled nor confused. Neither the Father nor the Holy Spirit is incarnate, but the Son. To the Father is born of the virgin a son, who was the Son by eternal and ineffable generation. But the Holy Spirit, which is the power of the Most High, overshadows the virgin and makes her pregnant. Thus we see the persons distinguished, though not divided–by their characteristics, rather than by the essence of divinity or by nature.[32]

A large number of proof-texts for the Trinity are identified in the gospel of John. According to Bullinger, John wrote his gospel to expose the errors of two opposing sets of heretics: those who taught that Christ was a mere man, the son of Joseph, and those who denied that he had truly become incarnate. In the prologue to the gospel, Christ is designated the Logos because through him God is made known. The word "beginning" in John 1:1 denotes not the moment of creation, as in Genesis, but eternity: the Son is generated from the Father "eternal from eternal, omnipotent from omnipotent, best from best, God from God, neither subsequent nor inferior to the one who begets him." By saying that the Word was with ($\pi\rho$ ς) God, John distinguishes clearly between the persons of the Father and the Son, unlike the ancient heretics Sabellius and Noetus. Conversely, by emphasising the Word's role in creation he makes clear that Christ is to be regarded as fully divine and in no way subordinate to the Father.[33] Further evidence of Christ's divinity is supplied by John 5:26, John 8:58 (where Jesus applies the divine name "I am," revealed to Moses in Exodus 3:14, to himself), John 10:30 (which Bullinger describes as signifying both the consubstantiality of and distinction between the Father and the Son), John 14:1, John 14:10-11, John 17:5 and John 20:28.[34] Christ's Jewish opponents are themselves shown to have recognised that, in calling himself the Son of God, he was laying claim to equality with God.[35] The gospel of John also contains testimonies to the divinity, personhood

32. *Sermonum Decades quinque*, f. 212[r-v]. Compare *In luculentum et sacrosanctum Euangelium domini nostri Iesu Christi secundum Lucam, Commentariorum lib. IX. per H. Bullingerum* (Zurich: Christoph Froschauer, 1548), HBBibl I, no. 174, f. 13[v]: "Est in his praeterea apertissimum adorandae trinitatis, praesertim autem distinctionis personarum euidentissimum argumentum. Mentio enim fit altissimi, filij dei, & spiritus sancti, atque hi tres unum sunt: non confunduntur tamen (propter unitatem) personae. Filius enim incarnatur, non pater, non spiritus sanctus, & ex spiritu sancto & Maria uirgine nascitur patris aeternus filius: interim tamen, indiuisa est trinitas, quia in deo est unitas non pluralitas."

33. *In diuinum Iesu Christi Domini nostri Euangelium secundum Ioannem, Commentariorum libri X. per Heinrychum Bullingerum [...]* (Zurich: Christoph Froschauer, 1548), HBBibl I, no. 154, f. 3[r]-5[r].

34. *In Ioannem*, f. 59[r], 94[v], 107[r-v], 134[r], 136[r-v], 188[v]-9[r]; *Sermonum Decades quinque*, f. 211[r], 229[r], 230[r], 231[r].

35. *In Ioannem*, f. 56[v]-7[r]; *Sermonum Decades quinque*, f. 21[v], 229[v]-30[r], 230[v]-1[r]. Compare

and dual procession of the Holy Spirit, notably John 14:16, John 15:26 and John 16:13-15. The first of these passages provides firm support for the church's teaching regarding the distinction of persons:

> What could be clearer than his saying, "I will ask the Father, and he will give you another comforter"? I, he says–the Son–will ask the Father, so that he may give you another comforter, whom he calls further on the Spirit of truth. The Father, Son and Holy Spirit are therefore distinct persons of the one deity.[36]

Bullinger sees trinitarianism as implicit also in the Acts of the Apostles and New Testament epistles. For example, the story of Ananias and Sapphira in Acts 5:1-6 demonstrates the divinity of the Holy Spirit, because the apostle Peter here equates lying to the Holy Spirit with lying to God.[37] In his *Commentary on Romans*, Bullinger argues that at the beginning of the letter Paul greets his correspondents in the names of both God and Christ "lest anyone should think that God is divided on account of Christ's incarnation or that Christ is less than God"; more generally, he interprets Paul's use of triadic formulations as an endorsement of the Nicene doctrine of the Trinity.[38] Romans 9:5, with its ambiguous syntax, is read in orthodox fashion as a declaration of the divinity of the Messiah,[39] while 1 Corinthians 8:6 is adduced as evidence that the "unity of God and the distinction of persons is not a human invention, but a testimony of God."[40] Again, when in 2 Corinthians 5:19 Paul says that God was in Christ reconciling the world to himself, "he recognises that Christ was not just a mere man, but also true God." In his exegesis of this passage, Bullinger insists that the presence of God in Christ is not to be compared to the indwelling of the prophets by the Holy Spirit: Colossians 2:19, with its statement that the fullness of divinity dwells in Christ, provides confirmation that the Son is equal in all respects to the Father.[41] This doctrine is reinforced in the opening verses of the letter to the Hebrews, which Bullinger ascribes to Paul. Although in Hebrews 1:2 Christ is described as God's heir, he is in no way inferior to the Father. The temporal inequality between human fathers and their sons is not mirrored in the eternal relationship between God and Christ, who are distinct in person but share an indivisible kingdom, over

---

In sacrosanctum Euangelium Domini nostri Iesu Christi secundum Marcum, Commentariorum lib. VI per Heinrychum Bullingerum (Zurich: Christoph Froschauer, 1545), *HBBibl* I, no. 170, f. 2ʳ.

36. *In Ioannem*, f. 139ʳ.

37. *In omnes apostolicas epistolas, divi videlicet Pauli XIII. et VII. canonicas, commentarii Heinrychi Bullingeri, ab ipso iam recogniti, & nonnullis in locis aucti* (Zurich: Christoph Froschauer, 1549), *HBBibl* I, no. 85, 380.

38. In omnes apostolicas epistolas, 5; *Sermonum Decades quinque*, f. 212ᵛ.

39. *In omnes apostolicas epistolas*, 78; *Sermonum Decades quinque*, f. 231ᵛ. Bullinger also opts to read Titus 2:13 and 1 John 5:20 as attributing the title "God" to Christ, *In omnes apostolicas epistolas*, 629; *Isaias*, f. 272ʳ; *In epistolas apostolorum canonicas septem commentarii Heinrychi Bullingeri* (Zurich: Christoph Froschauer, 1549), *HBBibl* I, no. 94, 106; *Sermonum Decades quinque*, f. 229ᵛ. However, in his New Testament commentaries at least, he follows Erasmus in rejecting the so-called Johannine comma (1 John 5:7) as spurious (*In epistolas apostolorum*, 103).

40. *In omnes apostolicas epistolas*, 179.

41. Ibid., 290; 484-5.

which they preside in equal power and glory. In the Father and the Son there is "nothing before, nothing after, nothing greater, nothing less."[42] For this reason, it is impossible that God should be worshipped without his Son, as the Jews and Turks falsely imagine.[43]

Bullinger's choice of a reading of scripture consistent with Nicene orthodoxy cannot be put down simply to his reverence for the Fathers and the exegetical tradition enshrined in their writings. More fundamentally, Bullinger is convinced that the Christian understanding of salvation makes sense only within a trinitarian context. Following Athanasius (and Zwingli), he argues that the efficacy of the atonement is dependent on Christ's full divinity, as the salvation of humanity "could not be achieved by a mere man."[44] In his *Commentary on Acts*, he insists that those who deny Christ's divinity are guilty of overturning the entire Gospel, because "if Christ were not God, he could not be our salvation or the object of our faith."[45] The third and fourth-century heretics Paul of Samosata and Photinus, who professed faith in Christ while refusing to acknowledge him as divine, are cursed, because scripture condemns anyone who places their trust in man rather than the one God.[46] In order that he might serve as the mediator between God and humanity, it was necessary for the incarnate Christ to be both true God and true man, as any mediator must hold something in common with both the parties between which he mediates.[47]

Bullinger's doctrine of the Holy Spirit is also expressed in soteriological terms. In the *Decades*, he describes the Spirit as co-operating with the Father and the Son to complete the work of sanctification in those who have been justified:

> For by him the fruit of God's salvation, completed in the Son, is sealed. Through the Spirit, our sanctification and cleansing is bestowed on us and channelled to us.[48]

The individual believer's awareness of the Spirit's personhood and role within the divine economy is thus intimately related to their experience of his presence within their lives. In his *Sermons on Jeremiah*, Bullinger makes the same point with reference to the Trinity as a whole. It is insufficient, he maintains, simply to acknowledge that God is three in persons, one in substance, wise and all-

---

42. Ibid., 647. Here Bullinger echoes the clause in the Athanasian Creed that states, "in this Trinity none is before or after the others: none is greater or less than the others."

43. *In omnes apostolicas epistolas*, 87-8 (referring to 1 John 2:22-3); *In Ioannem*, f. 58^{r-v}.

44. *In omnes apostolicas epistolas*, 290.

45. *In acta Apostolorum Heinrychi Bullingeri commentariorum libri VI* (Zurich: Christph Froschauer, 1540), *HBBibl* I, no. 45, f. 76^v: "Si enim Christus deus non esset, iam salus & obiectum fidei nostrę esse non posset. Proinde qui Christi diuinitatem negant, totum euangelium subuertunt." Compare *Sermonum Decades quinque*, f. 21^v: "nisi filius naturalis esset Deus, non posset esse saluator mundi."

46. *Ieremias fidelissimus et laborosissimus Dei propheta, expositus per Heinrychum Bullingerum, ministrum Ecclesiae Tigurinae, Concionibus CLXX. [...]* (Zurich: Christoph Froschauer, 1575), *HBBibl* I, no. 361, f. 117^v.

47. *Sermonum Decades quinque*, f. 22^r; *In Marcum*, f. 2^r: "Nisi enim dominus noster uerus & naturalis esset deus & homo, nunquam posset esse mediator inter deum & hominem, nunquam esset rex & pontifex omnium fidelium & saluator mundi."

48. *Sermonum Decades quinque*, f. 27^v.

powerful; rather, we must believe "that that one, triune, wise and all-powerful God is our God, showing us mercy, judging and justifying us."[49]

In all the works discussed so far, Bullinger's emphasis is on the "economic" Trinity–the Trinity as revealed in scripture and in God's unfolding plan for the salvation of humankind. Although Bullinger regards the Father, Son and Holy Spirit as distinct hypostases, rather than simply different modes of operation of a unipersonal God, he is wary of attempts to define relationships within the "immanent" Trinity too precisely. The closest he comes to doing this is in his use of patristic images designed to illustrate the distinction of persons. In the *Decades*, the *Compendium of the Christian religion* and the *Catechism*, Bullinger compares the Father to the sun, and the Son and the Holy Spirit to the light and heat that it produces, while in his *Commentary on Hebrews* he finds an analogy for the eternal generation of the Logos in the emission of a ray from the sun.[50] The source for both images is Tertullian, whose comparisons of the Trinity to a root, its stem and their fruit, and to a spring and the stream and river that flow from it, are also cited by Bullinger.[51] Less frequently, he refers to Augustine's analogy between the three divine persons and the human faculties of mind, memory and will.[52]

At the same time, Bullinger never ceases to remind his reader of the limited usefulness of such "similitudes": God's nature remains essentially mysterious and incomprehensible, except insofar as it has been revealed in scripture.[53] According to Bullinger, excessive speculation on the Trinity is not only disrespectful, but exposes those who engage in it to the grave risk of heresy. The orthodox doctrine of three persons in one substance is not to be explained, merely accepted, as it is not given to us to see the face of God in this life.[54] In the *Decades*, he condemns as sophists those who complicate the Trinity with "strange, curious and destructive questions": believers should rather content themselves with the knowledge "that there is one divine nature or essence, in which are the Father, the Son and the Holy Spirit."[55] Similarly, in his preface to the *Compendium of the Christian religion* he writes:

---

49. *Ieremias*, f. 74^v.

50. *Sermonum Decades quinque*, f. 213^r, 248^r; *Summa*, f. 25^r; *Catechesis*, f. 5^v; *In omnes apostolicas epistolas*, 647-8.

51. Compare *PL*: II:163-4.

52. See page 79 below.

53. *Sermonum Decades quinque*, f. 204^{r-v}: "Adferuntur quidem multae rationes physicae: sed maius & mirabilius perpetuò manet opus Dei, quàm assequatur cerebrum & eloquutio hominis. Nullus ergo hominum certum aliquid de Deo habere cupiens, in semetipsum descendat, aut humano innitatur iudicio. Alioqui semper colet figmentum cordis sui, stultitiam, nugas & deliria. Contra verò non potest non rectissimè de Deo sentire, iudicare & loqui, qui nihil sibi tribuit, nihil ex suo fingit cerebro, aut confictum ex capite alterius sibi sequendum deligit, sed in omnibus os Dei obseruat, reuelationemque Dei sequitur. Proinde veluti lege certa constitutum sit, non posse Deum rectè cognosci nisi ex verbo Dei: & Deum talem esse credendum vel recipiendum, qualem se ipse nobis in verbo suo reuelat. Nemo certè melius quid & qualis sit Deus dixerit, quàm ipse Deus." Compare Calvin, *Institutes*, I:142 (I:13).

54. *Sermonum Decades quinque*, f. 204^v-5^r; 214^{r-v}. Compare Calvin, *Institutes*, I:146-7 (I:13).

55. *Sermonum Decades quinque*, f. 211^v.

Our belief in God and the righteousness and salvation of mankind is not endless or uncertain. There is no need for us constantly to question it or to make up or seek out new things.[56]

Later in the same work Bullinger applies this point specifically to the Trinity. The doctrine that God is both one and triune is taught in scripture "so simply, truly and clearly," he argues, "that we should believe in its simplicity, rather than speculating on it, and wanting to know in this life more than God has revealed to us." Aware of the danger posed by such speculation, Christian rulers have for the past 1,000 years punished deviation from the orthodox faith as a capital crime—rightly so, in Bullinger's view, as Leviticus 24:15-16 prescribes the death penalty for such blasphemy.[57] Bullinger's conviction that harsh measures are sometimes required in the defence of orthodoxy was reinforced by his experience of contemporary antitrinitarianism, which from the early 1550s threatened to undermine the stability of the Reformed churches.

II. The Antitrinitarian Challenge

In the light of the reformers' call for a return to scripture and the practice of the primitive church, it was inevitable that some individuals should come to question the received doctrine of the Trinity. Ludwig Hätzer, an enthusiastic follower of Zwingli who went on to reject the magisterial Reformation in favour of Anabaptism, was one of the earliest thinkers to manifest antitrinitarian tendencies. In a hymn published in Sebastian Franck's *Chronicle*, he declared that God was not three persons, but one—sentiments that may have helped bring about his execution in February 1529.[58] Two years later Michael Servetus's sensational critique of Nicene orthodoxy, *On the errors of the Trinity*, was published by Johannes Setzer in Hagenau. The work met with almost universal condemnation, notably from Berchtold Haller, Martin Bucer and Johannes Oecolampadius.[59] Around the same time Johannes Campanus, a former Wittenberg student who had broken with Luther and Melanchthon over the Trinity during the late 1520s, published his *Restitution of divine scripture*. In this work, Campanus argued for a form of binitarianism, denying the personhood of the Holy Spirit and subordinating the Son to the Father.[60]

In 1534 the Savoyard preacher Claude d'Aliod was banished successively from Basle, Berne and Constance after attacking the Nicene Creed as an abomination on a par with the Mass. According to d'Aliod, the doctrine of the Trinity is

---

56. *Summa*, f. aii[v].
57. Ibid., f. 25[v]: "Diewyl dann die heilig Gschrifft die leer von der einigkeit vnd dryfaltigkeit Gottes / so einfalt / richtig / vnnd klar leert / söllend wir deren einfalt glouben / nit grüblen / vnnd hie in zyt mee wöllen wüssen vnd sähen / dann vns Gott geoffenbaret hat. Die Christlichen fürsten vnd oberkeiten / vor tusend jaren / habent recht vnd billich / by verlierung lybs vnd läbens verbotten / in disem artickel anders zů sůchen, sprechen vnd mit schmähung Gottes zů leeren."
58. George H. Williams, *The Radical Reformation*, (Kirksville, Mo.: Sixteenth Century Journal Publishers, 3rd ed. 1992), 301-3. In a letter to Bullinger dated 22 October 1534, Johannes Zwick noted Hätzer's denial of Christ's divinity (*HBBW* IV:373-4, no. 464).
59. Williams, *Radical Reformation*, 401-4.
60. Ibid., 404-5; 468-9.

nothing short of tritheism. God exists in only one person, the Father; Christ is not the incarnation of a second, pre-existent divine hypostasis, but a man indwelt by the plenitude of God's Spirit, who for that reason is termed God.[61] Bullinger, who had been kept informed of d'Aliod's activities by Berchtold Haller and Johannes Zwick, was sufficiently alarmed to rush out a defence of traditional Christology, entitled *An orthodox assertion of the two natures of Christ.*[62] This work, based on an oration given in the Zurich Grossmünster to mark the feast of the city's patron saints Felix and Regula, is of interest because, in seeking to establish Christ's divinity, Bullinger is also obliged to set out his position on the Trinity. Just as important, for our purposes, are the insights that the *Assertion* provides into Bullinger's heresiology. As will become clear, many of the arguments first articulated in this text were to be refined and expanded on by Bullinger in contributions to subsequent trinitarian controversies.

In a short preface to the *Assertion*, addressed to the ministers of the Zurich church, Bullinger makes clear his reluctance to delve too deeply into the mysteries of God's being.[63] When dealing with this matter in the past (the reference is to his recently published *Commentary on Hebrews)*, he has chosen not to respond to the heretics' detailed criticisms of orthodoxy, but rather to set out the truth simply and clearly. The first point of which all who embark on this task must be mindful is that the divine nature is beyond human understanding; Bullinger cites approvingly both Augustine's dictum that if God were comprehensible, he would not be God, and Jesus ben Sirach's warning against attempts to probe "higher things" and curiosity about things invisible. It is the responsibility of those charged with preaching God's word to proclaim his mercy, goodness, truth, omnipotence, wisdom and justice; salvation through Christ; the power of faith; and the virtues of the Christian life. Ministers are to be on their guard against the wiles of Satan, who will seek to divert their attention away from these useful tasks into "conflicts about words" and "consideration of curious and hidden things," with the sole aim of undermining the church.

This theme is developed in the main text of the *Assertio*, where Bullinger offers a theological explanation for the rise of heresy. The *Antistes* describes heresy as Satan's response to the collapse of idolatry and growth of the church following Christ's coming. With the survival of his kingdom at risk, Satan developed a new strategy to preserve it: taking advantage of human pride, superstition and ingratitude towards God, he was able to subvert the faith and split the church with heresies and schisms.[64] The circumstances that allowed heresy to emerge and flourish

---

61. Ibid., 469-72.

62. Haller to Bullinger, 3 May 1534 (*HBBW* IV:153-9, no. 370); idem, 7 May 1534 (ibid., 170-1, no. 373); Zwick to Bullinger, mid-August 1534 (ibid., 275-82, no. 424); idem, shortly after mid-August 1534 (ibid., 282-3, no. 425); Zwick to Bullinger and Konrad Pellikan, 9 September 1534 (ibid., 306-9, no. 435).

63. For the text of the preface, see *HBBW* IV: 336-7, no. 449.

64. *Vtriusque in Christo naturae tam diuinae quam humanae, contra uarias haereses, pro confessione Christi catholica, Assertio orthodoxa, per Heinrychum Bullingerum* (Zurich: Christoph Froschauer, 1534), *HBBibl* I 62, f. 4ʳ⁻ᵛ: "Aduentu enim Christi prostratus inimicus ueritatis sathan, uidens idola derelicta et per nimium credentium populum indies regnum suum destrui, atque templa quamplurima subuerti, neque illud incendium sanguine martyrum extingui posse,

in the early church have been repeated in Bullinger's own day, following the exposure of papist "idolatry."[65] Even the doctrines proposed by d'Aliod and his ilk are not new, but simply reiterations of earlier errors. Fortunately, the names and teachings of the ancient heretics have been preserved for the contemporary church by God as a warning against their modern imitators. Bullinger goes on to provide a short overview of Christological heresy within the early church, listing first those heretics who erred in respect of Christ's divinity (Noetus, Sabellius, Praxeas, Hermogenes, Arius, Photinus, Artemon, Eunomius, Aetius, Ebion, Basilides, Cerinthus, Carpocrates, Paul of Samosata and Theodotus) and secondly, those who failed to give due weight to his humanity: Marcion, Cerdo, Mani, Valentinus and, again, Arius, who is reported to have denied that Christ possessed a human soul. He also discusses the later, post-Nicene heresies of Eutyches, the Monothelites, Nestorius, Timothy and Apollinarius.[66]

Next Bullinger offers a summary of the catholic faith, based on the Nicene Creed but incorporating the Christological conclusions of Chalcedon, which leads into a consideration of the Trinity. Here Bullinger is again at pains to demonstrate the compatibility of the orthodox faith with monotheism. He notes that those who reject Christ's divinity do so for fear of professing a plurality of gods with the pagans, but this is to fall victim to yet another of Satan's deceptions. As Tertullian shows, Christians should be concerned at all times to balance their faith in the oneness of God with the preservation of the divine economy. The persons of the Godhead are three "not in rank, but in position; not in substance, but in form; not in power, but in appearance." They are distinct as regards their properties, but consubstantial in respect of their common deity; there is order within the Trinity, but no inequality.[67] Here, as in the *Decades* and his other systematic works, Bullinger finds analogies to the Trinity in nature: in the sun and the light and heat that it emits, in the root, stem and fruit of a plant, and in the human faculties of mind, memory and will. As usual, these images are accompanied by the caveat that the divine nature is not directly comparable to created things; the point, rather, is that we should believe what God wants us to believe about him, as revealed in the scripture.[68]

In the *Assertio*, Bullinger insists that only the doctrine of the Trinity properly expresses biblical teaching concerning the nature of God. "If there is no Trinity," he asks at one point, "to what do the terms Father, Son and Holy Spirit relate?"[69]

---

excogitauit nouam (ut Cyprianus ait) fraudem, ut sub ipso scilicet Christiani nominis et ueritatis titulo fallat incautos. Haereses ergo in hoc inuenit & schismata, quibus subuerteret fidem, ueritatem corrumperet, scinderet unitatem. Proinde quos detinere non potuit in uiae ueteris caecitate, eos circumscribit et decipit noui itineris errore."

65.   *Assertio*, f. 6ʳ: "Diu ille [Satan] ueterem ecclesiam quassauit persecutionibus tyrannorum, postea & haeresibus prophanorum quorundam hominum concussit. Idem uidemus illum & moliri & agere nostro etiam saeculo." In his preface to the collection *Valentini Gentilis teterrimi haeretici impietatum ac triplicis perfidiae et perjurii, brevis explicatio* (Geneva: François Perrin, 1567), Theodore Beza presents a very similar argument (see *Correspondance* VIII:234-58).

66.   Ibid., f. 7ʳ-10ʳ.

67.   Ibid., f. 15ʳ: "Pater solus a nullo est, filius a patre sine initio genitus est, ab utroque uero procedit spiritus sanctus. Trium tamen una est deitas, coaequalis maiestas."

68.   Ibid., f. 18ᵛ.

69.   Ibid., f. 18ʳ.

After citing some of his favourite proof-texts for the Trinity and the divinity of Christ (Genesis 1:26, Genesis 18:1-15, Psalm 33:6, Matthew 3:16-17, Matthew 28:19, Luke 4:18, John 3:34, John 15:26 and John 16:14), Bullinger outlines a series of more generic arguments for the co-equality and consubstantiality of Christ with the Father. Of particular interest are his attempts to turn back on the antitrinitarians the accusation of polytheism. In scripture, he points out, Christ is described as the source of life and salvation, is credited with the ability to forgive sins and is made the object of worship. The titles "God" and "Lord" are attributed to him. But the Bible also teaches that God is one (Deuteronomy 6:4), that there is no God but he (Isaiah 45:6) and that he will not give his glory to another (Isaiah 42:8). If these apparently conflicting truths are to be reconciled, we must conclude that Christ is one God with the Father, possessing the same divine prerogatives, and that where God is referred to without differentiation in scripture, the whole Trinity is meant.[70] The implication of this argument is that those who deny Christ's divinity while continuing to advocate his worship are themselves guilty of idolatry. In the *Assertio*, Bullinger pinpoints an inherent weakness of early antitrinitarianism, which subordinated Christ to the Father but attributed a derived, partial or honorific deity to him. The point was not lost on later Reformed defenders of orthodox trinitarianism or on the radicals themselves, some of whom sought to resolve this apparent inconsistency by ceasing to venerate Christ altogether.

Scattered references to the activities of early antitrinitarians such as d'Aliod are to be found in other works published by Bullinger during the 1530s. In his *Commentary on Galatians* (1535), the *Antistes* notes Jerome's use of Galatians 4:6 ("God has sent the Spirit of his Son into our hearts, crying 'Abba! Father!'") against heretics who contested the divinity of the Holy Spirit, adding that this error has now been revived by "certain smatterers and by idle men of ill will."[71] Of particular concern to Bullinger was Servetus's *On the errors of the Trinity*, against which he warns his readers in his *Commentary on 1 Corinthians* (1534).[72] In his earlier *Commentary on Hebrews* (1532) he lambasts "pests, irreligious men, hypocrites and most terrible blasphemers (I know not whether to call them demons)" who question the doctrines of the Trinity and the divinity of Christ. Although Servetus is not mentioned by name, his scandalous comparison of the Trinity to the three-headed Cerberus and other classical monsters provokes Bullinger into a defence of Nicene orthodoxy, which culminates with the denunciation of a string of ancient heresies.[73]

---

70. *Assertio*, f. 20[r-v]. Compare Bullinger's comments on Isaiah 55:5, where the same argument is put in the form of a syllogism: "Agnoscamus ergo patrem misisse filium ideoque distinctas esse personas uidelicet, mittentis & missi. Sed cum unus Deus adorandus sit & honorandus, & Christus perinde ut pater sit honorandus, consequens est patrem & filium in substantia unum esse Deum: cum non possit esse nisi unus uerus Deus" (*Isaias*, f. 278[r]). See also *In omnes apostolicas epistolas*, 459 (on Philippians 2: 6-11); 476-7 (on Colossians 1:15-19), 648-9 (on Hebrews 1: 2-3). In the *Decades*, the Holy Spirit's power of sanctification is adduced as evidence of his deity (*Sermonum Decades quinque*, f. 242[v]).
71. *In omnes apostolicas epistolas*, 380.
72. Ibid., 179.
73. Ibid., 649-50. It is unclear how Bullinger came by this information, as the comparison

The full extent of Bullinger's revulsion for Servetus's teachings was made clear following the Spaniard's arrest in Geneva in August 1553. A month later, the council of Geneva wrote to the ministers of the four Swiss Reformed churches (Zurich, Berne, Basle and Schaffhausen) requesting their opinion on the matter. Copies of Servetus's most recent published work, the *Restitution of Christianity*, and of various other documents associated with his case were sent for the ministers' perusal.[74] On 2 October Bullinger and his colleagues issued their response.[75] The Zurichers begin by asserting that the doctrine of the Trinity has been believed and handed down by the faithful "from the beginning of the world"; it is taught clearly in scripture and confirmed by the unanimous consensus of the catholic and orthodox church. After citing the revelation of the Father, Son and Holy Spirit at Christ's baptism as proof that God consists of three distinct divine persons in one essence, they denounce the heresy of the Patripassians and defend the Nicene Creed as a faithful record of apostolic teaching. Servetus himself is condemned for blaspheming the Trinity, for speaking disparagingly of the church Fathers Augustine and Athanasius, and for adding his voice to Jewish and Muslim attacks on Christianity. The orthodox doctrine that the Son exists "in his own hypostasis" from eternity is asserted against Servetus's belief in the generation of Christ's flesh from the substance of the Father. Finally, Bullinger and his colleagues proffer their view on what is to be done with Servetus. While not explicitly advocating the use of the death penalty against him, they make clear that his punishment should be severe, on the basis that for more than twenty years he has stubbornly resisted attempts to correct him. Providence, they claim, has provided the Genevan authorities with a golden opportunity to rebut the charge of heresy that has been levelled against the Reformed and to ensure that the Servetian poison spreads no further.

On 26 October, Servetus was pronounced guilty of Anabaptism and antitrinitarianism; the following day he was burned alive at Champel, just outside Geneva, in accordance with the prescriptions of imperial law. The sentence came as a shock to some elements within the Swiss churches, who feared the emergence of a "new inquisition" on Protestant territory, but Bullinger had no such qualms: for him, it was entirely justifiable in terms of the magistrate's *cura religionis*.[76] However, Servetus's death failed to have the desired effect of checking the spread of antitrinitarianism within Reformed ranks. Over the next few years, his ideas were taken up and developed by groups of Italian evangelical exiles who had settled in Geneva, Basle and the Rhaetian Freestate (Graubünden). Prominent

---

appears in neither of Servetus's early works, *De Trinitatis erroribus* and *Dialogorum de Trinitate libri duo*, but only in subsequent letters to Calvin and Abel Perrin, and in the *Christianismi restitutio* (406,581). Bullinger mentions it again in his unpublished *Trinitas Dei* (see page 96 below).

74. *CO* VIII:802-3.

75. Ibid., 555-8.

76. In a letter to Beza dated 30 August 1553, Bullinger suggested that the Genevan council was duty bound to put Servetus to death (Beza, *Correspondance* I:111-2, no. 36). For further details, see H. Fast, *Heinrich Bullinger und die Täufer: Ein Beitrag zur Historiographie und Theologie im 16. Jahrhundert* (Schriftenreihe des Mennonitischen Geschichtsvereins 7, Weierhof: 1959), 58-9; J. Wayne Baker, "Christian Discipline, Church and State, and Toleration: Bullinger, Calvin and Basel 1530-1555" in Oberman, *Das Reformierte Erbe* I:35-48.

among them was Matteo Gribaldi, a former professor of civil law at Padua who penned an *Apology for Servetus* as well as several antitrinitarian tracts. Although he claimed to be a follower of Servetus–going so far as to circulate some of his own works under the martyred Spaniard's name–Gribaldi developed a distinctive solution to the problem of the Trinity.[77] Repudiating the "sophistic" doctrine of consubstantiality, he argued that the persons of the Trinity were three separate beings or essences–in effect, three gods. At the same time, he drew a clear distinction between the Father, who alone is God "from himself" ("a seipso"), and the Son and the Holy Spirit who, although co-eternal with the Father, derive their divinity from him. Gribaldi's rationalistic scheme, dubbed "tritheism" by the orthodox, was to remain the dominant variant of antitrinitarianism until the mid-1560s. It was especially well received in the Italian church of Geneva, to which Gribaldi had written in September 1554 setting out his ideas.[78] By May 1559, the situation had deteriorated to the extent that Calvin and the Italian minister, Lattanzio Ragnoni, were forced to insist that members of the congregation subscribe to a rigidly orthodox confession of faith.[79] Two of the most outspoken dissidents, Giorgio Biandrata and Giampaolo Alciati, fled the city rather than face punishment; a third, Valentino Gentile, escaped Servetus's fate only by agreeing to a humiliating public abjuration.[80]

Initially, Bullinger was reluctant to lend credence to some of the direr warnings that he received about support for antitrinitarian ideas in the Italian exile community, with which he had developed a close relationship. In July 1555, he accepted as orthodox a confession of faith by the Sienese exile Lelio Sozzini, who had settled permanently in Zurich, even though he recognised that its wording was ambiguous.[81] Later the same year he approved a similar confession by Gribaldi, whom he also defended against accusations of Servetianism.[82] However, it is clear that Bullinger was becoming increasingly uneasy about the extent of antitrinitarian agitation and its effect on the Reformed churches. In a letter to Calvin dated 12 June 1554, he expressed approval for a death sentence handed down by the three Rhaetian Leagues against the antitrinitarian Anabaptist Il

---

77. Carlos Gilly, *Spanien und der Basler Buchdruck bis 1600: Ein Querschnitt durch die spanische Geistesgeschichte aus der Sicht einer europäischen Buchdruckerstadt* (Basle: Verlag Helbing, 1985), 298-318.

78. *CO* XV:246-8, no. 2018.

79. *CO* XVII:168-9, no. 2870; ibid. IX:385-8.

80. On these events, see John N. Tylenda, "The Warning that went unheeded: John Calvin on Giorgio Biandrata," *Calvin Theological Journal* 12 (1977), 24-62; T. R. Castiglione, "Valentino contro Calvino: Il processo del "secondo Serveto" nel 1558, a Ginevra" in Ludwik Chmaj ed., *Studia nad arianizmem* (Warsaw: PWN, 1959), 49-71.

81. Andreas Mühling, "Lelio Sozzini: Bemerkungen zum Umgang Heinrich Bullingers mit 'Häretikern'" in Athina Lexutt/Vicco von Bülow eds, *Kaum zu glauben: Von der Häresie und dem Umgang mit ihr* (Rheinbach: CMZ Verlag, 1998), 162-70; Edward M. Hulme, "Lelio Sozzini's Confession of Faith" in *Persecution and Liberty: Essays in Honor of George Lincoln Burr* (New York: The Century Co., 1931), 211-25. For the text of the confession, and Bullinger's comments on it, see Lelio Sozzini, *Opere*, Antonio Rotondò ed. (Florence: Olschki, 1986), 93-100; 240-6.

82. Bullinger to Beza, 3 December 1555 (*Correspondance* I:185-6, no. 69); Beza to Bullinger, 1 January 1556 (ibid. II:15-17, no. 71); F. Trechsel, *Die Protestantischen Antitrinitarier vor Faustus Socin*, 2 vols (Heidelberg: 1839/44), II:287.

Tiziano (commuted to banishment after the heretic renounced his errors).[83] Eighteen months later, he responded to some doctrinal queries raised by the minister of Pińczów in Little Poland, Aleksander Witrelin, with a tirade against Servetus, whose followers he designated "enemies of the Son of God, the Lord Jesus Christ, and of true religion." Bullinger described Servetus's theology as a mélange of ancient heresies contrary to both scripture and common sense, which he had disseminated through clandestine preaching and his published works; indeed, if Satan were to return to earth from hell, he would use the words of Servetus. Although it is the duty of ministers to attempt to bring those who have erred back to the right path through persuasion, in the case of incurable blasphemers like Servetus, "who mocked and insulted all instruction," the death penalty is entirely appropriate. Those who propagate Servetianism seek nothing less than the destruction of the church and true religion.[84]

These concerns are reflected in Bullinger's *100 Sermons on the Apocalypse*, first published in 1557. Significantly, the work is dedicated to precisely that group–the religious exiles–whose members had proved most susceptible to antitrinitarian heresy. In a recent article on the *Sermons*, W.P. Stephens notes both the strong Christological emphasis of the collection and the trinitarian context within which many of the references to Christ are set.[85] For example, Bullinger finds an allusion to the Trinity in the apostle's greeting to the seven churches of Asia (Revelation 1: 4-5): "he who is and who was and who is to come" is the Father, the seven spirits before God's throne denote the Holy Spirit, and Jesus Christ is of course the Son. This is balanced by God's subsequent description of himself as Alpha and Omega, which signifies his underlying unity.[86] The Trinity is again manifested in John's vision of the four living creatures gathered around the throne of God and the Lamb, which Bullinger compares with the revelation of the Father, Son and Holy Spirit at Christ's baptism:

> There is one throne, within which are contained the one seated, the Lamb and the Spirit. Because there is one throne, there is one divine essence and nature, one in power, majesty and authority. In short, there is one true and eternal God, who is blessed for ever, as Moses taught in chapter 6 of Deuteronomy and as all the prophets and apostles taught everywhere. In this single, undivided substance a most clear distinction of persons is also to be discerned. For there is one seated on the throne, and the Lamb, and the Holy Spirit who proceeds from them both.[87]

Shortly afterwards he sums up his understanding of the Trinity, in language redolent of the Athanasian Creed:

83. *CO* XV:157-8, no. 1967.
84. The relevant section of the letter is reproduced in Andreas Mühling, *Heinrich Bullingers europäische Kirchenpolitik* (ZBRG 19, Berne: Peter Lang, 2001), 232.
85. W. P. Stephens, "Bullinger's Sermons on the Apocalypse" in A. Schindler/H. Stickelberger eds, *Die Zürcher Reformation: Ausstrahlungen und Rückwirkungen. Wissenschaftliche Tagung zum hundertjährigen Bestehen des Zwinglivereins 1997* (ZBRG 18, Berne: Peter Lang, 2001), 261-80.
86. *In Apocalypsim*, 9.
87. Ibid., 65.

For the worshipful Trinity knows no confusion. The Father is God, the Son is God and the Holy Spirit is God. The Father is not the Son, the Son is not the Father and the Holy Spirit is neither the Father nor the Son, but the Holy Spirit. However, all three are one God, the Father in his hypostasis, the Son in his and the Holy Spirit in his. They do not constitute three gods, but three properties and persons in one undivided eternal essence. When Christ is described as being in the midst of the living creatures and of the elders, what is meant is that he is everywhere according to his divine nature, that he gives life and sustenance to all creatures, and that he is in the midst of his own and of his church. Just as we believe Jesus Christ to be a true man, so let us believe that he is true God, one in substance with God the Father.[88]

This endorsement of the orthodox faith is accompanied by a denunciation of the "monstrous and blasphemous Spanish sophistries of that most corrupt man Servetus," whose heresy Bullinger equates with those of Arius and Mohammed.[89]

Bullinger's fears about the consequences of allowing antitrinitarian ideas to gain a foothold within the Reformed churches were dramatically borne out by developments in Poland during the late 1550s and early 1560s. Following the accession to the throne of Sigismund II, who was sympathetic to the reformers, Protestantism had begun to register significant gains within the Polish-Lithuanian commonwealth, especially among the nobility. Bullinger himself corresponded with the aristocratic patrons of the Polish Reformed, the most powerful of whom was the palatine of Vilna, Mikołaj Radziwiłł. He was also in close contact with Francesco Lismanini, the former confessor to Queen Bona Sforza, whose links to the court made him an influential figure within the Polish Reformed church; indeed, Lismanini had first broken openly with Catholicism during a visit to Zurich in autumn 1554. Encouraged by reports from Lismanini and others, Bullinger had every reason to be confident of a bright future for Protestantism in the kingdom.

However, the Polish Reformation was blown off course by theological disputes within the Reformed camp, centring on the doctrine of the Trinity. The immediate source of the controversy was another Italian exile, Francesco Stancaro, who arrived in Poland from Hungary in May 1559. Stancaro was no antitrinitarian. In fact, there are many points of similarity between his understanding of the Trinity and that of Bullinger: both emphasise the unity of God's substance and the co-equality of the three persons, rather than their distinct roles within the divine economy. But Stancaro went a step further, arguing that the mediatorial office of Christ must necessarily be restricted to his human nature if the equality of Father and Son within the Trinity is to be preserved (on the basis that a mediator is inferior to the one with whom he intercedes).[90] Moreover, he did not hesitate to accuse those reformers who described Christ as mediator according to

88.   Ibid., 73.
89.   Ibid., 65; 73; 75.
90.   Stancaro's doctrine of the mediator is set out in his work *De Trinitate et Mediatore Domino nostro Iesu Christo* (Cracow: Scharfenberg, 1562). See also the analysis in Lorenz Hein, *Italienische Protestanten und ihr Einfluß auf die Reformation in Polen während der beiden Jahrzehnte vor dem Sandomirer Konsens (1570)* (Leiden: E.J. Brill, 1974), 89-97.

both natures (principally Calvin and Melanchthon) of subordinating the Son to the Father, like the heresiarch Arius. It was this charge, rather than the specific content of Stancaro's teachings, that provoked the Zurichers into taking issue with him publicly, in two official letters issued at the request of the Polish Reformed synod in May 1560 and March 1561.[91] In the second of these, in particular, they emphasised their acceptance of the orthodox doctrine of the consubstantiality and co-equality of the Father, Son and Holy Spirit, repudiating any suggestion of tritheism or subordinationism.

More alarming for the Zurichers than Stancaro's own views was the reaction that they elicited from some sections of the Polish Reformed pastorate. Many Poles accused Stancaro of teaching a form of Sabellianism and of converting the distinct Father, Son and Holy Spirit of scripture into modes of an undifferentiated "Deus trinitas." They also disliked his reliance on extra-biblical authorities, especially the *magister sententiarum* Peter Lombard, from whom his doctrine of the mediator was in large measure derived. The response of some Polish ministers was to emphasise the real distinction between the divine persons and, eventually, to question the whole notion of consubstantiality as traditionally understood. Whereas Calvin and the Zurichers resisted Stancaro's claim that to involve Christ's divine nature in the office of mediator is to make him inferior to the Father, the more radical of the Poles did not shy away from this conclusion–in effect, replacing the orthodox doctrine of the Trinity with subordinationist tritheism of the type pioneered by Gribaldi.

A key factor in fostering this development was the presence in Poland of Giorgio Biandrata. Following his flight from Geneva, Biandrata had sought refuge in Zurich, but he moved on when Bullinger demanded that he make his peace with Calvin and endorse the confession of Geneva's Italian church. In Poland, where he was well known as a former physician to the queen, Biandrata was received much more favourably. Hearing of this, Calvin denounced him to the Poles as a follower of Servetus, "worse than Stancaro," in the preface to the second edition of his *Commentary on the Acts of the Apostles* (August 1560).[92] However, with the help of his court connections, and supported by Radziwiłł and Lismanini, Biandrata managed to persuade the Polish Reformed synod that his views had been misrepresented. In September 1560, he was elected lay co-adjutor to the superintendent of the Polish Reformed church, Felix Cruciger. From this position, he was able to take advantage of the theological confusion to which the Stancarist controversy had given rise and garner support for his view that only a radical reformulation of the doctrine of the Trinity could restore unity to the church.

In his correspondence with the Polish Reformed, Bullinger repeatedly cautioned them against lending credence to Biandrata's protestations of orthodoxy. In May 1560, he told the evangelically minded Catholic bishop Jakob Uchański

---

91.   Epistolae duae, ad ecclesias Polonicas, Iesu Christi Euangelium amplexas, scriptae à Tigurinae ecclesiae ministris, de negotio Stancariano, & mediatore dei & hominum Iesu Christo, an hic secundum humanam naturam duntaxat, an secundum utranque mediator sit (Zurich: Christph Froschauer, 1561), *HBBibl* I, no. 421.

92.   *CO* XVIII:155-61, no. 3232.

that the Poles needed to be on their guard "not just against Stancaro, but against all those who with Arius and Servetus deny the divinity of Christ the saviour." Servetians like Biandrata were not to be listened to, but expelled as plagues on the church.[93] The following year he repeated the warning in letters to Radziwiłł and Cruciger.[94] In the second of these, Bullinger advises the Poles not to be taken in by those who simulate piety, but who are in fact "crammed with impious dogmas" and seek the destruction of true religion. Such persons are reluctant to reveal themselves as Arians, but in truth that is what they are. In a barely veiled reference to Biandrata, Bullinger notes that the Poles are at particular risk in this respect because their churches receive exiles from Italy and elsewhere. It is important that new arrivals should be examined carefully before they are admitted as church members, to ensure that they do not infect others with their errors. The Zurichers offer similar advice in their second letter to the Polish churches, where they urge the Poles to ensure that they are not duped by those who are exploiting the controversy over the mediator as an opportunity to win converts to heresy.[95]

Bullinger's anxieties were heightened by reports that he was receiving from doctrinal conservatives in Poland. In September 1561 Stanisław Sarnicki, a Reformed pastor in Cracow, confided that in a confession submitted to a recent meeting of the synod in Włodzisław Lismanini appeared to advocate "a pagan belief in three gods and Arianism, to the dishonour of the son of God."[96] The following year the simmering tensions between the orthodox and antitrinitarian wings of the Polish church came to a head. In March, Biandrata and Lismanini persuaded the synod of Książ to place a moratorium on the use of non-biblical language in relation to the Godhead, in the teeth of resistance from Sarnicki.[97] By the summer, a struggle for control of the church of Cracow was underway between Sarnicki and the rising star of the Biandratist party, Gregory Paul (Grzegorz Paweł).[98] This culminated in the publication by Paul of his *Table on the Trinity*, in which he argued that the Father, Son and Holy Spirit are not one God, but three distinct beings who share a common deity or divine nature.[99] In the course of 1563, the split became a fully-fledged schism, with rival orthodox and anti-Nicene synods meeting in Cracow and Pińczów respectively. Although that summer Biandrata left Poland for Transylvania, his place was taken by two of his former co-workers from Geneva, Valentino Gentile and Giampaolo Alciati, who continued to push the radical faction of the Polish church in the direction of "tritheism." In September the breach with orthodoxy was made official, when the

93. Theodor Wotschke ed., *Der Briefwechsel der Schweizer mit den Polen* (Leipzig: M. Heinsius, 1908), 108-9, no. 189.
94. *CO* XVIII:753-7, no. 3539; 757-60, no. 3540.
95. *Epistolae duae*, 51-2.
96. Wotschke, *Briefwechsel*, 129-33 (no. 228). Compare Maria Sipayłło, *Acta synodorum ecclesiarum Poloniae reformatorum/Akta synodów różnowierczych w Polsce*, 3 vols (Warsaw: 1966-83), II:119-23.
97. Stanislas Lubieniecki, *History of the Polish Reformation and Nine Related Documents*, George Hunston Williams trans. (Minneapolis: Fortress Press, 1995), 186-8; Williams, *Radical Reformation*, 1041-2; Hein, *Italienische Protestanten*, 160-1.
98. For details, see Lubieniecki, *History*, 188-98; Williams, *Radical Reformation*, 1042-6.
99. No copy of the *Tabula* survives, but Paul summarised its contents in a letter to the Zurichers dated 20 July 1563 (Wotschke, *Briefwechsel*, 197-202, no. 297).

Pińczowian synod adopted a confession in which the Nicene doctrine of consubstantiality was rejected as Sabellian.[100]

As the crisis within the Polish church unfolded, Bullinger and his colleagues intervened repeatedly to shore up the cause of orthodoxy. In a letter to Lismanini dated 29 April 1563, Bullinger affirmed the consistency of the Zurich church's teaching on the Trinity, defended the authority of the Athanasian Creed, and poured scorn on the attempts of some "tritheists" to find support for their views in the writings of the fourth-century Latin Father Hilary.[101] A week later, the Zurichers entrusted Christopher Thretius (Krzysztof Trecy), a former Zurich student who was visiting Switzerland to rally support for Sarnicki's campaign against the radicals, with a detailed statement of their position on the Trinity. In this work, entitled *A response of the ministers of the Zurich church to the arguments of the Italopolish Antitrinitarians*, Bullinger and his colleagues challenge directly the "tritheist" critique of Nicene orthodoxy.[102] The Zurichers claim that, like the third-century bishop Dionysius of Alexandria, some Poles in their enthusiasm to resist Stancaro's Sabellianism have facilitated the rise of the opposing heresy, Arianism. They deny that the orthodox doctrine of the Trinity is "sophistic" or amounts to a divine quaternity of one essence and three persons, as Gentile and others had suggested: God's essence is "most simple," but it is not to be abstracted from the persons of the Father, Son and Holy Spirit, all of whom possess it in its entirety. The Reformed accept that the divine persons are not to be confused, each being distinguished from the others by an "incommunicable characteristic." However, at the same time they affirm the orthodox principle that God is one in his works and will (*opera Trinitatis ad extra sunt indivisa*).[103] By stressing only the differences between the persons, the antitrinitarians leave themselves open to the charge of teaching "three essences or substances, or three spirits, or three gods." Some have suggested that the unity of substance between the Father, Son and Holy Spirit is comparable to the shared humanity of three men, but that is to make the persons of the Trinity not distinct, but separate. Attempts to interpret scriptural passages that speak of the one God without qualification as applying to the Father alone are similarly wrong-headed, as the New Testament makes clear that Christ is to be identified with the Jehovah of the Old.[104] The unity of the Godhead also requires that the western Christian doctrine of the dual procession of the Holy Spirit from both the Father and the Son be upheld.

100. *CO* XX:349-50, no. 4125. Hein gives the date as 8 October (*Italienische Protestanten*, 180-1).

101. Wotschke, *Briefwechsel*, 181-2, no. 280.

102. *Responsio ministrorum Tigurinae ecclesiae ad argumenta Antitrinitariorum Italopolonorum* (StA, E II 371, 931-5). As far as I am aware, this is one of the earliest documented uses of the term "antitrinitarian."

103. Compare *Sermonum Decades quinque*, f. 248ⁱ, where Bullinger argues that one and the same God is responsible for creation, salvation and the forgiveness of sins.

104. Compare *Isaias*, f. 271ᵛ: "Verùm sunt qui haec [Isaiah 54:5-6] referant non ad Christum Dei filium, sed ad solum patrem, quem aiunt solum esse Deum uerum, Christum uocari quidem Deum, sed non naturalem esse Deum. Atqui blasphemi sunt, qui ita sentiunt. Nam ut donemus haec dicta de patre, ab eo tamen filius in essentia non diuiditur. Est enim unus Deus pater, filius & spiritus sanctus, subsistens in tribus personis, unam nihilominus habens essentiam."

Accompanying the *Response* were letters addressed to the elders of the church of Little Poland and to Stanisław Myszkowski, the castellan of Sandomir, who was urged to remain in the "true orthodox and catholic faith." Ridiculing the radicals' claims to have recovered primitive Christian teaching, Bullinger called on Myszkowski to prevent them from inflicting more damage on the Polish churches by their teaching, which is "against the truth handed down in scripture and the creeds."[105] At Thretius's request, he also wrote to the Protestant voivod of Moldavia, Jacob Heraclides Despota, to warn him of the danger of allowing antitrinitarians to influence his religious policy.[106] In another letter, dated 15 June 1563, Bullinger advised the Polish general Stanisław Cikowski to respect the consensus of the early church regarding the Trinity and to avoid "curious disputation" about the divine mysteries.[107]

Despite the appeals of Bullinger and his Zurich colleagues, the heretical wing of the Polish Reformed church continued to gain adherents (including Cikowski, who threw in his lot with Gregory Paul).[108] In Lithuania, antitrinitarianism flourished with the support of Mikołaj Radziwiłł, who was nevertheless keen to seek dialogue with Bullinger. In October 1564, Radziwiłł sent the Zurichers works by Paul and another leading "tritheist," Jan Kazanowski, in order that they might be better informed about the issues at stake in the Polish trinitarian controversy. Radziwiłł argued that the radicals' position had been consistently misrepresented by their orthodox opponents, whom he blamed for the Polish diet's recent decision to banish "many most learned men, your brethren, exiled from other provinces for the sake of the gospel of Jesus Christ."[109] However, he maintained that there was still scope for resolving the two sides' disagreements through amicable discussion. According to Radziwiłł, the dispute centred on different understandings of God's unity: whereas the radicals saw it as deriving from the Father, as the fount of divinity, for Sarnicki and his followers it was underpinned by the doctrine of consubstantiality. Radziwiłł claims that the former view is more consistent with the teaching of the Fathers, especially Hilary; indeed, if only all parties could be brought to endorse Hilary's position on this matter, the Polish schism might swiftly be brought to an end. All that the radicals have done is to strip away scholastic excrescences from the doctrine of the Trinity and to return to the original Nicene understanding of the generation of the Son from the Father, which has been obscured by subsequent attempts to reduce the Father, Son and Holy Spirit to "mere relations, attributes and properties" within the Godhead.[110]

Bullinger and his colleagues responded to Radziwiłł's letter in March the following year. In their reply, they express sadness at the continuing divisions within the Polish church, which they attribute to the Poles' failure to heed their previous advice. In an implicit endorsement of the steps taken by the Polish authorities to remove foreign-born Protestants from the kingdom, they emphasise

105. Wotschke, *Briefwechsel*, 183-4, no. 282; 184-5, no. 284.
106   Erich Bryner, "Ein Brief Heinrich Bullingers an den Fürsten der Moldau aus dem Jahre 1563" in Oberman, *Das Reformierte Erbe*, I:63-9.
107.   Wotschke, *Briefwechsel*, 191-2, no. 293.
108.   Williams, *Radical Reformation*, 1045; 1081.
109.   The reference is to the edict of Parczów (7 August 1564).
110.   Wotschke, *Briefwechsel*, 226-31, no. 329.

the role of the Italian exiles in introducing heresy to Poland-Lithuania, accusing Biandrata and his compatriots of abusing the hospitality of the Polish Reformed and of reviving "old errors under new names." The Zurich ministers dispute Radziwiłł's "tritheist" reading of Hilary, which they see as a product of faulty exegesis. The radicals misunderstand Hilary because, rather than examining his works as a whole and within the wider context of patristic writing on the Trinity, they confine their attention to a few ambiguous passages. The result is that they fail to interpret "more obscure places ... by those that are clearer." There follows an orthodox confession of faith in God as one in "essence, divinity, nature, majesty, power and glory" and three in persons, "which the Greeks call hypostases." This doctrine in no way implies tritheism: the Father, Son and Holy Spirit are equally divine and co-eternal, but they are not "three gods or three lords distinct and subordinate in number, rank and office." The tritheists protest that the charges directed against them by the orthodox–that they teach a plurality of gods and at the same time deny the true divinity of the Son and Holy Spirit–are contradictory, but for the Zurichers this apparent contradiction is merely symptomatic of the incoherence of the tritheists' own ideas. As it is impossible that there should be more than one God, by excluding the Son and Holy Spirit from the nature of the Father the radicals preserve their divinity in name only. On the other hand, if all three persons are to be worshipped, as the tritheists maintain, even though they are distinct by nature, the consequence is polytheism. Once again, Bullinger highlights the fundamental tension in antitrinitarian thought: between the desire to exalt the Father as the unique fount of divinity, and the wish to preserve in some form the deity of the Son and Holy Spirit.[111]

During the second half of the 1560s, Bullinger remained in touch with events in Poland-Lithuania through his extensive network of correspondents. A final attempt in March 1565 to reconcile the conservative and radical wings of the Polish Reformed church merely highlighted the extent of their differences; the schism between the two groups was now permanent. Over the next few years, the antitrinitarian faction, now known as the *ecclesia minor* or Polish Brethren, drifted further from Reformed orthodoxy. Some groups espoused Anabaptist ideas. Others, including Biandrata and Paul, rejected tritheism for the proto-unitarian theology of Lelio Sozzini, who in an unpublished commentary on the Johannine prologue had denied the pre-existence of Christ. In a letter dated 16 April 1568, Paweł Gilowski, the senior Reformed pastor in Zator, informed Bullinger that the heretics were now split into three camps: followers of Lelio Sozzini, known as Samosatenes; more moderate "tritheists," many of whom were now returning to orthodoxy; and followers of Gentile, based mainly in Lithuania, who taught that the Son was "essentiated" from the Father but denied the personality of the Holy Spirit.[112] By this time Samosatene doctrines were also taking root in Transylvania, where Biandrata had succeeded in converting both the Calvinist superintendent Ferenc Dávid and King John Sigismund to antitrinitarianism. The news of

111. Ibid., 232-8, no. 332.
112. Ibid., 290-3, no. 378.

these alarming developments was passed on to Bullinger by his Hungarian correspondents Mátyás Thuri and Péter Melius, as well as by Beza and the Poles.[113] The task of combating this new variant of antitrinitarianism was undertaken not by Bullinger but by his son-in-law Josias Simler, whose monumental work *On the eternal Son of God* appeared in August 1568.[114] However, the issue of antitrinitarian heresy continued to preoccupy Bullinger during the final decade of his life. When Valentino Gentile was arrested by the Bernese authorities in June 1566, Beza asked Bullinger to add his voice to calls for Gentile's execution–a request with which the *Antistes* was happy to comply.[115] Later, Bullinger advocated the use of the death penalty against Johannes Sylvan and Adam Neuser, antitrinitarian ministers in the Palatinate who had attempted to make contact with both Biandrata and the Ottoman sultan.[116] In his *Sermons on Isaiah*, published in 1567, Bullinger alludes several times to the antitrinitarian menace and reiterates his support for the execution of Servetus, whose followers are described as worse than Muslims or Jews.[117] In a letter of August that year, he sought to persuade the Lithuanian magnate Jan Kiszka, who had begun to move into the antitrinitarian camp, of the merits of Nicene orthodoxy.[118]

More importantly, Bullinger's prolonged engagement with antitrinitarianism during the 1550s and 1560s forced him to reflect as never before on the implications of the scripture principle for Reformed doctrine. As his opponents continually pointed out, most of the technical terms used in relation to the Trinity–"essence," "substance," "person" and so on–had their origins in the discourse of Classical philosophy, rather than the Bible. From that, they were able to argue that their critique of Nicene orthodoxy was but the latest stage in the progressive restoration of apostolic Christianity, comparable with Luther's doctrine of justification or Zwingli's rejection of the real presence. The challenge for Bullinger was to safeguard his conservative vision of the Reformation enterprise by demonstrating the compatibil-

---

113. Thury to Bullinger, 28 March 1568 (*Miscellanea Tigurina*, 3 vols (Zurich: 1722-24), II.2:207-9); Melius to Bullinger, 27 April 1569 (Wotschke, *Briefwechsel*, 307-9, no. 402). For further details, see Williams, *Radical Reformation*, 1108-19; M. Balázs, *Early Transylvanian Antitrinitarianism (1566-1571): From Servet to Palaeologus* (Baden-Baden: 1996); E. Zsindely, "Bullinger und Ungarn" in Ulrich Gäbler/Erhard Herkenrath eds, *Heinrich Bullinger 1504-1575: Gesammelte Aufsätze zum 400. Todestag*, vol. 2: *Beziehungen und Wirkungen* (ZBRG 8, Zurich: TVZ, 1975), 361-82 (375-7).

114. On Simler's role as a polemicist against heresy, see Mark Taplin, *The Italian Reformers and the Zurich Church, c. 1540-1620* (Aldershot: Ashgate, 2003), 192-212.

115. Beza to Bullinger, 19 June 1566 (*Correspondance* VII:141-6, no. 476); Bullinger to Beza, 10 July 1566 (ibid., 172-6, no. 481).

116. Bullinger to Beza, 22 December 1570 (ibid. XI:298-9 [no. 812]). For more on this affair, see Christopher J. Burchill, *The Heidelberg Antitrinitarians* (Baden-Baden: 1989).

117. Ibid., f. 52^r; 166^r; 272^r. Explicit condemnations of Servetus also feature in Bullinger's refutation of Anabaptism, *Der Widertöufferen vrsprung* (Zurich: Christoph Froschauer, 1561), *HBBibl* I, no. 395, f. 55^v-7^r; in the *Second Helvetic Confession* (Niesel, *Bekenntisschriften*, 236; Cochrane, *Reformed Confessions*, 243); and in his preface to *On the eternal Son of God* (*De aeterno Dei filio domino et seruatore nostro Iesu Christo, & de Spiritu sancto, Aduersus ueteres & nouos Antitrinitarios, id est Arianos, Tritheitas, Samosatenianos, & Pneumatomachos, libri quatuor Iosia Simlero Tigurino authore* (Zurich: 1568), f. γ2^v- γ3^r.

118. The letter is published in Mühling, *Kirchenpolitik*, 331-3.

ity of the scripture principle with traditional trinitarian language and with the doctrine of God as expounded by the creeds, councils and Fathers of the early church.

III. The Trinity and *sola Scriptura*

In his *Assertion* of 1534, Bullinger explains the appearance of non-scriptural vocabulary in the creeds as a historical development, born out of the need to combat heresy within the early church. Initially, all that was required of believers was a simple confession of faith in the Father, Son and Holy Spirit. However, owing to the "curiosity of certain profane men," the church is now required "to express the same thing in more explicit words." For Bullinger, the distinction between the substance of what is said (*res*) and the words that are used to say it is crucial: the Reformed are not bound by the letter of scripture, but may use other vocabulary that articulates the essential truths contained in revelation.[119] In his *Institutes*, Calvin makes much the same point:

> If they call a foreign word one that cannot be shown to stand written syllable by syllable in Scripture, they are indeed imposing upon us an unjust law which condemns all interpretation not patched together out of the fabric of Scripture. [...] But what prevents us from explaining in clearer words those matters in Scripture which perplex and hinder our understanding, yet which conscientiously and faithfully serve the truth of Scripture itself, and are made use of sparingly and modestly and on due occasion?[120]

Another central theme of the *Assertion* is the compatibility between catholic Christianity, as defined by imperial law, and the teaching of scripture. Following Bede, Bullinger maintains that the decisions of the first six ecumenical councils concerning the nature of God and the person of Christ are to be received as authoritative.[121] Both here and in other works dealing with the Trinity, Bullinger backs up his arguments with lengthy citations from the Fathers, especially Augustine and Tertullian. At the same time, he is aware of the danger of compromising the central Protestant tenet of *sola scriptura*. In response to the charge that the papists, too, defend their errors with reference to early church tradition, Bullinger insists that the Reformed grant no independent authority to the councils and Fathers, whose statements are to be credited only to the extent that they reflect the teaching of scripture.[122]

These arguments are elaborated in his *Orthodox Response to Johannes Cochlaeus's book on the canonical scriptures and the authority of the Catholic Church*, published in 1544.[123] Here Bullinger replies directly to the charge–this

---

119. *Assertio*, f. 16ʳ: "[...] curiositas prophanorum quorundam hominum effecit, ut eandem rem nunc cogamur explicatioribus effari uerbis. Iam ut res non ex uerbis quibus effertur, sed ex ipso iure & re ipsa quae est, aestimatur: sic nimirum quilibet pius hoc negotium non ex uerbis, sed ipsa re ac ueritate aestimabit, qualibuscunque tandem efferatur uerbis."

120. *Institutes*, I:13, 124.

121. *Assertio*, f. 11ᵛ-12ʳ.

122. Ibid., f. 13ʳ: "Neque patribus neque conuentibus sanctorum nitimur, nisi quatenus constat illos consona scripturis & dixisse & statuisse."

123. The work was appended to the second edition of Bullinger's *De scripturae sanctae au-*

time from a Catholic controversialist–that the doctrine of *sola scriptura* undermines traditional Christian teaching on the nature of God: chapter 8 of the work is given over to proving "that the article of faith concerning the mystery of the worshipful Trinity is clearly contained in the canonical scriptures," while chapter 9 seeks to demonstrate that scripture teaches the consubstantiality of Christ with the Father. Again, Bullinger makes clear that the scripture principle is not to be confused with some naïve biblical literalism:

> For I understand the statement that everything is comprised in scripture to mean that from it, as from an inexhaustible treasury, all things necessary to religion may be derived. By comprised I mean collected, included and contained, such that all things may be shown in it or the necessary consequences may be deduced from it by clear and plain exposition or interpretation.

Of key importance is not the word, but the message of scripture:

> For who does not know that good men do not clash about words when there is proper agreement about issues of substance? And what, I ask, prohibits us from expressing things in clearer words, so long as those are faithful to the truth of scripture and reflect its meaning, especially when we are dealing with intricate and obscure matters? The pastors of the church have been forced, in response to quarrels about vicious teachings, with careful precision to devise terms for certain things that explain what is meant by them and leave quarrelsome persons with nowhere to hide. But those who reject such terms, and those who continually abuse them–thereby detracting from the absolute perfection of the scriptures–would seem to be equally foolish.[124]

At the same time, Bullinger is anxious to point out that many of the technical terms used to formulate trinitarian doctrine have close analogies in scripture. In Philippians 2:6, for example, Paul speaks of Christ as being "in the form of God," which is no different from saying that he is of one substance with God.[125] Similarly, in Colossians 1:15, Christ is termed "the image of the invisible God," which may be compared with the Nicene Creed's description of the Son as "light from light" and "true God from true God."[126] In Hebrews 1:3, the term "hypostasis" or substance is used to denote the nature of the deity.[127]

In the *Decades*, Bullinger attempts to define more closely the relationship between scripture and early church tradition. Prefaced to the work is a historical

---

thoritate, against which Cochlaeus had written the previous year. On the background to their dispute, see Ekkehard Mühlenberg, "Scriptura non est autentica sine authoritate ecclesiae (Johannes Eck): Vorstellungen von der Entstehung des Kanons in der Kontroverse um das reformatorische Schriftprinzip," *Zeitschrift für Theologie und Kirche* 97 (2000): 183-209.

124. *Ad Ioannis Cochlei de canonicae scripturae & Catholicae ecclesiae authoritate libellum, pro solida Scripturae canonicae authoritate, tum & absoluta eius perfectione, ueraque Catholicae ecclesiae dignitate, Heinrychi Bullingeri orthodoxa Responsio* (Zurich: Christoph Froschauer, 1544), f. 14$^{\text{r-v}}$.

125 *In omnes apostolicas epistolas*, 458; *Sermonum Decades quinque*, f. 230^{r}.

126 *In omnes apostolicas epistolas*, 476.

127. Ibid., 290; *Sermonum Decades quinque*, f. 21^{r}; StA, E II 371, 931^{v}. Compare Calvin, *Institutes* I:13, 122.

discourse entitled "Of the four general synods or councils," in which he describes how, following the Arian controversy, the churches were compelled "of very necessity" to produce a new, more tightly drawn statement of faith in addition to the Apostles' Creed that they had used hitherto.[128] The Nicene Fathers insisted on the use of the word "homoousios" to describe the relationship between the Father and the Son in order to expose the deceit of Arius, who pretended to affirm Christ's divinity but was not prepared to acknowledge him as consubstantial with God.[129] Once again, Bullinger insists on the consistency of the Nicene and later Creeds with scripture: the writings of the prophets and apostles were "the source, guide, rule and judge at all these councils, where the Fathers did not allow anything to happen according to their own will."[130] Although the terms Trinity, person, essence and substance do not appear in scripture, "the things to which those words refer are clearly contained and taught there."[131]

With the rise of organised antitrinitarianism during the late 1550s, Bullinger's position on the use of non-scriptural terminology hardens perceptibly. In the *Decades*, he appears at times to suggest that such language is permissible and helpful, rather than something to which the assent of all believers is required. Like Calvin, Bullinger is aware that the Greek and Latin Fathers differed in their use of the technical vocabulary, the Greeks preferring to describe God as one essence ($ουσ α$) in three hypostases, while the Latins opted for the formulation "one substance in three persons or subsistances." Such divergences may be tolerated, provided that there is agreement on the church's underlying teaching:

> We are not particularly worried about whether you call them [the Father, Son and Holy Spirit] substances, subsistences or persons, as long as you clearly express the distinction between them and their peculiar properties; confessing the unity without confusing the Trinity or robbing the persons of their properties.[132]

However, in later works Bullinger admits that experience has shown scripture and the Apostles' Creed to be insufficient as guarantors of doctrinal unity. At a time when the church is assailed by heretics, Christians may be required to demonstrate their orthodoxy by endorsing more explicit statements of faith, such as the Nicene and Athanasian Creeds.

Particularly instructive in this regard is Bullinger's response to a dispute that flared up in the Italian-speaking churches of Graubünden during the early 1560s. At the behest of its minister, Agostino Mainardi, the Reformed church of Chiavenna had decided that in future new members should be required to subscribe to an elaborate confession of faith that Mainardi had drawn up to combat the errors of the sacramentarian heretic Camillo Renato. A group of Mainardi's colleagues,

---

128. *Sermonum Decades quinque*, f. α5ᵛ-β3ᵛ.
129. Ibid., f. 229ᵛ.
130. Ibid., f. α5ᵛ.
131. Ibid., f. 211ᵛ.
132. Ibid., Calvin, similarly, expresses the wish that all technical terms might be buried, "if only among all men this faith were agreed on: that Father and Son and Spirit are one God, yet the Son is not the Father, nor the Spirit the Son, but that they are differentiated by a peculiar quality" (*Institutes*, I:13, 126).

led by the minister of Soglio, Michelangelo Florio, protested against this violation of "Christian freedom" by submitting to Bullinger a list of twenty-five questions, in which they expressed doubts about whether doctrinal error in respect of
the Trinity constituted sufficient grounds for excommunication and whether it
was reasonable to compel "uneducated and simple folk" to accept the complex
creeds of Nicaea, Athanasius and Pope Damasus.[133]

However, by now Bullinger had come to mistrust such appeals to biblical
simplicity; all too often, he believed, they masked a desire to legitimise the presence of antitrinitarians within the church. His suspicions are reflected in the Zurich church's official statement on the Chiavenna dispute, addressed to the
Rhaetian synod and dated 24 May 1561.[134] Here Bullinger defends the use by
ministers of extra-biblical terminology, comparing the creeds to a military symbol or watchword "by which we may tell who is on our side." In the early church,
no adult could receive baptism until they had been properly instructed in the faith
and had recited the creed; the Zurichers, too, require new arrivals to assent to certain articles of doctrine before taking them in.[135] At the time of the Arian controversy, "sectarians" argued that it was unreasonable to require the faithful to
endorse terms such as Trinity, person and consubstantial. However, the leaders of
the church rightly insisted on their use, "so that the orthodox truth might be expressed more clearly and heretical corruption excluded." On the authority of Athanasius, Bullinger argues that the church has the right to react to changing situations–
and the emergence of new forms of heresy–by formulating doctrinal statements
suited to dealing with them. The Reformed should take inspiration from the example of the early church, which responded to the misuse of the Apostles' Creed by
heretics by formulating more elaborate confessions of faith.[136] Bullinger concludes
that the historic creeds do not add to, but merely make explicit, what is taught in

---

133. For the original text of the questions, see StA, A 248.1. A copy is published in Trechsel, *Antitrinitarier*, II:417-19. See the discussions in Delio Cantimori, *Eretici italiani del in Cinquecento e altri scritti* Adriano Prospari ed. (Turin, Giulio Einaudi Editore, 1992), 282-3, and
Antonio Rotondò, "Esuli italiani in Valtellina nel Cinquecento," *Rivista storica italiana* 88 (1976),
756-91 (784-5).

134. *Tigurinorum Consilium ad Synodum Curiae*, published in Trechsel, *Antitrinitarier*,
II:419-28.

135. Bullinger is probably referring to the set of 15 articles (plus four articles on the sacraments), entitled *Capita confessionis Ecclesiae Tigurinae de praecipuis Christianae Religionis
capitibus, contra quam nemo quidquam in hac Ecclesia et Schola spargere debet* (StA, E II 381,
1369; copy in ZB, Ms. S 130, 14). In a letter to Thretius of November 1562, Stanisław Sarnicki
reports that at a synod in Cracow the previous month these articles had been adopted by the orthodox faction of the Polish Reformed, on Bullinger's advice (*CO* XIX:572-80, no. 3875). Articles 1 to 7 set out the doctrines of the Trinity, the dual procession of the Holy Spirit and the
eternal generation of the Son.

136. Compare the following statement in the Zurichers' letter to Radziwiłł of March 1565:
"Postremo sunt apud vos antitrinitarii, qui Serveti discipuli esse nolunt, habent autem propria et
peculiaria dogmata de deo. Interea tamen omnes hi, quos modo nominavimus, symbolum apostolorum agnoscunt et profitentur. Quare ut in veteri ecclesia, cum ariani, macedoniani, nestoriani
et reliquae pestes symbolum apostolorum verbo profiterentur, re ipsa autem suis dogmatibus illud
violarent, pii doctores necessitate adacti alias etiam confessiones fidei suae ediderunt, ita nos
quoque hoc tempore faciendum existimavimus" (Wotschke, *Briefwechsel*, 234).

scripture concerning the Trinity. Refusal to accept them is therefore tantamount to a rejection of scripture itself.[137]

Bullinger reiterates these points in two other texts from the 1560s: an unpublished work entitled *The Trinity of God, and the coequality in substance of the Father and the Son*, and his preface to Simler's *On the eternal Son of God*.[138] The principal target of the *Trinity*, which is prefaced by brief biographies of Servetus, Gentile and Biandrata, is the heretical doctrines of the Italian and Polish tritheists.[139] However, the work also provides evidence of the extent to which Bullinger's belief in the importance of creeds and confessions had been strengthened by his encounters with antitrinitarianism. In a section entitled "Confessions of faith" Bullinger argues that the church can no longer rely on the Apostles' Creed to safeguard orthodoxy against the activities of "cunning men," who twist its meaning in support of their own heretical notions. He continues:

> On account of such pests, the ministers of the churches have been forced to draw up brief formulas of faith, by which they may profess the received and apostolic teaching, and exclude and refute strange teaching. For that reason, certain terms have been included that reveal the true opinion of confessors, depending on whether they accept or reject them, and a great many creeds–the Nicene Creed, the Constantinopolitan Creed, the Creed of Chalcedon and others–have been added.[140]

Although some of the terms that appear in the creeds are not scriptural, their use is legitimate because scripture contains "what is expressed in those words."[141]

In his preface to Simler's *On the eternal Son of God*, Bullinger responds to the suggestion of an anonymous Catholic writer (known from other sources to have been the Polish Cardinal Stanislas Hosius) that antitrinitarianism is the inevitable consequence of the Reformed insistence on the primacy of the Bible. Once again, he grounds his argument in the fundamental distinction between the *verbum* and *res* of scripture. In scripture, he notes, we are taught that Christ was a true man, but free from sin; from that we may deduce that he possessed human flesh and a human soul, even though neither of those terms appears there. Similarly, if scripture identifies the Father, Son and Holy Spirit as the one true God, while at the same time teaching their distinct subsistence, what is the harm in using the words "Trinity" and "person" to express this reality? The acceptance by the Reformed of extra-biblical vocabulary is not a violation of the scripture principle, as in devising such terms the

---

137. Trechsel, *Antitrinitarier*, II:424: "Qui amplectitur ea, quae tradita sunt in scripturis sanctis de Trinitate deque incarnationis Filii mysterio et de Spiritu S.–non potest non eadem ratione eadem extra scripturas in Symbolis illis comprehensa atque tradita. Ergo qui Symbola haec respuunt, non videmus, quomodo sincere credant et sensu incorrupto retineant aut custodiant, quae in scripturis sanctis de illis ipsis capitibus sunt exposita aut comprehensa."

138. *Trinitas Dei, et patris filiique in substantia coaequalitas* (ZB, Ms. Car XV 20, 109-74); *De aeterno*, f. α2ᵛ-δ3ᵛ.

139. For example, that Christ is not the Jehovah of the Old Testament; that the Son is "essentiated" from the Father; and that the orthodox Trinity of three persons and one essence amounts to a quaternity.

140. ZB, Ms. Car XV 20, 117.

141. Ibid., 125.

Fathers and councils of the early church drew not on human tradition, but on the word of God itself.[142]

Conclusion

Because of the thoroughness with which Zwingli undertook the reform of worship, the sacraments, church government and Christian education during the 1520s, it is easy to overlook the essential conservatism of the Zurich Reformation. That conservatism is nowhere better demonstrated than in Bullinger's statements on the Trinity. The Reformation is sometimes presented as an attempt to replace the authority of tradition with the authority of scripture, but Bullinger would have seen this as a false dichotomy. Under the domination of the papacy, important aspects of the church's teaching had indeed been corrupted, but the core elements of authentic ecclesiastical tradition–above all, the doctrines of God and Christ–had survived intact. As Richard Muller points out:

> It is [...] entirely anachronistic to view the *sola Scriptura* of Luther and his contemporaries as a declaration that all theology ought to be constructed anew, without reference to the church's tradition of interpretation, by the lonely exegete confronting the naked text.[143]

Like his Protestant contemporaries and successors, Bullinger insists that everything necessary for salvation is contained in scripture. In scripture, "the universal Church of Christ has the most complete exposition of all that pertains to a saving faith, and also to the framing of a life acceptable to God; and in this respect it is expressly commanded by God that nothing be either added to or taken from the same."[144]

For Bullinger, the New Testament, rather than some ill-defined, orally transmitted body of doctrine, is the repository of apostolic tradition. The teachings of the Fathers and the first four (sometimes, six) ecumenical councils are to be respected, but only in so far as they are consistent with that of scripture. In his work *On councils* (1561), Bullinger distinguishes sharply between the authority of scripture and the authority of councils: whereas the scriptures are to be accepted absolutely, "on their own account," the decisions of councils must first be authenticated from revelation.[145]

---

142. *De aeterno*, f. α7ᵛ-8ᵛ. Compare *Ad Ioannis Cochlei [...] libellum*, f. 14ᵗ.

143. Richard A. Muller, *Post-Reformation Reformed Dogmatics*. vol 2: *Holy Scripture: The Cognitive Foundation of Theology* (Grand Rapids, Baker Books, 1993), 51.

144. Niesel, *Bekenntnisschriften*, 223; Cochrane, *Reformed Confessions*, 224.

145. *De conciliis. Quomodo apostoli Christi Domini in primitiua ecclesia suum illud Hierosolymis Concilium celebrauerint, & quanto cum fructu, quantaque pace: quomodo item Romani Pontifices in extrema mundi senecta, à quingentis & amplius annis, sua illa Concilia celebrauerint [...]* (Zurich: Christoph Froschauer, 1561), *HBBibl* I, no. 402, f. 103ᵗ⁻ᵛ: "Quamuis autem definitionibus de fide propositis nobis, per ista 4. Concilia oecumenica nihil prorus uelim derogatum, utpote qui illas citra omnem contradictionem recipiam, & venerer religiosissime, potiorem tamen authoritatem sanctis scripturis tribuo, quam ullis Concilijs. Illis enim sine alio testimonio, propter semetipsas, credo. Conciliorum uerò definitionibus non credo, nisi ea quae uel credenda uel facienda aut omittenda proponunt, per scripturas sanctas approbare possint."

However, Bullinger's understanding of *sola scriptura* is more nuanced than it appears at first sight. Because scripture is open to misinterpretation, the exegete is to be guided by what Bullinger–following Irenaeus and Tertullian–terms the "rule of faith." A clear statement of this principle is to be found in the third sermon of the *Decades*, where Bullinger declares:

> We say that the catholic religion involves not adding to or receiving in our expositions anything that others have alleged against the received articles of faith, as set out in the Apostles' and other most ancient creeds.

Christ's statement in John 14:28, "The Father is greater than I," is used to illustrate what that means in practice. Because it is "against the articles of faith to set up or allow any inequality in the divinity of the Father and the Son," the verse cannot be taken at face value, but must instead be referred to Christ's human nature.[146] In another work written around the same time, the *Thorough demonstration that the Evangelical Churches are neither heretical nor schismatic* (1552), Bullinger again emphasises the importance of the rule of faith as a criterion for determining the validity of particular interpretations of scripture. Here the rule is defined as "a universal, certain and agreed interpretation of scripture [...] which [the church] has faithfully passed on to all believers, so that they may understand it." When scripture speaks of God with reference to the Father, Son and Holy Spirit, for example, "the catholic faith and the church understand it to mean that God is one in essence and three in persons." If error is to be avoided, those who preach God's Word must be well versed not only in scripture, but in this "catholic understanding of the faith and the church," of which the Reformed are the modern custodians.[147] For Bullinger, the rule of faith is encapsulated in the 12 articles of the Apostles' Creed, more explicit formulations of which appear in the subsequent Nicene, Constantinopolitan and Athanasian Creeds.[148]

In this way, Bullinger manages to plot a middle course between the religious radicals, with their insistence on the plain letter of the Bible, and the Council of Trent, which established the parity of scripture and tradition as sources for authoritative church teaching. The decrees of the councils and writings of the Fathers are not to be appropriated wholesale, but "in so far as they are in agreement with the writings of the apostles, and in all things derived from them." However, where the Fathers offer scriptural backing for their opinions, they are to be honoured as witnesses to the historic teaching of the church on a particular issue.[149] For Bullinger, the selective use of the Fathers is entirely consistent with the scripture principle, as it is inconceivable that in respect of the core elements of doc-

---

146. *Sermonum Decades quinque*, f. 10ʳ. Compare *In Apocalypsim*, 56, where Bullinger rejects the Arian reading of Revelation 3:14 on the basis that one should not subvert the whole of scripture or dispute the articles of the creed and the living tradition of the apostles for the sake of one "little word." For that reason, the phrase "the beginning of God's creation" must be seen as relating to Christ's humanity.

147. *Das die Euangelischen Kilchen weder kätzerische noch abtrünnige sunder gantz rechtglöubige vnd allgemeine Jesu Christi kilchen syend grundtliche erwysung geschriben durch Heinrych Bullinger* (Zurich: Christoph Froschauer, 1552), *HBBibl* I, no. 259, f. 9ʳ-10ᵛ.

148. Ibid., f. 16ⁱ-17ᵛ.

149. *De conciliis*, f. 70ᵛ; *De aeterno*, f. α6ⁱ-α7ʳ.

trine—the Trinity and the two natures of Christ—there should be any conflict between the position of the early church and biblical teaching. For his antitrinitarian opponents, who saw the corruption of the church as beginning not with the rise of the papacy, but with the disappearance of the first generation of Christ's followers, Bullinger's approach entailed an unacceptable blurring of the distinction between scripture and tradition.

In his dogmatic works, Bullinger placed the received doctrine of the Trinity at the heart of Reformed teaching, while in his polemics against the antitrinitarians, he defended it against the assaults of radical biblicism.The motivations for Bullinger's continued faith in the Trinity were above all theological: in his view, it supplied the basic rationale for the doctrine of salvation through Christ. However, his insistence on the "catholicity" of the Zurich church also had a political and legal dimension. Ever since the establishment of the first Anabaptist conventicle in January 1525, Lutheran and Catholic apologists had accused the Reformed churches of acting as seedbeds for heresy. The Reformed background of most early antitrinitarians appeared to offer support for this charge, which was accompanied by demands that the Reformed be treated as heretics under Roman law. Throughout his career, Bullinger worked tirelessly to break the association between Zwinglianism and heresy, which he identified as perhaps the greatest obstacle to the spread of Swiss-style reform. The *Antistes* realised that the Reformed confession would make headway only if magistrates could be convinced of its legitimacy, antiquity and overall respectability. For that reason, the Zurich Reformation must be depicted as an exercise in continuity, rather than change. By emphasising the trinitarian and Christological orthodoxy of the Swiss churches, Bullinger sought to demonstrate the compatibility of their teachings with catholic Christianity as defined by imperial law: specifically, the anti-heresy edict of the Emperors Gratian, Valentinian II and Theodosius I (380), which is included in the prefatory material to both the *Decades* and the Second Helvetic confession.[150] In the process, he helped produce a unique Reformed synthesis of scripture and tradition, in which the scripture principle was upheld but heterodox interpretations were excluded by the operation of the so-called "rule of faith," central to which was the Nicene doctrine of the Trinity.

---

150. *Ad Ioannis Cochlei [...] libellum*, f. 52^r; *Grundtliche erwysung*, f. 18^r-19^r; *Sermonum Decades quinque*, f. β3^{r-v}; Niesel, *Bekenntnisschriften*, 221-2.

3

Bullinger's *Decades:* Instruction in Faith and Conduct

Peter Opitz

If a list of the most significant works of the Reformation was drawn up today, it is highly unlikely that Heinrich Bullinger's *Decades* would rank highly. Indeed, those who work on the sixteenth century, and on the Reformation in particular, have largely overlooked the *Decades*. Bullinger's most well known work has received scant scholarly attention.[1] By contrast, from the second half of the sixteenth century until well into the seventeenth century the *Decades* were one of the best-known theological works, performing a crucial role in the spread of the Reformed faith throughout Europe and beyond.[2] Although originally written in Latin, the *Decades* were soon translated into German, French, Dutch and English and became a familiar resource for countless Reformed preachers in the preparation of their sermons.[3] The book was also considered an essential possession for Reformed households; in the German and Dutch translations the *Decades* were termed a "house book" (*Hausbuch*) to be read in homes by families for instruction in piety and Christian conduct. The *Decades* were also to be found on Dutch trading vessels, which at times were required by law to have a "house book" on

---

1. As is well-known, there are numerous studies of Calvin and "Calvinism"; Zwingli's role is also by and large well established. By contrast, however there is a marked lack of literature on Bullinger's thought and influence other than studies which relate to England. The following list includes the small number of works which have addressed Bullinger's theology to date. For an introduction to this topic see Emidio Campi, "Bullinger, Heinrich" in Hans Dieter Betz et al. eds *Religion in Geschichte und Gegenwart: Handwörterbuch für Theologie und Religionswissenschaft* (4th ed., Tübingen: Mohr Siebeck, 1998-), I:1858f.; Fritz Büsser, "Bullinger, Heinrich" in *TRE* 7:375-87; W. H. Neuser, "Dogma und Bekenntnis in der Reformation: Von Zwingli und Calvin bis zur Synode von Westminster" in Carl Andresen ed., in association with Gustav Adolf Benrath, *Handbuch der Dogmen- und Theologiegeschichte*, (Göttingen: Vandenhoeck & Ruprecht, 1998), II:225-38. Without doubt Bullinger's work has received greatest attention in discussion of the *Second Helvetic Confession*, see Joachim Staedtke ed., *Glauben und Bekennen. 400 Jahre Confessio Helvetica Posterior. Beiträge zu ihrer Geschichte und Theologie* (Zurich: Zwingli Verlag, 1966); E. Koch, *Die Theologie der Confessio Helvetica Posterior* (Neukirchen: Neukirchener Verlag des Erziehungsvereins, 1968).
2. Walter Hollweg, *Heinrich Bullingers Hausbuch. Eine Untersuchung über die Anfänge der reformierten Predigtliteratur* (Neukirchen: Verlag der Buchhandlung des Erziehungsvereins, 1956).
3. cf. *HBBibl* I.

board; as a result Bullinger's sermons were carried not only to America but also to the Dutch overseas trading colonies in the Pacific.[4]

What follows in this chapter is not so much a detailed study of the *Decades* as a examination of the character of a book once held in highest regard by Reformed Protestantism, but now largely forgotten. I shall look at the *Decades* through four broad themes: first, the context within which the *Decades* were written and read; secondly, the intention behind the work and its structure; thirdly, the identification of several important and characteristic elements within the *Decades*, and, finally, this chapter will raise the question of the theological key to the *Decades*.

I. The *Decades* in the Context of Bullinger's Theological Works

The 800 folios of the *Decades* make it Bullinger's most extensive work in which he addresses all the important themes of Christian faith and life. Yet, to call it his "principal theological work" is too limiting, for it was neither Bullinger's intention to write systematic theology nor to go down in history as an original theological author. His works were written to serve the Reformation church in Zurich and across Europe. As a result, he composed a large number of works that repeatedly addressed the same theological points from different perspectives and for various audiences. This intention is evident in the *Decades*, which does not have a "systematic" character. For Bullinger, it was not the creation of a meticulously crafted and monumental work that was important; rather, it was his purpose to set out, justify, and defend the central content of the Reformed faith, which in his mind could not be separated from its practical realisation in the Christian life.

Bullinger performed his intended task in the *Decades* in a multifaceted manner, realising his many and varied roles as preacher, pastor, exegisist, teacher, advocate, polemicist, guardian of Zwingli's legacy, and evangelical irenicist. The *Decades* are the work of the "mature" Bullinger, and it is possible to identify three principal phases within his theology. The first phase when he discovered the evangelical faith began while he was studying in Cologne and continued into his Kappel apprenticeship.[5] This period is characterised by his reading of Luther's works written in the early 1520s and Melanchthon's *Loci* of 1521; this took place alongside his study of the works of Erasmus and the church fathers. Augustine, Chrysostom, Tertullian and Lactantius may have been the most important of these, but they were far from being the only church fathers he read.[6] The outlines of Bullinger's theology were inked in while he was in Kappel and owed much to his growing acquaintanceship with both Zwingli and Oecolampadius as well as to his engagement with early Christian history writing.[7] The

---

4. Hollweg, *Hausbuch*, 24-191.

5. Fritz Blanke/Immanuel Leuscher, *Heinrich Bullinger. Vater der reformierten Kirche* (Zurich: TVZ, 1990). The first part of the book is a reprint of Fritz Blanke, *Der junge Bullinger* (Zurich: Zwinlgi Verlag, 1940).

6. *HBD*, 6-8. On Bullinger's development in Kappel, see Susi Hausammann, *Römerbriefauslegung zwischen Humanismus und Reformation. Eine Studie zu Heinrich Bullingers Römerbriefauslegung von 1525* (Zurich/Stuttgart: Zwingli Verlag, 1970).

7. See J. Staedtke, *Die Theologie des jungen Bullinger* (Zurich: Zwingli Verlag, 1962).

piety of the late-medieval Catholic Church with its focus on the sacraments and the saints also played a crucial role in the formation of Bullinger's thought, for it was against this religious world that he would consistently write. Finally, this first stage was marked by the dispute over the Lord's Supper between Zwingli and Luther.[8]

The second stage can be dated from the mid-1520s to the mid-1530s when Bullinger was preoccupied with the theological concept of the covenant. The hermeneutical centrality of the covenant emerged in the *Studiorum ratio*[9] of 1528 and the *De prophetae officio*[10] of 1531, and it assumed a theologically central position in *De testamento*[11] of 1534. The opponents who had now come to the fore were, in broad terms, Anabaptists and separatist groups.

The third stage began in 1539 with the reworking of his *De origine Erroris*[12](*On the Origin of Error*), where we find that pneumatology clearly had become of vital interest to him–a process that paralleled Calvin's greater stress on the Spirit in the *Institutes* of 1539.[13] This third period saw the consolidation of Bullinger's position (and that of the Zurich church) against the Catholic Church, and at the same time an intensification of irenic efforts to create a greater understanding and reciprocal recognition between all Protestant confessions. Bullinger sought to do this without in any way compromising Zurich's theological positions. These efforts climaxed in 1549 with the *Consensus Tigurinus*, although, as was subsequently to become apparent, this agreement with Calvin marked a terminal point for this process.[14] It is to this phase in Bullinger's career that the *Decades*, which appeared between 1549 and 1552, belong.

In the preface to the *Decades*, composed in March 1549, Bullinger dedicated his first decade (ten sermons) to his colleagues in the Zurich church; this dedica-

---

8. *Heinrich Bullinger. Theologische Schriften*, vol. 2: *Unveröffentlichte Werke der Kappeler Zeit. Theologica*, J. Staedtke et al., eds, revised by H.-G. vom Berg et al., (*HBTS* 2; Zurich: TVZ, 1991).

9. Peter Stotz, *Heinrich Bullinger, Studiorum ratio–Studienanleitung*, 2. Teilband: *Einleitung, Kommentar, Register* (Zurich: TVZ, 1987).

10. *De prophetae officio, et quomodo digne administrari possit, oratio, Heinrycho Bullingero Authore* (Zurich: 1532).

11. *De testamento seu foedere Dei unico & aeterno Heinrychi Bullingeri breuis expositio* (Zurich: 1534). Charles S. McCoy/J. Wayne Baker, *Fountainhead of Federalism: Heinrich Bullinger and the Covenantal Tradition. With a Translation of De testamento seu foedere Dei unico et aeterno (1534)* (Louisville, Kentucky: Westminster/John Knox Press, 1991).

12. *De origine erroris libri duo, Heinrychi Bullingeri* (Zurich: 1539). By 1529 Bullinger had already published two works with the same title which were linked to the *Institutiones* of Lactantius. They were both concerned with the origin of the mass and veneration of images: *De origine erroris, in negocio eucharistiae, ac missae, per Heinrychum Bullingerum* (Zurich: 1528); *De origine erroris, in divorum ac simulachrorum cultu. Per Heinrychum Bullingerum* (Zurich: 1529). See W. Rordorf, "Lactanz als Vorbild Bullingers" in U. Gäbler/E. Zsindely eds, *Bullinger–Tagung 1975. Vorträge, gehalten aus Anlass von Heinrich Bullingers 400. Todestag* (Zurich: TVZ, 1977), 33-42.

13. W. Kolfhaus, *Christusgemeinschaft bei Johannes Calvin* (Neukirchen: Buchhandlung des Erziehungsvereins, 1939).

14. O. E. Strasser, "Der Consensus Tigurinus," *Zwingliana* 9 (1949): 1-16. U. Gäbler, "Consensus Tigurinus" in *TRE* 8:189-92; E. Busch, "Der Consensus Tigurinus (1549). Einleitung" in E. Busch et al. eds, *Calvin-Studienausgabe* (Neukirchen-Vluyn: Neukirchener, 2002), 4:1-10.

tion was retained in the complete edition of the work that appeared several years later. The *Decades* were intended to aid fellow ministers in the fulfilment of their revelatory, pastoral office, and Bullinger employed the medieval tradition of using collections of sermons to provide both homiletic guidance and material for the sermons of the frequently poorly-trained preachers.[15] In this endeavour Bullinger invoked the names of the well-known Dominican Johann Herolt (d. 1468) and the Franciscan Oswals Pelbartus (c. 1500), known as "Discipulus."[16]

Evidently Bullinger identified with his position as preacher in the Grossmünster, an office with the status and duties of a "primus inter pares" for the Zurich church with its rural chapters. His efforts were undoubtedly promoted by his recognition that following the Reformation the preachers, who, without exception, had grown up in the Catholic faith, still lacked the theological understanding and, in some cases, perhaps even the theological conviction, to be able to contribute effectively to the growth of the Reformed Zurich church.[17] It is unclear whether Bullinger in fact preached these fifty Latin didactic sermons. Although in his capacity as preacher at the Grossmünster Bullinger was responsible for the theological school, he did not teach there himself but rather left this to qualified masters such as Konrad Pellikan and Theodor Bibliander.[18] However, these printed sermons do imitate sermons given from the pulpit in that they are written in simple Latin and in that at certain points Bullinger addresses his public directly in introductory passages, and, indeed, he apologises in his conclusion for having once more preached for too long.[19] Nevertheless, in their final written form, the sermons appear to be literary fiction rather than a printed version of sermons delivered in the Grossmünster. This is confirmed by the fact that although Bullinger recorded his preaching activities in detail in his *Diary*, he makes no mention of giving such sermons–although he does record the printing of the *Decades*. Further, the fact that the sermons become increasingly long, including ever more quotations from the church fathers, and that the four sermons on the sacraments in the fifth decade were taken from a treatise written several years earlier and published by John à Lasco strongly suggests that it was written as a literary

---

15. The *Decades* were printed in four stages over two years. (1) The first two decades with preface are dated 1 March 1549. (2) The preface to decade 3 and the first two sermons of decade 4 is dated March 1550. (3) The preface to the remaining eight sermons of the fourth decade is dated August 1550. (4) The preface to the fifth decade is dated March 1551. The first complete edition appeared in 1552. On the title page the following appears: *Sermonum Decades quinque, de potissimis Christianae religionis capitibus, in tres tomos digestae, authore Heinrycho Bullingero, ecclesiae Tigurinae ministro* (Zurich: 1552). There is also an English translation: *The Decades of Henry Bullinger* H.I trans. (London: 1587), Th. Harding ed., (Cambridge: 1849). A critical edition of the 1552 edition of the *Decades*, as well as a translation into modern German (as part of the new translation of Bullinger's works), are in preparation. Both the edition and the translation will appear in 2004 from the TVZ.

16. *Sermonum Decades quinque*, f. α4ᵛ. Hollweg, *Hausbuch*, 47f.

17. *Sermonum Decades quinque*, f. α2ᵛ-α4ᵛ.

18. *Schola Tigurina. Die Zürcher Hohe Schule und ihre Gelehrten um 1550. Katalog zur Ausstellung vom 25. Mai bis 10. Juni 1999 in der Zentralbibliothek Zürich*, Institut für Schweizerische Reformationsgeschichte ed., (Zurich: Pano-Verlag, 1999).

19. *Sermonum Decades quinque*, f. 77ʳ.

work.[20] It is, however, worth considering that Bullinger may have started to deliver the *loci* sermons, perhaps within the context of the *Prophezei*, and that the first ten short sermons and the short explanation of the Creed may have been delivered orally from notes and subsequently written down. As the circle he was addressing widened, Bullinger may have moved to prepare the sermons only for publication, retaining, however, the oral form in the first and last elements of the sermons.

Once they became known on the European stage the *Decades* adopted a double role. On the one hand they offered an account of the Zurich Reformed faith in the confessional world of the mid-sixteenth century; while, on the other, the *Decades* were much sought-after and much read as a manual for education in the Christian faith. Even as literary sermons, the *Decades* served Bullinger's primary goal: not to enter into the realms of theology and polemic as deliberated in learned circles, but rather to contribute to the need to teach the faithful, without over generalising his subject. The growth in readership for the *Decades* is evident from the various prefaces written for the separate parts of the work. As mentioned, the preface to the first of the *Decades* was directed to the Zurich ministers and church; this local orientation, however, changed with the introduction to the third decade, written in March 1550, in which Bullinger addressed himself to the young Edward VI of England.[21] It was an attempt to influence the course of the English Reformation in its decisive phase, and in so doing, to bring Zurich's theology into the international arena.[22]

II. Intention and Structure

The *Decades* were written in the form of fifty individual *loci* sermons on traditional Christian catechetical subjects: the Ten Commandments, the Apostles' Creed, the Lord's Prayer, and the two Protestant sacraments. These fundamentals of the faith are explained in the tradition of Zurich Reformed theology and provide the framework for the depiction of the Christian life in all its dimensions and aspects. In this part of the essay I will provide an overview of the structure of the *Decades*, or rather their composition, beginning with the preliminary observation that it was typical of Bullinger's writings, and indeed fundamental to his theology, that the *Decades* can be divided in various ways according to various approaches.

In the first decade, which comprises the first ten sermons, Bullinger treats the Word of God, its origin, its being (sermons 1 and 2) and its effects: faith (sermons 4 to 9) and love (sermon 10). In his methodology Bullinger reflects the Reformed position that all legitimate discussion of God, the Christian faith, and the Christian life must begin with God's address to humanity. At the same time, Bullinger argues that Christian teaching does not begin with a metaphysical God,

---

20. *Absoluta de Christi Domini et Catholicae Ecclesiae Sacramentis tractatio* (printed 1551).

21. *Sermonum Decades quinque*, f. 86ᵛ-88ᵛ. The third dedicatory preface was also to the English king (f. 202ᵛ-203ᵛ); the dedication of the fifth decade is to Henry Gray (f. 285ᵛ-270ᵛ).

22. Hollweg, *Hausbuch*, 24-190.

but rather with his approach in the Word. Faith is based on this Word and thus on the God who speaks through the Word. The content of faith is in the acts of the triune God in the world as evinced in the biblical works. To demonstrate this, Bullinger incorporates a short outline of the Apostolic symbol (sermons 7 to 9) within his account of faith. As *regula fidei* (cf Rom 12.6) the Apostolic symbol summarises briefly and tellingly the biblical message of God in his love for humanity. It also forms a bridge to the theology of the church fathers, for even the oldest, such as Irenaeus and Tertullian, used this *regula fidei* as the criterion for true Christian faith in the debate with the "heretics" of their time.

Love is humanity's act of turning back to God and to one's fellow Christians; it is the fulfilment of the laws. Sermon 10 then leads to the fundamentals of Christian life, the Ten Commandments. It is the explanation of the Ten Commandments which occupies most space in the second and third decades, for here Bullinger addresses the law and all the questions which accompany it, such as the issue of the various forms of the law, its interpretation and its various theological applications, teachings on good works, on sin, and on Christian freedom. The Decalogue, therefore, serves as the springboard for the discussion of all essential aspects of Christian life, both individual and corporate.

In his treatment of the individual commandments Bullinger addresses concrete problems in Christian life and community. Issues range from the keeping of the Sabbath to the question of the legitimacy and duties of the Christian magistracy, the punishment of wrongdoers, war, the raising of children, respect between generations, the relationship of the Christian with rich and poor, and usury, to name but a few. From this emerge issues of individual ethics, social ethics and pastoral care. This extensive discussion of the law as Tora is followed by a sermon on the *evangelium* (sermon 31) and then Christian penitence (sermon 32). This makes clear Bullinger's intention to proceed in terms of salvation history: the Word of God was at the beginning, as spoken to the biblical fathers and remained unchanged for them–Bullinger finds its seeds in the Pentateuch. This was followed by the time of the law and then, with the appearance of Christ, by the time of the Gospel. The human response to the Word of God, both before and after the appearance of Christ, must always be in faith and love as an inseparable unity. Penitence is the result of hearing the Gospel, but it does not precede the Word of God as good news. At heart, penitence is no more than one element of faith whereby people turn to God and away from false ways.

This concludes the first element of the *Decades*. Running through these thirty-two sermons on the teaching of the Word of God and resultant human behaviour in faith and love is a correlation between the Word of God and the response of humanity. This correlation continues in the second part of the *Decades*. From sermon 33 Bullinger again addresses the Apostles' Creed, but this time at greater length. The last decade, sermons 41 to 50, is concerned with the Church. The catechetical use of the Lord's Prayer is explained here, as are the sacraments, which are treated at length. Bullinger addressed the Apostles' Creed twice, something that has been seen as a weakness in his systematic approach. However, this double treatment of the Apostles' Creed is a sign that during the period in which the *Decades* were written their audience changed. The preaching of the Reformed clergy in the Zurich church, designed to provide Reformed instruction and to instruct in a Reformed way of life, could be limited to the fundamental truths of the Apostles' Creed and had to concentrate on Christian behaviour.[23] By contrast, as a theological justification of the Zurich church for the wider European world a different approach was required, for Bullinger had to counter accusations of heresy against the Zurich theology with a strong emphasis on its conformity with the church fathers. The *Decades* also needed to place the controversial issue of the Lord's Supper in the wider European context, and Bullinger tackled this by including in the *Decades* (sermons 46-49) a treatise on communion that had been written some years earlier. This second part follows a discussion of God's Word and the hearing of this Word by men and women. It can therefore be understood both as the teaching of God himself, who loves and approaches humanity, and as the true human "religion" in the sense of the honouring of God. Bullinger's understanding of God merges into the treatment of providence and predestination and then leads into the teaching on true worship; the teaching on Christ leads into an explanation of the question of what it means to call oneself a Christian; the teaching on the Spirit concerns God's work in humanity; finally, the teaching of the Church treats the being and acting of humanity and the community in the body of Christ. Undoubtedly it was Bullinger's intention to have acknowledged both the salvific dimension of godly revelation and the "existential" godly relation of humans in whom faith and action are inseparable.

It is evident both from the intention of the work and its intended audience that the *Decades* had a dual purpose. The sermons were both teaching as preaching and preaching in the form of teaching. When Zwingli took up his position as *Leutpriester* (stipendiary priest) in Zurich on 1 January 1519 he also began his exposition of the Gospel of Matthew. From this moment the Bible and the story of Christ revealed within it would be the starting point of revelation and the standard against which Christian life would be measured. Throughout his life Bullinger continued this practice and preached in turn on each book of the Bible from start to finish. His awareness of his responsibility for the strengthening of the Reformed Zurich church is also evident in other ways: as early as 1532, when he gave his address on taking up the office, he distinguished between a sermon in the form of a homily with a continuous exposition of scripture verse by verse and a "thematic address" in which the central content of Christian life is explained in the form of a sermon, and thus also taught to the audience.[24] In the *Decades*, the "Prophetic office" was given more precise theological justification and was developed in particular in contrast to the Roman Catholic understanding of the office.[25] In keeping with this, Bullinger distinguished in a marginal note, where he wrote *De ratione docendi ecclesiam*,[26] between teaching as exposition of scrip-

---

23. Ibid., 233f.

24. "Ponimus itaque nos orationum genera duo, alterum quod expositione fiat, alterum vero quod themate propositio absolvatur … et rursus docendi genus esse duplex, alterum expositione scripturae constare, alterum effictione thematis." Cited by Hausammann, *Römerbriefauslegung*, 162. "Exposcunt non raro et tempora et rerum casus, ut thematis cum plebe agamus, et non scripturarum enarratione." *De prophetae officio*, f. XII[v.]

25. See the essay by Daniel Bolliger in this volume.

26. *Sermonum Decades quinque*, f. 305[r].

ture designed for those who were "advanced" and an elementary Christian teaching which consisted of the explanation of the principal points of the covenant, the Decalogue, the Apostles' Creed, the Lord's Prayer, and the sacraments, and which also addressed thematically the fundamental catechetical tenets.[27] Bullinger was aware that in doing this he was reaching back to the catechetical tradition of the ancient church.[28] The run of sermons that appear in Bullinger's *Decades* is to be understood as designed to provide the Zurich clergy with the means to create such catechetical sermons in accordance with the ancient faith. According to an entry in Bullinger's diary from March 1549 the first two *Decades* treat "de potissimis capitibus religionis nostrae."[29]

This elementary teaching must be preached to the people. In order to realise this, Bullinger brings on board classical rhetoric and puts it to work in the service of his teaching. Against the criticism that he unduly mingled theology with the profane arts, Bullinger points out in his *Studiorum ratio* that rhetorical rules were simply a peculiarity of human speech in which revelation should follow. Just as God must adapt to the rules of human speech in order to talk to man, so too must Christian revelation. Bullinger found additional biblical proof for such thematic sermons in Acts.[30] While still in Kappel Bullinger had written the unpublished "*De propheta*" where, with reference to Quintilian and Cicero's *De inventione* and *Rhetorica ad Herennium*[31], he had listed the specialist rhetorical terms and briefly addressed their significance.[32]

Bullinger held that the *exordium* should awaken the interest of the listener by pointing out the usefulness of the subject of his sermon; the minister should also prepare his audience to listen to his sermon by means of a short summary and by outlining the structure of the sermon that would follow.[33] Although the *narratio* is important for telling a story, it has no role in treating a categorical subject. The

---

27. "Comprehendit enim catechesis rudimenta fidei et doctrinae christianae, nempe capita foederis, decalogum, symbolum apostolorum, orationem dominicam, et brevem sacramentorum explicationem." *Sermonum Decades quinque*, f. 305[r-v].
28. "Veteres ecclesiae catechistas habuere peculiariter huic muneri consecratos. Commendavit autem nobis dominus in utroque testamento miris obtestationibus pubem, praecipiens ut ipsam tempestive et diligenter in vera religione instituamus ... Nullus certe fructus ab auditoribus catechesi non probe instructis expectari potest in ecclesia. nesciunt enim qua de re loquatur doctor ecclesiae, cum audiunt nominari foedus, praeceptum, legem, gratiam, fidem, orationem, sacramenta. Proinde maximam hic, sicubi alias, adhibere decet diligentiam. Perfectiorum doctrina versatur praecipue in expositione scripturae sanctae." *Sermonum Decades quinque*, f. 305[v]. The reference is clearly to Augustine's *De catechizandis rudibus* (*PL* 40:309-48; *CC.SL* 46).
29. *HBD*, 36, 27f.
30. *De prophetae officio*, f. XIII[r-v].
31. Hausammann, *Römerbriefauslegung*, 163.
32. "Secundi vero generis oratio, partibus absolvitur: Exordio, narratione, confirmatione et epilogo sive peroratione. Exordium vero finiunt esse partem orationis idoneae comparantem animum auditoris ad reliquam dicitionem. Narratio est rei gestae aut perinde ut gestae expositio. Confirmatio est qua et nostra confirmamus et aliena refellimus. Epilogus est artificiosa totius orationis conclusio." Hausammann, *Römerbriefauslegung*, 162.
33. "Attenti erunt auditores si de Christianis necessariis, utilibus rebus, item difficilibus aut involutis dicturum te adfirmes. Dociles facimus auditores, si brevi summa quae dicturi sumus, velut oculis subiiciamus, ostendamusque ordinem rerum dicendarum." Hausammann, *Römerbriefauslegung*, 163.

confirmatio by contrast was central, for it is here that the theme was to be stated and expounded upon and objections refuted. Finally, the *epilogus* is both a summary of the results and an appeal to the audience.[34] In addition he noted that such addresses could also contain an *excursus*.[35] While scripture is consistently the foundation of the thematic sermon, the sermon is the means by which the content of scripture is accommodated to the audience.[36]

It is evident that the sermons contained in the *Decades* are arranged according to these rhetorical categories, although to varying degrees. Bullinger usually begins with a short account of the theme, beginning often with the explanation of a fundamental term and its meaning in Hebrew and Greek, and then provides a definition or a summary of the points which he will address. He continues by developing the theme and by repudiating misunderstandings and errors. On occasion, for example when discussing the commandments, Bullinger includes long thematic digressions, or political digressions when addressing controversial topics. This is succeeded by explanations with biblical citations that as a rule abide by salvation history and to which quotations from the church fathers are added. Finally, the epilogue briefly summarises the material that has been developed in the sermon and addresses the audience, asking them to take that which they have heard to heart and to build upon it, or to allow it to lead into a request for the Holy Spirit. Explaining the Christian truth is always revelation. In so doing Bullinger was bearing in mind the Reformed view that the Word of God is a force, a dynamic address of God to humanity; the preached Word of God aims to make the life of the hearer part of God's history with humanity. This is evident not only in the form of the sermons of the *Decades,* but also in their content. Whenever Bullinger discusses doctrine, including the teaching on the natures of Christ or the characteristics of God, this is done with an existential dimension and with a kerygmatic goal. His treatment of predestination is typical:[37] he follows Ambrose's *De vocatione gentium*[38] and not Augustine's attempt at a rational solution. His position is simple and consistent: God did not divide men into "two Books" in advance, but rather offers salvation to all, just as Christ died for all men, and all are called to faith. For Bullinger, it would be nothing more than speculation if one were to move beyond this kerygmatic basis.

The point of such thematic sermons is fundamentally no different from any sermon: it is to teach (*docere*), to admonish (*hortari*), and to console (*consolari*).

---

34. "Porro peroratio sive epilogus constat duabus rebus: Enumeratione et adfectu. Enumeratio est brevis eorum quae tota oratione sparsim dicta sunt repetitio summaria. Affectus est vehementior animi conmotio." Hausammann, *Römerbriefauslegung*, 164.

35. Ibid., 164.

36. "Scriptura sane ac veritas sola, citra contraversiam, materia est prophetae. Inutilis autem fuerit materia, nisi intrumento expoliatur et redigatur in usum. Instrumentum vero istud prophetae oratio est. Per eam enim id quod animo concepit, quodque ex scripturis pro auditorum captu et commodo, congessit: oratione clara et praesenti rei accommoda, audiatoribus proponit." *De prophetae officio*, f. XIII^v.

37. This is one of the few areas of Bullinger's theology which has received some attention. See Peter Walser, *Die Prädestination bei Heinrich Bullinger im Zusammenhang mit seiner Gotteslehre* (Zurich: Zwingli-Verlag, 1957); C. P. Venema, *Heinrich Bullinger and the Doctrine of Predestination* (Grand Rapids, Mich.: Baker Press, 2002).

38. The real author is not known, but it is often assumed to be Prosper of Aquitaine.

In *De propheta* Bullinger was already following classical rhetoric with its trinity of *docere*, *delectare* and *movere* and corrected it on the basis of 1 Corinthians 14:3.[39] The *aedificatio* is treated as doctrine while it has the character of an address and its goal is the building up of the church.[40] The *adhortatio* is at the same time admonishment; it is admonishment to remain in hope, patience, and trust, but also to do good works.[41] The trust resides in the proclamation of Christ's reconciliation and in the return to Christ.[42]

The *Decades* treats what Bullinger has already stated in *De propheta* as the question of the application of the proclamation of Christ.[43] The *aedificatio* is most clearly found in the presentation of Christian doctrine, as well in the indication of injustice,[44] so that it is on the one hand the refutation and rejection of heresy and error whilst, on the other, the affirmation of orthodox teaching.[45] Bullinger treats *adhortatio* with the biblical text from 2 Timothy 4:1-5 and he comes near to the traditional rhetorical *movere*,[46] while the explanation of *consolatio* is connected to the text from 2 Timothy 2:24.[47]

For Bullinger the theological teaching on the Word is based on the living God who comes to humanity and brings the "way of life."[48] This is demonstrated by the manner in which Bullinger orders his treatment of the Word of God, Gospel, and Law in the following schema: origin (*origo/causa*), nature (*natura*), effect (*virtus, effectus*). The suggestion that Bullinger's theology marks a strong shift

39. "Paulus ergo eo modo quo nos sumus prophetam tractaturi, quid sit propheta dilucidissime sic explanat I. Corint. 14: "Qui prophetat hominibus liquitur aedificationem et exhortationem et consolationem." Proinde is verus est propheta qui aedificat, hortatur et consolatur." Hausammann, *Römerbriefauslegung*, 177.
40. "Itaque aedificationem, quam primam fecit ordine Paulus, nominare potes, certam in deum deductionem, sive per evidentem demonstrationem, sive per sanam doctrinam factam adeo ut ipsa salutaris aedificatio doctrina sit. Liquet ergo quod primum prophetae officium est docere." Ibid.
41. "Est autem hortatio aliud nihil, quam admonitio ad populum facta, ut semen acceptum spe, patientia, munditia, aliisque bonis operibus colat, deum tentare, ei difficere, male agere, carnemque sectari desinat." Ibid.
42. "Iam et propheta consolatur. Quoties pavefactos peccatores ad Christum reducit. Ut qui est agnus dei tollens peccata mundi, aut quoties territas hominum mentes, cordatas esse iubet. Id faciunt prophetae, proposita dei immensa misericordia, apostoli vero proposito propiciatore Christo ... Utcumque tum res habeat, hoc unum ante omnia exigimus, ut ex scripturis petita sit consolatio et in Christum deducat..." Ibid.
43. *Sermonum Decades quinque*, f. 305ᵛ (Marginal).
44. "Ergo ad perfectiorum doctrinam pertinet non tantum scripturae sanctae expositio, sed et dilucida vel maxime perspicua dogmatum vel rerum christianarum demonstratio, in primis autem clare de poenitentia et remissione peccatorum in nomine Christi doctrina item obiurgatio opportuna et acris, vel gravis se prudens scelerum accusatio." *Sermonum Decades quinque*, f. 305ᵛ.
45. "... confutatio quoque errorum et haeresum oppressio, assertioque doctrinae orthodoxae ... Neque enim satis est simpliciter docere religionem veram, nisi eandem quoque constanter inculcando urgeat, defendat atque conservet doctor ecclesiasticus" *Sermonum Decades quinque*, f. 305ᵛ⁻ʳ, with reference to Tit 1,10f.
46. "Opus est itaque adhortationibus creberrimis, ut quod ecclesia per doctrinam frequentem et perspicuam intellexit vel prosequendum esse, vel fugiendum, adhortatione ferventi accensa et impulsa constanter prose,quatur vel refugiat." *Sermonum Decades quinque*, f. 306ʳ.
47. Ibid.
48. Edward A. Dowey, "Wort Gottes als Schrift und Predigt im Zweiten Helvetischen Bekenntnis" in Staedtke, *Glauben und Bekennen*, 235-50.

towards Reformed Orthodoxy cannot be sustained by an examination of his writing: Bullinger will not allow Christian doctrine to be reduced to exact dogmatic statements.

III. Characteristic Features

Now that something has been said about the nature and purpose of Bullinger's *Decades* we need to turn to some of the key characteristics which shape its content.

Humanist Learning in the Service of the Proclamation of the Gospel, Doctrine and Polemic

In his student days Bullinger had already come under the influence of humanism. His theology and thought were considerably shaped by the humanist teaching on textual criticism, the use of languages, the precedence of language over conceptual exactness and rigorous logic, as well as the use of history and the examples of classical historians. Bullinger greatly esteemed Erasmus, Melanchthon, and other humanists, and he readily adopted the *loci* method, which linked the rhetorical dimension with historical thought. During his time at the monastery at Kappel Bullinger had begun to engage in scriptural interpretation along humanist principles, and the most important result was the above mentioned *Studiorum ratio* of 1528. This hermeneutical confidence, which can hardly be called a naïve biblicism, is best demonstrated in the third sermon of the first decade, in which Bullinger, after two sermons on the Word of God, comes to the question of the proper interpretation of scripture.[49]

The Importance of the Hebrew Bible

Central to his humanist hermeneutic was the importance of the Old Testament. Bullinger's principle of *ad fontes* meant above all the Bible. Bullinger was clear that all the New Testament authors, most notably Jesus himself, referred to the Hebrew Bible, and that the Word of God was a history of the tradition of this Word. The whole New Testament, according to Bullinger, is nothing more than an interpretation of the Old.[50] However, the Old Testament is also to be seen as containing self-interpretation in which the prophetic books interpret the Pentateuch.[51] The Bible, therefore, is a history of salvation. It is a witness to the unity of God's work and words since the fall of humanity. It is a book that develops, and yet never contradicts itself and reaches its highpoint with the appearance of Christ.[52] For Bullinger the content of scripture is not Gospel and Law, but a

---

49. "De sensu et expositione legitima verbi dei, quibus modis et rationibus exponi possit." *Sermonum Decades quinque*, f. 8ᵛ.
50. It is so formulated in *De scripturae negotio* from 1525, see *HBTS* 2:25.
51. Peter Opitz, "Hebräisch-biblische Züge im promissio-Verständnis Heinrich Bullingers" in *Historische Horizonte* S. Lekebusch/H.-G. Ulrichs eds, (Emder Beiträge zum reformierten Protestantismus 5; Wuppertal: Foedus, 2002), 105-17.
52. A. A. G. Archilla, *The Theology of History and Apologetic Historiography in Heinrich Bullinger. Truth in History* (San Francisco: Mellen Press, 1992).

covenant that is and remains a covenant of grace in which Christ is the scopus. Bullinger saw his evidence for this not only in the Bible itself but also in the conflict of the church fathers with the heretic Marcion. He looked to the way in which Irenaeus and Tertullian stressed the unity of God in the Old and New Testaments.[53] It was typical of Bullinger that when he makes a doctrinal point he never merely uses an Old Testament passage and then adds the proof from the New. His method is always to demonstrate the essential link and continuity between the relevant Old and New Testament passages. The result is that most of the New Testament is interpreted in light of the Hebrew Bible and given new insights.

Consensus with the Early Church

In the *Decades* Bullinger makes frequent reference to the most important of the Church councils: Nicaea, Constantinople, Ephesus, and Chalcedon. He also provides a summary of the *regula fidei* of Irenaeus and Tertullian and the Imperial decree "Cunctos populos" of Theodosius the Great.[54] Throughout the *Decades* Bullinger stresses that his, and the Zurich, theology, was "orthodox" and "catholic."[55] Thus it was crucial for Bullinger that he demonstrate that all, in particular controversial, theological statements, could be referenced to the early church writers. Above all loomed the figure of Augustine, who was for Bullinger the most important church father. There is hardly another Reformer for whom Augustine was such a dominant author as Bullinger, who not only frequently cited the Bishop of Hippo, but referred to him in virtually all theological matters.

Tertullian is also central to Bullinger's thought, but he must be seen alongside Ambrose (and Pseudo Ambrose), Lactantius, Chysostom, and others. It is certainly true that all the Reformers made use of the church fathers, both in their polemic against Rome and in the dispute over the Lord's Supper. In Bullinger's case, however, this was not simply a means for him to reinforce his own position; from the beginning it is clear that his theology evolved out of the study of the church fathers and that he was wholly persuaded that the message of the fathers was utterly relevant to the Church of his day.

The Consolidation of Anti-Papal Polemic and Reformation Irenicism

Following the publication of the fifth decade Bullinger wrote to Vadianus on 8 March 1551, "As I know all too well, the Papists will take greater offence [from my work] than they have before…"[56] Against the background of the Council of Trent and the religious politics of the 1540s and 1550s it is clear that Bull-

---

53. See Bullinger's early writing *Verglichung der vralten vnd vnser zyten kaetzereyen* (Zurich: 1526).
54. *Sermonum Decades quinque*, f. βʳβ6ʳ.
55. Edward A. Dowey, "The Old Faith: Comments on One of Heinrich Bullinger's Most Distinctive Treatises" in Willem van 't Spijker ed., *Calvin: Erbe und Auftrag. Festschrift für Wilhelm Neuser zu seinem 65. Geburtstag* (Kampen: Kok Pharos, 1991), 270-8.
56. "Ut autem sat scio papistas me nunc offendisse gravius quam antea unquam…" *CO* 14, 71.

inger's work was moving in the direction of confessionalism. Bullinger hoped to win converts from the Roman faith to the Reformed religion but he had no expectations of regaining those associated and mandated parts of the Swiss Confederation that had been forcibly returned to the Catholic faith. Inside the Protestant lands, including German Lutheran territory, Bullinger did not regard the confessional borders as fixed.

In particular he had in mind the debate over the Lord's Supper when he wrote to Vadianus that he hoped "in the four sermons on the sacrament to have done something to persuade [them] to see the error of their ways when they have condemned us as heretics and sacramentarians."[57] Bullinger had devoted a great deal of time to the sacraments in his four sermons. On the one hand he had defended Zwingli's position, in which he paid particular attention to the little considered later works, such as the *Fidei expositio*[58] and the writing against Eck.[59] On the other, he stressed the consensus with Calvin, whose name he intentionally mentioned and whom he quoted.[60] This was a significant departure from Bullinger's way of working, which was never to quote contemporaries in his theological works. The sermons show Bullinger in a non-polemical mood as he outlined the Reformed position on the body of Christ, which can only be the human body and the body of the resurrected, as the Creed states. At the same time he stressed the spiritual presence of the body of Christ in the sacrament, which not only Zwingli, Calvin, and Oecolampadius had held to, but which was also the position of Luther, and the great church father, Augustine.

The Unity of the Christian Life

We have already mentioned Bullinger's belief in the unified witness of the Bible to God's revelation. To this we must add Bullinger's emphasis on the unity of God and of his Word: God does not contradict himself but speaks in corresponding terms, because there is one divine Word and one will to save which fall under the categories of "promise," "law" and "Gospel." All of these reveal God's will that humanity return to community with God. It is with this purpose that Bullinger speaks of his three uses of the law; law does not bring death but leads in different ways to life.[61] This emphasis on the unity of the divine will is mirrored in the Christian life with its unity of faith and love. Faith and love do not follow from one another but are identical and are the work of the same spirit, which dwells in each person through faith. This leads to the question of Christian ethics, which was so heavily debated in Lutheran circles. For Bullinger, life is constant activity in trust, hope, truth, and obedience. Although Bullinger places the Gospel above the law he could reverse the catechetical order; for it concerns the life in the Spirit of God according to his Word. The unity of the Christian life is not limited to individual piety and the imitation of Christ, but it leads also to

57. "Spero in his, maxime sermonibus quatuor de sacramentis, me fecisse operae pretium, et peccatum suum intellecturos qui nos damnant pro haereticis et sacramentariis etc." *CO* 14, 71.
58. *Z* VI/5:140-62.
59. *Z* VI/3:249-91.
60. *Sermonum Decades quinque*, f. 377ʳ.
61. Decade 3, sermon 8 (*Sermonum Decades quinque*, f. 136ʳ-149ᵛ).

the unity of the individual with communal living. Naturally Christian life and love take place within the concrete framework of the communal life, which in their external circumstances Bullinger associated with the civic community. For Bullinger, as for the other reformers, community was conceived in terms of the *corpus christianum*. Bullinger believed that the civic as well as the political aspects of society had their particular roles according to scripture and that the "Christian magistrate"–either as king or city council–had its prophetic counterpart in the minister of the Word, whose role was to remind the magistrates of their duties. It was from this standpoint that Bullinger rejected any separate authority for the church in matters of excommunication or in keeping people from the sacrament. The role of the minister was to invite and not to exclude the people from the Lord's Supper.

The Gospel as Freedom to Do Good Works

With great consistency Bullinger focused on the Reformed teaching on the Word of God and human faith, and as a result he emphatically rejected the position on the Lord's Supper held by Luther at the end of his life. Nevertheless it is not entirely satisfactory to speak of Bullinger's position as being simply that God gives and the human person receives passively in faith. Bullinger ceaselessly stressed that this movement–the *sola gratia*–was the basis of all Christian faith and living. Humanity is so entirely passive in the face of God's grace, that Bullinger stated that the divine grace brings humans to life (*vivificatio*) and that each person is reborn in God's grace (*regeneratio*). This awakening to a new creation is a crucial part of Bullinger's theology, for as each person receives God's grace he/she becomes a liberated, responsive, and freely acting person.[62] That person is free to do good; that is, and this is repeatedly stressed, the person is free to do God's will. As soon as the person is awoken to the new life, he/she progresses down the road of life. Bullinger sought to unite the Reformation teaching on *sola gratia* with the theology of the Hebrew Tora on the basis of Pauline and Johannine pneumatology.

The Dual Handling of God with Humanity through the Word and Spirit

For Luther faith proceeds from the Word in its proclamation, while for Zwingli the inner working of the Spirit has priority over the Word, but in Bullinger's thought there is an attempt to unite these two positions.[63] More clearly than Zwingli he made reference to Romans 10:17, but in keeping with Zwingli he held to the importance of John 6:44. Bullinger always distinguished between the working of God from inside and from outside; in his teaching on the Church (in-

---

62. "...libertate christiana liberante nos a malis non a bonis." *De gratia Dei iustificante nos propter Christum, per solam fidem absque operibus bonis, fide interim exuberante in opera bona, Libri IIII. ad Sereniss. Daniae Regem Christianum, &c. Heinrycho Bullingero authore* (Zurich: 1554), f. 72ᵛ.
63. G. W. Locher, "Praedicatio verbi Dei est verbum dei" in idem, *Huldrych Zwingli in neuer Sicht. Zehn Beiträge zur Theologie der Zürcher Reformation* (Zurich: Zwinlgi Verlag, 1969), 275-87.

ner and outward marks),[64] the sacraments[65] and the law, the inner and outer are not seen as opposites but as closely linked aspects. In other words, one refers to the other. The whole of Bullinger's theology has a dynamic that is built around the work of God in Word and Spirit.

IV The Theological Heart of the Decades

Is it possible to reduce Bullinger's thought to an essential core? This takes us to the question of what forms the theological heart of the *Decades*. It is often maintained that Bullinger was not really much of a theologian, but rather a preacher and a pastor. Indeed, looking at the *Decades* with its synthetic rather than analytical character, one would be tempted to accept this judgement. In his other theological works Bullinger could, and did, organise his *loci* in a different manner; we find this in his *Summa*, which was intended as a simplified summary of the *Decades*, but where in fact the *loci* are organised in a different order. Indeed the *Decades* is repetitious as, for instance, Bullinger treats the Apostles' Creed twice. At other points in the sermons he makes reference to other places where he has treated a particular theological point in greater detail.

Can we say that the covenant is the centre of the *Decades*? Certainly Bullinger treats the subject, but in contrast to his earlier writings the covenant appears in a more limited and pedagogical light.[66] Greater emphasis is given to pneumatology: that is sanctification, vivification, and communion with Christ.[67] Almost all of Bullinger's theological works bear on their title page the quotation from Matthew 17:5 but reformulated to make a theological point: "This is my son *in whom I am reconciled*. Listen to him!"[68] This was the heart of his teaching: to preach reconciliation in Christ and to bring the penitent to the Word of God. The demand, "listen to him" was Bullinger's message. For the *Decades* it meant that this message could not be reduced to a system of *loci* rigorously organised. Rather, each sermon must be understood as a piece of the circle that has as its centre point Christ and his message. Bullinger's message was drawn from this middle point. He did not interest himself in a linear system and a repeated treatment of the Apostles' Creed or any other subject would not have struck him as a mistake. Where Christ's Gospel is preached faith and love take root and people

---

64. Fritz Büsser, "Der 'oekumenische Patriarch' der Reformation. Bausteine zu Bullingers Lehre von der Kirche" in W. H. Neuser/H. J. Selderhuis eds, *Ordentlich und fruchtbar Festschrift für Willem van 't Spijker* (Leiden: J. J. Groen, 1997), 69-78.

65. J. C. McLelland, "Die Sakramentslehre der Confessio Helvetica posterior" in Staedtke, *Glauben und Bekennen*, 368-91.

66. On this point, see J. Wayne Baker, *Heinrich Bullinger and the Covenant: The Other Reformed Tradition* (Athens, Ohio: Ohio Univ. Press, 1980). Criticism of this view is found in P. A. Lilliback, *The Binding of God. Calvin's Role in the Development of Covenant Theology* (Grand Rapids: Baker Press, 2001).

67. M. S. Burrows, "'Christus intra nos Vivens'. The Peculiar Genius of Bullinger's Doctrine of Sanctification," *Zeitschrift für Kirchengeschichte* 98 (1978): 48-69; Fritz Büsser, "Zürich–'Die Stadt auf dem Berg.' Bullingers reformatorisches Vermächtnis an der Wende zum 21. Jahrhundert," *Zwingliana* 25 (1998): 21-42; Büsser, "Der 'oekumenische Patriarch'."

68. "Hic est filius meus dilectus, in quo placata est animus mea. Ipsum audite!" For example in *Antwort an Burchard* (1526), (*HBTS* 2, 143).

are brought into the circle of the Word and Spirit and established as the "new created" on the road to life. This road is not only towards individual fulfilment but also towards communal living, whose social character and structures are likewise built upon the hearing of the divine Word. Bullinger's message is essentially practical and is part of the Reformation rejection of speculative theology.

There is still much work to be done: the various theological aspects of the *Decades*, the contribution of the *Decades* to the history of theology and piety, and the influence of the *Decades* on posterity all await further research.

4

Bullinger's Vernacular Writings: Spirituality and the Christian Life

Bruce Gordon

"This is my beloved son in whom I am reconciled. Listen to him!" These words, taken from Matthew's account of the transfiguration of Christ (Matt 17:5), appear on the title page of all of Heinrich Bullinger's printed works. The text, one of only two occasions in the New Testament when God the Father speaks directly to the Apostles, lies at the heart of Bullinger's near fifty years of preaching and pastoral care in Zurich.[1] It formed the lens through which he viewed himself and his calling as Christian, minister, and head of the Zurich church; it declared God's merciful and creative revelation of his Word, his Son, and his reconciliation with the world through Christ. In his *Summa*, Bullinger offers the following gloss:

> God the heavenly Father has given his only Son Jesus Christ as the only, and eternal advocate, mediator, defender and protector. To the Father he is the greatest, most beloved, most worthy and most pleasing. Nothing is lacking in him which a true mediator and advocate should be. He is lord of all, is friendly (*fruntlich*) and merciful to all poor sinners, he invites all to himself and promises them all truth and love.[2]

For Heinrich Bullinger, Christian spirituality was about the reality of the relationship between God's beloved Son and the lost children of creation. God's disposition is to save all–an attitude captured by the repeated use of the term "*fruntlich*" and its cognates–but not all will be saved, for most reject the Son who has been sent. This chapter will explore the spiritual grammar and vocabulary developed by Heinrich Bullinger as he attempted to craft the Reformed understanding of the Christian life.

Far from limiting human possibilities, Bullinger saw God's revelation of his Son as a new framework for human responsibility and activity. At Caesarea Philippi Christ had asked his disciples, "Who do you say I am?" God now answers

---

1. The other occasion is at Christ's baptism when God uses almost exactly the same words, see Matthew 3:17.

2. *Summa christenlicher Religion. Darinn uß dem wort Gottes one alles zancken und schälten richtig und Kurtz anzeigt wirt was einem yetlichen Christen notwendig sye zů glouben zů thůn und zů lassen ouch zůlyden und sáligklich abzůsterben* (Zurich, 1556), f.rii^v. *HBBibl* I, no. 283.

this question by proclaiming the one in whom he is pleased and through whom he has established his relationship with humanity. Yet, the keen eye will note that the version of the text which appears on the title page of Bullinger's printed works is not a direct quotation from scripture, for the verb "to be pleased" has been intentionally replaced with "to be reconciled" (*versôhnen*).[3] The alteration is easily overlooked, but it is not insignificant, and in this change we find an interpretive moment that reveals a central theme in Bullinger's understanding of the Christian life. The Latin version of Bullinger's motto has a slightly different emphasis and reads, "This is my beloved son in whom my soul is reconciled; listen to him."[4] To listen means both to be attentive and to obey, and this captures the essential character of Bullinger's spirituality–the co-operation or partnership between God and humanity.

Without doubt, the reconciliation of God and humanity was a gracious act of divine provenance, entirely unmerited–on this Bullinger would yield no ground. Yet, within the vast corpus of vernacular literature that Bullinger produced during his tenure in Zurich we find the reformer in a different key. Bullinger stretches the essentially Augustinian framework of his theology to focus on the human response to the divine act of communication and to aver human activity in the partnership offered by God.[5] The imperative voice of *audire (horen)* captures Bullinger's sense that God has reached across the divide to form a partnership with humanity. Shaped by words and actions, in which each person bears responsibility for living the Christian life, the use of the verb "to listen" unites the passive and active elements of the human response. God speaks (reveals) and the human person first receives passively, but this passivity then gives way to an active response, the reply of gratitude. Rejecting pure quiescence on the part of humanity, Bullinger strove to find a vocabulary for human activity in the face of an omnipotent, omniscient God.

Our understanding of Matthew 17:5, which Bullinger wore as a spiritual badge through his long years as head of the Zurich church, requires attention to the full biblical account of the transfiguration. Christ brings Peter, James, and John to a mountain where he appears, clad in white, conversing with Moses and Elijah: Moses represents the old covenant to be fulfilled in the death of Jesus, while Elijah is the restorer of all things. The scene ends with Christ's explanation of the Old Testament prophecy to the three Apostles; he grimly predicts that his will be the way of suffering.

The importance of Matthew 17:5 to Bullinger is evident when we look to the interpretation offered by Zwingli in his last, and most significant, theological work, the *Fidei expositio* of 1531. In his treatment of the forgiveness of sins, Zwingli refers to the parallel passages of Matthew 17:5 and 3:17 (John's baptism of Christ) as unequivocal proof that God alone can and has forgiven the sins of

3. The 1531 Zurich Bible version of Matthew 17:5 reads: "Das ist mein lieber sun in welchem ich ein wohlgefallen haben, dem sôllen ir gehôrig sein."
4. "Hic est filius meus delectus in quo placata est anima mea, ipsum audite." Bullinger's versions of the German and Latin became standard in the Zurich Bibles after 1534.
5. On Bullinger's vernacular literature see Bruce Gordon, "'welcher nit glouPt der ist schon verdampt': Heinrich Bullinger and the Spirituality of the Last Judgement," *Zwingliana* 29 (2002): 31, note 10.

the faithful. For Zwingli, God has announced that Christ is his son, and it is on account of his pleasure in him that his mercy will be upon those who stand in Christ. It was a proclamation to the whole world, therefore "it cannot be, that they [the people] do not know that to them who trust in God the mercy of the forgiveness of sins has been given through Jesus Christ, who is our Lord and Brother."[6] The formulation is typically Zwinglian and carries the essential dualistic argument that both shaped the nature of the Zurich church and formed the basis of Bullinger's pastoral message. God has spoken to humanity with unmistakable clarity; responsibility now rests with each individual as to whether he/she will live in faith or perish in unbelief.[7] Through the thousands of pages of his printed works this, for Bullinger, remained the essential point. He saw the world as divided between the saved and the damned, separated by one crucial distinction–faith in Christ. This perspective informed every word and phrase that Bullinger preached and wrote. He took little interest in the infernal fate of those who rejected God–though from the 1550s he did not shy from threatening those who opposed him with damnation–but devoted himself to the formulation of a vocabulary of spirituality for the faithful.[8]

The significance of the transfiguration for Bullinger is further explained by the iconic roles played by Moses and Elijah, who were interpreted by the Zurich reformers in a manner indicative of the way in which they read the Old and New Testaments. In his 1554 commentary on Matthew Bullinger discusses the appearance of Moses and Elijah as the joint witnesses of the law and the prophets to the reality that Christ is the Son of God.[9] The *Prophezei* in Zurich was devoted to the exposition of the Hebrew Bible, and the fruits of its early labours of the 1520s became apparent in 1531 with the publication of the Zurich Bible, which contained the newly translated books of the Old Testament.[10] The Hebrew Bible was read in Zurich, as it was in the Upper Rhine textual community, in a highly Christological manner.[11] This is most evident in Bullinger's theological and pastoral writings, where he marshalled scriptural evidence by placing texts from the Old and New Testaments alongside one another in order to demonstrate the way in which the Old prefigures the New, and that the New holds the interpretative key to the Old. In their treatment of the Old Testament the Zurich writers showed great eagerness to detect the presence of Christ in the ancient prophecies.[12]

6. *"Fidei expositio,"* Z VI.5 In his exposition, Zwingli uses the Latin translation "Hic est filius meus dilectus, in quo placor."

7. Bullinger's notes are found in two volumes, ZB, Ms. Car 152 and 153. I am grateful to Dr Urs Leu of the ZB, who brought these notes to my attention.

8. Gordon, "Spirituality of the Last Judgement," 49-50.

9. *In sacrosantum Iesu Christi Domini nostri evangelium secundum Matthaeum, Commentariorum libri XII per Heinrychum Bullingerum* (Zurich, 1554), 166ᵛ-167ʳ.

10. Traudel Himmighöfer, *Die Zürcher Bibel bis zum Tode Zwinglis (1531). Darstellung und Bibliographie* (Veröffentlichungen des Instituts für Europäische Geschichte Mainz, Abteilung Religionsgeschichte 154; Mainz: von Zabern, 1995, 154).

11. On this understanding of the Bible, see Bernard Roussel, "La Bible de 1530 à 1600" in Guy Bedouelle/Bernard Roussel eds, *Le temps des Réformes et la Bible* (Paris: Beauchesne, 1989), 125-289.

12. On Hebrew scholarship in Zurich, see Christoph Zürcher, *Konrad Pellikans Wirken in Zürich* (Zurich: TVZ, 1975).

Bullinger's version of Matthew 17 declared the unambiguous Christocentrism of the Zurich church. Commentators on Bullinger's theology rarely fail to note the centrality of the life and work of Christ in his writings.[13] Much of the story of Bullinger's tenure as head of the Zurich church involved disputes relating to the person of Christ: the Lutheran accusation of Nestorianism, the Anabaptist controversy over the Christian life, and the anti-trinitarian debates of the 1550s and 1560s.[14] This long and wearisome series of battles was mapped in Bullinger's work: in his theological writings he strove to affirm the doctrines of the ancient councils of the church, in particular the Chalcedonian formulation of Christ's natures,[15] in the endless dispute with the Lutherans over the Lord's Supper Bullinger sought to explain how Christ was physically at the right hand of the Father while spiritually present in the sacrament; the Christian life, in Bullinger's eyes, was a process by which a person becomes more "Christ-like" and "in Christ."[16]

The use of Matthew 17:5 was neither a decorous platitude nor a humanist confection, but rather expressed the heart of Bullinger's Christocentric spirituality. The textual dynamic lies in the relationship between speaking and hearing. God speaks and humanity must hear. There is a delicate balance of the imperative and the voluntary that attempts to resolve the tension between the absolute authority and power of God and human responsibility and action. This emphasis on verbal communication was a particular theme for the Zurich reformers who devoted themselves to the Word and words. The human response is determined by the command "listen to him," but for Bullinger listening was also freedom; it offered the opportunity to work in co-operation with God.

Although Bullinger's language of spirituality was grounded in the co-operative relationship between God and humanity, it was not his intention to suggest that this was in any way a partnership of equals. Nevertheless, Bullinger presents a robust defence of human agency that asserts, even in the face of an essentially Augustinian position on the fallen nature of humanity, that there is a role for men and women in salvation. Spirituality, therefore, occupies the shadowy land between the two poles of Bullinger's thought: the supreme sovereignty of God and the depravity of humanity. In his vernacular writings from the mid-1530s Bullinger sought to forge a language for the Christian that balanced divine power and human responsibility.[17] This involved a mixture of active and passive

---

13. Joachim Staedtke, *Die Theologie des jungen Bullinger* (Studien zur Dogmengeschichte und systematischen Theologie 16; Zurich: Zwingli Verlag, 1962), 140-200.

14. See in particular Mark Taplin, *The Italian Reformers and the Zurich Church c. 1540-1620* (Aldershot: Ashgate, 2003).

15. See Mark Taplin's essay in this volume.

16. On this last point, see Mark S. Burrows, "'Christus intra nos Vivens'. The Peculiar Genius of Bullinger's Doctrine of Sanctification," *Zeitschrift für Kirchengeschichte* 98 (1978): 48-69.

17. Most of these printed works were taken from his sermons. During the 1550s in particular there was a torrent of vernacular pastoral works from Bullinger's hand on all aspects of the Christian life. Examples of such works are: *Von rechter Hilfe und Erretung in Nöten* (1552), *Von wahrem beständigen Glauben* (1552), *Von der Verklärung Christi* (1552), *Von rechter Buße oder Besserung des sündigen Menschen* (1553), *Vom heiligen Nachtmal* (1553), *Vom Heil der Glaübigen* (1555), *Das Jüngste Gericht* (1555), *Bericht, wie die Verfolgten antworten sollen* (1559), *Von der Bekerung des Menschen zu Gott* (1569), *Wider die schwarzen Künste* (1570),

language and a wide range of metaphors, none of which were to be understood as terms of systematic theology. In the vernacular Bullinger found the malleable vocabulary by which he could express his pastoral message.

The terms "Christian life" or "spirituality" are not part of Bullinger's language, and, indeed, they imply a modern attitude wholly foreign to him. Nevertheless, with their suggestion of the distinction between the meditative and the active, the two terms do help us to understand the manner in which he treats religion in his pastoral works. In the fifth sermon of the fourth decade Bullinger comes to speak of "adoration." He describes, in true Zwinglian fashion, the means by which the body expresses the spiritual adoration of the heart:

> Because the outward gesture or habit of the body is commonly framed according to the inward quality of the mind, and the outward habit of the his body which addores submits, yields, and makes subject him that worships to him who is worshipped; therefore adoration is translated likewise to the inner man: so that to adore is to reverence and respect God, to bequeath ourselves wholly unto him, and to cleave inseparably unto him, upon him only and alone to hang in all things, and to have recourse unto him in all our necessities whatsoever.[18]

True adoration flows from the heart, and the true friendship of Christ and the believer is an inward, spiritual relationship given expression in prayer. Yet, the transforming power of this relationship must extend to the body and actions in the world. The Christian life, if Bullinger were to use that term, could be described as the realisation in the world of that interiority, which we call spirituality.

The central metaphor used by Bullinger to describe the life of a Christan is of a "trial" (*Bewährung*). This image can be, and is, deployed in several ways. Fundamentally, it refers to the daily suffering of individuals in a hostile world. Although Bullinger had a humanist's interest in the curiosities of creation, and a fascination for history, he did not at all share Calvin's sense of the wondrousness of the world.[19] For Bullinger, creation is a dark vale dominated by demonic forces and populated by unbelievers, for whom there can be no salvation; salvation can only come from an external, alien light that penetrates the darkness of sin. The dualist language characteristic of Zwingli runs strong in Bullinger's vernacular writings: only God is good, whilst all that is created reeks of sin, and consequently there is distinct repugnance for the material and bodily. The love of God redeems, transforms, and fills those who receive his grace. Faith and love are hardly separated, for it is love that is the first fruit of faith; it is love that creates the possibility of relationships:

Von höchster Freud und größtem Leid des jüngsten Tages (1572), *Von der schweren Verfolgung der christlichen Kirchen* (1573), *Predigten über den 130. und 133. Psalm* (1574).

18. *The Decades of Henry Bullinger*, translated [from the Latin], Thomas Harding ed., 4 vols (Parker Society; Cambridge: CUP, 1849-2), decade IV.v.199. All quotations from the *Decades* are taken from the Parker Society translation.

19. On this point see the essay by Christian Moser in this volume. On Calvin, see William J. Bouwsma, *Calvin. A Sixteenth-Century Portrait* (Oxford: OUP, 1988), 168-70.

The love of God works in us a will to frame ourselves wholly to the will and ordinances of him whom we love most heartily. Certainly, it is pleasant and sweet to him that loves God to do that which he perceives acceptable to God, if it be done. He that loves reverences in his heart the one whom he loves. His eye is never off the one he loves. In always and in all things he wishes for his beloved. His only joy is to talk with God and to hear the words of God again as he speaks in scripture.[20]

Clinging, cleaving, grasping–these are the terms used by Bullinger to describe the physicality of the relationship between the believer and God. Each person must hold on for dear life as one progresses through the dark wood of human existence. At the same time, that tenuous physical hold on God is balanced by the manner in which the believer is in love with God. The eye does not wander and the two wills become one.

The image of the trial is also integral to Bullinger's explanation for the presence of suffering in the world. In short, suffering exists on account of sin as both a punishment a nd a test. In his vernacular, pastoral work Bullinger deftly shifts the image of God he wishes to bring before the people: the loving, patriarchal God who offers his Son for all of humanity frequently gives way to the Old Testament vision of the punishing God who pours down his wrath upon the faithful and unfaithful alike. Bullinger frequently alights upon the subject of death, never failing to remind his audience that mortality is the price of sin, and that sin has a terrible human cost: plagues, illness, war, and destitution.[21] At the same time, he also saw the hand of God testing the faithful in a Job-like manner. Those who respond by demonstrating their complete trust in Christ will survive, but their reward will not be in this world, a point that Bullinger made to the French refugees after the Massacre of St Bartholomew's Day, when he counselled patience in the face of adversity.[22] Human suffering is not redemptive, but serves to remind men and women of their separation from God.[23] In this world it is a rod for the backs of believers and non-believers alike, with the sole distinction that for those with faith it is an essential preliminary stage of spiritual development. It excoriates any faith in the self or human ability and leads to the essential recognition that

20. *Decades*, decade 1.x. 182.

21. Hans Ulrich Bächtold, "Gegen den Hunger beten. Heinrich Bullinger, Zürich und die Einführung des Gemeinen Gebetes im Jahre 1571" in Hans Ulrich Bächtold, Rainer Henrich, and Kurt Jakob Rüetschi eds, *Vom Beten, von Verketzern, vom Predigen. Beiträge zum Zeitalter Heinrich Bullingers und Rudolf Gwalthers* (Zug: Achius, 1999), 9-44; Bruce Gordon, "'God killed Saul': Heinrich Bullinger and Jacob Ruef on the Power of the Devil" in Kathryn Edwards ed., *Werewolves, Witches and Wandering Spirits. Traditional Belief and Folklore in Early Modern Europe* (Kirksville: Truman State University Press, 2002), 155-79.

22. *Von der schweren langwirigen verfolgung der Heiligen Christlichen Kirchen* (Zurich, 1573), *HBBibl* I, no. 575.

23. Although Bullinger wrote to the French Protestants towards the end of his life, this was by no means the first time he had treated the theme of human suffering. In 1552 he printed a sermon on Matthew 18 entitled *Von rechter Hilfe und Errettung in Nöten* (Zurich, 1552) *HBBibl* I, no. 260. The sermon was directed towards German Protestants during the tumultuous period of the Interim. Seven years later, in 1569, he published a work with sixty-one questions on how a Christian should answer a persecutor, *Bericht, wie die Verfolgten antworten sollen* (Zurich, 1559), *HBBibl* I, no. 386.

God alone is good. Yet even as a first step towards the Christian life human suffering can only have meaning when united to the efficacious suffering of God's Son. This unity is brought about by the conversion of the person to God by which, in Bullinger's almost mystical language, there is a fusion with Christ. At that point human suffering is made holy.

The prominence of suffering in Zurich theology is largely a post-Zwingli phenomenon, and, indeed, it may have had much to do with the catastrophe of 1531. Zwingli had written on the subject in his 1523 *Exposition of the Articles*, but it was not central to his conception of the Christian life.[24] Rather, the theme of Christ's suffering (*leiden* or *lyden Christi*) emerges prominently in the 1530s in the work of Leo Jud, whose devotional and pedagogical writings deeply influenced the young Bullinger.[25] Jud appropriated the medieval Passional to the Reformed tradition in his 1534 work *On the suffering of Christ*, an extensive devotional treatment.[26] The language that he used became central to the spiritual vocabulary of the Zurich writers. It was during the 1530s, when Jud and Bullinger worked together closely in the preparation of devotional texts for the clergy and laity, that the distinctive spirituality of the Zwinglian reformers took shape.

In line with late-medieval thought, Bullinger preached and wrote that human suffering reflected God's nearness, not distance, and that it must be borne in imitation of Christ, without complaint.[27] Suffering forms part of the passive element of the relationship between God and humanity and is reflected in the key terms used by Bullinger to denote how it should be endured by the Christian: patience (*geduld*), obedience (*gehorsamkeit*), and humility (*demut*). These terms express aspects of the virtues of Christ, and they are to be imitated, a concept that Bullinger repeatedly uses and which may well have come from Jud.[28] Imitation is not mere emulation but a unitative engagement of both the senses and the intellect with the object imitated. Thus, for Bullinger, this entailed an entering into Christ through the rejection of the self. This repudiation brings into view an apparent tension or even contradiction, for whilst Bullinger's spirituality is clearly an attack on the self, the form of imitation and the relationship with Christ is mediated through the language of human emotions. These emotions have been ennobled by the life of Christ. Denial of the natural self creates new possibilities, however, such as friendship (*freundschaft*) and the reception of the fullness of Christ

24. Zwingli's most significant treatment of suffering is found in article 18 of the *Exposition*, Z II:111-57.

25. On this see Bruce Gordon, "Transcendence and Community in Zwinglian worship: the Liturgy of 1525 in Zurich" in R.W. Swanson ed., *Continuity and Change in Christian Worship* (Studies in Church History 35; Bury St Edmunds: Boydell and Brewer, 1999), 128-50.

26. *Des lyden Jesu Christi Gantze uss den vier Evangelistenn geeinigte historia mit Christlicher klarer und einfalter usslegung, darinn die frucht und nachvolg dess lydens Christi angezeigt, ouch mit geistrychenn gebaetten geprysen unnd gelobt wirdt, Geschriben durch Leonem Jude, diener des worts der kilchen Zürich* (Zurich, 1534).

27. On late-medieval concepts of suffering, see Caroline Bynum Walker, *Fragmentation and Redemption. Essays on Gender and the Human Body in Medieval Religion* (New York: Zone Books, 1992), and Mitchell B. Merback, *The Thief, the Cross, and the Wheel. Pain and the Spectacle of Punishment in Medieval and Renaissance Europe* (London: Reaktion Books, 1999).

28. On imitation, see Staedtke, *Theologie des jungen Bullinger*, 213-4.

(*Vollkommenheit*).[29] The transformation of the self from an "I" (ego), which sees the world through its own immediate concerns, to a self which is lodged in Christ is achieved through conversion.

This Christian life, therefore, has two convergent dynamics. It is a battle against evil in the world in which each person seeks to withstand the assaults of the devil, who constantly works to undermine the faith of God's elect. At the same time, it is also a process of conversion in the Augustinian sense. The purpose of the Christian life is to realise God's Word in the world, to take it from the page of the Bible and allow it to dwell in the inner person from where it will guide the outer actions of that person.

What gives both trial and conversion their legitimacy is their place in God's Word, the unity and coherence of which is, for Bullinger, the absolute foundation of the Christian life. This belief is reflected in the schematic outline of his theology, the organisation of his loci, in which the preeminence of the Word of God is reflected. Scripture was always the first locus to be treated.[30] For Bullinger the whole relationship with God's Word involved movement, the transmission from the printed word of the Bible to its realisation in the world through the mediation of the Spirit. This made the humanist disciplines of textual analysis, translation, and communication (rhetoric) integral to the Christian life. This found expression in the *Prophezei*, which has rightly been identified as the heart of the Zwinglian church.[31] Although this institution evolved into a school for prospective ministers, the original concept remained intact. Recent work on the *Prophezei* has placed less emphasis on its role as an educational institution and more on its character as a fraternity of learned men committed to the exegesis of the Old Testament in the service of the church. It was a community of prayer, a model, according to Zwingli and Bullinger, of what God requires of humanity. In the *Prophezei* we find the confluence of humanist, *Devotio moderna*, and Cistercian influence. It was devoted to what Thomas à Kempis called "useful learning," employing the humanist tools of philology and textual exegesis with reverence for the scriptures. The end, however, lay with the application of the scriptural message to daily life, and that is why the final stage of the *Prophezei's* work was a vernacular sermon in which the lay people could be instructed in the meaning of

29. Bulliger devoted a whole work to the subject of Christian perfection (*Vollkommenheit*) in his *Der Christenheit rechte volkommenheit* (Zurich, 1551), *HBBibl* I, no. 251. The work was intended as a "summa" of the life of Christ to demonstrate that he was sent as the saviour of humanity and to serve as the perfect example of godly living. On Bullinger's understanding of *Vollkommenheit*, see Staedtke, *Theologie des jungen Bullinger*, 212-3. Staedtke sees this as an example of how Bullinger reworked classic elements of *Devotio moderna* theology.

30. On this point see Ernst Koch, "Die Heilslehre der Confessio Helvetica Posterior" in Joachim Staedtke ed., *Glauben und Bekennen: vierhundert Jahre Confessio Helvetica Posterior* (Zurich: Zwingli Verlag, 1966), 278-99.

31. Himmighöfer, *Die Zürcher Bibel bis zum Tode Zwinglis*; Fritz Büsser, *Die Prophezei. Humanismus und Reformation in Zürich. Ausgewählte Aufsätze und Vorträge. Zu seinem 70. Geburtstag am 12. Februar 1993* (ZBRG 17; Berne: Peter Lang, 1994); Michael Baumann und Rainer Henrich, "Das Lektorium, sein Lehrkörper, seine Studenten" in Hans Ulrich Bächtold ed., *Schola Tigurina. Die Zürcher Hohe Schule und ihre Gelehrten um 1550. Katalog zur Ausstellung vom 25. Mai bis 10. Juli 1999 in der Zentralbibliothek Zürich* (Zurich/Freiburg i. Br.: Pano, 1999), 24-27; Karin Maag, *Seminary or University*, 130-3; Gordon, *Swiss Reformation*, 232-9.

an Old Testament passage for them.

Essentially what emerged from the biblical exegesis of the *Prophezei* was a model for the Christian life. It is the activation of the Word in the world through the inspiration of the Spirit and it takes place within the community, or fraternity, of scholars committed to the common cause of Christ's church. Scholarship and the Christian life cannot be separated because both depend upon the Spirit. Yet, for Bullinger and his circle in Zurich, scholarship was the essential underpinning for the creation of the Christian community because through translation and biblical exegesis the Word is made digestible for men and women, who receive it in sermons, catechisms, and (where possible) in reading the Bible. Biblical exegesis, conducted under the guidance of the Spirit, reveals the mode of living demanded by God. The external transmission from scripture to the message preached initiates the inward movement towards conversion of the believer:

> Now there is no one who is so blind who cannot see that the preaching or doctrine of the truth is required to stir up repentance in us, to teach us what God is and to whom we must be turned; what the goodness and holiness is to which we must be turned; who the devil is, what evil and wickedness is, from which we must be turned. And lastly, what it is in our minds and lives which must be amended, and how it is to be altered and amended.[32]

Bullinger saw the Christian life as involving the recovery of the whole person. It creates the possibility of harmony between that person's inner and exterior natures in order that words and deeds reflect the thoughts of the heart. The route to this balancing of the inner and outer person is through a self-knowledge which is, following Augustine, nothing other than coming to know one's self as one is known by God. A person comes to this standpoint through self-examination, which is a judging of one's self by the standard by which God judges humanity: scripture. Scripture reveals God's judgement as well as his commandments on how to live, and each person must confront the crucial decision as to whether he/she will accept it. Against the backdrop of his predestinarian thought, Bullinger stresses the momentous nature of this decision. To accept scripture as God's Word is to place one's life outside one's self, to make it subject to the divine perspective alone.

Near the end of his life Bullinger dedicated a work to the subject of conversion and in many ways the text forms a useful summary of his writing and preaching on the subject.[33] The small work consists of a series of sermons on Acts 8, the story of the Ethiopian eunuch, and it is one of Bullinger's most powerful and extensive considerations of the themes of conversion and spirituality. Conversion, he begins, can happen at any moment in a person's life–the place and timing are entirely up to God. Those who are converted, however, are only those who have been predestined by God to eternal life, who are few in number,

---

32. *Decades*, decade IV, ii, 56.

33. *Von der Bekerung deß menschen zů Gott und dem waaren Glouben vi. Predigen gethon von Heinrychen Bullingeren dieneren der kyrchen Züyrch über das 8. Capitel der Geschichten der heiligen Apostlen von der Bekeerung deß Herren uß Morenland durch den heiligen Apostlen Philippum...* (Zurich, 1569), *HBBibl* I, no. 561.

and who are made holy by the "free election and mercy of God."[34] Conversion, therefore, is the actualisation of a possibility created by God. Yet, there is a crucial human element in the process, for men and women are brought to God by the preaching of ministers, whose principal role is to facilitate conversions (*die menschen zuo bekeeren*). Bullinger's extremely high view of preaching is well known, culminating in his title for section four of the *Second Helvetic Confession*: "To Preach the Word of God, Is the Word of God."[35] The appropriate response of the individual to the Word and to the minister is obedience and thanksgiving.[36] Philip in seeking to convert the Ethiopian provides an example for all Christians who are bound to bring others to Christ through scripture:

> Firstly, and most crucially, we desire from God that he grant us in our hearts the spirit by which he fills Holy Scripture; and that he inwardly illuminates us with true understanding and outwardly provides us with accounts of God-fearing men and true teaching, which open us to the true understanding of his Word.[37]

The centrality of scripture requires that it be properly interpreted:

> The correct, true conversion is based on the proper knowledge of Jesus Christ, namely that we through scripture understand and know that God has given his son to us poor sinners for our salvation, reconciliation, and sanctification, and it is through him that we have our sins removed, justification, all mercy and goodness and eternal life.[38]

The reward of this conversion is the fullness of Christ, which Bullinger refers to as a form of "perfection" in Christ (*volkommenheit in Christo*). This perfection does not imply that the faithful do not remain sinners, but rather that they have obtained a fullness of unity with Christ in which that person is utterly focused on God, who provides for everything. "They turn to God and his Son alone with their whole hearts...."[39] The key to this is the imitation of Christ's humiliation (*erniderung*) on the cross:

> Those who understand and believe that they have been raised up by the humiliation of Christ and saved by his suffering and death from eternal death and suffering will no longer be outraged by Christ's humiliation. For they will now understand that the humiliation and suffering of Christ are the true means to sal-

---

34. Ibid., f. cvi^v.
35. Bullinger's own comment on the statement "To preach the word of God, is the word of God" reads as follows: "Wherefore when this Word of God is now preached in the church by preachers lawfully called, we believe that the very Word of God is proclaimed, and received by the faithful; and that neither any other Word of God is to be invented nor is expected from heaven: and that now the Word itself which is preached is to be regarded, not the minister that preaches; for even if he be evil and a sinner, nevertheless the Word of God remains true and good." (*Second Helvetic Confession*, chap. 1, section 4).
36. *Von der Bekerung*, f. biii^v.
37. Ibid., f. dii^v
38. Ibid., f. ei^i.
39. Ibid., f. ei^v.

vation. Now they will be thankful.[40]

In humiliating himself Christ purifies each believer. This word purity *(reinigkeit)* forms a central part of Bullinger's language and echoes the Zwinglian commonplace that each person must be pure as God is pure. Christ has made humiliation the way of the Christian, who in imitating him not only participates in the gift of grace but also redeems his/her own existence. Christ's humiliation led to the purification of the faithful: they, in turn, purify themselves through the rejection of the self and the ways of the world. Human activity is not separate from the divine, but is made holy through proper imitation.

The suffering of Christ is not an abstract ideal, for Christ was beaten, pierced, bled, and suffered in agony, and he did this for each person. Bullinger continuously emphasises both the reality of Christ's suffering and the fact that human sin was its cause. Christ's suffering was deeply personal. He endured it for each man and women, and the memory and contemplation of the suffering of Christ confronts every man and women with the horror of what was done for them. It is not sufficient to believe that Christ is the Redeemer, but one must take to heart that he is a personal Redeemer.[41]

To deny the human dimension of suffering on the cross was, according to Bullinger, tantamount to a rejection of the Christ who, according to scripture, suffered physically and spiritually. In his description of the wounds of Christ we find some of the most powerful language in Bullinger's writings.[42] Both Heinrich Bullinger and Leo Jud could convey a sense of tears and rage when contrasting the physicality of Christ's sacrifice with humanity's indifference. The water and blood that flowed from Christ's side on the cross were, for Bullinger, the essence of life and purification:

> As blood preserves life and water cleanses and purifies, so we have from the suffering and death of Christ the cleansing *(reiniget)* of our sins and eternal life. The wounds of Christ are our guarantee of the redemption of our sins.[43]

Christ is not only the sacrificial offer for the sins of humanity, but also the example to all Christians of how they should face their trials, for he demonstrated "the greatest humility, wonderful patience and obedience",[44] and "he provided all the faithful with an example of how they should conduct themselves in all their suffering."[45] Herein lies the essential difference between human and divine suffering. At best, those who have suffered on account of their faith are examples to others; their suffering is not efficacious. Bullinger quotes Pope Leo on the martyrs of the Church:

"Although the death of many saints is precious in the sight of the Lord, yet the

40. Ibid., f. evii[v]
41. Ibid., f. gv[r].
42. Ibid., f. gv[v]
43. Ibid., f. gviii[r]
44. Ibid., f. hv[v]
45. Ibid., f. hvi[r]

127

slaughter of no man in the state of sin is the propitiation for the sins of the world." Again "The righteous have received, not given, the crowns of glory: and of the great constancy of the martyrs have sprung many examples of patience, not the gifts of righteousness: for their deaths were singular; neither did any one of his ending pay the debt of another, since there is one Lord Jesus Christ, in whom they are all crucified, dead, buried, and raised up again."[46]

In the *Decades* Bullinger reiterates a point that he would continue to make throughout his life. God has ordained three things as essential for a true church: the preaching of the Word, prayers, and the administration of the sacraments.[47] Prayer, the sacraments, good works, and the good death form, for Bullinger, the active side of the Christian life. Without doubt, however, it is prayer that he regarded as the foundation of spiritual living. Bullinger follows Zwingli in his appropriation of Augustine's definition of prayer as "the lifting up of the heart to God."[48] Prayer is a work of faith. In his extensive treatment of prayer in the *Summa*, Bullinger reviews the biblical evidence, beginning with the Old Testament and moving through the Gospels and Epistles.[49] From this he draws the preliminary conclusion: "Prayer is nothing other than a heartfelt or inner (*einbrustig*) dialogue of the heart with God whereby the faithful seek something from God... and give praise and thanks."[50] The word dialogue is crucial. Bullinger's understanding of the Christian life as human co-operation with God is grounded in the essential dialogue between the two partners. Prayer is the conscious articulation of the human response with two components: praise and thanksgiving. God is to be praised as the source of all goodness, while each Christian must give thanks for his mercy. Bullinger's draws his guidelines for praying from Philippians 4.[51]

Prayer is the first act of obedience and must be offered by Christians alone, with the family, as well as publicly in church. Although it is the first obligation, it cannot be strictly ordered. Bullinger argues that the location, timing, and form of prayer belong to the freedom of a Christian, for these are matters of the Spirit and depend on necessity (*notturfft*) and devotion (*andacht*). This freedom, however, does not extend to the option of not praying, for the liberty of the Christian is not contempt for God (*verachtung gottes*). The Christian has no claim on God. This relationship is a dialogue initiated by God, and for a person to enter it he/she must have a disposition grounded in humility (*demut*), lowliness (*niederträchtigkeit*), and nothingness (*nichtigkeit*). The starting point must be a confession of sin and recognition of God's grace. Bullinger cites the prayer of Daniel, who begins his supplications with fasting, sackcloth, and ashes.[52]

Whenever he discusses prayer in his pastoral works Bullinger raises an objection he must have encountered innumerable times as a minister: why, if it is nec-

---

46. *Decades,* decade IV, ii, 95.
47. Ibid., decade V, v, 165. At the start of Bullinger's treatment of prayer.
48. On Zwingli and prayer, see Samuel Lutz, *Ergib dich ihm ganz - Huldrych Zwinglis Gebet als Ausdruck seiner Frömmigkeit und Theologie* (Zurich: TVZ, 1993), 15.
49. *Summa christenlicher Religion.* f. vi[v].
50. Ibid., f. qi[r].
51. The key text is Philippians 4:6: "The Lord is near: have no anxiety, but in everything make your requests known to God in prayer and petition with thanksgiving."
52. *Summa christenlicher Religion,* f.qii[v]. The prayer is found in Daniel 9:4-27.

essary to pray, does God often seem deaf to those prayers? His reply, this time from the *Decades*, is characteristic:

> Therefore, when we are not delivered, and do not obtain our desires, it is certain that God so desires it, and that it is profitable for us that this should be. By this means he hears our prayers, when he hears us: for our prayers tend only to the end that things go well for us. God, since he is only wise, knows what can profit and what can hurt us, and does not give us what we ask. Yet by not giving us what we ask he is granting what is good for us. Therefore, the lawful prayer of the faithful is always effectual and obtains its purpose: the Lord grants to his that which he knows to be good.[53]

Prayer is about the divine and human wills. It is the means by which men and women acknowledge and meditate upon God's goodness and mercy. Bullinger is most concerned to demonstrate that what matters most about prayer is that it be offered freely and in faith. In prayer God seeks a partner who enters into the dialogue willingly (*frywilliger diener*). Yet, as in all other aspects of his spirituality, Bullinger treats prayer as having a purgative quality. As a person progresses in prayer there is a diminishing need for external props and structures. Maturing in prayer involves a casting off of the self and of language itself; eventually it is a unity of the heart with Christ for which Bullinger uses the term *vereinigt*. All prayer, properly, is "from the heart" (*in irem hertzen*) but, in its highest form, it should imitate the silent, contemplative prayer following the example of Christ (*nach byspil Christi*). It becomes a more immediate relationship that Bullinger characterises as friendship. Prayer is the language of a friendship that is signified in the world through the sacraments and works of love.

Bullinger explicitly speaks of how the sacraments act as visual expression of the world of prayer:

> The Lord has established this meal (*Nachtmal*) in order that the church might retain a fresh memory of his death through which he redeemed, fed, watered, and saved us. He wishes that we should do what he has taught us to do, that we should believe, praise him and give thanks.[54]

The believer receives the body of Christ in a spiritual manner, for although Christ had a human body and suffered physically on the cross, he, in the classic Zwinglian formulation, is now physically at the right hand of the Father. His presence in the world, therefore, cannot be through any visible form, but in the hearts of the faithful alone, to whom, through the Holy Spirit, he communicates all the benefits of his "holy body" and suffering:

> It is also a sacramental eating not only when the believer has inner faith that Christ's death is his life but also when from outer faith he comes to the Lord's Table or at the Lord's Supper sits and obediently and joyfully receives the meal according to His Word as a sacrament of the true body and blood of Christ,

---

53. *Decades*, decade V, v, 171.
54. *Summa christenlicher Religion*, f. uvi^v-vvii^r.

which for his salvation was given for him on the cross and poured out.[55]

The Lord's Supper also reminds Christians of their duties and of the unitive power of love:

> In the Lord's Supper we are also reminded of our duty (*pflicht*) and obligation (*schuld*), that we are a community of Christ which has been purified through the body and blood of Christ and which lives in Christ (*yngelybet*). Therefore we also eat from the bread and drink from the cup drink so that we might promise our brothers and sisters that we are one with them and that we will serve them in love.[56]

In eating and drinking together the community is united in the Holy Spirit. For Bullinger the sacraments reflect the equality of all believers and are the principal means of reconciliation within the body of believers. He retained a particularly Swiss attitude in that baptism and the Lord's Supper indicate citizenship in Christ's church and that in their performance one makes a powerful public statement of one's love of God and neighbour. The power of the Spirit in signifiers was for Bullinger very real; the same force that draws together the parishioners as one body also enables the fraternity of scholars to interpret and explicate God's Word.

In prayer a person expresses gratitude and repentance, while through the bread and wine he/she is fed and united with fellow Christians in faith. To this must be added the subject that dominates many of Bullinger's vernacular texts on the Christian life: good works. Although he never wavered from his Augustinian understanding of salvation, Bullinger was deeply sensitive to the criticism that predestination could engender spiritual arrogance, contempt, or even despair. Good works formed an essential aspect of human co-operation, for through these works God's love was to be realised in the world. In commenting on 1 Peter I and Acts 15 Bullinger states that God has made our hearts pure through faith, but with that purity comes the command that each person must do good works. Failure to act in the world is contempt for God's forgiveness:

> The faithful should at all times, in particular when in danger and *wiederwartig-keit*, trust God the almighty, then they should call out in all their requests, thanksgiving for all that is good. Then they should devote (*ergeben*) and offer themselves (to God) and walk only according to his will, abandoning their own will and rejoicing in him alone. These are above all the greatest (*allerherrlich-sten*) works of faith.[57]

Good works come from an ordered life. They are, on the one hand, acts of love towards others, and, on the other, a means of constraining the flesh. Bullinger transfers the mystical language of purgation into the world, describing how a person is made holy through the doing of God's commandments. The two terms

---

55. Ibid., f. uviii[v].
56. Ibid., f. viiii[i].
57. Ibid., f. xiv[v].

that he employs are redemption (*heiligung*) and purification (*reinigung*): both liberate from the flesh (*fleisch tufel*) and the world. Without this purgative process no one will see God. These two terms, however, are not the same and Bullinger adds, mindful of the Anabaptists, that God has not primarily called humanity to purity, but to redemption. The Christian life is essentially a battle against the devil, the world, and the flesh and is above all a life of penitence (*bussfertig laeben*). In the third decade good works are treated under the rubric of "Christian liberty". Bullinger writes:

> Now, therefore, we said that good works are indeed wrought by them that are regenerate, to the glory of God, the ornament of our life, and the profit of our neighbour. For the Lord in the Gospel prescribes this end to good works when he said, "Let your light so shine before men, that they may see your good works, and glorify your Father which is in heaven." ...For it is true, that the apostles of Christ sought to persuade us to put off the old man and put on the new which is created in the image and likeness of God. ....And as he requires good works at our hands, so, if we do them, we on the one hand please and delight him, and, on the other, he honours us again, as may be proved by many testimonies of holy scripture. [58]

This passage touches on essential Bullinger themes: the faithful doing God's will because they are created in his image, and, the reciprocity between God and humanity. God honours those who do that which pleases him–a powerful echo of Bullinger's motto from Matthew 17:3. Each person can become the "son" in whom the Father is well pleased.

Those who refuse this way live in what Bullinger describes as *Mutwillen*, a sort of rash mischievousness. Such a disordered life will be punished. Bullinger returns to the subject of suffering, but this time from a different perspective. Nonbelievers in the world are rejected for their lack of faith, but for the faithful the hand of God serves to wake them from their slumber and to remind them of his will. Punishment is an aspect of self-realisation, for the faithful become aware that they do not suffer as innocents, and that they deserve to suffer much more than they have. The elect have a fundamentally different view of suffering, for they know that God has taken their sins away and that what they now endure is a test of their faith, an incentive to be obedient and do good works.

The human response to all events in the world must be shaped by love, love of God and of one's neighbour. Without love no one can fulfill the commandments or see God. Good works are those things that please God and are demanded of all; Bullinger denies that good works are done by separate religious orders but argues that they are done in the world by people. To each estate of society belongs different tasks: the clergy must preach the Word of God, correct error, plant God's Word, admonish, punish, visit the sick, look after the poor, study earnestly, pray, bring the people to prayer, carry out their office in a friendly manner. The princes must fear God, gladly support the Word of God and read it themselves, seek God's guidance, be fair to those who come before them.

---

58. *Decades*, decade III, ix, 356.

Officials of the state must also fear God and be fair with the common people.[59]

There is no doubt that Bullinger saw life as preparation for a good death. The faithful on earth are like gold awaiting purification and polishing. At the root of all his pastoral advice was the recurrent theme that God knows all that has taken place in each person's life, all the suffering endured, and that faith will be repaid in the next life. Bullinger expected little from this world, and even as a young(ish) man he gave expression to a pessimistic view of human life in his *Bericht der krancken*, which was printed in 1535.[60] Here he makes very clear his position that illness and death are a punishment of God for the sinfulness of humanity.[61] The darkness inherent in Bullinger's sense of the world is evident in his assurance that death is not simply a punishment, but a release from this world. In death God seeks to have his own return to him so that they might enjoy eternity.[62]

Illness is not merely disease but a means by which God warns people about their sinfulness. For Bullinger it even has the positive function of allowing men and women to begin the process of separation from the world–a world about to be judged most harshly. Thus Bullinger sees death as another aspect of God's paternal love and faithfulness (*vaetterlicher trüw und liebe*).[63] This raises the problematical relationship to medicine which was common among the Protestant writers of the sixteenth century. For Bullinger, medicine is indeed a reflection of the fact that God works through natural means, but the danger inherent in this, as one might expect from a follower of Zwingli, is that people will put their trust in the means and not the author. The doctor can only bring about healing if it is God's will that a person recover from an illness, therefore all trust must be placed in God.[64]

For Bullinger death is a release from the sinful world of the flesh and its approach is to be greeted with thankfulness. He refers to death as the path from "prison to freedom, from misery and need to joy and peace, from disunity to unity, from danger to security, from earthly injustice to heavenly, eternal confirmation (*bestendigkeit*), from darkness to light, from human community to the company of angels, yet as such it is a proper passage from death to life."[65]

In a typical piece of advice, Bullinger turns to those who feel distraught at the prospect of being separated by death from their wives, children, and friends. Bullinger's first response, as ever, is a rather cold reminder of the biblical message from Matthew 19:37-9 that those who love their parents before God are not followers of Christ. For Bullinger this is yet more evidence that these people have their hearts set on earthly things above heavenly. Having made his point,

---

59. On Bullinger's attitude towards political morals, see the contribution of Emidio Campi in this volume.

60. *Bericht der krancken. Wie man by den krancken und sterbenden menschen handlen/ ouch wie sich in yeder inn siner kranckheit schicken unnnd zum sterben rüsten sölle kurtzer unnd einfallter Bericht Heinrychen Bullingers* (Zurich, 1535), *HBBibl* I, no. 73.

61. On the *Bericht*, see Andreas Mühling, "'Welchen Tod sterben wir?' Heinrich Bullingers *Bericht der Kranken* (1535)," *Zwingliana* 29 (2002): 55-68.

62. *Bericht*, f. aiii^v.

63. Ibid., f. avi^r.

64. Ibid., f. aviii^v.

65. Ibid., f. bii^v.

however, Bullinger moves into a more pastoral tone and advises men that they must make provision for their families by drawing up wills as a precaution against sudden death.[66] He then counsels the dying:

> Therefore ought those who are ill have no doubts about God's trust and care, and they ought with earnest prayer give over their wife and child into God's protection and help that He protect them according to his mercy.[67]

The message is ever the same: trust in God and God will act in your life for the good. That good is not in any way to be understood in material terms, but as leading to the true purpose of human existence, salvation and eternal life. A person must surrender him/herself entirely to the will of God and be obedient to the teaching of the Bible. Illness and death cannot be seen as anything other than part of the trial (*Bewehrung*) which, as discussed, marked for Bullinger the whole framework of the Christian life. To fear such things is to demonstrate a lack of faith. It is a message that can seem cold, but to understand Bullinger on his own terms we need to remind ourselves that this is only one part of the equation. The greater reality is God's boundless love for humanity and the promise that if one turns to him all will be well. For Bullinger, the personal concerns of existence in this world are nothing compared to what is on offer for eternity. It is an entirely unmodern view that can easily mislead the reader into assuming that Bullinger had little regard for human life.

Towards the end of *Bericht der Kranken* Bullinger offers a prayer to be uttered by those near to death. The prayer is a good example of the emotive language of Bullinger's devotional writings and it encapsulates the essence of his spirituality:

> Because you, O Lord, Almighty God, and Heavenly Father have instructed us through your true eternal Word that you will not abandon any who cry to you in need, so I cry to you alone with my request and beseech you in your eternal truth through Jesus Christ, Your Son, our Lord, that you do not abandon me, your poor creature, at my end. If my illness does not lead to death, grant me patience in my situation that I may feel (*erzeugen*) your hand, that I may rise again and always have you before my eyes and make myself better (*moge*); if I am to die, you have given me body and soul and you have the power, according to your eternal and good will, to take them back again. Take from me all trust and care for earthly things that I might lightly leave them and place them according to your holy order in the good hope that all will be well with them. I also praise you and give thanks that right up to this hour you have preserved me with your fatherly love and faithfulness, and with your trust and protection heard all my requests, in particular all who have carried out my business. I willing forget and forgive all offences against me, and ask you O Lord that you be merciful to all men who confess their sins, and protect your faithful. Also that in my life I have often sinned against you, for this I am sorry and seek your mercy and charity, which you have given us through Jesus Christ, who has given us eternal life and paid for our sins, and you have promised that those who trust in the Son of God

66. Ibid., f. bvii^{r-v}.
67. Ibid., f. ci^r.

will have eternal life. So I believe in Jesus Christ, your only Son our Lord, true God and man in one Redeemer of the whole world: I renounce all other comforts, help, and assistance. I hope for eternal life through the forgiveness of sins. O Lord, increase my faith and help my unbelief. Protect from the world of evil and do not lead me into temptation, strengthen me in my weakness and do not abandon me in my madness, but show me your righteousness in Your Son our Lord Jesus Christ (at your right hand), who has given us a certain promise that we will come to you in heaven. Therefore, I give myself wholly to you with body and soul, I praise and thank you for your mercy and charity, for without doubt I know and believe you will awaken this poor mortal body from death on the Last Day. Take my soul into your hand in my last hour as I now commend it to you, O Lord God, have mercy on me and take me from this death to eternal life, through Jesus Christ Our Lord.[68]

This prayer expresses the spiritual grammar Bullinger sought to impart to his church. These lines tell us as much about the man as we are able to glean from his diary and correspondence. The mask of the Reformation patriarch slips and reveals a person clinging to Christ, fearing the darkness of the world, and begging for forgiveness. Bullinger had a profound sense of the majesty of God. Like Peter, John, and James before the transfigured Christ, he throws himself to the ground in fear. But fear gives way to joy, and Bullinger's spirituality rests in an emotive grasp of the friendship offered by God by which humanity, in all its weakness, is made noble. Little of that joy was to be found in this world, where Christians would continue to struggle and require mutual support in the face of the demonic forces of persecution, illness, physical hardships, and unbelief. Bullinger the pastor and writer found it easy to decry the ways of the world, from which he expected no good, but to the end he struggled to express the hope he regarded as central to religion. Bullinger speaks explicitly of the emotions; they flow strongly through the veins of his prayers. There is rawness in the emotional character of the prayer; the self is to be denied and overcome yet God's love is encountered and felt in the midst of a person's life. It is a deeply intimate moment between God and the individual but it is never stripped of the context of other human relations within the community. The emotions are not to be denied, for they are made holy when a person becomes Christ-like, obedient to the will of God, and filled with the spirit. God and humanity have become friends, a relationship of equals, and in the vernacular works of Heinrich Bullinger the Reformed tradition found a human and humane articulation of its spirituality.

68   Ibid., f. eiv^r-ev^r.

5

Bullinger and Worship: "Thereby Does One Plant and Sow the True Faith"

Roland Diethelm

Even members of the Swiss Reformed churches are unlikely to think that their tradition has made much of a contribution to either the history of liturgy and or its importance for the worship of the Church today. While Roman Catholics, Anglicans, Lutherans, and even French Calvinists have a strong sense of the significance of liturgy, when it comes to the German-speaking Reformed tradition the tendency has been to examine worship and liturgy in the context of daily life. The absence of liturgy from mainstream academic research has become programmatic largely because for the liberal theological tradition liturgy remains something of an embarrassment. Recent work has done little to alter this standpoint, although there has been a clearer understanding of the connection between worship and culture, which has led to a greater appreciation of the Reformed liturgy.[1] However, in the metatheory at the heart of the recent work of a prominent scholar of Reformed liturgy it is clear that the subject is really about "preparing for daily life."[2] This rather blinkered view demonstrates little understanding of the historical richness of the Zurich liturgy and it misses opportunities for innovative research.[3] To switch metaphors, the field must now be properly surveyed, new paths established, and test holes drilled in the ground.

In this article I shall attempt to begin that survey of the field of liturgy and in particular examine the state of research on Reformed worship in Zurich. I hope this will enable me to draw attention to various desiderata in the scholarship. With this in mind, my intentions are first, to ask what constituted liturgy, and then, secondly, to determine who was involved in liturgy and to examine its place in the institutional life of the city-state of the sixteenth century. Further, I shall explore the sources for the study of liturgy in order that we might glimpse the richness of the liturgical life in the "Christian city of Zurich." From this starting point I wish to develop two themes more fully: community and communication -

---

1. Ralph Kunz, *Gottesdienst Evangelisch Reformiert. Liturgik und Liturgie in der Kirche Zwinglis* (Zurich: Pano, 2001).

2. Alfred Ehrensperger, *Gottesdienst: Visionen-Erfahrungen-Schmerzstellen* (Zurich: TVZ, 1988).

3. An example is found in the booklet Okko Herlyn, *Theologie der Gottesdienstgestaltung* (Neukirchen-Vluyn: Neukirchener, 1st ed.,1988, 2nd ed.,1992).

the communication of the prophet with his community - and covenant and *civitas*, the spirituality of the new Reformed clergy in Zurich.

In order to assess accurately the achievements of the reformers in liturgical affairs we need to begin with the historical contexts for their writings. The crucial question of continuity and change in the liturgy can only be properly explored once we have a good sense of that which existed before Zwingli, Jud, and Bullinger began their dramatic reform of worship in the 1520s. We begin our investigation with the pre-Reformation form of preaching service which existed in the Upper Rhineland and which cultivated a common sense of worship in the cities of Strasbourg, Basle, Berne, Zurich, and Constance.[4] This shared form of worship does not, however, wholly support the thesis of Hermann Waldenmaier, found in every survey of Reformed liturgy written since the First World War and uncritically repeated in every study of the provenance of Reformed worship, that Ulrich Surgant's *Manuale curatorum* of 1502 was the model for this Upper Rhineland preaching service.[5] It is evident that during the 1520s the Reformation, despite the profound theological break, retained continuity with late-medieval texts and formulations. Unlike the early writings of the Protestant reformers against the mass and in favour of purging the liturgy of all objectionable dogma, the early liturgical reforms are remarkable for the absence of polemical language against the Catholic Church. The reason for this was the considerable degree of continuity between late-medieval and Reformed forms of worship. Was this continuity, as found in the liturgies in Zurich and Strasbourg, really grounded in the Basle work of Ulrich Surgant? Certainly, many of the alterations in form and wording which emerged between 1519 and 1528 were entirely uncontroversial. But there is a problem with dating our sources. How far did Huldrych Zwingli[6] and Heinrich Bullinger[7] delve into the history of liturgy in order to date and analyse the individual sections of the mass that were retained? The sources do not permit a satisfactory answer. The 1528 *Order and Practice of the Churches in Zurich*, for example, offers no concrete evidence. It may still prove possible to locate a link between the influential liturgy of Ulrich Surgant and the work of Huldrych Zwingli/Leo Jud, but in order to do this much more research needs to be done on the background to the liturgies of 1523 and 1528.[8] Until this is done Waldenmaier's interesting thesis cannot be considered anything more than suggestive conjecture.

To begin, an investigation of the roots of liturgical reform in Zurich during the 1520s is essential to our treatment of Heinrich Bullinger's understanding of

---

4. On the Upper German exegetical community, see the essay by Daniel Bolliger in this volume.

5. Hermann Waldenmaier, *Die Entstehung der evangelischen Gottesdienstordnung Süddeutschlands im Zeitalter der Reformation* (Schriften des Vereins für Reformationsgeschichte 34, no. 125 and 126; Leipzig: Kommissionsverlag von Rudolf Haupt, 1916).

6. *De canone missae epichiresis*, 29.8.1523 (*Z* II = *CR* 89: 552-602).

7. *De origine erroris* (*HBBibl* I, no. 10-14).

8. The standard work on liturgical reform in Strasbourg, which in many ways paralleled Zurich, is René Bornert, *La Réforme protestante du Culte à Strasbourg au XVIe siècle (1523-1598). Approche sociologique et Interpretation théologique* (Studies in Medieval and Reformation Thought 27; Leiden: Brill, 1981).

worship and liturgy, for it forces us to consider the importance of the role played by both oral and other unknown traditions in Zwingli's reforms. For example, we can think of the development of public, or general, confession between 1523 and 1535. In Leo Jud's 1523 formulation there is only one sentence, namely the biblical absolution from the parable of the Prodigal Son (Luke 15). In 1528, however, there is already a more detailed text that seems more akin to Surgant's formulation of 1502.[9] The simplest explanation, next to the possibility that Surgant was the source or that the innovation was due to the biblicism of Leo Jud, is that in 1528 for the first time what was actually said in the service was, for the first time, written down. If this assumption is true, we have a clear foundation for the evolution of the Zurich liturgical texts: the oral traditions and practices were written down as they were appropriated by the Reformed tradition, but this process did not happen at once. Therefore, it is clear that the surviving Zurich church orders do not in themselves form a satisfactory basis for the study of the thought and actions of the second-generation reformers in the field of liturgy. The creativity of Heinrich Bullinger and his generation cannot be explained on the basis of a comparative study of extant documents alone, for these documents only dimly reflect a vibrant oral tradition in the city that was only committed to paper in a piecemeal manner, giving a false sense of evolution. Using the surviving documents in isolation, one could arrive at a distorted picture of liturgical development in Zurich which would look like this: the reforms of 1523 brought a clean break with the medieval past, but during the course of the sixteenth century there were endless revisions by which many of the medieval practices expunged between 1523 and 1525 were gradually reintroduced into the Reformed liturgy. This is the picture of liturgical reform in Zurich that has been painted by scholarship, but I wish to argue against it on the grounds that it is based on a questionable use of sources.

The history of liturgy cannot be studied with recourse to either written or oral sources exclusively. There was a complex interplay between the two that must be understood in terms of the institutions in which the liturgy was performed. Research on Reformed liturgy, particularly for non-eucharistic services, has not to this point made use of the links between literary analysis, theology, and social history. The whole Reformation in Zurich must be examined in light of liturgical history in order for us to understand which institutions were linked to which forms of liturgy. A good example of the failure to do this is the manner in which Bullinger's *Decades* have been understood. Scholars are still unclear as to the purpose of the work and whether, or where, its sermons were preached. Many have understood the title *Hausbuch*, given to the *Decades* by the German translator Johannes Haller, to mean that the sermons were intended for the family table as devotional or instructional reading. There are, however, other possibilities that arise out of the evidence for the complex lines of communication among Bullinger's colleagues and friends.

Similarly, we need to look again at the *Prophezei*, the Zurich pedagogical institution founded in 1523 with the council's mandate *Christian Appearance and Order*, which since 1525 was the heart of the Zurich Reformation. That the

---

9. *CR* 91:697f.

Prophezei was originally a theological school and the "spiritual centre and political heart of the theocracy" has long been established.[10] However, the daily life of the institution has never been researched, although we know the order of service for "daily public Prophecy-worship," known simply as the "Prophecy." It was a morning service in which the fruits of the work undertaken by the clergy on the Latin, Hebrew and Greek editions of the Old Testament were explained to the people in the vernacular. The liturgical form of the service was extremely simple. The canonical prayer in its late-medieval form was declared by Zwingli to be a "verlönet tempelgebätt" meaning paid sung prayer, and in the printed description of liturgy we find his comment "so we have abolished the canonical prayer and the Latin singing of offices and replaced them with the prophecy according to the teaching of Paul."[11] Modern scholars of church history have thought that these older monastic forms were to be replaced by "pure, appropriate understanding." It is important to note that the Zurich reformers understood "replace" to mean "supplanted" and not that the new forms were in any way the liturgical equivalent of that which was being removed.

The vehemence and thoroughness with which Heinrich Bullinger defends the canonical prayer in his monumental chronicle of Zurich history, however, allows for a different interpretation. He argues that the *Prophezei* had inherited the *Obligatorium*, the requirement for the canons to gather for communal prayer. The Reformed canons, chaplains, and fellows were now to gather for the obligatory exegesis of scripture as the medieval canons had done for canonical prayer.[12] We do not yet fully understand what form of communal life (*vita communis*) lay behind this gathering, but there was clearly, in Bullinger's understanding, an historical and spiritual continuity between the late-medieval institution of the chapter of canons and the Reformed *Schola Tigurina*.

Martin Brecht has sought to portray the Zurich *Prophezei* as the successful fulfilment of the Lutheran ideal that never succeeded in Wittenberg.[13] The temporal proximity of the two institutions of the "Prophecey" and the "preaching service" rules out the possibility of such dominating influence. In early spring, or at least by Pentecost, 1523 Luther published his *On the Order of Worship in the Community* in which he suggested alterations in worship which were remarkably similar to those announced in Zurich in September 1523 (and then later from 1525). There is no extant text from Luther that would allow us to make a persuasive connection between the developments in Wittenberg and Zurich. This is not to say that there were not connections, and Brecht's supposition does have some textual support in Luther's formula for Baptism, which was adopted in Zurich through the work of Leo Jud, who seems to have been the man responsible for the German language formula of the liturgy. Further, we know that Jud and Bullinger were very close in their ideas.[14]

10. Jacques Figi, *Die innere Reorganisation des Grössmunsterstiftes in Zürich von 1519 bis 1531* (Affoltern am Albis: J. Weiss, 1951), 107.

11. *CR* 91:701,19-21.

12. Figi, *Die innere Reorganisation*, 101.

13. Martin Brecht, "Die Reform des Wittenberger Horengottesdienstes und die Entstehung der Zürcher Prophezei," *Zwingliana* 19/1 (1991/2): 49-62.

14. Preface to *De propheta libri duo*, 1525 (ZB, Ms. A 82.1).

Although the Wittenberg reforms did have some influence in Zurich we must also bear in mind that there were other institutions located closer to Zurich that played a more direct role. First of all we need to look to the young, reform-minded Cistercian Abbot Wolfgang Joner in Kappel am Albis, which lay a few miles south of Zurich. Joner had summoned the young Heinrich Bullinger to aid in the education of his monks. In January 1523 Bullinger introduced in Kappel an institution similar to the *Prophezei* which would emerge later in Zurich. In Kappel, however, Bullinger's vision took shape alongside the offices of the monks, to which he was closely connected as a member of the monastery.[15] Through both Abbot Joner and the young Bullinger the Erasmian ideal was being realised in Kappel. Thus, although it remains an open question whether Luther's writing had moved the Zurichers during 1523 to give their biblical *Lectorium* the form of a *Prophezei*, what we do know is that the influence of Bullinger's Kappel years was decisive. In Bullinger's 1532 handwritten agenda for the daily morning worship there are four lines that are taken directly from the monastic offices. They read as follows:

In nomine Patris et filii et spiritus sancti, amen. Deus in adiutorium meum intende, domine ad me festina. Domine labia mea aperies, et os meum annunciabit laudem tuam. Salvem fac domine populum tuum, et benedic hereditati tuae, et rege eos et extolle illos usque in aeternum.

This text was not adopted in the official printed version of the service and is not to be found in Bullinger's personal agenda from 1563. There is no doubt, however, that Bullinger conceived of the new communal worship in terms of an historical evolution of the monastic offices. It is fascinating to consider whether Bullinger's gloss on one of the above lines that "in its place is the *Prophezei*" is more than simply a reference to the obligatory nature of the service for those who held canonical livings. Perhaps it contained the ideal of a new *vita communis reformata*? The *Prophezei* was for the Reformed clergy, from Zwingli to Bullinger, as well as for their followers, the cornerstone of the communal life as well as a crucial liturgical event.

In this context it is also worthy of note that the text from 1 Corinthians 14:40, which was the biblical foundation of the *Prophezei*, was to be found on the title page of the printed text of the Zurich liturgy throughout the sixteenth century: "All things must be done in a fitting and orderly manner." This was Paul's teaching to the community at Corinth on the nature of worship. This text, however, occupied a controversial place in Zurich as the Anabaptists used it in 1525 in their arguments in favour of lay preachers. Zwingli's objection to lay preaching is well-known; he argued that in order to preach the Gospel one must have an adequate knowledge of Hebrew and the Old Testament, and it was to serve this purpose that the *Prophezei* was founded. The anti-Anabaptist use of 1 Corinthians 14 by Zwingli and then Bullinger was intended to save the church from the radicals; the idea that one must be able to understand the Old Testament in the original language of the *ecclesia vetus*, the language of Israel, became in Zurich the de-

15. *HBRG* I:92 and *HBD*, 8:2-9.

marcation point between the official clergy and the Anabaptists. It was a sign that one belonged to a chosen people ruled over by a legitimate government advised by the prophets, and not to a separate troop of "true and persecuted Christians," in whom all and none are prophets. It was in this context that the early reformers shaped their work, including their liturgical reforms. Crucial and typical for Bullinger was the term *legitime* and the formation of the image of the wise prophet (*propheta sapiens*). His intention was not merely to exclude others but to build the Church.

From the beginning of his tenure as head of the Zurich church we find that Bullinger's liturgical work was already focused on the cultivation of three things: the sermon, biblical exegesis, and the presentation of the evangelical faith. These would remain the heart of Bullinger's work during his forty-three years as minister in the Grossmünster. The *lectio continua* method was the basis for Bullinger's preaching, with the exception of the occasional sermons for feast days and certain free-standing works such as the *Decades*. Bullinger practised the *lectio continua* principle throughout his career, but more fascinating is the question of the logic by which he chose the books of the Bible for his sermons. This choice, as well as the manner in which he interpreted texts, expressed the creative potential in the new Zurich order. What can we say about that order? Let us begin with an incident recounted in Bullinger's *Reformation History*:

> In this time two citizens of Zurich, Heinrych Röüchli the Seckelmeister and Hans Füßli, welder of church bells and cannons, when they heard that Zwingli was preaching on the Gospel of Matthew, made their way to the Grossmünster with all haste to hear him, and after the sermon they said publicly that he (Zwingli) was a far more faithful preacher of the truth and that he spoke about things as they really are.[16]

We know that when Zwingli took up his post in Zurich he introduced the principle of *lectio continua*, which was a radical departure from the use of the medieval lectionaries. This moment was both a liturgical and, as Bullinger made clear in his account in the *Reformation History*, a political event.[17] The citizens mentioned by Bullinger, Röüchli and Füßli, had previously stayed away from worship, but now, following Zwingli's sermons, came with zeal ("mit flyß") Clearly these laymen had understood, as many others in Zurich had, the significance of Zwingli's changes. Bullinger refers to the political implications of liturgical reform later in the same account:

> How and what he preached from the start until the year 1523 (that is for four years) he [Zwingli] recalls in his *Archeteles* in the following manner: when I first came to Zurich I preached on the Gospel of Matthew, then the Acts of the Apostles in order that one might learn how the Gospel was planted from the start and the Christian church built. Then I preached through the Epistles of Paul to the Corinthians, then Timothy, as they instruct the churches so that the flock of Christ learn of their duties and sins. Then, as there were things that were not

16. *HBRG* I:13.
17. Ibid., 30f.

right and well, according to the faith I preached on the epistle to the Galatians and then on the other letter of Timothy. Then that no one might despise the teaching of Paul because he was not one of the twelve I preached on the two letters of Peter in order to show how all the Apostles spoke with one voice and taught the same. Then I preached on the Letter of Paul to the Hebrews in order that men might learn of the great things that Christ has done for us, that he is alone our high priest, the sufficient sacrifice for our sins, our only mediator, advocate, and priest, and that we have all in Christ.[18]

What we have here is Zwingli's outline of how preaching serves in the building of the Christian community. In reflecting on these events, Bullinger saw the preaching and liturgical changes initiated by Zwingli as the essential basis for subsequent reforms: iconoclasm, as well as the abolition of the mass and the veneration of the saints. In addition, preaching was seen as the foundation for a new understanding of the office of minister integral to the new church, church discipline, and the renovation of the church year. How did Bullinger lead the church through these changes and what use did he make of the freedom to choose the biblical books for his sermons? In considering Zwingli's statements we learn much about what was to become Bullinger's practice.

Until recently our understanding of how the sixteenth-century clergy around Bullinger understood themselves and their work has been hampered by scholars' narrow theological perspective that surely these ministers must have seen themselves in light of the anticlericalism that had fostered the Reformation. The confessional orientation of the scholarship in which the Reformation break with the medieval past is heavily stressed has, until recently, prevailed. However, more recent work on religious mentalities in the early-modern period offers us a different viewpoint: we are beginning to understand how the ministers viewed themselves both as *symmystae* in service to the Word of God and in terms of their differences from the communities which they served. This leads us to the issue of the liturgical reforms as both a rejection of the medieval mass and also a self-conscious reorientation of the Zurich church towards a newly-discovered tradition; liturgical events in Zurich can be understood as both a polemical rejection of Catholicism and the formation of a new tradition.

The break with the mass liturgy and the introduction of a new preaching service was, as mentioned above, a common concern of all the evangelical reformers of the Upper Rhine. It was understood to entail the reintroduction of a form of worship that was faithful to God's command for the abolition of false worship, which was a creation of human and ecclesiastical traditions. In the realm of theology this was given expression in the close connection made by Bullinger between the true worship of God and the true knowledge of God: those who practise the *verus dei cultus* alone properly know God. In this theological respect the liturgical reforms were conceived of as a radical break with the past, for in the scholastic tradition worship and prayer were clearly connected to the Christian life. Bullinger, in contrast not only to the scholastics, but also to Calvin and Mel-

18. Ibid.

anchthon, handled worship in the context of the knowledge of God.[19] He certainly shared the Augustinian high regard for worship with its insistence that the human person without God is condemned to a life of sin.[20] There is a stark choice to be made: either one takes up the Word of God or one does not: there is no place for a contemplative or neutral "third way." Thus worship has a central role for both Bullinger's understanding of God and his anthropology, and he had to formulate a theological and liturgical articulation of what had taken place in the Reformed abolition of the mass. The central act of the church must be an expression of true doctrine. The sermon, in Augustine's words, must be the presentation of the *doctrina Christiana*, through which the servant of the Word, according to the *Order or practice of the Zurich church* "teaches, admonishes, punishes, and consoles."

Nowhere is the condemnation of the mass and canonical prayer more sharply formulated than in Bullinger's comments in the *Second Helvetic Confession*:

> *Horas canonicas ... nescivit vetustas ... Sed et absurda non pauca habent, ut nihil dicam aliud, proinde omittuntur recte ab ecclesiis substituentibus in locum ipsarum res salutares ecclesiae Dei universae.*[21]

Yet, how far was this polemical rejection of the mass reflected in the practice of worship as it evolved in Zurich? Polemic and practice are often quite separate things and we find that the picture that emerges is more complex and nuanced than one might expect. The *Ave Maria*, for example, long continued to be used in the churches together with the Lord's Prayer, in accordance with usual medieval practice. Latin prayers likewise remained in use and many were reintroduced, and singing, except in the city of Zurich, continued to be a central part of worship, even in churches under Zurich control. The radical nature of theological reform was not entirely reflected in the liturgical forms found in sixteenth-century Zurich.

In order to measure the degree of continuity that shaped Bullinger's liturgical work we must once more turn to the practice. As a useful case study, let us take the tradition of singing mentioned above. If we look at scholarship on the subject we get the following account. Music in the church remained part of worship in communities very close to the city of Zurich, such as Winterthur, Stein am Rhein, and Schaffhausen. Moreover, the hymnal produced in Constance and used in these churches was printed in Zurich. These were all churches that were very much under Zurich's influence and the reluctance of Bullinger to interfere in this matter reflected his view that singing was adiaphora. He did occasionally engage with the subject in his writings, often approaching it from an historical perspective, and his consistent view was that in the Latin West there had been no tradition of singing similar to the East. Thus, in a typical Bullinger formulation, what

---

19. A example is found in sermon 35 of the *Decades: Sermonum Decades quinque, de potissimis Christianae religionis capitibus, in tres tomos digestae, authore Heinrycho Bullingero, ecclesiae Tigurinae ministro* (Zurich: 1552), *HBBibl* I, no. 184.

20. Martin Klöckener, "cultus," in *Augustinus-Lexikon*, 2: col. 157-66.

21. E.F.K. Müller, *Die Bekenntnisschriften der reformierten Kirche* (Leipzig: A. Deichert, 1903), 214, 40-45.

was not used in the old church did not need to be introduced in the contemporary church. Thus Zurich remained without singing in the churches until 1598, when it was re-introduced.

This view of the abolition of singing in Zurich, drawn largely from Bullinger's own words, has become the standard position thanks to the research of Markus Jenny. But a more expansive use of available documents demonstrates that Jenny's presentation of Zurich in the sixteenth century is not entirely accurate. I quote from the Zurich School Ordinance of 1532:

> above all the schoolmasters must ensure that schoolboys with all zeal, truth, and seriousness are brought up in the fear of God, discipline, and piety.

Then the following:

> every morning the school should raise itself up with a clear, discernible voice with Our Father, and then at the close of the school day, about the fourth hour, end with a Psalm. On Tuesdays, Thursdays, and Saturdays, however, one should sing the *carmina*, as is the old practice.[22]

In Bullinger's own liturgical agenda from 1563, which is a slight revision of the 1535 order, we find in his handwriting other prayers and a collection of Latin and German texts alongside which he has written "*Ex Hymnis Ecclesiasticis.*" Along with these we find a collection of hymns of Fortunatus.

Thus we are left with a series of intriguing questions. Before the re-introduction of singing into the Zurich churches at the end of the century were Latin hymns being sung? If so, where? Certainly the Zurichers were slow to remove the Ave Maria - it was still to be found in the agenda of 1535, but by 1563 it was gone. It is not improbable that it disappeared with the confessionalisation of Mary following the Council of Trent.[23]

If we ask how Bullinger understood this central issue of continuity and change in liturgical tradition we find the sources give a somewhat contradictory response. We know that in the description of worship found in the *Reformation History* Bullinger emphasises the changes found in the new preaching service,[24] but in his account of the Grossmünster chapter, in the *Tigurinerchronik* a different picture altogether emerges. In the latter work Bullinger puts the emphasis on continuity with the medieval chapter and its canons. He explores the background of the chapter, in particular its original obligation to provide teachers and preachers of Holy Scripture. Bullinger also chronicles its decline and restoration under the reforms of the provost Felix Frei. This continuity had a particular purpose, for it was Frei, along with the canon Heinrich Utinger, who had been prominent in the summoning of Zwingli to the Grossmünster in 1518. Restoration and the re-

---

22. *Order and Regulation of How in Future One Should Establish the Studies and Other Affairs of the Schoolboys in the Zurich Grossmünster School*, StA G I 75, 42f.

23. On the adoration of Mary and related issues, see Emidio Campi, *Zwingli und Maria: eine reformationsgeschichtliche Studie* (Zurich: TVZ, 1997).

24. *HBRG* I:12f.

form of the canons were not, in Bullinger's eyes, contradictions, but belonged to the same goal: the restoration of the biblical office of the prophet.[25]

Pamela Biel has written extensively on the nature of the pastoral office in Zurich. She has described both its theory and practice, as well as how the minister found himself between his role as preacher of the Word and representative of the church among the people. In his parish the minister had to interpret scripture to the people, a profoundly liturgical act. According to Biel, following the 1535 ordinance the key liturgical moments were the sermon (*predig*), the *Prophezei* (*prophecey* or *lezge*), the marriage service, Baptism, the Lord's Supper and the Common Prayer (*Gmein baett*). In his role as representative of the state the minister had, according to Biel, his "third sacrament," which was to ensure true penance—the punishment of sin. Biel describes this as the "civil servant" in his liturgical role. Closely connected to this was the place of the synod, the principal instrument by which Bullinger led the clergy. In his exegesis of the letter to the Hebrews in 1532 Bullinger laid down the principles of the Zurich clergy. He clearly placed the Reformed clergy in the tradition of the Levitical priesthood of the Old Testament.[26] This connection was finally made explicit in the 1565 sermons on the Book of Daniel.[27] For Bullinger the Levitical priesthood was in the first instance an aid to Moses, who sought to teach the people the laws of God. The later Jewish priesthood, and in particular the sacrificing priesthood of Jesus' day, was, in Bullinger's account, a corruption of this tradition. Biel's understanding is supported by Bullinger's tone in his Grossmünster chronicle, which we can summarise as follows: the activities of the Apostolic prophetic priests were a Reformation in which they sought to restore the Mosaic intention for the priesthood. This became the justification for the abolition of the mass and the introduction of the sermon. The purpose of this office has remained unchanged from biblical times, and Bullinger saw his reforms as standing in the tradition of the restoration of the original Mosaic priesthood: Zurich has restored the ideal of priesthood that was embodied in the relationship between Christ and Israel. This figure of the prophet was originally conceived for the old covenant between God and Israel, but it had been damaged by the infidelity of the people, just as the Christian ministry had been desecrated during the Middle Ages by papal corruption. For the Israelites the disintegration came through integration with the Canaanites, while for the medieval church it was caused by the usurpation of worldly power by the clergy.

It was not Bullinger's intention that the clergy should be made subordinate to political authorities, but this soon became part of Reformed teaching and practice. So how did Bullinger defend his ecclesiastical ideas against the venal interests of the Zurich council? Hans Ulrich Bächtold has provided the essential study of Bullinger's relations with the Zurich magistrates,[28] while Figi has studied the

---

25. Heinrich Bullinger, *Von den Tigurineren und der Stadt Zürych sachen VIII Buecher*, part 1, book 4, chaps 3, 4 and 9 (ZB, Ms. A 92, 125-33 and 144-50).

26. On this see the contribution of Daniel Bolliger to this volume.

27. Pamela Biel, *Doorkeepers at the House of Righteousness: Heinrich Bullinger and the Zurich Clergy 1535-1575* (ZBRG 15; Berne: Peter Lang, 1991), 118, 124.

28. Hans Ulrich Bächtold, *Heinrich Bullinger vor dem Rat. Zur Gestaltung und Verwaltung des Zürcher Staatswesens in den Jahren 1531 bis 1575* (ZBRG 12; Berne: Peter Lang, 1982).

reorganisation of the Grossmünster chapter. In contrast to these studies, however, I do not see the contacts between the council and church as either aggressive or confrontational. Thus I am also less inclined to emphasise the dramatic nature of Bullinger's failure to defend the church against the magistrates. On the whole Bullinger succeeded in getting what he wanted and with his interventions (*Fürträge*) he developed an efficient means of communication with the magistrates. For example, in 1571-2 Bullinger was able, with the assistance of the council, to introduce a Common Prayer and thereby obtain from the magistrates an order that the people be required to attend church twice as often as had previously been prescribed. Bullinger's will, in which he explained the nature of worship, was read to the council, and the magistrates accepted his position.[29] It was laid down by the council that in the rural areas the Ten Commandments should be read out and preached upon, as was the custom in the city.[30] That the council had no doubt about the use and purpose of worship for their subjects was due to Bullinger's work. An explained absence of more than two weeks by one subject could lead to the suspension or removal of that person's legal rights. Some of the magistrates, however, felt themselves to be above these regulations and did not attend church regularly. This distressed Bullinger greatly, for not only was it a bad example to the people, but there were also serious consequences, for a people which does not come before God as one cannot be pleasing to him.[31] Bullinger wished to make the further point that Christian teaching, the *doctrina Christiana*, was as binding upon the magistrates as it was on the rural farmers–all are subject to God's commands regardless of station. The magistrates in turn greatly resented any use of the pulpit to attack their policies or conduct, as they demonstrated in their quarrel with Leo Jud at the start of the 1530s. This had been at the centre of Bullinger's compromise with the ruling authorities in Zurich when he assumed office in 1532. Bullinger had sought to maintain the freedom of the clergy to preach whilst ensuring that the ministers would not use the pulpit to stir up the subjects against their political masters. It was for this purpose that the intervention, or *Fürtrag*, was used as a mediating device between the ministers and the magistrates.[32] In his preaching Bullinger often read the riot act to the Zurich council when the opportunity arose from the text. For example, his sermons on Deuteronomy continually reminded the various estates of their duties before God and how they must take these responsibilities more seriously. Week after week Bullinger appeared before the people to explain the role of the council in a Christian republic and the obligation of the people to be obedient. In the sermons on Isaiah, Bullinger, over the weeks, continued to identify the sins of the Israelites and the royal house of Judah with the failings of the Zurich council.

What is significant for our purposes is the manner in which Bullinger ever more explicitly emphasised the priestly nature of the preaching office. This

29. For an example *HBBibl* I, no. 734f. Bullinger's will has been partially printed in Pestalozzi, *Heinrich Bullinger* (Elberfeld: 1858), 618-22.
30. ZB, Ms. B 27.
31. Biel, *Doorkeepers*, 114 ff.
32. On this point see the detailed discussion found in Bächtold, *Bullinger vor dem Rat*, esp. 23.

priestly character embraces the prophetic office: the prophet reveals the will of God and convicts the people of their sins before God. Therefore, it is important for our understanding of liturgy that Bullinger had no intention of breaking completely with the medieval tradition of the Christian priesthood. Much more significant is how he understood that priesthood, and his belief that there was a need to restore the Levites to their proper role as servants of God.

If we look briefly to the sources for our investigation we find that there is a rich seam of material pertaining to liturgical life in the "Christian city of Zurich." The Reformed church year was essentially concentrated on Sundays and weekday services as well as on those festivals of the medieval church associated with Christ. However, the attempt to retain only feast days that could be justified from the Bible could not be sustained, and in Zurich we find celebrations for the Apostles, as well as the patron saints of the Grossmünster, Felix and Regula. In addition there was a range of other traditional church festivals that although not officially sanctioned remained popular with the people through until Bullinger's death. Even Bullinger himself preached regularly on these occasions.[33] Religious practice in Zurich was a balance between official teaching and surviving traditional celebrations.

The Lord's Supper was reduced to the three or four most significant festivals of the church year and had nothing to do with the weekly rhythm of worship. The celebration of the Lord's Supper on these major occasions emphasised their importance to the Reformed church year, and in Zurich theology these festivals were associated with the major pilgrimage celebrations of the Old Testament. This meant that the requirements set down in the reforms under Josiah, in which the people of Israel were required to come three times a year to the Temple in Jerusalem, were made normative for the Zurich church.[34] Bullinger was hesitant about making the connection between the Reformed Lord's Supper and the reform of worship in the Old Testament too explicit, largely, it seems, because it would have been highly controversial. In reply to a question from Konrad Ulmer, the head of the church in Schaffhausen, who wanted to know why the Swiss Reformed did not celebrate the Lord's Supper weekly, as the Lutherans and Calvinists did, Bullinger admitted that weekly celebration was certainly justifiable on theological grounds, but after forty years he had no desire to alter the established practice, as this could lead to renewed controversy.[35]

It has been suggested that the liturgical reforms of the Reformation brought about an overwhelming concentration on the Sunday preaching service. This may have been somewhat truer for the rural areas where the attendance of the people at services was dependent on the availability of the clergy, but for the city the evidence does not bear it out. We find that in the Grossmünster alone that there

33. ZB, Ms. Car I 206b.
34. *Sermonum Decades quinque*, sermon 49 (*De coena domini*) and sermon 26f (*De lege caeremoniali*, in particular f. 120ʳ) as well the *De institutione et genuino eucharistiae usu* (ZB, Ms. A no 3d, f. 86ᵛ): "... Veterum opinio. Hinc veteres festivitatem hanc, alij sijnaxim alij unionis tesseram, alij communionem, alij vero eucharistiam nominarunt. Nullus vero omnium Deum, carnem, Christum, sive sanguinem dixit. Eucharistia festivitas, non quotidianum convivium.."
35. Heinrich Bullinger to Konrad Ulmer: 17 October 1567, Konrad Ulmer to Heinrich Bullinger: 7 December 1567, *Correspondance*, 8:268ff.

were approximately 624 services a year.[36] Clearly there was a great deal of co-operation between the principal churches of the city (Grossmünster, Fraumünster, and St Peter's), which between them organised the preaching of the Gospel in Zurich.[37] The differences between the weekly and the Sunday services were not,

36. Biel, *Doorkeepers*, 113.
37. StA, E II 54, 247.
   Uff Sontag predgend
   1552 Ioan. Baptista

Zum grossen münster	Bullinger
Zü S. Peter	Walthart [Rudolf Gwalther]
Zü dem frowen münster	Wolff [Johannes Wolf]
Zü den predigern	Hanns Jac[ob] Wick
Zü Mittentag	Haller [Wolfgang Haller]
Zü Abendt	Lavater
Uff montag	
Zü früyer predig Zuo S. Petter	Walthart
Zü spater predig	Zwyngli [Ulrich Zwingli jnr]
uff zinstag	
Zü früyer predig zuo S. Petter	Walthart
Zü spater predig	Bullinger
uff mittwoch	
Zü früyer predig zuo S. Petter	Walthart
Zü spater predig	Caspar Hirt
uff donstag	
Zü früyer predig zum münster	Haller
Zuo spater predig	Wolff
vff frytag	
Zü früyer predig	Bullinger, münster
uff sampstag	
Zü früyer	Lavater
Mittag imm Sammling	Wick
Abend	Zwyngli

Following this another document at StA, E II 54, 249:
   Uff Sontag predigend
   1550

Zum grossen münster	Bullinger
Zü S. petter	Rodolff Walthart
Zum frowen münster	L. Lavater
Zü den predgeren	Ioan. Wolffius
Umb Mittentag	M. Otth Werdm. [Otto Werdmüller]
Zü der abend predig	M. V. Zwyngli
uff montag	
Zü früyer predig	Walthart zü S. petter
die spaaten predig thuot	Zwyngli
vff zinstag	
Zü früyer predig	R. Walthart zuo S. petter
die spaaten predig thuot	Bullinger
uff mittwoch	
Zü früyer predig	M. Otth Zum Münster
die spaater predig thuot	Zwyngli
uff donstag	
Zü früyer predig	Lavater Zum Münster
Die spaater predig thuot	Jo. Wolff

therefore, very great. The recital of the confession of faith (Apostles' Creed) and the reading out of the names of the recently deceased was reserved for Sunday, as were the mandates from the council requiring the people to attend church. These alone distinguished the Sunday service from those held during the week.

Now we should investigate where church services in Zurich from the middle of the sixteenth century were actually held. Alongside the established churches in the city and the *Prophezei* (or *Lectorium* of the *Schola Tigurina*), we know from the school ordinances that worship took place in the German and Latin schools of the Grossmünster and Fraumünster. In addition, worship was held at the twice-yearly meetings of the synod. Further, there were special worship services for special days in Zurich, such as the feast of Charlemagne (28 January), the swearing in of the council before Christmas (*Natalrat*), and the feast of John the Baptist (*Baptistalrat*).

The Lord's Supper celebration in communal worship was organised according to the guilds and the estates.[38] The liturgies for these events still await proper examination. Yet it is one thing to say how many services there were, but quite another to say what these services looked and sounded like. From the surviving sources we know, for instance, that baptism and marriage did not take place as part of the regular services in the Grossmünster, but were generally conducted by assistants, such as the deacons. At the same time the memorial services for the dead seem to have been part of Sunday worship and ministers did not appear at the graveside.

From 1571 the council required all the people to attend a penitential service on Tuesdays. If we look for the roots of this service there are some clues in an agenda from 1563 that has a series of Latin prayers entitled *Confessiones peccatorum*. Are these to be connected to extraordinary and casual official public confession of sin that we know from the *Wickiana* to have taken place? This remains to be determined. The same agenda from 1563 contains other prayers that raise the question of how effectively we are able to glean from the surviving sources a clear picture of liturgical life in Zurich.

What attitudes lay behind these services of worship? This is a difficult question to answer, but in the order of prayers for the schools we have an excellent witness from the period:

> Firstly, because fear of God is the starting point of all wisdom, and because the Apostle James tells us that all wisdom comes from God, so it is essential above all that the young boys are brought to the proper fear and knowledge of God, and

---

uff frytag	
Zü früye predig ist geordnet	Bullinger
Uff sampstag	
früye zum münster	Lavater
Mittag im dem Samling	Wolff
die abend kinder predig thuot	M. Ottho

38. According to Julius Schweizer, *Reformierte Abendmahlsgestaltung in der Schau Zwinglis* (Basle, 1954), 82f. Clearly, Schweizer assumes that part of Zwingli's reform, as set out in his programmatic work "Action oder bruch des nachtmals ... 1525" (*CR* 91:16,13-16) was put into effect. This is not found in Ludwig Lavater/Johann Baptist Ott, *De ritibus et institutis Ecclesiae Tigurinae* (Zurich: 1702; Zurich: TVZ, 1982), 53.

in addition after they get up early they recite the prayer that Our Lord Jesus Christ has taught us so that through the whole day they may receive the fruits and wisdom of his teaching. The students ought to do the same in the evenings when they go to sleep, and in particular they should consider what they have done that day and thereby seek God's mercy. When this is done then each student ought to examine himself in all earnest and ask of himself what he learnt that day. [39]

In addition to this ideal for the students we have evidence of private spirituality, for example the prayer of Heinrich Bullinger for his son, who was abroad. This was a model of spirituality for a member of the clergy. Another example is the letter of one Adolf von Baar, who had written to Bullinger in October 1563 asking the Zurich church leader to pray both publicly and privately that he might find an appropriate wife. [40]

Bullinger does not seem to have expended a great deal of energy defending theologically the liturgical practices or prayers employed in Zurich. Conrad Klauser, with Bullinger's support, wrote a book on prayer in 1553. Ludwig Lavater, as his marginal notes demonstrate, studied Klauser's book with great attention. In 1559 Lavater wrote his great apology for the church order in Zurich, *On the rites and institutions of the Zurich church.* He provided two reasons for writing the work: first because the Zurich church had been accused by others of heresy, and, secondly, to provide an example for those other churches which looked to Zurich as a model.

Our information on the services of worship in Zurich from the middle of the sixteenth century is largely dependent on Lavater's *On the rites and institutions of the Zurich church,* as well as the series of agendas mentioned previously. The first agenda dates from 1528, but during Bullinger's life other agendas were printed in 1535, 1563 and 1570. From the surviving printed and manuscript copies of the agendas it has been possible, as the work of Leo Weisz and Markus Jenny has demonstrated, to trace the changes and developments that took place. [41] What remains to be done is for the liturgical revisions to be placed in the context of contemporary events in Zurich. What circumstances, we might ask, led to the revision of the liturgy being issued by the council?

From the documents we can reconstruct the liturgical evolution in Zurich as follows. From the first synod in Zurich in June 1528 all the ministers and preachers were given a copy of the liturgy for worship held in the city churches. This was intended to be binding upon the ministers in the rural parishes. Following his appointment to the Grossmünster in 1532, Bullinger made a copy of the prayers used in the Grossmünster, and this early text provides the best evidence for what the preaching service looked like. It was clearly an outline of the two/three preaching services a week which Bullinger himself led. Bullinger continued to

39. *Zucht ordnung für die knaben amm Cappeller hoff uff verbesserung vnnd gefallen vnser herren gestellt* (StA, E I 14.1, no. 1 and 2).
40. StA, E II 377, 2405. My thanks to Rainer Henrich for bringing this letter to my attention.
41. Leo Weisz, "Heinrich Bullingers agenda," *Zwingliana* 10/1 (1954-8): 1-23; Markus Jenny, "Bullinger als Liturg" in Ulrich Gäbler/Erland Herkenrath eds., *Heinrich Bullinger 1504-1575*, vol. 1 (ZBRG 7; Zurich: TVZ, 1975), 209-30.

revise this document throughout his time in office and the last dated note is from 1575, the year of his death. In that year he added, poignantly, a prayer for those who suffered from serious illness. In this document Bullinger wrote down several significant dates: "19 June 1525" as the start of the *Prophezei* and "1528" as the date of the synod in April of that year, which had met under the leadership of Zwingli and Leo Jud. It was at this synod that Bullinger had taken the oath of office. This seems to have been Bullinger's most important agenda, the one from which he worked.

In 1535 a new official agenda was printed and distributed. It likewise underscored the obligatory nature of conducting Reformed worship for the former priests. Bullinger returned to the topic forty years later during his quarrel with the council over the Lord's Supper in the old Dominican Church in Zurich. At that time the council rejected a revision of the Lord's Supper.[42] Perhaps the printing of an unrevised version of the agenda for the Lord's Supper was the consequence and end of a failed reform attempt. In any case, foreign events seem to have played a crucial role, as we can see from the apologetic nature of the preface to the agenda. 1535 marked the height of the Anabaptist catastrophe in Münster and the flight of many of the survivors to Strasbourg. It was also a low point in the ongoing conflict between Bullinger and Luther over the Lord's Supper. The year also saw the start of Reformation movements in Horburg, Reichenweiher, and Montpelyard, all towns in which Bullinger was acting as an advisor. It is certainly possible that the reprinting of the agenda in 1535 was intended to serve as a model for these diverse audiences.

The agenda of 1563 was printed on parchment, a sign of its great value and of the expectation that it would be long in use. It contains only a few alterations from the 1535 agenda. It is of note that Bullinger made notations on both the 1535 and 1563 printed agendas, as well as on the manuscript from 1532, and the Common Prayer of 1571. We are, therefore, in possession of two agendas that were revised by Bullinger himself over the course of time. It is possible that the 1563 agenda was printed to coincide with the introduction of the Reformation in the Palatinate, but this cannot yet be definitively proved. Certainly the text harmonises well with two contemporary documents: Ludwig Lavater's account of the conflict between the Zwinglians and the Lutherans over the Lord's Supper from 1524 to1563, and the *Second Helvetic Confession*. In all of these texts from the 1560s certain themes are prevalent: the innocence of the Reformed in the quarrel with the Lutherans and the orthodoxy of the Zwinglian church.

What do these agenda tell us about the liturgical life and development in Zurich during the middle decades of the sixteenth century? Many of the surviving copies give us the names of their owners as well as the occasional revision or addition. It is clear that ministers used these documents when conducting worship and that the alterations reflect the necessary changes made for the services. These documents also provide other fascinating clues about church life in Zurich. For instance, from some we are able to trace the introduction of certain of Bullinger's prayers into parish worship. A good example is the liturgy for the first anniver-

---

42. StA, E II 440, 493 (quoted in Bächtold, *Bullinger vor dem Rat*, 333).

sary of the lost battle of Kappel on 11 October 1531. From one note we know that the Psalm prayer *Ubi est zelus tuus* was required.

Another crucial date was the prayer *Conversi* of Augustine, which often, though not always, marked the end of Bullinger's sermons. In the agenda of 1563 Bullinger included it without commentary under the title *Post concionem*. In his handwritten agenda of 1532 he wrote beside it the date "7 November 1537." The link between the prayer and these notes is significant. During this period fell the unseemly quarrel over the *First Helvetic Confession* (1536) by which the Swiss had hoped to find some form of coexistence with Luther. The autumn of 1537 also brought Martin Bucer's attempt to force the Swiss to agree to the *Wittenberg Accord*, an act that earned him the enmity of Bullinger. What had particularly offended Bullinger was a letter from Bucer to Luther in which the former denigrated the Swiss theology of the Lord's Supper. Bullinger complained to Myconius in a letter of 4 November 1537:

> Every day we are weighed down by new writings, but I stand by the Basle Confession and its interpretation to Luther. I will confess no other. Others may wish to write a thousand confessions, but this one is enough for me. I am satisfied that each should stand by his own confession, which I will not accept or reject. What is not opposed to us I shall not judge. But I cannot understand Bucer's confession. I have no idea what it is intended to achieve. I confess this to you in friendship, but you can bear my simplicity. You, dear Myconius, should not be fearful of this new tragedy. We will remain united, it is just that I will not support this new endeavour. God knows my heart. He knows what I seek and this he will judge on the last day! I have written to Bucer, but I do not understand his endless correspondence. What I do understand is what Melanchthon writes and that pleases me, particularly what he has written on the sacrament.[43]

It is perhaps with this in mind that Bullinger composed the following Latin prayer:

> *CONVERSI ad Dominum Deum Patrem omnipotentem puro corde ei quantum potest parvitas nostra maximas atque veras gratias agamus, praecantes toto animo singularem mansuetudinem eius, ut preces nostrae in beneplacito suo exaudire dignetur inimicum quoque à nostris actibus et cogitationibus sua virtute expellat, nobis fidem multiplicet, mentem gubernet, spirituales cogitationes concedat et ad beatitudinem suam perducat. Per Jesum Christum filium suum dominum nostrum qui cum eo vivit et regnat in unitate spiritussancti Deus Per omnia saecula saeculorum. Amen.*
> *7 Novemb. MDXXXVII*

We find further entries for 1546 and 1567. In both cases these entries have an intercessory character. In 1546 the reference is to the looming Schmalkaldic War in the Empire, while in 1567 it was the persecution of the Huguenots in Lyon that Bullinger had in mind. In both cases the prayers added to the agenda are men-

---

43. Quoted in Pestalozzi, *Heinrich Bullinger*, 202.

tioned in his correspondence.[44] The prayers often form a response to bad news in the form of a penitential confession to an angry God. They seek sympathy for those suffering without attempting to bring about political or military intervention. They also have an international character, although they were often adapted for local use. We know through the correspondence between Zurich and Geneva that parallel prayers were an established practice: both churches would share a prayer for a particular event or occurrence. A good example of how these prayers could be used in services has been recently analysed by Hans Ulrich Bächtold in his study of the Tuesday worship during the economic and social crisis of 1572.

Further connections raise some fascinating possibilities. We have already noted the use of Psalm 9, which was introduced in the 1573 agenda. Clearly there was for Bullinger some connection between the Psalm and the massacre of St Bartholomew's Day. Bullinger was deeply engaged with the consequences of the massacre in the Empire and his principal text on the subject, *On the Persecution of the Church*, was written as a commentary on the Psalm. Pestalozzi, Bullinger's famous biographer, wrote in 1858:

> As the horror of the massacre in 1572 spread from Paris across France Bullinger was fearful that similar events could take place in the empire. Bullinger was deeply pained in reflecting on the devastating effect the massacre had had on the faithful, especially the more vulnerable. It was to encourage these threatened believers that he wrote the above-mentioned *On the Persecution of the Church* (1573), in which he laid out the grounds for persecution as well as for God's punishment of the persecutors. The text also contained Bullinger's admonition to the faithful to remain in perseverance, a key Zwinglian word. In his dedication to Count Ludwig von Sayn-Wittgenstein, Bullinger wrote: It is with great pain that I have realised that every faithless and dreadful bloodbath in France could be the cause of many similar events in German lands, so that many might begin to doubt the truth of our religion and teaching. It is in order to strengthen the doubters that I have written this text." The fact that the Protestants in France were able to save their church despite the catastrophe of St Bartholomew's Night was for Bullinger a miracle. He was not able to attend their synods so he wrote to them in a fatherly manner, admonishing them to unity and simplicity in their teaching and worship and to remain faithful in the face of all that might befall them.[45]

We turn now to the communication of the prophet with his community and examine this dialogue in both its theological and social historical contexts. We have already noted our surprise at the degree to which Bullinger fastened his view of the clergy to the model of the Levitical priesthood in order to explain his understanding of ministers as servants of the Word. This position corresponds with the current view in scholarship that the introduction of the priesthood of all believers

---

44. Heinrich Bullinger to Ambrosius Blarer, 21.7.1546, edited in *Briefwechsel der Brüder Ambrosius und Thomas Blaurer 1509-1548*, vol. 2 (Freiburg i. Br.: 1910), 476f. On his correspondence with Beza, see "Bullinger-Zeytungen," 17.10.1567, edited in *Correspondance*, 8:267f. Also see Heinrich Bullinger to Konrad Ulmer, 17.10.1567, edited in *Correspondance* 8:268f.

45. Pestalozzi, *Heinrich Bullinger*, 441f.

and the rejection of the sacrificial priesthood of the mass did not have the effect of depriving the clergy of their position as mediators between the laity and God. The unique aspect in Zurich was the retention of the late-medieval public confession of sin, which in other south German cities was greatly diminished. In Zurich this confession remained part of the liturgy and was placed after the sermon, while the Strasbourg model put confession at the start of the service, as it was for the mass. Here it was originally directed towards the people by the celebrant, while in Zurich the old public confession remained intact. This character of Zurich worship was greatly strengthened by the introduction of the Common Prayer for the Tuesday service in 1572. The priestly character of the minister remained an essential element, although Zurich clearly belonged to the religious world of Upper Rhine Protestantism. The other cities tended more towards the models of church discipline constructed by Bucer in Strasbourg and Blarer in Constance. The collective penitential services in Zurich contrasted with the individual character of penitence favoured for the Lord's Supper in Strasbourg and Geneva. The Zurich minister remained a part of the repentant community as its priest.

These liturgical practices were backed up by the developing theology in Zurich. In the Zentralbibliothek in Zurich there is a two-volume manuscript from the hand of Bullinger that was clearly a blueprint for the *Decades*.[46] In twenty *loci* Bullinger drew up a list of the most important theological propositions together with the relevant biblical texts and commentary from the church fathers. If we compare what Bullinger has to say on penitence and confession in these loci and then in the *Decades* there are some fascinating insights. For the most part the material is in agreement, and in both cases the *Exhomologese* of the Early Church was used. In the case of the loci collection, however, it is used to deny the historical validity of individual confession as well as auricular confession, while in the *Decades* it is used to bolster the Reformed teaching on penitential practices.

From the middle of the sixteenth century there was a perceived need for greater rigour in confession and this was reflected in intensified church practices in Zurich, as Bächtold has discussed. What Bächtold has found in his social historical analysis of the Zurich church fits well with Biel's study of Bullinger in the 1530s. Bullinger was moving towards his firm conviction that the preacher is the mediator between God and his people and that in this office he holds the full authority of discipline.[47]

The richness of the sources enables us to use Bullinger's Isaiah sermons as an example of how in the Zurich church the transition was made from exegetical work to communication of scripture to the people. From Zwingli's *Archeteles* it was clearly established in Zurich that the *episcopus*, or minister, was bound by *lectio continua* to the interpretation of the whole biblical book, but that this also gave him the freedom to choose on which book he wished to preach. Zwingli's intention with his text *Archeteles*, which was addressed to the bishop of Constance, was to demonstrate that he, Zwingli, had assumed episcopal authority on account of the bishop's negligence. The choice of biblical book was a sign of official competence, and in his *Reformation History* Bullinger cited not only the

---

46. ZB, Ms. Car 152 and 153.
47. Biel, *Doorkeepers*, 134.

lectio continua itself, but also its value in building the community. For Bullinger the establishment of preaching, the building of parishes, the *doctrina Christiana*, and contemporary history formed a seamless robe. The Isaiah sermons are particularly useful because we have such an abundance of material, including the commentaries of Oecolampadius and Bibliander, which have been preserved through Bullinger's notes on Bibliander's lectures delivered between 1548 and 1562. We also have Bullinger's sermons as recorded by Wolfgang Haller and Rudolf Gwalther, which were published in Latin translation with prefaces. For anyone wishing to study the liturgy in Zurich in the sixteenth century, it is crucial that considerable attention be given to both extant texts and the processes of communication. Although scholars have persuasively demonstrated that the sermons were neither exegetical nor academic lectures, they have not yet been entirely successful in determining what exactly they were. Because the documents that detail the communication process from biblical exegesis to both the sermon in the parish church and the instructional literature have survived intact, it is now possible to establish the proper character of the sermons.

In the example appended at the end of this chapter we get a sense of Bullinger's rhetorical style as he equates Israel, the Apostolic Church, and the contemporary situation in Zurich in which he is criticising the council. In his critique of Christendom and the Swiss Confederation, he says to Zurich "what is being done in our city?" (*"Quid in nostra urbe factum?"*). This break with the authorities does not lack clarity. In this matter Bullinger hardly used church discipline less than Calvin or Bucer. The office of the key, as the sermon was designated in Reformed thought, was forceful in its application. The zealous preacher was protected in his work by proper exegesis.

We return to the question of what "liturgy" meant in the lives of men and women in the sixteenth century. It was a regulated, public, and practical communication with God. Bullinger's creativity in the liturgical field can be measured by both his prayers, which were closely bound to contemporary events, and his choice of biblical books for preaching. This enables us to have an insight into the spirituality shared by Bullinger and his congregation in the Grossmünster.

To close I would like to present two documents which have not yet received any attention. One is an addition to Bullinger's 1532 and 1563 agendas. They form a rich collection of prayers in Latin that are often drawn from older traditions of sacramentars (medieval books with some liturgical texts for the mass) including the Milanese (Ambrosian) liturgy. The collection is organised according to the evangelical church year, but its underlying principles have not yet been examined. The other text is a prayer book (*Baettbuechlin*) put together by Johannes Wolf in 1623. It has over one hundred pages and two hundred prayers, of which a considerable number are by Heinrich Bullinger.[48] In the preface reference is made to a prayer book that is now lost and to which there is no bibliographical reference. Wolf says that he is presenting an expanded version of Bullinger's personal prayer book, which he greatly treasured.

Even if our conclusions must remain speculative, the survival of one exemplar of the prayer book and the specific use of the Latin prayers presents us with

---

48. *HBBibl* I, no. 720.

evidence for the liturgy of the clergy and those laity who could read German, but not Latin. The Latin prayer collection also points to the liturgy of the clergy. One look at the rubrics for the prayers shows that many of them originated from the prayers for votive masses–prayers that were intended for particular occasions. The collects were not necessarily taken from the prayers for the Eucharist nor were they to be used in that context. Under the title *Gratiarum actio* may lie a form of worship that is still unknown to us.

Gratiarum actiones:

DEUS, cuius misericordiae non est numerus et bonitatis infinitus est thesaurus, tuae piissimae maiestati pro collatis nobis donis gratias agimus, tuam semper clementiam exorantes, ut qui te invocantibus postulata concedis, eosdem non deserens ad praemia futura disponas. Per Iesum etc.

ORATIOnum nostrarum petitionem cum gratiarum actionibus suscipe, Domine, quaesumus, et praesta, ut quos exaudire et incolumes servare dignatus es, ab omni in posterum animae et corporis adversitate custodias, utque per haec tua beneficia, quae nobis conferre dignatus [36 recto] es, tuum nomen semper magnificemus et in tuo amore servitioque semper crescamus. Per Christum etc.
Gregor. Homilia in Ezech.5.

GRATIAS tibi reddimus, Domine Deus creator noster, de bonis, quae accepimus, tibique cum Isaia propheta suppliciter dicimus: Omnia opera nostra operatus es in nobis. Bona enim nostra tua sunt opera. Cuius miseribus¿ non suffecit, ut nos exigeres, nisi et temetipsum pro nobis inclinares. Si enim coaeternus patri Deus non fieres homo in tempore, numquam homo temporalis saperet aeterna. Descensio ergo veritatis tuae ascensio facta est humanitatis nostrae. Damus ergo tibi gloriam, damus tibi laudem, qui vivis et regnas etc.
M: Homil.:

DOMINE Iesu iuste, quem advoca- [36 verso]tum apud patrem habemus, iustos nos defende in iuditio, qua nosmetipsos cognoscimus et accusamus iniustos. Non enim in fletibus, non in actionibus nostris, sed in advocati nostri patrocinio confidimus. Qui vivit etc.

This is not necessarily a Eucharistic prayer. Rather, the repeated use of thanksgiving in prayer makes it likely that a form of thanksgiving service was regularly held in Zurich. Thus we must consider that alongside the known penitential services in Zurich there was also a regular service of thanksgiving. How did it stand in liturgical relationship to the other services? That remains to be discovered.

This survey of the untrod territory of Reformed liturgy leads to a final observation concerning future research. There remains in practical theology, since D.F.E. Schleiermacher, a distinction between sermon and liturgy; in other words, liturgy and homiletics have been divided. In the sixteenth century no such distinction was made, and if we are to understand the liturgical culture that developed in Zurich after the Reformation it is crucial to approach liturgy in a more holistic manner, mindful of the interplay of exegesis, theology, sermon, and current events. This initial inquiry has pointed to the essential connection between prayer and communication processes as the essence of liturgy.

Appendix

(EXPLICAT MAGIS) WIE sij zur huoren worden und landet schliesslich bei denen, die tonangebend für den Verfall verantwortlich seien: *PRINCIPES tui. Die es weeren sottend, warend die bösten, der küng, fürsten vnnd rädt.*

CONCIO VII
15. Febr. 1562.
Quomodo meretrix facta est etc.
(...)
Haec ita examinanda sunt vt ad nos quoque refferamus. Ein spiegel nützt nüt / so man Jnn nit brucht. Ita et Scriptura.
(...)
EXPONIT QUALIS FUErit Ierusalem. FIDELES. Es stuond zuo den alten zyten wol vm dstatt vnds land, sij warend gloübig vnd trüw an Gott, wie ein frommer gmahel am anderen, den er lieben, In eeren hat vnd dienet. Also wared sij gegen Gott vnder dem David, sij glouptend allein in Jnn, namend keine götzen an, vernuogtend sich gotz vnd sines diensts. hattend weder Baal, Moloch, Astarot etc. [33 verso] vnder Aza vnd Iosaphat reformiertends wider vnd tatend wider hinweg was vsgericht was. Sij hattend ouch herrlich lüt Inn der oberkeit, fromm glert trüw lerer vnd diener, ward als bij inen funden was zuo eer vnd guoten dienet.
Also ists etwan in Helvetia gstanden / ein fromm vfrecht schlecht volk gsin / burger, lantlüt, hantwerchs lüt. Es ist dess wuosts vnd läbens nüt gsin.es ist ein ruom gsin allenthalben, von grechtigkeit vnd früntligkeit, mit wägwisen vnd sicherheit, das man ouch gseit das einer dörfft gold an ein stäken durchs land tragen.
SED QUID NUNC. wie ists als zur huoren worden? [34 recto] Das wort hand wir noch / so man vbel handlen, hushat, verdirbt. Ein huor ist die vntrüw ist an Jrem man / nit hushat, rennt, loufft, kein guotz anfacht, den guoten man äfft vnd bedört.
Wie was es mit Ierusalem? Sij benuogtend sich gotz vnd seines diensts nit, wustend wenigs von Christo, namend götzen an, machtend cappelen vnd älter als neber zuohin. Es was inn der oberkeit nüt guot mee, schelmen vnd buoben, die got vnd dem volck nüt nachfragen, sunder Jrem pracht vnd gwalt. daneben was alle bueberij.
Wie stats ietz inn der Christenlichen kilchen? sij ist abtrünnig worden, huerig worden, Christi nit bemuegt, vil creaturen / fürpitt vnnd opfer angenommen. die kilch hat es nit tan, sed mali homines qui ... nomine ecclesiae. Es sind wenig nüwer hereren mee / wenig frommer lüten mee, kein gricht noch recht.
Ita et in Helvetia ...: Amissa [34 verso] verus laus. Vn weise wie es stat. Summa es ist als zur huoren worden. Es ist kein trüw vnd grechtigkeit mee. Man nimpt gelt von fürsten vnd herren / henkt sich an sij, hilft inen zuo irem muotwillen, daneben achtet man keiner pündten noch nach purschaften. das gat nieman zhertzen / dem fragt nieman nüt noch.
Wie stats vmmb gricht vnd recht? So iemands rechts bgert, mag er nit darzuo kommen. Ein anderer muos gält han wil er recht han.
Wie ist man so vnfrüntlich, hässig, vnfridlich vnd verachtig worden; wie vil schrijend der friden welle vns verderben; Sich wie es gat.

Also ists etwan vm die Christenlich kilchen gstanden, die gar trüw an Christo
vnd gloübig gsin. 2.Cor.11. desponsavi vos uni vivo etc. es war grosse trüw, hat
keine creaturen angruefft, kein andere fürpitt noch opfer ghan dann alein christi,
fromm gsin vnd allem bösen gwert vnd vorgsin.
Ita fit in toto Christiano orbe et Germania quoque.
Was hoffart / pracht, muotwillen wirt mm triben, von burgeren vnnd pueren. fürsten vnnd herren hand etwan nit so vil dran tan.
Quid ın nostra urbe factum? *wer vor ein liebe hat zuo gotz wort vnnd ein ijfer,*
der gieng darzuo, dorfft reden, kam für, [35 recto] ietz kan der nit für kommen /
muos e, fürchten, nieman darff nüt me reden.
EXPLICAT MAGIS WIE sij zur huoren worden.
...
Diewijl da von der oberkeit har kumpt, stat er an sij.
PRINCIPES tui. Die es weeren sottend, warend die bösten, der küng, fürsten vnnd
rädt. So ein husvatter vnd husmuoter trüncken vnnd verruocht / so gat das gantz
hus ze schijteren. Ita in populo. So der apt dwürffel leit, so spilt der Convent.
Ideo vocat vos
Disertores, abtrünnig, von got, vonn sim wort, vom glouben, wottend ouch nit
das mia inen Inredte. Vide ca. 30. Hoc adhuc fit [36 recto] man seit den Predi-
canten nütt von bscheidenheit. Man seit, man muog luogen wie man inen thuege.
Oderunt ministros.
Gmeinder den dieben / nit der offnen diiben die man henckt, sonder der grossen
die mit wuocher, bschiss vnnd faltsch vmgand. Eph.4. sij wared ire gsellen, lies-
sends machen, warttend inen nüt. So du nit werst ein vbel so wirst ouch dess
teilhaftig, fures so sij gmein hand, latrones so sij einanderen verwarend, finnt
consortes peccati et poenae. Ita hic. ex magistratu liggend mit denen wuoherer
under der teki.

157

6

Bullinger on Church Authority: The Transformation of the Prophetic Role in Christian Ministry

Daniel Bolliger

One aspect of Heinrich Bullinger's life and work much emphasised in recent scholarship is his extraordinary influence over the church in Zurich. His position as a learned and prolific theologian and leader of the church was unrivalled.[1] Without his enormous influence as an "opinion leader" it is clear that the Reformation in Zurich would have been silenced, if not in 1531, then at some later point during the sixteenth century. This chapter will explore the theological and historical development of Bullinger's understanding of his institutional role and his acceptance of an unusual, quasi-episcopal position in the Zurich church. The question of Bullinger's official position in Zurich is central for our understanding of the question of authority within the Reformed church. We know that Bullinger worked hard to ensure that there would be a smooth transition of church leadership after his death; he did this through both his will[2] and his late historical writings, in which he presented as his legacy his view of the Reformation and heavily emphasised his own role as an eyewitness to the events described.[3] Nevertheless, the position that Bullinger passed to Rudolf Gwalther in 1575 had greatly evolved from 1531 when the young preacher from Bremgarten had assumed office. During the intervening forty years Bullinger had moulded the role of chief minister (or *Antistes*, as it was later called), subtly but decisively moving it away from Zwingli's conception of the prophet towards his own understanding of a bishop. The shift took place for theological, exegetical, and ecclesiastical reasons which I shall attempt to map in this chapter.

If we begin with Bullinger himself, it is impossible for us to judge how far his domination of the Zurich church was a result of personal ambition as, quite naturally, this was not a subject he would have addressed. Likewise, in investigating the extent to which his position as chief minister was reflected in the official documents of the church, we might paraphrase Foucault's dictum: the reformer is

---

1. Pamela Biel, *Doorkeepers at the house of Righteousness. Heinrich Bullinger and the Zurich Clergy 1535-1575* (ZBRG 15; Berne: Peter Lang, 1990); Andreas Mühling, *Heinrich Bullingers europäische Kirchenpolitik* (ZBRG 19; Berne: Peter Lang, 2001); Bruce Gordon, *The Swiss Reformation* (Manchester: Manchester Univ. Press, 2002), esp. 348.
2. Pamela Biel, "Heinrich Bullinger's Death and Testament: A Well-planned Departure," *Sixteenth Century Journal* 22 (1991): 3-14.
3. See the essay by Christian Moser in this volume.

hardly part of the Reformation discourse. Given the nature of events in the 1520s, the reformers were extremely nervous about openly discussing episcopal authority, for in Reformed ecclesiology it was unthinkable for the chief ministers, or *Antistes*, to be singled out for a special office. Bullinger dealt with this question of terminology by choosing to refer to himself as "(a) servant [*minister*] of the Zurich church." He only started to discuss the distinctive office that he personally held when, in a series of publications, he came to treat the subject of church offices. Nevertheless, in examining his statements on his office we find that remarkable modifications were made during his career. The principal difference lay in the manner in which the office of the minister developed from prophet to that of a servant of the church. The change may appear to be only terminological, but what lay behind it was the evolving character of both the Zurich church and Bullinger himself. Over the course of his tenure as first minister Bullinger had to come to terms with the hierarchical character of the biblical offices of the pastorate whilst attempting to remain true to his belief in the equality of all ministers.

From 1523 Zwingli aggressively employed the concept of the prophet in the fierce debates over the proper understanding of theological authority. The reformer of Zurich took aim at the authority of ecclesiastical hierarchy in the interpretation of scripture by stressing those passages of the Bible where the Greek word *propheteuein* in the New Testament appears, mainly 1 Corinthians 14. This term ("prophesying") he understood exclusively as a corporate, i.e. not hierarchical, manner of interpreting the Bible. The Zurich New Testament of 1524, an adaptation of Luther's *Septembertestament* made under Zwingli's direction, replaced Luther's translation *weyssagen* or *Weyssager* (which means having an *immediate* inspiration) with *prophezeyen* or "prophet," which, for Zwingli, meant being inspired to explain the scriptures.[4] This change was made no less than seventeen times and was directed against the bishop of Constance, to whom Zwingli wanted to prove that he and his friends were legitimately and correctly interpreting the Bible. The authority of the Zurich reformers rested on two points: they were prophets, and that anyone could refute a doctor or prelate who contradicted scripture, even if this contradiction bore the weight of ecclesiastical tradition.

Bullinger's first work on the office of the prophet, *De propheta libri duo*, was written in June 1525 and followed Zwingli in its rejection of the Anabaptist attempt to equate prophetic with lay exposition of scripture. Although *De propheta libri duo* was a work of considerable length, political circumstances precluded its publication.[5] In the work Bullinger distinguishes, on the one hand, between the prophet as an Old Testament seer or a New Testament *episcopus* and, on the

---

4. Traudel Himmighöfer, *Die Zürcher Bibel bis zum Tode Zwinglis (1531). Darstellung und Bibliographie* (Veröffentlichungen des Instituts für Europäische Geschichte Mainz, Abteilung Religionsgeschichte 154; Mainz: von Zabern, 1995), 180-4.

5. *De propheta Heilrÿchii [sic] Bullingeri libri duo. In hisce duobus libris, quos prophetae titulo appellamus, veluti per transennam expositum reperies, veri prophetae offitium: et quid eum promoveat, ut doceat aperte, ut frivulos adhibeat, atque consternatos animos sublevet consolando, cum aliis quibusdam imprimis huc pernecessariis. Quorum indicem versa pagina reperies. J[esu]. Addita est Leonis Tigurinorum episcopi, in hosce libros, ad lectorem prefatio. [...] 1525.*

other, as an interpreter of the Bible according to 1 Corinthians 14.[6] This distinction was later more precisely defined, but in 1525 Bullinger held the prophet to be primarily an expositor of scripture and then a preacher. Accordingly, the *De propheta* is divided into two sections to cover these aspects of the prophetic office. The first book demonstrates how the prophet comes to a proper understanding of a biblical passage through an accurate reading achieved through conformity to the proper rules of exegesis. The second book concerns how the prophet is able to transmit this knowledge to the wider public in a persuasive manner. The speech (*oratio*) is described by Bullinger as the "tool of the prophets", just as Zwingli in 1529 had described the prophetic work as the art of exposition connected to the rhetorical method.[7] While many aspects of these tools (type, construction, and figures of speech) are associated with the names Quintilian and Cicero, all uses of rhetoric as ends in themselves are rejected–a subtle but clear repudiation of the humanist tendency towards an obsession with rhetoric for its own sake. For Bullinger, the tools of classical learning were valid only when applied to the search for Christian truth: he not only insisted on the fundamental importance of classical tools for the interpretation of texts and their rhetorical presentation, but also eagerly worked to demonstrate their application. While Zwingli tended to stress the effects of the rhetorical arts over their form, Bullinger devoted much more time to arranging them in a precise order so that they might be used. This reflected the pedagogical skills that Bullinger had honed during his years as a teacher at the Cistercian monastery at Kappel.

It is clear that to some extent his *De propheta* contains elements of a deeply moving, if not very dramatic, spiritual autobiography. The Kappel Bullinger was tormented by the question of religious authority that had begun to trouble him in Cologne from 1519. In *De scripture negotio* of 1523, written as a fictitious letter by Bullinger's Abbot Joner to a friend, Joner describes how he discovers that even the fathers trusted only in the authority of scripture. Bullinger then declares his desire to follow the Bible–a decision that gives him a wonderful experience of the sweetness and completeness of scripture–and resolves to leave behind all the doctors, schools and councils in favour of God's Word. This renunciation was highly significant for the young scholar who, in a spiritual crisis, craved a stable foundation, and even admitted that he almost despaired of life. In the work, Bullinger is emphatic about the complete coherence of scripture; he insists, following Luther, that every passage can be understood with the aid of another.[8] This formal notion of scriptural sufficiency is enhanced in *De propheta* by a detailed marshalling of verses on biblical coherence. While the second part of the first book on the prophet as expositor deals with the correct understanding of the different sorts of biblical texts, almost the entire first half is dedicated to the subject of biblical unity. These early developments and influences proved of the greatest

6. *De propheta*, [ZB, Ms. I, 3 (7)]: "Sed in novo quoque Testamento hi etiam dicebantur prophetae, qui scripturarum sensum populo apperiebant [...] Nobis de eo propheta sermo sit qui publice interpretatur, qui docet, hortatur et consolatur."

7. His preface to the prophets, in *Z* VI/2:289-312, stresses the importance of comprehensible translation along rhetorical principles.

8. He uses several quotations of Augustine and one of Hilary of Poitiers that reappear in *De propheta*, and later in *De prophetae* and many other writings.

importance to the later evolution of his understanding of the clerical office. The unity of scripture is a key presupposition for the unity of the evangelical ministry, which in turn was charged with bringing proof of scripture into the world. Yet, at this stage of Bullinger's life, the insistence on scriptural omnisufficience became so pronounced that the young scholar displayed a slight arrogance. Whereas Luther and Zwingli knew exactly why they had rejected the scholastics, according to Bullinger, in the introductory three chapters of *De propheta,* the medieval churchmen *are* suspect because of the mere presumption that their works are not biblical enough. At this stage of his intellectual development *sola scriptura* had an almost ideological note and was in danger of degenerating into a mere *petitio principii prophetizandi.*

De prophetae officio

Bullinger's next significant treatment of the prophetic office was an elaboration of his earlier position of 1525 in which the concept of the prophet was fundamentally expanded and more deeply grounded in his theology.

The occasion on which he first presented this new conception of prophecy could not have been more important to both his personal career and Zurich's wavering path as a Christian commonwealth. On 28 January 1532 the recently appointed *Antistes* delivered his programmatic oration *De prophetae officio et quomodo digne possit administrari oratio.*[9] It was certainly a remarkable moment, for although Bullinger had shown brilliant promise, he was still a relatively young man and untested in his new office. It was important for him to introduce himself to many of his colleagues, as well as to the prominent people of Zurich, not only as a orator, but, more crucially, as a leader. The occasion was the feast of Charlemagne, which had been celebrated in Zurich since time immemorial. The city was a centre of Caroline veneration in the Holy Roman Empire.[10] The enthusiasm of the people for emperor had certainly not diminished in the late middle ages and there is evidence that devotion was growing in the decades before the Reformation.[11] What exactly happened to the celebration in the years after the iconoclasm of 1525, during which the signs of veneration for Charlemagne were violently removed from the Grossmünster, remains unclear.[12] What we do know for certain is that in 1532 the old feast day was still being celebrated (or had been reintroduced) in a revised form: the audience for Bullinger's Latin

---

9. *De prophetae officio et quomodo digne possit administrari oratio* (Zurich: Froschauer, 1532). The text will be found in a modern German translation in Emidio Campi et al. eds, *Heinrich Bullinger: Schriften* vol. 1 (Zurich: 2004).

10. Two generations after Charlemagne was canonised (1165) the Großmünster chapter had already acquired (1233) his thumb from his sepulchre in Aachen. This led to a regular collective celebration of his day of death.

11. In 1405 a second prebend to the altar was endowed by canon Niklaus Trütler; cf. Andreas Meyer, *Zürich und Rom. Ordentliche Kollatur und päpstliche Provisionen am Frau- und Großmünster 1316-1523* (Bibliothek des Deutschen Historischen Instituts in Rom 64; Tübingen: Niemeyer, 1986), 549.

12. What we know for sure is that the second chaplain of the altar, Laurentius Moser, held his prebend until 1531, when he probably died–but this proves nothing more than that he was still provided an income in order to prevent there being another beggar in the city.

oration was not, however, the people of Zurich, but the canons of the Grossmünster college, the ministers of the city, and, perhaps, some of the rural ministers.[13]

Even though the guild of canons, and of ministers, gathered in the Grossmünster formed a more or less closed body, Charlemagne's Day remained an event of pre-modern *civic* religion.[14] In celebrating Charlemagne as a saint and divine monarch, as well as the founder of the chapter and its school, Zurich was also celebrating herself, her origins and traditions, and was seeking to rescue her troubled dignity after the disaster of Kappel. 28 January was something like a civic holiday, and when it approached in 1532 the people hungered as never before for a new interpretation of events, confirmation of their identity, and a sense of the city's purpose in history. It was quite a challenge to meet the implicit and explicit demands of the moment, and if we suppose that Bullinger was invited to give the speech only after his nomination as *Antistes* on 9 December, it is clear that he did not have long to prepare the text. Yet the result was a lucid, well-balanced, and coherent statement on a deeply controversial subject.

If we compare the section titles of *De prophetae* to those that Bullinger gave to the text of *De propheta* of 1525, we can grasp the structure and nature of the 1532 oration. In *De prophetae officio* Bullinger provides a simple–by this we mean a single rather than a double–thematic speech in classical form. The opening *exordium*, with its *captatio benevolentiae* and *status*, is followed by the *confirmatio*, then the *cohortatio*, and, finally, the epilogue.[15] *De propheta* proposes an alternative designation–*propositio, confirmatio, confutatio*–for the same structure. This revision fits the purpose of *De prophetae officio* because it is able to express how the second and third parts of the work are clearly related to each other as two sides of the same coin, i.e. the same prophetical task.[16] In the *confirmatio* the prophet is supposed to be a good exegete or doctor, whereas in the *confutatio* his *officium* suddenly turns into that of a pastor or bishop. The methodological explanations of the *confirmatio* are almost entirely taken (though par-

---

13. This in turn established (or continued) a new tradition, which was to last exactly three centuries. In addition to the speeches already known–listed by F. Büsser, "J. H. Hottinger und der Thesaurus Hottingerianus," *Zwingliana* 22 (1995): 85f.– there must have been many speeches for the feast of Charlemagne (*Karlstagsreden*), the text of which are to be found in the ZB or StA. The identification with Zurich's alleged roots in the Carolingian Renaissance grew so strong that from the 17th century the theological school was called Schola Carolina. See Anton Largadièr, "Das reformierte Zürich und die Fest- und Heiligentage," *Zwingliana* 9 (1953): 497-525.

14. A vernacular version of the speech was never printed. It was clearly a speech for the erudite. The identity which Bullinger gives to the prophet might seem to have something of the modern sense of "intellectual snobbery," indeed Bullinger does not at all feel inhibited to consider the prophet's hearers as a "stulta [...] plebecula cuius proprium est raro aut prorsus nihil sapere, immanis [...] et indomita multorumque capitum belua" (f. 15ᵛ).

15. Compare Quintilian. III,9,1; Cicero., Inv. 1,14,19. See also S. Hausammann, "Die Rhetorik im Dienst der reformatorischen Schiftauslegung," *Kerygma und Dogma: Zeitschrift für theologische Forschung und kirchliche Lehre* 20 (1974): 305-14.

16. *De prophetae officio*, 34b: "Et rectius meo iuditio hanc partem nonnulli contentionem nuncupavere, cuius partes sint, propositio, confirmatio, confutatio. Sic ut propositio sit thema, status sive questio. Confirmatio thematis declaratio. Confutatio vera pars est qua adversariorum tela excipiamus. Porro peroratio sive epilogus constat duabus rebus, enumeratione et adfectu; enumeratio est brevis eorum que tota oratione sparsim dicta sunt repetitio summaria. Affectus est vehementior animi commotio."

tially rearranged in their order) from the first book of *De propheta*. This reminds us of the late Fritz Blanke's pointed declaration that Bullinger's theology was already set *before* he came to Zurich.[17] Although this is rather an overstatement, the text of *De prophetae officio* is indeed to a large extent woven out of citations, fragments, and even whole paragraphs from earlier writings of Bullinger, principally *De propheta libri duo*, but also from the *Studiorum ratio* and other writings. The groundwork for the above-mentioned innovations in the 1532 oration was laid in the thinking of the young Bullinger. This also explains how Bullinger was able to produce such a sophisticated oration in such short order.

Bullinger's elaboration of the prophetic office in 1532 grew out of both his own earlier writings and those of Huldrych Zwingli. In his booklet *On the preaching office* of 30 June 1525 Zwingli had brought a pastoral dimension to the exegetical duty of the prophet.[18] Because his own original anti-hierarchical view of prophecy was increasingly used against him, Zwingli had to diversify his position. Therefore, he maintained that only after the elected pastor had spoken, and then only if he was in error (contradicted scripture), did members of the community have the right to prophesy.[19] The pastoral, authoritative aspect of the prophetic office was now as important to Zwingli as its doctrinal function. By linking the two, Zwingli sought to unify two aspects of the prophetic concept that throughout church history had existed at various times in harmony and dialectical opposition: the prophet as teacher *and* pastor.[20]

Bullinger followed Zwingli very clearly in this direction. Having placed the teaching and pastoral functions in his *Studiorum ratio* of 1528 on a more equal level than in 1525, in 1532 he completely aligned them in the introductory *status* by repeating his or Zwingli's arguments of 1525. The Hebrews, Bullinger writes, called the prophets seers because they could see into the future, whereas the bishops or *epi-scopoi* (in Latin *speculatores*) must see into the situation of their parishes. This theory used by Bullinger, even though Jerome was its ingenious creator and it was commonly used throughout the late middle ages, was, however, based on a highly speculative and rather equivocal etymological similarity that could not really settle the argument. Consequently, Bullinger also provided another, more convincing link, citing Jeremiah 1:9, a verse already mentioned in *De propheta*, in the *Studiorum ratio* and by Zwingli, where God places the prophet "to uproot and tear down, to destroy and overthrow, to build and to

17. Fritz Blanke, "Die Theologie des jungen Bullinger," *Neue Zürcher Zeitung* 1962, Nr. 4467.

18. Z IV:397,33-398,7. Translated: "Therefore we have two types of prophetical office. On the one hand, as the prophets in the Old Testament prevented the evil and planted the good; so do the wardens or pastors in the New Testament. Therefore the prophetical, the episcopal and the evangelists' office are all but one. The other prophetical office is when in big churches they disclose the sense of scripture, first in the Old Testament, when there is a meeting to learn the Bible. This is not common now, yet if God permits, this will begin with us in Zurich in only a few days. [...]."

19. For Zwingli, they could not earnestly claim to be real prophets because they did not master Hebrew, which since the Apostles' time was an indispensable mark of office (*nota prophetae*).

20. On this point, see Lucerna Schlosser, *Lucerna in caliginoso loco. Aspekte des Prophetie-Begriffes in der scholastischen Theologie* (Veröffentlichung des Grabmann-Institutes, new series 43; Paderborn: 2000).

plant." Bullinger understood this passage to mean that the prophet has both a positive and a negative role, a programmatic opposition which is explained by the two main parts of the oration. What the doctor teaches the minister must defend.

The Covenant and the Pastoral Office

This dialectic of teaching and defending did not successfully draw out the more attractive aspects of this new pastoral side to the prophetic office. Bullinger, therefore, connected the pastoral and teaching aspects through another essential development indicated in *De prophetae officio*: covenant theology. Bullinger clearly applied covenant theology both in his teaching on scriptural interpretation and in his treatment of the pastoral office of the prophet.

Already in 1523, referring to Romans 10:4, Bullinger cautiously employed the traditional term *testamentum* (covenant), in his writing. At the beginning of his interpretation of the letter to the Hebrews in 1526 he openly declared that the New Testament is the fulfillment of the covenant with Israel. He then proceeded further in this direction by responding to a question which, although only implicitly posed in the 1532 oration, was present in all the new disciples of the humanist *philosophia christiana* of the 1520s: if the New Testament is *the* important part of the Bible, what is the purpose of the rest of scripture? Bullinger's answer lay in the covenant of God and humanity, culminating in God's testament in Christ, which is the overall *status* of scripture as a whole. Therefore, and correspondingly, the *status* of every precept, story, pericope or letter, in short, of every passage of the Bible refers, if adequately interpreted, to this great basic *status* (the covenant). The prophet is responsible for linking the traditional medieval understanding of the divine covenant or testament with the new principle of scriptural sufficiency. This unity, according to Bullinger, is only possible through the adoption of a new methodological approach, which is the true task of the prophet.

In proposing this solution, Bullinger refined his previous position found in chapter 20 of the *Studiorum ratio* of 1528, entitled: *De unico scripturae scopo, ad quem omnia bibliorum referantur.*[21] Clearly, Bullinger was reflecting more deeply on the issue of scriptural coherence and on how to integrate tensions between differing biblical texts into his somewhat naive earlier conceptions. Such reflections were typical for the development of the Reformation movement in general, for reformers in the several wings of the movement read the Bible very differently, and each felt a growing need to supplement the formal principle of scriptural interpretation with a material one. Bullinger's way was simply to deny any tension between the formal and material aspects: for him, the material principle of the covenant proved and guaranteed the formal principle of sufficiency of the Bible and *vice versa.*[22] The link between the two is the prophet.

---

21. Chapters 21 to 28 of this work all serve this goal to a certain extent, characterising the relationship of the different groups or sorts of biblical books to the *testamentum*. Whether this method was ever achieved *completely*, in practice for each single pericope or chapter is another question.

22. This is why he held the Old Testament in such high esteem not only the legal parts of it, but also the historical books, as he stresses in *De prophetae officio* very clearly. It proves that the

In Bullinger's argument the logic could be further extended. Just as the prophet in covenant theology mediates between the formal and material scripture principles, so too can these mediate between the contrasting sides of the prophetic office. Whereas the *confirmatio* in the oration develops, as we have seen, the positive task of the prophet, the *confutatio* deals with the negative side of this same prophetic duty. Where the scripture principle is disrespected, the prophet has to intervene in uncovering and rebuking this offence. The manner in which Bullinger describes this twofold duty can be regarded as a treatment of the question at first for the formal,[23] but then also for the material aspect.[24] This reveals to us the symmetrical structure of Bullinger's *confutatio*. In other words, an error is a violation of the formal while a vice is a deviation from the material scriptural principle. This is embedded in another symmetry: the teacher-prophet has to present these principles from the pulpit, while the pastor-prophet has to combat all deviations through contact with the people.

Bullinger then had to devise a means of combining the two aspects. First, we note an important difference from the third section to the fourth: those who constantly err, who reject the Bible as a formal principle, are always already *outside* the Church. The prophet, Bullinger declares, has to watch that these inveterate sinners do not infect the healthy body of the faithful. Those who commit sins, on the contrary, should by all means be kept *within* the community by the Church. If they have to be rebuked, Bullinger says, that should happen in all prudence. Only public crimes should be publicly named from the pulpit, and then in a constructive rather than a vengeful manner. This mirrored the medieval differentiation of heretics from sinners: heretics, who simply and obstinately reject tenets of faith, are outside the Church, while sinners, who are too weak to live according to the rules of faith, remain inside. The ethical ideals of the 1532 oration were not original, as the evils Bullinger denounces appeared in dozens of lay pamphlets of the period. But again, what is new, as in the first section, is the manner in which Bullinger combines these ethical norms with the covenant. And his conception of the divine covenant has a dual structure, as he explains extensively in the *Studiorum ratio* and later works: God offers a covenant in order to share his love with his partners, but he will punish those who abandon the covenant. The covenant is strictly mutual, and if the human partners of the covenant do not respect this mutuality, the relationship becomes negative. Naturally the punishment or judgement is intended to bring back to the fold those in danger of deserting the

---

covenant was at all times the centre of divine action and in turn that the earlier appearance of the covenant in the Old Testament meant that this was a legitimate and necessary part of scripture. The external form of the New Testament as a written text was also much more important to him than for other reformers. See S. Hausammann, "Anfragen zum Schriftverständnis des jungen Bullinger im Zusammenhang einer Interpretation von 'De scripturae negotio'" in Ulrich Gäbler/Erland Herkenrath eds., *Heinrich Bullinger 1504-1575. Gesammelte Aufsätze zum 400. Todestag*, vol. 1: *Leben und Werk* (ZBRG 7; Zurich: TVZ, 1975), 29-48.

23. In the second section–*de erroribus impugnandis et tollendis*–Bullinger declares that every *doctrinal* error is mainly or simply a violation of the formal principle. His recipe against this consists merely in demonstrating that a certain wrong opinion is against scripture. The mass, the Anabaptists, and any other heresy is to be combated by scripture.

24. The third and the fourth sections–*de flagitiis accusandis* and *scelera protrahenda esse*–present *flagitia* and *scelera* as violations of the material principle, the divine covenant.

covenantal community. In other words, the negative, potentially threatening side of the covenant has the purpose of enforcing its essentially positive character. And this, by analogy, is true of the negative side of the prophetical task too.

Zwingli and Oecolampadius as Models

After a passionate *digressio* against the abuse of church goods and an appendix on the necessity of rhetoric, which again is mainly drawn from *De propheta*, Bullinger concludes the *confutatio* by praising above all perseverance (*constantia*), drawing upon a stoic-humanistic conception of virtue.[25] Perseverance and endurance are especially needed in difficult times, while a spirit of defeat is to be rejected, and this is to be seen in several figures from the early church (Athanasius), the New Testament (Paul), and, not least, the Old Testament (Isaiah). This takes us to the beginning of a series of biblical role models of whom, for Bullinger, Zwingli was the most recent. The epilogical *encomium* for Zwingli is nothing other than a continuation of this lineage of biblical heroes and is introduced as such: "why do I refer to old examples when there are new ones, who are the most perfect?" Not only in his life, but in the manner of his death, Zwingli was an example! His violent death did not necessarily prove the failure of his work and faith, as so many of his critics thought and stressed.[26] This speech on Zwingli's death was a sort of delayed funeral oration and burial. As no form of official memorial service had taken place, Bullinger must have felt consciously or unconsciously that there had to be an official farewell that would also mark the commencement of his term of office. This perspective is interestingly mirrored in the compositional relation of the *encomium* to the entire speech: the four subsections in the epilogue indicated in the margins are identical with the marginal heading at the beginning of each section of the entire speech. The epilogue thus has the structure of a fugated coda and the effect of an intense repetition of Bullinger's own ideals: Zwingli embodied the perfect ideal of a prophet in combining the positive and the negative aspects of the prophetical task in his greatest action, his Reformed appropriation of the covenant. In tearing down the old illusory idols (by which Bullinger meant the saints as well as the sacraments) Zwingli had pointed to God's real covenant–he had uprooted by planting and had planted by uprooting.

If the content of Bullinger's 1532 oration had been largely inspired by Zwingli, its form came from another source. The printed version seems to have been modelled on a recent publication by the one person who (besides Zwingli) is mentioned with reverence in the oration: Johannes Oecolampadius's *Epistola paraeneutica* of 1528 to the pastors of the Basle countryside.[27] In 1528 the situa-

---

25. Ibid., f. 26^v-27^r.
26. Prominent among them was Martin Bucer, to whom Bullinger repeated in a personal letter the arguments developed in this epilogue (*HBBW* 2,2, no. 62, 42-4:44).
27. *Ioannis Oecolampadii ad fratres qui evangelium Christi in agro Basiliensi annunciant epistola paraeneutica ut vitae doctrinaeque ac ceremoniarum puritatem in omnibus sectentur* (Basel: Valentin Curio, 1528). German (vernacular) translation, probably by Oecolampadius: *Ain Sendbrieve Johannis Oecolampadij / an ettliche Brüder / so das Evangelium in Basler landschafft predigen* (s. l.: 1528).

tion in Basle had become critical for the reform party, and Oecolampadius understood that there would either be a complete breakthrough or a complete failure for the Reformation. In his oration Oecolampadius sought to reach out to assure and strengthen his fellow clergymen, who were cut off from the most recent information and were, in all likelihood, disoriented. The situation was similar to that faced by Bullinger at the beginning of 1532, but Oecolampadius's approach was clearer and more focused. The Basle reformer addressed every single pastor by name and added a German translation of his text so that all might understand him.[28] Although Bullinger did not draw from Oecolampadius's oration directly, his topics, put in a different order, are basically identical. For Bullinger, Oecolampadius held the very office that he was now to assume. Passionately interested in biblical prophecy, the head of the Basle church had written in a similar situation a letter to his rural clergymen, which must have encouraged Bullinger to compose his oration. Both works therefore–and probably not by coincidence–follow the classic form of a bishop's pastoral letter. The frame of reference was no longer the diocese but the city and her surrounding territory.[29] Bullinger's colleagues not only willingly accepted this episcopal missive, but beseeched him to publish the text and to make it available to the rural clergy. Because Bullinger had shown himself in this speech to be Zwingli's successor as the ideal prophetic type, he was treated as a bishop with the right to decide on matters of doctrine.

The Civic Context and Scriptural Exegesis of the 1530s

Zurich was by no means the only city-state where we encounter this tendency towards episcopacy in the notion of prophesying. In virtually all its neighboring Protestant civic republics a similar process is to be found. According to a persuasive thesis of Bernard Roussel, there existed something of an "école rhénane," an exegetical community in the cities along the Rhine, in which the interpretation of the biblical prophets gained an overarching importance.[30] Roussel names the following as members of this confraternity: Konrad Pellikan, Sebastian Münster, and Johannes Oecolampadius in Basle, Wolfgang Fabricius Capito and Martin Bucer in Strasbourg and Zwingli in Zurich. Other, secondary, figures included Simon Grynaeus in Basle and Jean Rabus and Elias Schradäus in Strasbourg. These men were friends who not only shared their learning, but also in some cases even wives (although not simultaneously!). In all these cities there were similar institutions in which they read and interpreted the Bible and through which they founded a new academic tradition. Among these, Zurich was the most

---

28. Probably these were at least partially the ministers in whose parishes Oecolampadius's deacon Hieronymus Bothanus had recently conducted a visitation, to which he alludes in a long Pauline *prooemium*.

29. Seen in this light, it is no surprise that Bullinger's Synodal Ordinances of October 1532, which were written down a few months later than *De prophetae officio*, reiterate much of it E. Egli ed., *Actensammlung zur Geschichte der Zürcher Reformation in den Jahren 1519-1533* (Zurich: 1879), no. 1899, 825-37; especially II: *Von der leer und leben der*.

30. Bernard Roussel, "La Bible de 1530 à 1600" in Guy Bedouelle/Bernard Roussel eds, *Le temps des Réformes et la Bible* (Bible de tous les temps 5; Beauchesne, Paris: 1989), 125-89: 227-33.

prestigious centre, but Basle was both earlier in really applying the new teaching style (through Oecolampadius's interpretation of Isaiah from April 1523) and more original in setting the new prophetical tone. The "school members" not only had a humanist background in common but also a passion for the Hebrew language and culture, and a clear preference for the Old Testament prophets. Of course they may have had lesser motives: Hebrew was a more prestigious language than Greek and in addition probably provided the only real chance in the field of biblical exegesis to escape the shadow of the prince of humanists, Erasmus. But mainly they wanted to legitimise their new urban church model, as Roussel says. Already in the first and probably most important work of the "school," Oecolampadius' commentary on Isaiah, Jerusalem is a typological model for the city-church and for every godly church:[31] "De plus M. Bucer, H. Zwingli, J. Œcolampade, W. F. Capiton "inventent" un type nouveau d'églises urbaines, où ils jouent le rôle exposé de "pasteurs / docteurs." La compétence du bibliste le désigne pour exercer de hautes charges au sein de l'Eglise."[32]

This south German context provides the first answer in our investigation of the basis of Bullinger's domination of the church in Zurich. He had assumed an office that was not intentionally created for him, but which, not only in Zurich but in all the cities of the Reformation in Upper German lands, had served the purpose of legitimating the place of the chief minister in church administration. It is all the more important that this concentration on the prophetic office and covenant theology appears, at least superficially, to have been wholly abandoned in Bullinger's later writings on the subject, such as the relevant sections from the commentaries on the New Testament of the mid-1530s, the treatise *De scripturae sanctae authoritate* of 1538, the crucial sermons in the fifth of his magisterial *Decades* of 1549, and, finally, article 18 of the *Second Helvetic Confession* of 1566. Nevertheless, the modified understanding of the Christian ministry of the Bullinger's years was still profoundly influenced by the "prophetic approach" of the earlier period. Let us now turn to the changes that began to appear after the 1532 oration.

Bullinger's work on the New Testament, in particular the Epistles, must have made him uncomfortably aware of the limited biblical basis for his erstwhile understanding of the prophetic office: prophecy is a category which is found in the new covenant, but by no means does it have the prominence it was given in Zurich and other places during the 1520s. If Bullinger wanted to be taken seriously in his conviction of the unity of the whole Bible he could not escape the New Testament. In his exposition of the letters of Paul, which he undertook in the

---

31. It is interesting that Ludwig Hätzer, a man of the community-oriented left wing of the reform, translated Oecolampadius's commentary into the vernacular. This in turn challenged Zwingli and Luther to complete as quickly as possible their own translations. In this sense as well, Oecolampadius and the Rhenish Old Testament specialists were key stimuli for Zurich's preoccupation with the prophets, as well as for Bullinger's speech of 1532.

32. Roussel's thesis does not hold in every case. In the 1520s Luther (for example) became a well-known exegete of the prophets and the fact that Melanchthon's theory of a prophet is not so very different from that of, for example, Bullinger at least calls into question the theory of exclusiveness of the Rhinelanders in this matter. Further research will hopefully throw more light on to such similarities and dependencies.

mid-1530s, he frequently came to the theme of the Christian ministry, placing a great deal of emphasis on the relevant New Testament texts which suggest that there is only one office in the Church. Here we find again the original foundation of his thought: the prophetic office as the basis of the coherent unity of scripture. However, Bullinger continued to make this point even where the Bible seems to suggest otherwise. This conscious disregard for the obvious meaning of the text provides us with an excellent example of what can be seen as a rather shocking aspect of Reformation biblical exegesis not unique to Zurich. In Bullinger's case, his interpretation of Ephesians 4:11 goes entirely against the grain of the biblical text.[33] While the apostolic author clearly speaks of different offices among different groups, Bullinger sees only a need to differentiate in the various situations of proclamation, that is to say to apply virtual differentiation.

De scripturae sanctae authoritate (1538)

If the biblical commentaries of the 1530s had started to expose problems with the Zurich understanding of the prophetic office, external circumstances also began to play a role. In his first truly international text, the polemical *De scripturae sanctae authoritate* of 1538, dedicated to Henry VIII of England, Bullinger was forced to think about the problem in a new way.[34] The previous concentration on the prophetic office, so important in the Upper Rhine/Swiss context, clearly had little relevance for English or Catholic readers, who are also implicitly addressed in the text. Bullinger needed a broader basis for his understanding of the office of the minister that embraced not only the whole Bible but also the historical ways of thinking that were central for the English and Catholic churches and that did justice to the actual variety of church offices, a fact which could no longer be denied by a Reformed polity. How the proclamation office in the Christian Church was to be conceived and practised as a functional unity was now to be placed in the broader historical argument in a more plausible manner which reflected more accurately the reality of church life. Thus Bullinger set out to demonstrate how God, in his dealings with his people, had at different times emphasised different aspects of the one office in order to suit the changing needs of the faithful. In the first chapter of the second part of *De scripturae sanctae authoritate* the prophetic office is explained and essentially the older arguments are repeated. The prophetic office is equated with the priesthood and above all with those who have proclaimed the Word of God, for the *prophetae* or *ministri* have existed at all times since the beginning of world. The Roman appeal to antiquity needed to be overcome and, therefore, Bullinger claims that the Protoplastes was the first prophet.[35] The principal ancestors of the Christian preachers of the Word were the Levites, who were

33. *In D[ivi] Pauli ad Galatas, Ephesios, Philippen[ses] et Colossen[ses] epistolas Heinrychi Bullingeri Commentarii* (Zurich: Froschauer, 1535), [Ad Ephesios], Cap. IIII, f. 158^{r-v}.
34. *De scripturae sanctae authoritate, certitudine, firmitate, et absoluta perfectione, deque Episcoporum [sic], qui verbi divini ministri sunt, institutione et functione, contra superstitionis tyrannidisque Romanae antistes, ad Sereniss[imum] Angliae Regem Heinrychum VIII. Heinrychi Bullingeri Libri duo* (Zurich: Froschauer, 1538).
35. *De scripturae sanctae authoritate*, f. 67^r.

given the primary tasks of teaching the law and of intercessing, and only after that of serving the temple cult.[36] The biblical texts used by Bullinger to prove this lineage of Christian preachers would hardly convince in modern eyes, but for Bullinger this historical argument had aquired a clearer form since its first expression in his commentary on Hebrews of 1526. The argument had now become the central thesis in his understanding of the covenantal foundation of the prophetic office, according to which the Levites were directly replaced by Christian preachers. Because the Christian office contains in itself all the essential functions that its historical predecessors held disperately.

The differences between the covenants do not rest primarily in the concept of the offices, but much more in the fact that the office bearers in the old covenant were united in and led by a high priest, who in the New Testament is replaced by Jesus Christ. Because the new high priest is in heaven at the right hand of God the Father, any reference to his direct representative on earth is nothing short of blasphemy, a position that Bullinger emphasised polemically towards the end of his text.[37] Just as the high priest in the Old Testamant determined that the Levites should serve in teaching,[38] so Christ called the Apostles to be teachers to the nations.[39] Therefore, in Bullinger's view, all duties and services of the Church are derived from the Levitical/Apostolic office. All "orders" (*ordines*) in the church office are merely forms (*species*) of one and the same office (*ministerium*) as Bullinger continued once again to explain in reference to Ephesians 4:11.[40] It was on this basis that Bullinger vehemently rejected every aspect of ecclesiastical hierarchy with its privileges, as well as doctoral degrees for theological teachers. Part of Bullinger's argument against these degrees was based on the small number of stipendia available for Zurich students,[41] but his main argument was a variation on the exegetical/covenantal position of the whole text. This was that the church fathers had taken up the injunction to teach originally given to the Levites. Schools, Bullinger argued, belonged to the contemporary church as they had to the early church.[42]

---

36. Ibid., f. 69ʳ.

37. Already two years before the publication of *De scripturae sanctae authoritate* northern Europe was made aware of a planned general council in Italy. See Rudolf Pfister, "Zu Bullingers Beurteilung des Konzils von Trient" in Gäbler/ Herkenrath, *Heinrich Bullinger*, 1:123-40, 124f. It is both theologically and psychologically interesting that the second edition of the text in 1544 contained a defence against Cochlaeus' *Replik*, which had appeared after the first edition.

38. *De scripturae sanctae authoritate*, f. 68ᵛ.

39. Ibid., f. 79ⁱ.

40 Ibid.

41. Bullinger's letter to Rudolf Gwalther of 29 November 1540, ZB, Ms. F 37, f. 405ⁱ⁻ᵛ.

42. Bullinger's emphatic historisising of his understanding of the church office can also be understood as the foundation of his approach to church politics, which is only hinted at in the purely prophetic speech of 1525. It was essential for Bullinger that Christian educational institutions be properly administered in the community because their leadership was a Christian duty. This position was greatly strengthened by Bullinger's ability to demonstrate the antiquity of the argument that those who held church offices were also charged with teaching- even though his fight for relative autonomy of the schools stands in some logical contradiction to the Reformation party's policy of thorough secularisation. As Hans Ulrich Bächtold emphasises: "The Chorherrschaft was in a fact a unique case in the Zurich Reformation," *Heinrich Bullinger vor*

The *Decades*

In sermons 43 and 44 of the *Decades*, in which he treats the application of the office of the Christian ministry, Bullinger develops the themes set out in *De scripturae sanctae authoritate*.[43] In contrast to his earlier works, it is hard to miss the fact that the prophetic element, once so dominant, is now definitely relegated to the background. The role of the prophet is stripped of all pastoral qualities: prophets are either given a particular and unusual revelation and able to speak of the future, as in the Acts of Apostles, or they are the types of figures mentioned in 1 Corinthians 14 who have unique qualities for the interpretation of scripture.[44] Bullinger either abandoned the other aspects or transferred them to the pastors or doctors; thus he had made a fundamental distinction between those who performed the daily offices of the church and those who had the particular calling of a prophet. It is in this light that we should examine his late work on the books of the Old Testament, in which the prophets appear more clearly in their individual and historical contexts and ever more, as in the case of Daniel, are understood as predictors of the future as in antiquity when they were deliverers of *dicta-probantia* and welcome examples of virtue. The extent of this diminution of the prophetic office from *De prophetae officio oratio* became clear fifteen years later in the *Second Helvetic Confession*, when the readers quite remarkably have to be assured that the prophets "still exist today"![45]

In contrast to his earlier works we find in the *Decades* that Bullinger has distributed the duties of the Christian ministry to several offices, not only between persons but between God and humanity. Both are *cooperarii* (1 Cor 3:9);[46] and Bullinger was so persuaded by the cooperation of humans in the proclamation of the Gospel and the defence of spiritual exegesis that he did not hesitate to use the language of natural law: *Suum cuique!*–to each his own part.[47] God's part is to reveal himself in his Word, while the role of men and women is to co-operate. God does not in any way bind himself to creation, a position derived from the Franciscan/Augustinian tradition which Bullinger had appropriated from Zwingli and expressed in both the *First and Second Helvetic Confessions*.[48] God does, however, require people who are partners from free choice and who take seriously the ministry in order to ensure the proper and true propagation of the Gospel. What the Reformers emphasised, however, was not

dem Rat. Zur Gestaltung und Verwaltung des Zürcher Staatswesens in den Jahren 1531 bis 1575 (ZBRG 12; Berne: Peter Lang, 1982), 113.

43. *Sermonum Decades quinque, de potissimis christianae religionis capitibus, in tres tomos digestae, authore Heinrycho Bullingero, ecclesiae Tigurinae ministro* (Zurich: Froschauer, 1552).

44. *Sermonum Decades quinque*, 3, f. 295ʳ.

45. *Confessio et expositio simplex orthodoxae fidei 1566, XVIII: De ministris Ecclesiae, ipsorumque institutione, et officiis, in: Bekenntnisschriften und Kirchenordnungen der nach Gottes Wort reformierten Kirche*, ed. Wilhelm Niesel, (Zurich: 1938, reprinted 1985), 254,23-25: "Prophetae quondam praescii futurorum, vates erant: sed et scripturas interpretabantur. Quales etiam hodie adhuc inveniuntur."

46. *Sermonum Decades quinque*, 3, f. 293ʳ.

47. Ibid., f. 292ᵛ.

48. *Non alligat*; Compare Berndt Hamm, *Zwinglis Reformation der Freiheit* (Neukirchen-Vluyn: Neukirchener, 1984), 42f., note 192.

the ability or talent of individuals to carry out the preaching of the Gospel, but rather that God wills to have them and to cooperate with them. From this there is a distinct tendency towards egalitarianism. In all its manifestations the ministry serves the purpose of being both the unifying power and visible unity of the Body of Christ. It is not only the equality of those who hold offices with one another that is emphasised by the theological position that they are engaged in a common enterprise and must therefore cooperate with one another, but also a certain equality of bishops or presbyters (ie. ministers) on the one hand, and elders on the other.[49] This functional equality is given programmatic expression in a marginal comment to, as well as the main text of, Article 18 of the *Second Helvetic Confession*: *una et aequalis potestas ministrorum* ("the authority of the ministry is one and equal.")[50]

Although Bullinger pursued this line of the equality of offices, it is possible to find in his *Decades* evidence for distinctions between the offices. For instance, the diaconate was closely connected to the ministerial office and was not a separate office, as was made clear in Ludwig Lavater's book on the rites of the Zurich church, in which the diaconate is discussed together with the ministerial office. Nevertheless, it is not identical with the ministerial office, as would be later explained in a separate article of the *Second Helvetic Confession*.[51] Also the laying on of hands, which Zwingli had already sought to preserve in 1525, was reintroduced in the *Decades*. Bullinger's sense of the importance of this act underlined his intense interest in the considerable role of the church in the ordination of its servants, who did not receive their call either from themselves or from outside the church community. Ordination, preaching, and teaching can only take place within the context of the church, as Bullinger argued in the *Decades* not only against the spiritualists, but also against other "independent" forces and tendencies. Ordination exists only because there is an order which is the foundation of the church as an institution. It was this line of argument which legitimised the particular place of the *praepositus* among the ministers.[52] He is the first among equals only according to the structure of the church, which is designed to maintain proper order. This position is not embodied in the person, but rather he is the person chosen to hold it. It is important to note that for the first time Bullinger clearly speaks of his own position as chief minister in the *Second Helvetic Confession*.[53] The office holder must ensure that the voices of his fellow

49. *Sermonum Decades quinque*, 3, f. 295^r.
50. *Confessio*, 257, 1f.: "Data est autem omnibus in ecclesia ministris una et aequalis potestas sive functio."
51. Ludwig Lavater, *De ritibus et institutis ecclesiae* (Zurich: Froschauer, 1559). The text was edited and expanded by Johann Baptist Ott (1702), translated by Gottfried Albert Keller, *Die Gebräuche und Einrichtungen der Zürcher Kirche* (s. l., s. a.), 28: "Further the individual districts, or chapters, have their own deacons. With this name we do not mean the minister but the representative of the minister. They stand in for the minister when he is ill or when for some reason he is not able to perform his tasks. The deacon is to perform the teaching ministry and dispense the sacraments."
52. *Sermonum Decades quinque*, f. 290^v.
53. The crucial text is the following: *Confessio*, 257,8-11: [Marg.]: "Ordo servandus." [Text]: "Interea propter ordinem servandum, unus aut certus aliquis ministrorum, coetum

ministers in gatherings of the clergy are accorded equal weight. This is the first time that Bullinger began to write about the role of leading ministers; why he did so so late and in such a modest manner must now be our subject of investigation.

The Office of Chief Minister

Bullinger's concept of the pastoral office owed much to the changing circumstances of his life and work and reflected the interplay between his intentions and the compromises he was forced to make. Bullinger had first taught in Kappel and sought, as Zwingli had previously done, to use the new prophetic style in order to legitimate his interpretation of the Bible. He had then assumed office in Zurich and adapted Zwingli's concept to a comprehensive, integrated, and ecclesiastical prophetic office that he united with the central theological concept of the covenant. In dialogue with the English church, and in conflict with the Roman, he sought to formulate an integrated but anti-hierarchical understanding of the church ministry in which he took up the historical arguments of these churches and used them to support his own case. In his great pedagogical work, the *Decades*, and in the *Second Helvetic Confession* he set forth his mature and comprehensive view of the church office, one which sought to embrace not only the real needs of the church but also the foundations of his theology.

Through all of these changes and modifications there are two consistent lines of thought. The first is that the holder of the office must do nothing other than bring the Word of God, and in this he is bound exclusively to the Holy Spirit, through whom scripture is given and inspired. This was always at the heart of Bullinger's thought on the church office: it is found in the first part of *De propheta* of 1525, the first section of his speech *De prophetae officio* of 1532, the first part of his diatribe *De scripturae sanctae authoritate* of 1538, and in the first sermons of the *Decades*. From this follows Bullinger's second principle, that as each holder of the office is subject above all to the Holy Spirit, there is no theological ground for a hierarchy of church offices. Everything else, in Bullinger's eyes, is not only false, but an attack on the fundamentals of Christian teaching, the scripture principle, and a scandal (even anti-Christian).

Although these two points formed the foundation of Bullinger's thought, over the course of time he considerably varied the manner in which he understood their relationship to one another. During his career as head of the Zurich church this second point, enmity towards church hierarchy, became increasingly prominent. The concept of office remained fairly consistent, but one marked trend in Bullinger's writings was a decreasing emphasis on the particular qualities of individuals holding that office. In modern terms, we could say that he "democratised" his view of church offices. This meant that not only could the star humanist become a minister but so too could less educated men. Bullinger moved away from a particular conception of the individual for the ministry; he played down the theme, so heavily stressed at the beginning of his career, of the

---

convocavit, et in coetu res consultandas proposuit, sententias item aliorum collegit, denique ne qua oriretur confusio, pro virili cavit."

qualifications which a minister must have to hold office. In his early writings These qualifications were seen as the essential guarantee of the Christian ministry. the Reformation linking of the office to scripture was fundamentally grounded in the competence of an individual to interpret the Bible. Along with a good knowledge of languages, by which he could recognise incorrect interpretations of scripture, the prophet must also be able to demonstrate the coherence of the Word of God. To this end he had himself to be consistent and courageous, as Zwingli and the prophets of the Old Testament had been. In brief, a prophet is an especially talented and important interpreter, as the later Bullinger would always maintain.[54] From the *Decades* onwards, however, a different tone was evident in Bullinger's writings, which stressed the shared role of the ministers in the church in pursuit of one goal, the building of church unity through the edification of the community. Bullinger had already made this point in his oration *De prophetae officio*: love is more important for a prophet than the knowledge of languages.[55] Despite the clear references to the classical Roman basis for a collegial, corporate undestanding of life and to the Augustinian hermeneutic of the Christian rules of love, this shift in Bullinger's thought might appear to be an apology for the mediocre, or even poor, quality of the ministers in Zurich. But in the *Decades* we find a clear declaration of fraternal interdependence based on the differing talents of the ministers.

This throws new light on the authority of the prophet in the early Reformation. After the clear break with the authority of the bishop of Constance there was a power vacuum in Zurich which was not only legal but, more importantly, spiritual. The disaster of the Battle of Kappel in October 1531 only served to heighten the sense that the old episcopal authority had to be restored in some manner.[56] As with the other cities of the Upper Rhine and the Swiss Confederation, Zwingli had sought to find a concept which was not only biblical but which had been intensively used in the Middle Ages.[57] On account of its original context in the Old Testament, and because it did not emphasise aspects of the priesthood, the concept of the prophet was extremely welcome. Nevertheless, in view of the power vacuum in Zurich it was hardly conceivable that this new office could be considered in any other than episcopal terms. In agreement with Roussel one could certainly argue that the early Reformation "prophets" were not princes of the church, but in fact, and particularly in Zurich, they were an emergency initiative as territorial bishops in the city republic.[58] It is

54. See note 44 above.

55. *De prophetae officio*, f. 10r-10v.

56. The disastrous effects which could result from such a power vacuum were evident in the small city of Schaffhausen, which was economically dependent on both Zurich and Constance. In the absence of a skilled theologian comparable to Bullinger there were close to ten years of bitter conflict between the Lutheran Bavarian Erasmus Ritter and the Reformed Benedikt Burgauer from St Gall. As Gordon has written: "the least attractive aspect of the evangelical Reformation [was] its vulnerability to personality conflicts in the absence of established lines of authority," Gordon, *The Swiss Reformation*, 114.

57. Schlosser, *Lucerna in caliginoso loco*.

58. It is highly significant that from the diverse statements by Jerome on the clerical office in his commentary on 1 Timothy (*PL* 26, 596B) in the *Decades* Bullinger concentrates on those which refer explicitly to the urban context of the episcopacy of the Early Church: "Observandum

hardly surprising that the strongest manifestation of the prophetic office in Zurich, Bullinger's 1532 speech *De prophetae officio*, was delivered on the most important of civic occasions, the feast of Charlemagne, during the greatest crisis of its church.

It is also hardly a coincidence that Heinrich Bullinger, with his growing conception of the church, also increasingly distanced himself from the concept of the prophet. The Grossmünster chapter, which was once the place where the Zwinglian/Bullingerian concept of the prophet could be realised, lost much of its ecclesiastical influence during the sixteenth century and increasingly became a comparatively autonomous school. In its place, the synod, the deans, and not least the rural parishes became increasingly important.[59] These were areas that required the bishop, not a prophet. The slow but clear shift towards collegiality meant a decentralisation of the church: the ministers were institutionalised communally and became officials of the state. As Zurich developed as a territorial church during the sixteenth century its ministers were no longer focused on the Grossmünster. The development of his thought had led Bullinger to recognition of the diversity of offices, but against this was his strongly Swiss anti-hierarchical sentiments. The creation of the office of first minister, or *Antistes* (a name which Bullinger himself did not use), was not about a centralising of the old office but rather, in contrast, an extension of the process of desacralisation and the removal of hierarchy: the principal authority of the *Antistes* was to guarantee the collegial authority of the ministers. There was, of course, a certain paradox in this. The only hierarchical office in the church was founded as a defence against hierarchy. Nevertheless, this came about as Bullinger had to explain his own position in Zurich from which he dominated the church. This influence was, however, embedded in the institutional changes that he had developed but lay in his own enormous personal influence. It was with the territorial consolidation of the church that it became possible to resolve the tension between equality and inequality of church offices. It was at this moment in history that the formal differences of the offices could be asserted alongside their material unity.[60]

We need to introduce a note of caution. Certainly the development of the Reformation in Zurich seems to fit into the classical Weberian categories of the ideal types of prophet and priest and the role of the charismatic leader in the development of new religious movements. The initial phase of prophetic enthusiasm, which can lead to violence, leads to a crisis following its demise that can be

---

est autem beatum Hieronymum non loqui de Romana monarchia, sed de episcopis singulis, in urbibus singulis super presbyteros constitutis." Jerome himself translated the Bible text (1.5: *per civitates*) with *per singulas urbes*. Interestingly, Bullinger also explicitly compares particular churches (or, rather, parishes) with cities. See *Sermonum Decades quinque*, f. 281ᵛ: "Porro particulares vel singulares ecclesiae sunt velut oppida vel urbes in regno aliquo. Copia urbium non scindit regnum."

59. The standard work here is Bruce Gordon, *Clerical discipline and the rural reformation: the synod in Zürich, 1532-1580* (ZBRG 16; Berne: Peter Lang, 1992).

60. See the stimulating study by Martin Hauser, *Prophet und Bischof. Huldrych Zwinglis Amtsverständnis im Rahmen der Zürcher Reformation* (Ökumenische Beihefte zur Freiburger Zeitschrift für Philosophie und Theologie 21; Freiburg: Universitätsverlag, 1994). Pamela Biel, *Doorkeepers*, also attempts to develop an historical-biographical orientated sketch of Bullinger's understanding of both the ministry and his position.

handled only by consolidation and systematic regulation by the priest figure. As Weber and his students, in particular Pierre Bourdieu, emphasise, prophetic charisma does not arise spontaneously or without context but rather is closely linked to profound change and crisis situations.[61] Likewise Bullinger's genius lay precisely in his ability to retain the creative force of the prophetic ideal of the early Reformation through a lifetime of leadership, though he was forced by circumstances to refine it.[62] Although the prophetic aspect of his life manifested itself in the first half of his life, while the priestly became more prominent in the second, it was Bullinger's particular talent to be able to unite them. It is impressive that in many lands where the Swiss Reformation had its influence many of the clergy demonstrated this talent. The extent of Bullinger's influence, however, through his understanding of the ministerial office still needs to be properly researched. We lack detailed studies of the relationship between the church's preaching and the interests of political rulers in the Reformed lands in the period from the Reformation to the Enlightenment. They might well, as the recent research into this question in Lutheran lands has shown, yield some surprising results.[63]

61. Pierre Bourdieu, "Eine Interpretation der Religion nach Max Weber" in his *Das religiöse Feld* Andreas Pfeuffer trans., Stephan Egger et al. eds, (édition discours 11; Constance: UVK, 2000), 11-37: 31.

62. This was demonstrated most clearly in Bullinger's reaction to the four Meilen Articles before his election in Zurich in 1531.

63. Most recently, Alexander Bitzel, *Anfechtung und Trost bei Sigismund Scherertz. Ein lutherischer Theologe im Dreißigjährigen Krieg* (Studien zur Kirchengeschichte Niedersachsens 38; Göttingen: Vanderhoeck & Ruprecht, 2002), 14. For the late sixteenth and seventeenth centuries he speaks of "the observation by many authors of the fearless stance of Lutheran pastors against the authorities."

Part II: Humanism, Politics and Family

7

Bullinger's Early Political and Theological Thought: *Brutus Tigurinus*

Emidio Campi

Introduction

In *Ab urbe condita* the great Roman historian Titus Livy (59BC-17AD) describes the events which followed the rape of Lucretia by Sextus, son of King Tarquinius Superbus, and her subsequent suicide in c.510BC.[1] Lucius Iunius Brutus drove the tyrannical king out of Rome and founded the Republic. According to Livy's account, the people elected Brutus and Lucretia's husband, Lucius Tarquinius Collatinus, consuls. Supported by the patriciate and by Porsenna, King of the Etruscans, the Tarquin family attempted to regain power. Brutus' two sons were amongst the conspirators, and, informed of the conspiracy by a slave, the father's response was decisive: his two sons were executed.

Although this passage from Livy is relatively short, it addresses ethical and political issues that have inspired Western authors[2] from Virgil to Petrarch, from Machiavelli[3] to Voltaire[4] and on to Alfieri,[5] whose *Bruto primo* was, tellingly, dedicated to George Washington. In the Swiss Confederation it was also common to use such much-loved ancient material to illuminate contemporary concerns. The story of Brutus can be found for the first time in the sixteenth century in the

---

1. Titus Livius, *Ab urbe condita* (lat./ger.). Liber I. *Römische Geschichte.* (Stuttgart: Reclam, 1981), I, 56-60:167-81. Sixteenth-century editions: *Romische Historie vss Tito livio gezogen* (Mentz [= Mainz]: 1505), f. 18ᵛ-20ᵛ; *Römsche History* (Strasbourg: 1507), f. 24ᵛ-26ⁱ; *Romische historien Titi Livij mit etlichen newen translation auss dem Latein. so kurtzuerschinen jaren zů Meyntz imm hohen Thůmbenstifft erfunden hiezů gethon; fast lüstig zů lesen vnd fruchtbarlich allen den: so inn tugent: manheyt oder ritterlichen thaten jr leben üben wöllen* (Meyntz [= Mainz]: 1530), f. 21ʳ-23ʳ.

2. Reinhard Klescewski, "Wandlungen des Lucretia-Bildes im lateinischen Mittelalter und in der italienischen Literatur der Renaissance" in Eckhard Lefèvre/Eckhard Olshausen eds., *Livius. Werke und Rezeption. Festschrift für Erich Burck zum 80. Geburtstag* (Munich: Beck, 1983), 313-35.

3. See Niccolò Machiavelli, *Discorsi sopra la prima deca di Tito Livio*, Francesco Bausi ed. (Edizione nazionale delle opere di Niccolò Machiavelli, Sezione 1, Opere politiche 2; Rome: Salerno 2001).

4. Voltaire, *Brutus* (1730).

5. Vittorio Alfieri, *Bruto primo* (1786/9?); see also Emilio Cecchi and Natalino Sapegno eds, *Storia della letteratura italiana* vol. 7: *Il Settecento* (Milan: 1988), 923-1040, esp. 1030-1.

anonymous work *Urner Spiel von Wilhelm Tell,*[6] in which distinct parallels are drawn between the liberation of the original part of the Swiss Confederation and the rape of Lucretia and the subsequent fall of the Tarquin family. Another example of this genre is provided by the first edition of the *Descriptio Helvetiae* (1514) by the humanist Heinrich Glareanus, for whom William Tell was the Swiss Brutus.[7] In 1527 Hans Sachs turned the story of Lucretia into a play, although his intention was not to stress the political message of the events, but rather to provide a memorial to the model virtues of Lucretia.[8]

Heinrich Bullinger provided one of the most impressive dramatic retellings of this ancient story during those years. It was written while he was a teacher at the monastery school in Kappel am Albis. The drama was entitled "A fine play on the history of the noble Roman woman Lucretia, and how the tyrannical king Tarquinius Superbus was driven from Rome, and in particular on the steadfastness of Junius Brutus, first consul of Rome."[9] *Lucretia and Brutus* would be the only drama in Bullinger's opus, and although it was not one of his most successful works, literary critics have reckoned it amongst the most beautiful and most original stage works "which Switzerland possesses, along with Manuel, in terms of dramas for the sixteenth century."[10] Although up until now this work has received little attention, even a brief glance at the text reveals the potential for a

6. Max Wehrli ed., *Das Lied von der Entstehung der Eidgenossenschaft. Das Urner Tellenspiel* (Aarau: Sauerländer, 1952).

7. Heinrich Glarean, *Helvetiae descriptio et in laudatissimam Helvetiorum foedus panegyricum* (Basle: Adam Petri, 1514), Werner Näf ed. and trans., (St. Gallen: Tschudy, 1948). A second edition with the commentary of Myconius and dedicatory poem by Vadianus appeared in 1519 in Basle, published by Froben with the title: *Descriptio de situ Helvetiae et vicinis gentibus [...]*.

8. Hans Sachs, "*Tragedia von der Lucretia auss der beschreybung Livij*" *(1527)* in Horst Hartmann ed., *Heinrich Bullinger–Hans Sachs: Lucretia-Dramen* (Leipzig: Bibliographisches Institut, 1973), 99-110. On Hans Sachs, see Berndt Hamm, *Bürgertum und Glaube. Konturen der städtischen Reformation* (Göttingen: Vanderhoeck & Ruprecht, 1996), 181-231.

9. [Heinrich Bullinger], *Ein schoen spil von der geschicht der Edlen Römerin Lucretiae / vnnd wie der Tyrannisch küng Tarquinius Superbus von Rhom vertrieben / und sunderlich von der standhafftigkeit Iunii Bruti / des Ersten Consuls zuo Rhom / vff Sontag den andern tag Mertzens / im 1533 jar / zuo Basel gehalten* (Basle: Thomas Wolf, 1533). cf. *HBBibl* I, here 39-41. The first reprint of this edition was Jakob Bächtold, *Schweizerische Schauspiele des sechzehnten Jahrhunderts* vol. 1 (Frauenfeld: J. Huber, 1890), 105-69. A second edition is Horst Hartmann, *Heinrich Bullinger–Hans Sachs: Lucretia-Dramen*, 39-97. In this paper I shall quote from the Hartmann edition. As I have had the original edition to hand, I have come across two transcription errors: 50, v.26: Hartmann "mit" while the original has "mir"; 51, v.12: Hartmann "man" while original has "myr." This Bullinger text has not yet received any attention in church history circles, but there are some interesting contributions from the field of German literary studies: the important dissertation of Käthe Hirth, *Heinrich Bullingers Spiel von "Lucretia und Brutus" 1533* (Phil. Diss, Marburg: 1919), is not only useful for its examination of language and meter, but also looks into the sources, the humanist elements and the political orientation of the work. Also authoritative is the study by Remy Charbon, "Lucretia Tigurina. Heinrich Bullingers Spiel von Lucretia und Brutus (1526)" in *Antiquitates Renatae [...]. Festschrift für Renate Böschenstein* Verena Ehrich-Haefeli et al. eds, (Würzburg: Königshausen und Neumann, 1998), 35-47.

10. Jakob Bächtold, *Geschichte der deutschen Literatur in der Schweiz* (Frauenfeld: J. Huber, 1892), 306; Charbon, *Lucretia Tigurina*, 46, refers to the text as "one of the most significant examples of Swiss historical-political drama."

more detailed examination. It is readily apparent that this is Bullinger's version of current political and religious problems and how they should be clothed, but in a classical tale. In addition, both the events and the characters in the play can be examined in light of one of the most important developments in recent writing on the Reformation: issues of communication and the formation of opinion through the culture of festival and popular drama.[11] The aim of this paper is twofold: first, it will examine Bullinger's intentions in his reworking of the story of Lucretia and Brutus; secondly, and in the context of additional material produced during Bullinger's time in Kappel, it will seek to identify and examine additional motives which contribute to our understanding of Bullinger's early political and theological thought.

Bullinger's Reworking of the Story of Lucretia and Brutus

I. Context

The original of Bullinger's work is no longer extant. The lack of a manuscript is not, however, hugely problematic as there exist two printed versions of the play, one from Basle and the other from Strasbourg, and there is little variation between them.[12] Although neither copy bears the name of the author, this is not a contested matter. The title page of the copy held in the Zentralbibliothek in Zurich has the following handwritten comment by Johann Jakob Simler, the founder of the eighteenth-century Simler Collection: "written by Herr Bullinger while he was still in Kappel, taken from him and performed against his will in Basle." This comment was based on a letter written to Bullinger on 11 February 1533 by Oporinus and is confirmed and expanded by Bullinger's own entry in his diary.[13] According to this diary, although he was in Kappel for less than six years, during this time he wrote more than fifty works, long and short and in German and Latin. Included in a list of these works, and amongst those in German, appears *Brutus sive Lucretia, Germanico carmine scripta tragoedia, quae postea anno domini 1533 Basileae publice a civibus acta est et impressa sine meo nomine.*[14]

Although it is clear that this work was conceived during Bullinger's years in Kappel, we lack the necessary evidence to pinpoint accurately when it was written. However, in light of similarities with other works by Bullinger and the play's allusions to contemporary events in Zurich, it seems most likely that the work was written in the late autumn of 1526,[15] although there is little in the way of hard evidence to substantiate this conjecture. It has been suggested that the work

---

11. On this see Peter Rusterholz, "Fastnachtsspiel und Reformation. Die Metamorphosen des Fastnachtsspiels im Widerstreit der Disziplinen" in Heinrich Schmidt et. al. eds, *Gemeinde, Reformation und Widerstand. Festschrift für Peter Blickle zum 60. Geburtstag* (Tübingen: Bibliotheca Academica Verlag, 1998), 243-60.

12. Hartmann, *Heinrich Bullinger–Hans Sachs: Lucretia-Dramen*, 32-3.

13. *HBBW* III, no. 190.

14. *HBD*, 15.

15. Charbon, *Lucretia Tigurina*, 35.

was written in 1528, but this guess is equally uncertain.[16] Despite all my efforts I have been unable to find any further evidence to enable a precise dating of the work, and for the moment we have to be satisfied with the likelihood that it was written between late autumn 1526 and 1528.

II. The Circumstances for the First Performance

It is unlikely that a work written in Kappel was for the pupils alone. Rather, the intended audience would have included all those associated with the monastery school, for it is well-established that it was not only the pupils themselves who attended the lessons given by Bullinger, but also other members of the monastic community as well as individuals from outwith the religious house, even from neighbouring Zug.[17] As will be demonstrated here at greater length, essentially this piece of theatre was written for propagandistic purposes. Indeed, it is possible to take this interpretation even further and to demonstrate that this dramatic work, with its strong desire to mould opinion, is a fine example of the methods of communication and persuasion employed at the time of the Reformation.

Lucretia and Brutus was never performed in Kappel, though it has not yet proved possible to establish why. There is, however, evidence that the manuscript was taken without Bullinger's approval and published by Thomas Wolff in Basle in 1533. On 2 March the play was performed in Basle and drew large crowds.[18] A short time later it was also performed in Aarau, and again received an enthusiastic reception.[19] Ignored for more than 400 years, the work was performed again at the outbreak of the Second World War in 1939 at the initiative of the student theatre of the University of Basle. Several performances in Basle and Zurich were well received. In a review of the performance in the *Neue Zürcher Zeitung,* a critic wrote "the amateur actors, students at the University of Basle, put right an ancient wrong when they brought their production of this work back to Zurich and performed it on the central staircase of the University to an audience composed primarily of academics–indeed they performed the work so perfectly that the spirit of the author must surely have forgiven Basle for the theft of the manuscript and the illegal public premiere which followed."[20] Yet gentle chaffing on the origins of this piece and humorous asides on the impact of Basle pronunciation on the Zurich ear cannot distract from the fact that it was not the well-established rivalry between the two Swiss cities that was at the forefront of the public's mind at the time of this performance. The "contemporary relevance" of

16. The dating is primarily from Hirth, *Heinrich Bullingers Spiel von "Lucretia und Brutus,"* 28. The scholarly foundation of this assertion is not persuasive. Joachim Staedtke, *Die Theologie des jungen Bullinger* (Zurich: Zwingli Verlag, 1962), 292 remarks that Bullinger "placed the drama at the end of his catalogue," and from this he concludes that it was intended for the year 1528. This is conceivable, but it does not rule out the possibility of an error in the ordering of the catalogue. As a result, we are still not able to date the work precisely.

17. Fritz Blanke/Immanuel Leuschner, *Heinrich Bullinger. Vater der reformierten Kirche* (Zurich: TVZ, 1990), 60.

18. See Basler printers listed in note 9.

19. Hirth, *Heinrich Bullingers Spiel von "Lucretia und Brutus,"* 5.

20. *Neue Zürcher Zeitung,* 6 December 1939, no. 2065, 3.

the piece lay rather, as Bullinger himself had written, in the issue of "how freedom, once obtained, can be upheld against all tyranny and oligarchy." A closer
examination of the play makes this very evident.

III. Content

The play is written in traditional rhyming couplets and covers 32 quarto sides,
recto and verso–about 1555 verses in total. It comprises a prologue (Bll. 1b-2a,
Hartmann, 39-40), two distinct acts (Bll. 2b-31a, Hartmann, 41-60, 60-95) and a
short instruction for the players (Bll. 31b-32a, Hartmann, 96-97). On the title
page there is a woodcut of the coat of arms of Basle and the insignia of Wolff's
printing house. As I will explore later, it is not simply by chance that a mercenary
soldier appears behind both these insignia.

The prologue, with its references to Bullinger's sources and purpose, is important for understanding the meaning of the play. Bullinger refers specifically to
the first and second books of Livy's *Ab Urbe condita* and to the fourth and fifth
books of the Roman history of Dionysius of Halikarnossos (c 60BC to c7AD), a
Greek rhetorician who lived in Rome. Although on the whole Bullinger does not
move far from these ancient historians, he does not slavishly follow them: when
they do not agree with his views, he simply deviates from them. Bullinger lays
this out clearly in the introduction:

> This play is taken from the first and second books of T. Livy's *Ab urbe condita*
> and out of the fourth and fifth books of Dionysius's *Antiquitates*, and it places
> before our eyes how tyranny came to rule among a certain people. Tarquin is a
> tyrant, and he therefore brought the Romans in many ways into despair as Iunius
> Brutus demonstrates in his speech after the death of Lucretia. His tyranny will
> also be illustrated through the violation of Lucretia; this will also be shown
> through his conduct and debauchery. To this end a poem by a peasant is ap-
> pended which is from neither Livy nor Dionysius. Its purpose is to show that in a
> dreadful circumstance something positive can come forth. He turns into a joke
> that which is truly serious, namely how a tyrannical, godless man violently deals
> with the poor people. The greater the offence, the greater and more horrific the
> punishment. Thus is Tarquin, on account of his dreadful deeds, driven away by a
> great uprising.[21]

The first act, which is only about one third of the total play, is dedicated to
the tale of the eponymous Lucretia, who, although she embodies the ideal of female morality, is not the central dramatic figure in the play.[22] Instead, Bullinger is
primarily concerned to bring to the fore the theme of the struggle for freedom
inspired by the spirit of patriotic virtue. To some extent the title of the play is

---

21. Hartmann, *Heinrich Bullinger–Hans Sachs: Lucretia-Dramen*, 39,2-21.
22. Ibid., 60,31-36: " ... Ihr Christen wyber / btrachtend das Laβt ee hingon den lyb zuo
grund Eee jhr brechen eelichen pund Land üch vff erden nichts verfüren Ee sôl jhr sterben / dann
verlieren Dem man syn eer...."

misleading, for the story of Lucretia is only a preamble, explaining the occasion for Brutus' subsequent actions in the cause of freedom.[23]

The play is opened by the herald, who warns the audience that they should expect something which is neither lightweight nor extravagant. At his request the writer reads out a short account of the story of Lucretia as contained in the ancient sources. Lucretia is young, beautiful and true to her husband Collatinus. Sextus Tarquinius, the son of the king, is entranced by her beauty and falls deeply in love with her. While her husband is doing military service, Sextus finds a pretext to gain entry to her house in the night. Bullinger throws a veil over Sextus's abuse of her trust and her rape. He decides instead to replace this incident with a court scene in which a poor peasant is cheated of his just rights by Tarquinius Superbus and his son Sextus. The meaning is symbolic: the example of the peasant is used to show how a regime without conscience violates its subjects, and that the arbitrary and brutal use of force by a tyrannical regime leads to its own downfall.

In the meantime the news of the outrage committed against Lucretia reaches her father and husband in the army camp. They hurry home, accompanied by their friends Brutus and Publius Valerius, and discover Lucretia in the depths of despair. She tells them of the disgrace which has been done to her, protests her innocence, calls for revenge and stabs herself. At this point Brutus enters the fray. He interrupts the laments of her family to call for the expulsion of the Tarquin. At the marketplace and standing beside the body of Lucretia, Brutus denounces in raging words the scandalous acts of the ruling family and calls on the people to expel the tyrants and to take responsibility for the country into their own hands. The first act closes with the call to the citizens to participate in forming the new social order.

While Lucretia is the heroine of the first act, Brutus is the central character of the second. This second act is about 1000 verses long, two-thirds of the total length of the play. It is here that the dramatisation of the central theme of the play is to be found: "how freedom which has been won can be retained against all tyranny and oligarchy." This act covers the attempts of the citizens to secure their state and defend it against both internal and external enemies. At the beginning the herald commands the council to act justly. This is followed by the confirmation of the constitution of the newly founded republic. At its head there are to be two "Consuls or Burgermeister" who will hold office in rotation and to whom the council, elected from members of the guilds, will answer; the council in turn is to make decisions on matters of great political weight in conjunction with the citizens. Elected as consuls by the people, Brutus and Collatinus have hardly had time to take up their office, when it seems the Republic is in danger of falling back into the slavery it has just escaped. Envoys of the king who has just been expelled attempt to ingratiate themselves, but are turned away. Rich wastrels, merry fellows, beggars, young men who support the king and, in particular those who received pensions and mercenaries, who have been paid by the former king and appear in "foreign clothes," unite to bring back the old order.

---

23. As Bullinger notes in his diary (*HBD*) "Brutus sive Lucretia," the political direction of the work is evident.

The most vociferous participants are the sons of Brutus, Titus and Tiberius, who have grown up knowing nothing but luxury and idleness, and now curse the new Republic. However, the conspiracy is discovered by a faithful slave and the rebels are taken prisoner. In the climax of this scene, carefully crafted for its full impact, the sons of Brutus are condemned by their own father and delivered into the hands of the hangman (Hartmann, 83-6); Collatinus is removed from office on account of his indecisive and cowardly behaviour and is banished from the city. The Republic has proved itself to be both unassailable and virtuous in its response to a plot hatched by outsiders from both the highest and lowest social classes. At the end Vindices, the slave whose actions had bought the conspiracy to light, is rewarded with his freedom. He is given the status of citizen and is even equipped with a sum of money for his new life. Brutus, who has successfully defended his position, can say with justice to the council:

Now we have ordered all things
So that we may in future more easily rule.
And when we remain faithful and true
So will fortune and salvation come to you.[24]

Politics and Theology in Lucretia and Brutus

I. The Historical and Political Background

It would be inaccurate to suggest that Bullinger's play is no more than just an entertaining literary exercise without any contemporary social or political relevance. As mentioned earlier, there is evidence that the play was written after late autumn 1526. If we set it against the context of Zurich in the years between 1525 and 1526, and in particular bear in mind daily religious life and internal political developments, we can discern the links with the politics of the day as well as the intentions of the author.

In 1525 and at the height of the Zwinglian Reformation, Zurich was isolated both confessionally and politically within the Confederation. The criticism of Zurich that was voiced by other members of the Confederation was clearly audible. This censure focused on the ecclesiastical changes that had recently been introduced in Zurich: the dissolution of the monasteries and introduction of state-run poor relief, the abolition of the mass and new regulations for the celebration of communion, withdrawal from Episcopal jurisdiction and introduction of a new order for the morals court (*Ehegericht*), and the opening of the *Prophezei*, the Zurich theological school. The conflict between the politics of the Confederation and Zurich[25] was made evident by the presence of three delegations from the Catholic Confederates in Zurich between September and November 1525 attempting, without success, to convince the council to reintroduce the mass and

24. Hartmann, *Heinrich Bullinger–Hans Sachs: Lucretia-Dramen*, 94,25-95,2.

25. See René Hauswirth, "Zur politischen Ethik der Generation nach Zwingli," *Zwingliana* 13 (1971): 305-42, here 311. What Hauswirth argued for the generation after Zwingli was already true for the years 1525-6 and held for this whole period.

the old order.[26] This conflict was also evident in the arduous negotiations over the annual reaffirmation by oath of alliances within the Confederation. A more serious problem was the growing isolation of Zurich within the Confederation on account of the city's lone stance against mercenaries and pensioners. Zwingli was well known as a bitter opponent of mercenary service and pensions from foreign lords (including the papacy).[27] As early as 1522, and in part as a result of Zwingli's strong influence, the council in Zurich had introduced a general prohibition of mercenary service unique in the Confederation,[28] in September 1524 the ruling had been made even stricter and it was upheld stringently in the following two years.[29] Zurich's stance was opposed most vigorously by the Catholic Confederates Uri, Schwyz, Unterwalden, Zug, and Lucerne, where mercenary service, together with pensions, formed a lucrative source of income that these Confederates were neither willing nor able to surrender. As the attack on mercenary service had particularly strong religious underpinning, the Catholic Confederates hoped it would be possible to have Zwingli outlawed and the Reformation condemned in the name of the Confederation as a whole. At the diet of 1526 a disputation was held in Baden (19 May–9 June)[30] at which the majority of the members of the Confederation did indeed condemn Zwingli's teachings as erroneous. This condemnation was, however, worthless as Berne, Basle, Schaffhausen and, naturally, Zurich itself refused to put their names to the verdict. The disputation had, however, made evident that the Confederation was deeply divided by the religious question. When Berne, St Gall, Basle, and Schaffhausen also joined the Reformation in 1528-9 the partitioning along confessional lines was unmistakable.

In 1525-6 the conflict in Zurich between church and politics also reached its climax. Through spring and summer 1525 the rural hinterland was besieged by complaints from the peasantry, which included many who were supportive of Anabaptist teachings. Amongst their demands were the abolition of serfdom and of the small tithe and the removal of lower justice and introduction of the free election of pastors. The revolt was resolved without recourse to arms, in part as a result of repressive measures and in part as a result of a variety of concessions to the peasants. The armed conflict between the authorities and the peasantry which took place in southern Empire was therefore not replicated in the Confedera-

---

26. See Oskar Farner, *Huldreich Zwingli,* vol. 4: *Reformatorische Erneuerung von Kirche und Volk in Zürich und in der Eidgenossenschaft* (Zurich: Zwingli Verlag, 1960), 87.

27. On this, Georg Gerig, *Reisläufer und Pensionenherren in Zürich 1519-1532. Ein Beitrag zur Kenntnis der Kräfte, welche der Reformation widerstrebten* (Zurich: Leemann, 1947); Hermann Romer, *Herrschaft, Reislauf und Verbotspolitik. Beobachtungen zum rechtlichen Alltag der Zürcher Solddienstbekämpfung im 16. Jahrhundert* (Zurich: Schulthess, 1995); Olivier Bangerter, *La pensée militaire de Zwingli* (ZBRG 21; Berne: Peter Lang, 2003), esp. 36-122.

28. Emil Egli, *Actensammlung zur Geschichte der Zürcher Reformation* (Zurich: 1879; republished Nieuwkoop: 1973), no. 215, 293.

29. Egli, *Actensammlung,* no. 575.

30. Leonhard von Muralt, *Die Badener Disputation 1526* (Leipzig: M. Heinsius 1926); Gottfried W. Locher, *Die Zwinglische Reformation im Rahmen der europäischen Kirchengeschichte* (Göttingen: Vandenhoeck, 1979), 182-7.

tion.[31] However the Reformation in Zurich was still opposed by a significant grouping. It was in this tense atmosphere that in May 1526 Hans Buelmann rode through the Grossmünster and cursed Zwingli as a "rogue, thief, heretic, traitor and murderer of souls."[32] Opposition to the Reformation came from both the Anabaptist movement, against which the council took decisive action in 1526, and the Catholic clergy of the Grossmünster and Fraumünster. The latter included, for example, the canon Jakob Edlibach, and it was Edlibach's defence of the mass which was Zwingli's target in his work *Responsio brevis...in qua de eucharistia quaestio tractatur* of 14 August 1526.[33] The political opposition naturally also included many who were members of wealthy families, but it proved particularly attractive to those who were interested in the retention of mercenary service and in the income from pensions. Mercenary service was still an attractive proposition for many people and as the pensioners retained numerous connections with influential figures in the Catholic Confederate states, this circle of opponents presented a significant threat to the Reformation and the politics of the Zurich council. Zwingli himself acknowledged this in a sermon on 12 March 1525.[34] He renewed his attack in mid-September 1526, when from the pulpit he accused those who received pensions and those involved in the mercenary trade of seeking to thwart the Reformation and its growth within the Confederation.[35] His denunciations were directed against a number of individuals concerned with the mercenary trade, but it was concentrated on one man in particular: the influential city councillor Jakob Grebel (c1460-1526).[36]

Yet while Grebel's actions as a pensioner did count as misdemeanours, Grebel himself was by no means fully opposed to the Reformation. He was a moderate man concerned about the crisis of conscience, afflicting both the leading figures in the city and the common people, brought on by Zurich's isolationist politics. He was greatly disturbed by the radical political direction taken by Zurich. In addition, the Reformation had affected him personally: his son Conrad had alienated himself completely from his family and later became leader of the Anabaptist movement in Zurich. The new edge to Zwingli's sermon had the desired impact. The council prepared itself to take the decisive step against those who received pensions and those who supported mercenary service. An investigative commission was formed and those who supported mercenary service—designated *grex catilinaria* and traitors to the fatherland by Zwingli, on the model of Cicero—underwent a harsh interrogation that included the use of torture. The trial of Jakob Grebel resulted in the death sentence, although in fact there was not

31. See most recently, Andrea Strübind, *Eifriger als Zwingli. Die frühe Täuferbewegung in der Schweiz* (Berlin: Duncker und Humblot, 2003), 426-39.

32. Egli, *Actensammlung*, no. 580; see Locher, *Die Zwinglische Reformation*, 175.

33. *Z* V:317-58. Edlibach's text is printed there, 323-41.

34. *Z* III:584-9.

35. Zwingli to Oekolampadius on 29 November 1526, in *Z* VIII:779-83.

36. Hans Georg Wirz, "Familienschicksale im Zeitalter Zwinglis," *Zwingliana* 6 (1934-38), 194-222, 242-71, 470-99; Walter Jacob, *Politische Führungsschicht und Reformation. Untersuchungen zur Reformation in Zürich 1519-1528* (ZBRG 1; Zurich: TVZ, 1970), 173-7; Martin Haas, *Huldrych Zwingli und seine Zeit* (Zurich: TVZ, 2nd ed., 1976), 192-7.

sufficient evidence to justify capital punishment.[37] On 30 October 1526 Jakob Grebel was beheaded at the Fish Market. The judgement was very evidently politically motivated: his execution was a warning sent out by the campaign against mercenary service. Yet if Zwingli hoped that the lesson to be learnt from Grebel's death would have lasting impact, he was to be disappointed. Only one day after the condemnation of Jakob Grebel, several of his fellow-accused were pardoned–apparently the council did not want to push too far. There was no rush to proceed with further trials of those receiving pensions and those who recruited mercenaries–a year later several cases were still outstanding. Contemporaries criticised the severity of the action taken against Grebel, and this criticism could also be heard within Zurich itself. Felix Grebel, brother of Jakob and a council member and knight of the Holy Sepulcher, immediately relinquished his seat on the council, demonstratively surrendered his citizenship of Zurich, and left the city to live in Rapperswil.[38]

Bullinger's work functions on two levels: it both describes events in some detail and also takes an unambiguous and active stance on the social and political issues of the day.[39] For example, at the end of the first act Bullinger places particular emphasis on the alliance of peasants and citizens, a clear reference to the settlement between Zurich and the rural territories which followed the peaceful conclusion of the peasant unrest of 1525. This union of interests was a defining feature of this highly significant year.[40] In the play the scene set in Markus' home in which the conspiracy is planned not only reminds the audience of the tensions which accompanied the victory of the Zwinglian Reformation in 1525-6, but describes with some force the intrigues amongst unconvinced members of Zurich's ruling elite which had come to light in the course of the process against the supporters of mercenary service in October 1526.[41] The background for Legate Drances attempts at bribery clearly underscores the deeply felt revulsion at the oligarchy–military, economic and clerical–and its involvement in the business of war.[42] However, within the play there seems to be a direct reference to the diplomatic mission of the under-secretary Joachim Amgrut, a well-known opponent of Zwingli, and his mission to Rome in 1525 to claim from the papacy long overdue payment for mercenary services.[43]

There are similar points of reference in the political measures undertaken after the fall of the kingdom in order to maintain political and social order. Bullinger lays out clearly his ideal of a democratic state which is based on the

---

37. Egli, *Actensammlung*, no. 1050. For a treatment of the process, see Georg Gerig, *Reisläufer*, 53-69 and Leo Schelbert, "Jacob Grebel's Trial Revisited," *Archiv für Reformationsgeschichte* 60 (1969), 32-64.

38. Jacob, *Politische Führungsschicht*, 171.

39. Charbon makes the same argument, even though he uses different terminology, when he judged that the Lucretia was a "classicalisation of contemporary issues," Charbon, "Lucretia Tigurina," 45.

40. Hartmann, *Heinrich Bullinger–Hans Sachs: Lucretia-Dramen*, 58-60; see also Strübind, *Eifriger als Zwingli*, 429-31.

41. Hartmann, *Heinrich Bullinger–Hans Sachs: Lucretia-Dramen*, 73-81.

42. Ibid., 78.

43. See Locher, *Die Zwinglische Reformation*, 179 and Jacob, *Politische Führungsschicht*, 101.

fundamentals of the Roman republican constitution but which at the same time is clearly reflective of the political and social order in Zurich at the time of the Reformation. While this is evident in the method of election of both mayors and councillors, Bullinger also places particular emphasis on referenda carried out by the council in the first years of the Reformation in order to ensure popular support.[44] The removal of Collatinus from consular office on account of his failure to act decisively at a time of crisis can in part be viewed as an example drawn from history to give legitimacy to the (unjust) punishment of Councillor Grebel who had failed to abide by the prohibition on pensions. And certainly there can be no doubt that the contrast between Brutus and Collatinus was intended to provide two very different models of authority which represent the conflict between different political and social groupings. It was Brutus who embodied the ideal magistrate at the head of the community.

> And here will be briefly shown
> How authority ought to be used
> For the common use and virtue
> For freedom and justice
> That there ought to be a man of perseverance
> The like of whom has not been seen.[45]

It still cannot be established with any certainty whether Bullinger's positive appraisal of authority, set against the backdrop of the events of 1525 and in particular the official persecution of the Anabaptists, was either an intentional or a subconscious rejection of the radical forces within the Zurich reformation which rejected the institution of authority for Christians. Without doubt, however, Bullinger's ideas were drawn from the same debates as Zwingli's works *On divine and human righteousness* of 1523 and the section *On the magistrate* in the *Commentary on True and False Religion*. Authority is not just an emergency measure put in place to counter the evil in humanity, but rather an institution with moral and educational purpose.[46] Brutus' passionate appeal for unity amongst the people of Rome both recalls traditional Swiss legends about the evil actions of the representatives of Habsburg power and the struggle for freedom undertaken by the original members of the Confederation and exhorts contemporary members of

---

44. This is correctly emphasised by Hirth, *Heinrich Bullingers Spiel von "Lucretia und Brutus,"* 26 and Charbon, "Lucretia Tigurina," 40, note 20: "Apart from the explicit equating of "Consul" and "Burgermeyster" and "Lictoress" with "Weybeln or stattknecht" (64) there is also a reduction of guilds from 24 to 12 without company of the Constaffel. Bullinger translates "SPQR" as "Ein Rodt vnd gmeind der Statt Rom" (81). Further, the abolition of the standing army (64) and the right of the people (*Burger*) to be consulted during important matters (64) need to be mentioned. The latter is the so-called "Volksanfragen" when the inhabitants of the rural areas were consulted by the ruling magistrates, such as in the summer of 1526 when they were asked about the relationship to the 5 Inner States."

45. Hartmann, *Heinrich Bullinger–Hans Sachs: Lucretia-Dramen*, 62,3-8.

46. "Von göttlicher und menschlicher Gerechtigkeit," in Z II:458-525. "De vera et falsa religione commentaries" in Z III:590-912, esp. 867-88. See also the relevant treatment by Arthur Rich, "Zwingli als sozialpolitischer Denker," *Zwingliana* 8 (1969): 67-89 and Berndt Hamm, *Zwinglis Reformation der Freiheit* (Neukirchen-Vluyn: Neukirchener, 1988), 116-20.

the Confederation to maintain their unity.[47] This appeal can, however, also be seen as propaganda in support of Zwingli's ambitious ideal for the Confederation in which the Reformed faith would provide the foundation for unity of both religion and state.

It is not surprising that it occurred to Bullinger as schoolmaster in Kappel to turn his hand to drama. His intention was not simply to present the story of Lucretia and Brutus to a new audience as entertainment and a lesson in history. Indeed, his purpose, as a fellow-worker of Zwingli, was to use well-known historical material to illuminate the concrete events of the Reformation in the crisis years 1525-6. He clearly recognised the potential for high drama and effective dramatisation that this story provided and used it to the full. At the same time Bullinger the humanist clearly also enjoyed the perspective provided by history.[48] It is, however, startling to see that in this work the author neither treated the original material as an end in itself, nor imposed aesthetic or literary values upon it. Bullinger's desire to use the vehicle of drama to bring to the people the ideal of the rebirth of the Confederation from pure Christian teachings is evident in both solemn and more lighthearted exchanges within the play which contain here a Biblical echo or there a clever, but not condescending, comment. The reader can see very clearly that Bullinger constantly seeks to win over his audience to his own position while exposing and countering opposing opinions. In light of the highly controversial subject matter, it is hardly surprising that Bullinger's presentation is not without a degree of partisanship with a rather one-sided presentation of opposing views and polemical declarations. In this the play was hardly unusual, but rather a typical example of the processes of communication in the Reformation. The play is a game of hide and seek designed to appeal to as wide an audience as possible; in the end, however, all is revealed to the audience, who are left in no doubt as to the message of the play. When this message is fully digested it will reshape the political ethos of the audience.[49] It should also be noted that Bullinger was able to evaluate the varying accents of the sources available to him (Titus Livy and Dionysius of Halikarnassos), using their individual characteris-

---

47. Hartmann, *Heinrich Bullinger–Hans Sachs: Lucretia-Dramen*, 62,15-63,24.

48. On the ordering of the material historically, see the excellent dissertation by Christian Moser, *"Vil der wunderwerchen Gottes wirt man hierinn sâhen." Studien zu Heinrich Bullingers Reformationsgeschichte* (Diss., Zurich: 2002), 155-70.

49. This attempt to influence public opinion was not only through the theatre but is found in other, less speculative, communication processes. This is seen in a letter from Bullinger to Max Rosen of 5 February 1525 (*HBBW* I, no. 63, 16-64). Rosen was a young prominent burgher in Frauenfeld. In the letter Bullinger sets himself strongly against mercenary service, invoking the biblical text Deuteronomy 27:25 to justify his attack on the immorality of those who receive pensions–gifts from foreign lords–and who shed innocent blood. Another example is Bullinger's devotional text *The Highest Good* of 1528 in which he warns against the moral, political, and economic dangers of pensions. Heinrich Bullinger, *Das Höchste Gut*, Joachim Staedtke ed. and trans., (Zurich:1955), 21-22. On this, see Robert Walton, "Heinrich Bullinger, Repräsentant der reichen Bauern und seine Beziehungen zur städtischen Obrigkeit" in Siegfried Hoyer ed., *Reform, Reformation, Revolution* (Leipzig: Karl-Marx-Universität, 1980), 132-42.

tics in a remarkably mature manner in order to enlist the tale of Lucretia into the service of contemporary political circumstances in the Confederation.[50]

The drama *Lucretia and Brutus* was not the only place in his early works where Bullinger commented on communal government and the duties of the authorities. The example of Brutus is cited explicitly in a work of August 1526, published in Zurich at Zwingli's insistence, *Früntliche Ermanung zur Grechtigheit wider alles verfelschen rychtigen gerychtes.*[51] Here the word justice (*Gerechtigkeit*) is used not so much in addressing the theological problem of justification, but rather in examining "civil and state justice"; in other words, the relationship between authority and law. The duty of this office is contrasted with tyrannical government: such authority seeks not the realisation of its personal will, but rather the knowledge, protection and implementation of justice as the bedrock of communality. Here, as in the play, Bullinger stresses his view that justice must be placed before any unfettered attempt to exercise power. Bullinger summarises the situation thus: the magistrates should be like an "Egyptian judge," in other words a "an upright, magnanimous, humane person (so that one knows how to punish) who neither through opportunity, force, or payment is moved, and never deviates from the way of righteousness."[52] The power of the sword of which Romans 13 speaks is given by God to the authorities alone to enable them to defend the innocent and to confine and punish the unjust. The Anabaptist belief that Christians cannot hold magisterial office is therefore wrong and must be rejected. Bullinger makes specific reference to Brutus, arguing that Brutus' actions reflected his acute awareness of justice and the communal good. Therefore, just as Brutus did not spare the Romans his only son, so should no one refuse to offer themselves. Bullinger also thought very highly of the wars of liberation of his Swiss ancestors–Morgarten, Sempach, Naefels–against malicious nobility, against those who perverted the course of justice and against tyranny. And he admired greatly the traditional order, in other words the alliance system of the Swiss Confederation that committed the members of the Confederation to a policy of common protection against all foreign rulers and formed the Confederation into an overarching protective community based on justice. For Bullinger the corruption of this consciousness of freedom, justice, and community presented a real threat to the Confederation. One of his foremost concerns was therefore how the Confederation could solve the moral and political problems that it faced at the beginning of the sixteenth century. Bullinger's view of the relationship between state and church is characterised by his overriding desire to demonstrate the religious foundations of the political ethos and of the magisterial office. It is with this conviction that he admonishes the authorities:

Therefore I take my leave and desire that you desire, according to God's will, justice and the highest covenant of our faith, and that you seek in your office to

---

50. Hirth, *Heinrich Bullingers Spiel von "Lucretia und Brutus,"* 8. On Bullinger's use of historical material in his writing, see Moser, *Studien zu Heinrich Bullingers Reformationsgeschichte,* 134-52.

51. *HBBibl* I, no. 2; see Staedtke, *Die Theologie des jungen Bullinger,* 281.

52. Hartmann, *Heinrich Bullinger–Hans Sachs: Lucretia-Dramen,* Aiiij[v].

observe God and his unsurpassable justice, remaining by God's Word, and keeping him before you as God, Lord, and Judge.[53]

Bullinger addressed the same theme in greater detail in a work written in 1525 but published, anonymously, for the first time only in 1528. This was the piece entitled *"Anklage und ernstlisches Ermahnen Gottes."*[54] He takes as his starting point the Confederation as a unity and from this he develops, along the same lines as Zwingli, three interconnected ideas:[55] that the origins and continued existence of the Confederation are products of God's benevolent care, that the present members of the Confederation have left the path beaten by their predecessors whose nature they thus disowned, and that God is calling these members of the Confederation to repentance and renewal. Bullinger uses the political events of the day to highlight the crisis into which the whole country has descended. The greatest outrage to be found in society, he stresses, is the pension and mercenary income that he deems not only the exercise of the judgement of God on society,[56] but also, and above all else, reprehensible on account of its catastrophic ethical results:

> If you refuse to understand I must recount it to you, what you have achieved with your wars and pensions. I will not speak of my honour and empire but will constrain myself to the worldly consequences of what is happening. First, no one can be deceived that the origin of this lies in evil; you see daily that the wars bring nothing worthy. Look, rather, at what the fruits of the mercenaries are: they play games of fortune, they swear, they blaspheme, they are drunk day and night, they lie with prostitutes and adulteresses. In short, they destroy the whole order of honour and discipline.[57]

In addition Bullinger points out the economic and political damage caused by mercenary service and pensions. As a result of military service, youth fit to work

53. Ibid., C iiij^v.
54. *HBBibl* I, no. 3-9. The content and importance of the text, as well as its printing history and influence, have been thoroughly examined in Fritz Büsser, "Bullinger als Prophet. Zu seiner Frühschrift 'Anklag und Ermahnen'" in Fritz Büsser, *Wurzeln der Reformation in Zürich. Zum 500. Geburtstag des Reformators Huldrych Zwingli* (Leiden: 1985), 106-24. See also the careful study of Hans-Ulrich Bächtold, "History, Ideology and Propaganda in the Reformation: the Early Writing 'Anklag und ernstliches ermanen Gottes' (1525) of Heinrich Bullinger" in Bruce Gordon ed., *Protestant History and Identity in Sixteenth-Century Europe* vol. 1: *The Medieval Inheritance* (St Andrews Studies in Reformation History, Aldershot: Ashgate 1996), 46-59. The date of the work is difficult to determine more precisely than the end of 1525. See Bächtold, ibid., 48-49, note 12. In the following passages I cite the transcription made by Hans-Ulrich Bächtold of the text found in the ZB (Ms. A 73). This text is a copy of the apparently lost original Bullinger manuscript.
55. See Eduard Jakob Kobelt, *Die Bedeutung der Eidgenossenschaft für Huldrych Zwingli* (Zurich: Leemann, 1970), and Ulrich Gäbler, "Die Schweizer–ein 'Auserwähltes Volk'?," in Heiko A. Oberman et al. eds, *Reformiertes Erbe. Festschrift für Gottfried W. Locher zu seinem 80. Geburtstag* vol. 1 (Zurich: TVZ, 1992), 143-55.
56. f. 13. As in the letter to Max Rosen (note 49) Bullinger uses Deut. 27:25 to prove that the pension lords who received unlawful gifts and who were responsible for the shedding of blood were damned.
57. Hartmann, *Heinrich Bullinger–Hans Sachs: Lucretia-Dramen*, 16.

the land are not available, prices rise, and capital accumulates in the hands of an oligarchy that can shape both internal and foreign policy to its own ends. This grouping is therefore currently failing to fulfill its responsibilities to the community and is leading the country into ruin:

> You have no democracy any more. Rather, oligarchy and the pension lords rule over the people, who receive no pensions. All others remain silent, and no one is honourable, pious, and true as he should be for his community and fatherland. No one takes this disastrous situation seriously and no one will do anything for the common good.[58]

At the heart of Bullinger's *Anklage*, however, lies his call for repentance and renewal from the members of Confederation. For Bullinger there is a very strong connection between faith and moral behaviour. True faith means not just the recognition of the existence and nature of the one God and a reliance, both trusting and reverential, on God who has revealed his mercy to humanity through Christ. From faith would also come a sense of duty towards one's fellow human beings. For Bullinger, therefore, the renewal of the Confederation was not possible without the justice which comes from true faith, a justice which has at its heart a sense of the communal spirit, the defeat of self-interest, and is manifested daily through activities both in and for the community.[59]

While this is of significance for the Confederation as a whole, it is of particular relevance for the actions of the authorities, whose first and most significant task, drawing on the medieval idea of the state, is the care of the common good. It is typical of Bullinger that these duties are fulfilled when the magistracy acts to protect law and punish wrongdoing. The magistrate has not to act in accordance with his own understanding, rather he is bound so closely to the law that the office of secular authority is at heart indistinguishable from that of judge. Both judge and regent should be lovers of justice who judge the people on the basis of justice. According to the *Anklage* the principal tasks of authority are strict adherence to justice and love of the communal good founded on this justice; these are to be accompanied by strength of character and spirit. Those entitled to be officeholders within the state are to be distinguished by these political virtues.[60]

---

58. Ibid., 41-42.

59. "Daran lyt aber der waar, mir wolgfellig dienst, das du vff mich allein såhist, mich erkennist, mitt waarem glauben, als das eynig, volkommen, oberist guot, von dem alles guots, vnd vssert dem nützig guots sye, das ich sye der eynig Gott, der allmechtig schôpffer aller dingen, die ewige krafft, die alles in allem thůt, die vnuerzylt macht, die alles durchtringt, erfüllt, vnd an allen orten gegen wirtig ist, vnnd das Barmhertzig gůt, das dem menschen wol wil: vnd darumb auch mynem eynigen liebsten sun für die wållt hin in todt geben hab. Darumb jr mich allein foerchen soellend, anbetten, vnd vereeren, auch eynig anrůffen in allen üwerem anligen. Das ist der waar vnd geråcht Gloub in mich. Der verschaffet denn das du dem nachkumpst das obgemeldet ist, vβ der Prophecy Jsaie mynes dieners. Dann der recht Gloub leeret: Jr sôllend üwere nåchsten lieben als üch selbs / jnen helffen vnnd beraaten sin, sy nit beleydigen noch betriegen. Jr sôllend die Armen beherbergen, jr sôllend sy trôsten, spysen, trâncken, vnd bekleyden. Jr sôllend üweren naechsten wytwen vnd weysen byston zum råchten, vund niemants lassen kein gwalt beschåhen." (f. 23-24).

60. "Rychter und regenten sôllend jr haben, das sy das volck rychtind mitt gerechtem gerycht. Darum wo ir in allem volck gottsfôrchtig lüt habend die nit glychßner sind, sunder eins

Brutus is included in the list of great men of ancient times and biblical accounts who ruled according to the norms of justice and law; he is depicted as the embodiment of political virtue: O you (the Swiss) should be like the late Brutus and Themistocles–that is how it should be.[61]

A comparison of the concept of authority contained in the *Ermahnung* and in the *Anklage* with the instructions for those participating in the play *Lucretia and Brutus* readily reveals that the characteristics of just authority in both are drawn from the same well of virtues. In his portrayal of Brutus Bullinger seeks to highlight his bravery, his confidence-inspiring way of life and his sense of justice according to which all receive what is justly theirs.[62] This gives further force to the position taken at the start of this paper: even if this play had little direct impact on the contemporary situation, its contribution, when placed alongside his early works, to our understanding of Bullinger's concept of authority in his early years must not be overlooked.

II. The Theological Dimension

This discussion must not be allowed to leave the impression that Bullinger's early writings were concerned only with the justification of the constitution of the Swiss Confederation and, primarily, with the situation of Zurich. There is another angle to this material that remains to be highlighted; this will also throw additional light on the sources available and bring to the fore Bullinger's central concerns. Along with reflections on the nature of the state, there is another issue that pervades every aspect of these works: the fulfilment of God's call for righteousness and justice within the political community. This brings us to the fundamental issue for Bullinger, for the Zurich reformation and for Reformed political ethics as a whole: the distinction between God-given justice and human justice. The problems in determining the precise interdependence between the *iustitia divina* and the *iustitia civilis*, or rather the definition of their relationship, are particularly evident in Bullinger's concept of authority.

It is possible to say, in broad terms, that Bullinger's understanding of authority was not taken from the Bible alone. Rather his ideas expressly flowed from biblical conceptions to those of ancient theorists of the state who, even without recognising the will of God, held that the commonweal should be ruled according

---

uffrechten vollkomnen hertzens: die dapffer redlich lüt sind und nit forchtsam, die ab yedem tröuwen erschräckend, sunder die mann sind, wie Cato was und David: die standhafft sind, nit biegsam, hüt eins wellend, morn ein anders, die starck sind, und manns hertz habend, nit fråfel Jugurthe: die wyß sind, das recht wol wüßend: die liebhaber der gerechtigkeyt sind, fygend des unrechten und mütwillens, ouch trüw und waarhafft, nit schwåtzer und falsch, die ouch den gmeynen nutz liebend, dem gyt ghassz sind, und gar kein gaaben nemmend: die richtig im rechten fürgond, alles das thünd was die gsatzten vermogend und billigkeit, niemants darumb ansehend. Ja wo jr soemlich lüt habend, die setzend in grycht und rath." (f. 37).

61. f. 43.

62. Hartmann, *Heinrich Bullinger–Hans Sachs: Lucretia-Dramen*, 96,8-11: He "soll von lyb vnd gmůt ein herrlich dapffer man syn / ernsthafft, ruch / ghrecht / grådtz über das vnrecht / ja / das er sich nit erbetten laßt / vnd doch den güten früntlich sey."

to justice and the law. However, it was fundamental to Bullinger, as to all other Reformers, that authority stemmed from the command of God and as such was an effective element of God's providence. Such authority is therefore not subordinate to spiritual authority on earth, but rather must be exercised independently, although, of course, in full responsibility before God. It is important to recognise that this principle struck at the heart of the medieval concept of the two swords in which spiritual authority held precedence even in temporal matters (*plenitudo potestatis papae in temporalibus*).[63] It was Bullinger's view, based on Romans 13, that magistrates were the servants of God, responsible for the realisation of his order.[64] Bullinger gave them the title "Elohim"[65] in order to demonstrate their particular responsibilities before God. They were not to implement their own will, but rather to execute God's will for justice. The status of the magistracy is made particularly clear through a comparison, often used in ancient times, with the father of the household, who is responsible for the protection and care of the community within his house.[66]

Based on his unshakable conviction that authority derives from God, Bullinger believed with equal intensity that those under this authority were bound to obedience. At the same time, however, he indicated the boundaries which magistrates had to observe. In both *Lucretia and Brutus* and in the *Ermanung* Bullinger repeatedly demonstrated, in numerous sentences and with succinct allusions, that those in authority, just like all people, were under the eternal justice of God and that those who exercised power could do so only as permitted by God. These are the grounds for Bullinger's striking dramatulurgical portrayal of the Tarquin as they stepped beyond the boundaries of their God-given competencies, their tyrannical rule destroying that which they were bound to maintain and maintaining that which they were bound to destroy. It is made clear that in this situation resistance is a risk which must be taken. Like Zwingli, but unlike other reformers, Bullinger called upon the people, and in particular citizens who were imbued with a sense of justice, to resist power exercised unjustly. There is a good example in the *Anklage* of Bullinger's bold and radical position on active opposition to tyrannical authority, and even on the murder of tyrants:

> Now you [the Swiss] know well the guilt of the pension lords with their deeds and spilling of blood. Perhaps one could be merciful with them if they, in future, renounced that shedding of blood and the selling of men, and if they gave to the poor and fairly distributed those goods acquired by blood. When they do not do this, if they never seek peace, and do not apologise, then can we do nothing

---

63. See Ulrich Duchrow, *Christenheit und Weltverantwortung. Traditionsgeschichte und systematische Struktur der Zweireichelehre* (Stuttgart: Klett, 1970), chap. III, 321-435.

64. Bullinger, *Ermahnung*, f. Ajjjj'.

65. Bullinger, *Anklage*, f. 21: "Jr soltend Elohim (das ist Gôtter) sin, mine statthalter in gricht vnnd gerechtigkeyt, in sorg, ernst, gûte, vnnd straff ..."

66. Ibid., f. 21: "Jr im regiment, soltendt üch nit alles gewalts vnderwinden als Landtsfürsten, üwer lannd ist nit ein Oligarchia, sunder ein Democratia, ein Commun. Darumb sôltend jr üwers armen volcks Patres (das ist vâtter) sind: üwer volck soltend jr halten wie mitbürger, ja sy lieben wie kind, vor schaden vergoumen, versehen das weder sy noch jr annaemind, von dannen mitt der zyt ein schad entston moechte". On the significance of the terms "Democratia" and "Commun," see Kobelt, *Die Bedeutung der Eidgenossenschaft*, 51-65.

other with them than as Solomon dealt with Joab, when he cut off his head. It is certainly better not to fill the land with wild bloodhounds, for this would only bring chaos, wailing, hunger, war, and misery.[67]

The primary duties of the secular authority should constantly be impressed on them: the *cura religionis,*[68] the maintenance of peace,[69] care of the communal well-being and protection of the freedom of both the citizens and the community. Bullinger was well aware of how difficult it was to make the political powers act in accordance with God's justice. According to Bullinger it was the duty of the Christian community to impress this need upon the political authorities and to support them in the execution of their legal and judicial responsibilities in the spirit of the commands of the Bible. This issue was at the heart of both *De propheta libri duo,*[70] written in 1525 but unpublished, which addressed the issue of the true prophetic office, and the *Ermahnung.* In these works and in various ways Bullinger elucidated the close ties between the church community and the political community, and between the office of minister and the office of the magistrate. Church and civic community must be understood as different entities, but they are not two entirely separate bodies based on fundamentally different principles, but rather two elements of the same organism. Although their tasks are separate, they themselves are indivisible. For Bullinger, both bodies draw on the same model of justice and righteousness in which directions for behaviour within the community and the moral principles of the individual form a single unit. There is therefore a common concept of human community that provides the basis for both the church community and the community of citizens and is in accordance with the Christian-biblical foundations of the community of justice. In the church community righteousness comes primarily from internal agreement achieved through faith and, therefore, this community can act as a model for the community of the state.

For Bullinger, the civic community is not just a political body with powers of compulsion; rather, and above all, it is also a moral community that through renewed recognition of God's commands enables its members to emulate the righteousness of God, over and above human justice. The boundary between actions based on genuine religious faith and those based purely on the will for political power is clearly drawn. The *iustitia divina* with its biblical commandments should not be applied indiscriminately or blindly to the day-to-day process of political decision-making. Bullinger's intention is not the clericalisation of society, let alone the creation of a theocracy in the sense of rule by the clergy. Rather, it

67. Bullinger, *Anklage*, f. 43. See 1 Corinthians 2:5-6 and 2:29-34.

68. Ibid, f. 39: "Wenn aber der gwalt, der das houpt vnd oug ist, also heylig vnd gsund ist, so müß es demnach vmb den lyb (vmb üch dz gmeyn volck) wol ston. Dann sicht er eynig vff mich, vff die gsatzen, vff myn wort..." and *passim.*

69. Bullinger, *Ermahnung,* f. B^V.

70. ZB, Ms. A 82. Cf. Staedtke, *Die Theologie des jungen Bullinger,* 275-6 and Pamela Biel, *Doorkeepers at the House of Righteousness. Heinrich Bullinger and the Zurich Clergy 1535-1575* (ZBRG 15; Berne: Peter Lang, 1991), 200-3. On Bullinger's later text from 1532 on the same theme, see Fritz Büsser, "De prophetae officio. Eine Gedenkrede Bullingers auf Zwingli" in Fritz Büsser, *Wurzeln der Reformation,* 60-71.

was his contention that the Christian community must watch over secular matters and raise its voice whenever it sees injustice. On the other hand, if both church and secular communities are founded on common principles and both accept the principle of scriptural authority, then it may seem superfluous to have an autonomous church order, for this can be the responsibility of the authorities as the guardians of justice. With this opinion on the relationship between church and state Bullinger clearly rejected the Anabaptist position that the Christian community should be formed outwith the secular sphere or that the individual should remain apart from all offices of authority. It was central to Bullinger that the *iustitia divina* was not a *res interna*, but rather also a *res publica*. The Reformation was to serve society; it was to enable the renewal of the civic community. And in turn this also meant that as long as the authorities were seeking to fulfill the tasks which God had given them, their actions were in the service of God.

This chapter is not the place to discuss whether Bullinger's desire to define the true relationship between God's law and human law, and between church and state could be realised without pause or without alteration. As the history of the Reformed churches and of Protestantism as a whole demonstrates, the issues which Bullinger addressed would be raised time and time again. The lasting contribution of his early works is twofold: the realisation that human law, or the office of political authority, could no longer lay claim to final authority and that it is by nature changeable and must remain changeable. As a result Bullinger's reworking of the story of Lucretia and Brutus in his early writings is more than just an episode in the history of interpretation of the ancient Roman legends; he endows the legend with timeless significance.

8

Heinrich Bullinger's Efforts to Document the Zurich Reformation: History as Legacy

Christian Moser

Heinrich Bullinger as Historian

Alongside his time-consuming pastoral duties, his unending work in expounding the Bible, and the constant demands of church politics, Heinrich Bullinger devoted himself to the study and writing of history.[1] This fascination with history and in particular with getting down on paper a correct account of events was a central part of Bullinger's life and his role in the reformation of the church, and there is little doubt that a deeper understanding of his passion for history will enable us to explore and understand more fully his life and thought. Bullinger's printed works demonstrate clearly the centrality of history to his thought, but another as yet untapped source is the rich body of work in manuscript which he left behind. Many of his printed works concentrate on historical theology and church history, and they reveal what he described in his own words as his "great joy and appetite" for the past and his zeal for historical research.[2] A good example of this is his 1539 work *Concerning the origin of*

1. The literature on Bullinger's engagement with history, its importance for his thought, and his work as a historian is limited. There is the work of Joachim Staedtke, "Die Geschichtsauffassung des jungen Bullinger" in Ulrich Gäbler/Erland Herkenrath eds, *Heinrich Bullinger 1504-1575. Gesammelte Aufsätze zum 400. Todestag*, vol. 1: *Leben und Werk* (ZBRG 7; Zurich: TVZ, 1975), 65-74 and Hans Ulrich Bächtold, "History, Ideology and Propaganda in the Reformation: the Early Writing 'Anklag und ernstliches ermanen Gottes' (1525) of Heinrich Bullinger" in Bruce Gordon ed., *Protestant History and Identity in Sixteenth-Century Europe*, vol. 1: *The Medieval Inheritance* (Aldershot: Ashgate, 1996), 46-59. Above all, see Aurelio A. Garcia Archilla, *The Theology of History and Apologetic Historiography in Heinrich Bullinger: Truth in History* (San Francisco: Mellen Press, 1992). This essay is largely drawn from the author's unpublished dissertation on Bullinger's Reformation history writing: Christian Moser, *"Vil der wunderwerchen Gottes wirt man hierinn sähen": Studien zu Heinrich Bullingers Reformationsgeschichte* (Diss., University of Zurich: 2002).
2. This great interest in the history of his "fatherland" is indicated by Bullinger himself in his letter of dedication to Samuel Tillmann of his history of the counts of Habsburg, the monastery of Königsfelden and the Sempach War (ZB, Ms. A 142, f. 1-69): "Years ago, as I was younger and able to do more work, I had a great joy and appetite in the history of our fatherland, the common Eidgenossenschaft." The dedication is printed in Emil Blösch, "Ein Brief H. Bullingers," *Anzeiger für schweizerische Geschichte*, new series 5 (1887): 108f., quotation is found on 108.

error, in which he undertook an historical examination of the medieval origins of error in the doctrines of the Lord's Supper, the veneration of saints, and the mass. His purpose was to explore the historical context of what he regarded as crucial lapses in the history of the church.[3] This was by no means his first effort, for in 1526, under the pseudonym Octavius Florens, he had written his *Comparison of the ancient heresies with those of our day.*[4] The later works which would be distinguished by his historical interests include his treatment of church councils, *On Councils,*[5] and his analysis of the problem of persecution in the church, which he wrote following the massacre of St Bartholomew's Day.[6] In all these works there is an explicit use of history, and his arguments are built upon his interpretation of the past designed to reveal error in the church's history and to throw light on contemporary debates. This was especially important for Bullinger in defending the Reformed faith in the growing confessionalism of the sixteenth century.[7] The head of the Zurich church worked hard to demonstrate that the teaching of his church was absolutely consistent with the doctrines of the Apostolic faith of the early church.[8] In both the more familiar printed works on

---

3. *De origine erroris libri duo Heinrychi Bullingeri. In priore agitur de Dei veri iusta invocatione et cultu vero, de deorum item falsorum religionibus et simulachrorum cultu erroneo. In posteriore disseritur de institutione et vi sacrae coenae Domini et de origine ac progressu missae papisticae, contra varias superstitiones pro religione vera antiqua et orthodoxa,* Zurich 1539 (*HBBibl* I, no. 12). Earlier editions of the text appeared in 1528 and 1529 (*HBBibl* I, no. 10f.). In this article reference will be made only to the first editions of Bullinger's works. Further information about subsequent editions and translations is readily to be found in *HBBibl* I.

4. *Verglichung der uralten und unser zyten kåtzeryen, zů warnen die einfaltigen Christen durch Octavium Florentem beschriben,* Zurich 1526 (*HBBibl* I, no. 8).

5. *De conciliis. Quomodo apostoli Christi Domini in primitiva ecclesia suum illud Hierosolymis concilium celebraverint [...], quomodo item Romani pontifices in extrema mundi senecta, a quingentis et amplius annis, sua illa concilia celebraverint et quanto cum damno perturbationeque fidelium, brevis ex historiis commemoratio [...],* Zurich 1561 (*HBBibl* I, no. 402). Compare Bullinger's announcement in his preface (Ibid., f. 2ᵛ): "commemorabo in hoc opere ex historiis, quid de conciliis ab annis 1500 celebratis ipsa veritas testetur".

6. *Vervolgung. Von der schweren, langwirigen vervolgung der heiligen christlichen kirchen, ouch von den ursachen der vervolgung und vermanung zur gedult und bestand, sampt erzellung der raach unnd straaff Gottes wider die vervolger [...],* Zurich 1573 (*HBBibl* I, no. 575). The intention which Bullinger pursued with his publication is expressed in the following passage: (Ibid., f. 2ᵛ): "Dorumb zů besserem bericht, trost unnd entscheid wil ich mit Gottes hilff uß heiliger gôttlicher geschrifft und alten gloubwirdigen historien, ouch erfarung der zyten, erzellen unnd verzeichnen, was die heilig christenlich kirch von anfang der geburt Christi biß zů disen unseren zyten von wågen unsers heiligen, waaren, ungezwyffleten christenen gloubens erlitten, ouch was grossen glücks unnd faals, fürgangs und sygs, der ermelten kirchen fynd und widerwertige durch und von Gottes verhångnuß gehebt, doch zů letst ire straff ouch entpfangen habind etc."

7. See for example "Christian Moser, Ratramnus von Corbie als 'testis veritatis' in der Zürcher Reformation: Zu Heinrich Bullinger und Leo Juds Ausgabe des *Liber de corpore et sanguine Domini* (1532)" in Martin H. Graf/Christian Moser eds, *Strenarum lanx: Beiträge zur Philologie und Geschichte des Mittelalters und der Frühen Neuzeit* (Zug: Achius, 2003), 235-309.

8. Compare the text *Das der Christen gloub von anfang der wålt gewåret habe, der recht und ungezwyflet glouben sye [...],* Basle 1537 (*HBBibl* I, no. 99). On this point, see J. Wayne Baker, *Heinrich Bullinger and the Covenant: The Other Reformed Tradition* (Athens, Ohio: Ohio Univ. Press, 1980), 55-64; Edward A. Dowey, "The Old Faith: Comments on One of Heinrich

theology and church history, and in the voluminous body of manuscripts which have yet to receive scholarly attention, Bullinger demonstrates his consuming interest in the past and his will to deal with current issues and problems through the lens of history.

Bullinger's historical works were not limited to the history of the Church. A major part of his corpus is made up of profane historical works that are more directly concerned with institutions and the history of particular lands. Naturally, Bullinger himself made no distinction between his ecclesiastical and profane historical writings, although it has been the former and not the latter that have attracted scholarly attention. This inattention to the profane histories has much to do with the fact that these works, and the extensive material that belongs to them, have, with a few exceptions, never been printed. Various types of writings make up the body of Bullinger's historical work that he left as a legacy to the Zurich church.[9] There are the histories of particular religious houses, such as his 1526 *Annales sive Chronicon Coenobii Cappell*, concerning the Cistercian monastery at Kappel, where Bullinger worked as a teacher from 1523 to 1529.[10] He also wrote a history of the Benedictine house of Einsiedeln and its abbots.[11] In addition to the history of religious houses there are Bullinger's accounts of Zurich and Swiss history, such as his *Erste Schweizerchronik*, which he wrote between 1530 and 1531.[12] This was followed almost forty years later by his comprehensive accounts of the Swiss Confederation (1568, 1572-4).[13] Another type of writing was Bullinger's analysis of contemporary events, such as his history of Anabaptism,[14] which appeared in 1560, and his *History of the Reformation*, which we shall discuss at length below. Finally, Bullinger's interest in universal history and historical chronology is represented by a work which appeared in 1565 under the name *Epitome temporum*, but was preceded by a preparatory work in 1544.[15]

Bullinger's Most Distinctive Treatises" in Willem van 't Spijker ed., *Calvin: Erbe und Auftrag. Festschrift für Wilhelm Neuser zu seinem 65. Geburtstag* (Kampen: Kok Pharos, 1991), 270-8; Garcia Archilla, *The Theology of History*, 8-36.

9. I can only refer here to a selection of Bullinger's historical writings; for a full account and information on the location of the texts, see Moser, *Studien zu Heinrich Bullingers Reformationsgeschichte*, 19-26.

10. The manuscript is found in StA, E II 437, f. 130r-146r. The later editions and partial editions are found in *HBBibl* I, no. 744f.

11. *Von dem kloster zů den Eynsidlen und sinen aeppten*, ZB, Ms. A 127, 17-63 (undated).

12. *Gemeiner Eydgnosschafft, deß grossen und allten pundtes in obren Dütschen landenn harkummen, allte geschichten und trüw, besondere und gemeine thaten, mitt kurtzer und warhafter histori, durch H. B. beschryben*, ZB, Ms. A 47. See Hans Georg Wirz, "Heinrich Bullingers erste Schweizerchronik" in: *Nova Turicensia: Beiträge zur schweizerischen und zürcherischen Geschichte* (Zurich: Höhr, 1911), 235-90.

13. Compare with the works cited below pages 204-5.

14. *Der Widertöufferen ursprung, fürgang, secten wåsen, fürnemme und gemeine irer leer artickel [...]*, Zurich 1560 (*HBBibl* I, no. 394).

15. *Epitome temporum et rerum ab orbe condito, ad primum usque annum Iothan regis Iudae: in qua praecipue attinguntur, quae pertinent ad sacras literas illustrandas et ad veram antiquamque religionem et eius certitudinem, progressum item et mutationem, cognoscendam. [...]*, Zurich 1565 (*HBBibl* I, no. 430).

The History of the Reformation

One of Bullinger's principal historical endeavours was to document the history of the Zurich Reformation. This took shape in his *Historia oder geschichten, so sich verlouffen in der Eydgnoschafft, insonders zů Zürych, mitt enderung der religion und anrichten christenlicher reformation, von dem jar Christi 1519 biß in das jar 1532 [...]*, the aforementioned *Reformation History*. Bullinger commented on the completion of the work in his *Diary* in 1567: "On 10 November I completed my Zurich history of the reformation of the Church from 1519 to 1532. It is written in German and is extensive."[16] Extensive is certainly the correct word, for Bullinger's manuscript, which is to be found in the Zentralbibliothek in Zurich, comprises two massive volumes that run to over 1600 pages.[17] In contrast to Bullinger's entry in his *Diary*, the manuscript gives 20 March 1564 as the completion date.[18] On the basis of internal evidence, such as the dating of events in 1567, this date of 1564 seems rather unlikely.[19] Bullinger himself solved the problem of contradictory dates when he described the process by which he wrote the work. He worked backwards chronologically, so that he had clearly finished the section on the Second Kappel War in 1564, while the remaining parts were completed in 1567. Bullinger writes:

> In writing the text I have written first the last part, the Second Kappel War, then the First Kappel War, and the Reformation from 1519 to 1529. Then I worked on the description of the Old Zurich War and the following events through to the Swabian War. Afterwards, I wrote the history of the period from the founding of the Swiss Confederation to the Old Zurich War. Finally, I expanded the remaining period, that is from 1500 to 1519. When this was done I had finished the history completely from the beginning of the Confederation in 1306 through the 226 years to 1532.[20]

This account of the order in which he wrote the *Reformation History* is taken from the preface to his *Eidgenössische Chronik*, which Bullinger completed a year later and in which he described pre-Reformation Zurich and the Swiss Con-

---

16. "10. Novemb. absolvi historiam Tigurinam de reformatione ecclesiæ ab a. D. 1519 ad 1532; Germanice scripta est et magna." *HBD*, 87.

17. The manuscript is found in ZB, Ms. A 16 & 17. As with all of his larger historical works, this remained unprinted. An edition was not prepared till the nineteenth century: see *HBRG*. Indices of places, names, and subjects were prepared later: *Register zu Heinrich Bullingers Reformationsgeschichte (ed. J. J. Hottinger und H. H. Vögeli)*, prepared by Willy Wuhrmann (Zurich: 1913).

18. ZB, Ms. A 17, 756.

19. cf. *HBRG* I:32, 230.

20. "Imm schryben hab ich zum ersten das letzt an die hand genommen und beschriben den anderen Capplerkrieg, darnach erst den ersten sampt der erzellung von der reformation vomm iar Christi 1519 bis in das iar 1529. Daruff hab ich gearbeitet amm Zürychkrieg und was dem gefolget biß nach dem Schwabenkrieg und hie erst bin ich gestanden an disen anfang der Eydg[noschafft] und inn ußgefůrt biß an Zürychkrieg. Zůletzt hab ich ouch hinzů gethan, was noch überig was von dem 1500 iar biß zů dem iar Christi 1519. Hiemitt ist die history gantz und volkommen worden vomm anfang der Eydgnoschafft vomm iar Christi 1306 durch 226 iar biß zů dem iar 1532." ZB, Ms. A 14, f. 27ᵛ.

federation.[21] However, only four years later Bullinger replaced this chronicle, which had been quickly drafted and was not complete, and wrote once more on the same time period. This was the two-volume *Tigurinerchronik*, written between 1572 and 1574. To this massive history Bullinger appended a history of the Grossmünster chapter and a copy of his *Reformation History* in two further volumes.[22] On 14 December 1574 Bullinger handed over the four volumes to the members of the Grossmünster chapter.[23]

Bullinger's *Reformation History* covers the period 1519 to 1532/3 and treats the history of the Zurich Reformation in the context of both political and ecclesiastical events in the Swiss Confederation and crucial foreign events. The account begins with a reflection on the relationship between ecclesiastical and political institutions in Zurich before the Reformation,[24] a short biography of Zwingli including a report on his appointment as stipendiary priest (*Leutpriester*) in Zurich.[25] The book ends with Zurich's defeat in the Second Kappel War, the negotiations over the possibilities and limits of evangelical preaching,[26] the confusion over the Zurich mass mandate of 29 May 1532,[27] and the May synod of 1533.[28]

The heart of Bullinger's account lay in the development, implementation, and consolidation of the Reformation in Zurich and the subsequent discussions, confrontations, and revolutionary changes in the ecclesiastical and political spheres. Bullinger gives the two Kappel Wars a great deal of coverage and the period from 1529 to 1531 comprises more than half the work. The focus of Bullinger's interest was the events in Zurich, although his extensive contacts throughout the Confederation enabled him to draw on information about the course of events in other areas. Bullinger's attention to the reformations in Basle, Berne, Graubünden, and Solothurn, however, was not sufficient to make his work a history of the Swiss Reformation, but he did succeed in providing a broader Swiss context for the de-

---

21. The manuscript of the *Eidgenössische Chronik* is in ZB, Ms. A 14 & 15.

22. The work is divided up as follows: The *Tigurinerchronik* in ZB, Ms. Car C 43 & 44 is in Bullinger's hand, while the *History of the Grossmünster Chapter* (also in his hand) in ZB, Ms. Car C 44, 787-941 and the copy of the *Reformation History* in the hand of Israël Stäheli is found in ZB, Ms. Car C 45 & 46. On this copy and its author, see Hans Ulrich Bächtold, "'Ein fine hand zü schriben.' Glanz und Elend im Leben des Schönschreibers Israël Stäheli, †1596" in Hans Ulrich Bächtold ed., *Von Cyprian zur Walzenprägung: Streiflichter auf Zürcher Geist und Kultur der Bullingerzeit* (Studien und Texte zur Bullingerzeit 2; Zug: Achius, 2001), 115-43, esp. 134-7.

23. "Den 28. Septembris endet ich die 6 bücher von den Tigurineren und der statt Zürich sachen. Darzu tat ich ouch historien der reformation des stifts zum Großen münster, ouch 2 partes oder teil von dem Cappeler krieg und reformation; warend 4 bücher. Die übergab und schankt ich den herren pflägeren, dem verwalter und ganzem capitel zum Großen münster den 14. Decembris, die es mit großem dank annamend. Dise 4 bücher hab ich unglöuptlich bald, fast in 2 oder 2½ jaren, näbend minen predigen und vilfalten geschäften, durch Gottes gnad vollendet." *HBD*, 118 (entry for the year 1574).

24. *HBRG* I:3-6.

25. Ibid., 6-13.

26. Ibid., III:322-9.

27. Ibid., III:329-43.

28. Ibid., III:343-8.

tailed account of events in Zurich.[29] The opposition to the Reformation in the Inner Catholic states as well as the various military campaigns and battles in which the Swiss took part were of particular interest to Bullinger. On the European stage, the struggle in Italy between Charles V, the papacy, and Francis I, is given a prominent place, though these events are viewed through the lens of Swiss participation in the military campaigns. As to the Empire, his interest is almost entirely limited to the development of the Reformation.

The result is a remarkably broad documentary history of the Zurich Reformation which makes use of a wide range of sources. It was the Swiss equivalent to the *Commentary on the state of religion and of the states under Emperor Charles V* by the Strasbourg diplomat and historian Johannes Sleidanus.[30] The political and confessional tensions of the second half of the sixteenth century made it impossible for Bullinger to publish his history, although it seems that he might never have intended for it to be printed. Nevertheless, in spite of its length the work was frequently copied by hand till the nineteenth century and influenced subsequent historical writing on the Zurich Reformation. In the Reformed tradition Bullinger's *History of the Reformation* was a fundamental resource for historical knowledge of the period and soon established itself as the canonical narrative of the Zurich Reformation.

Stages of Development

To understand the provenance of his *History of the Reformation*, we have to look back far beyond the 1560s, when Bullinger wrote the text, to the time of his succession to the position of preacher in the Grossmünster following Zwingli's death and Zurich's defeat in the Second Kappel War. It is characteristic of Bullinger's engagement with history that he spent his life, particularly after becoming head of the Zurich church, gathering different types of material that documented past and contemporary events. In the dedication of his *Tigurinerchronik* to the Grossmünster chapter, he describes the early stages of gathering the material which formed the crucial beginning point of his historical work and his own formation as a historian:

> Beginning forty years ago, and ever since then, I have laboured as much as I have been able to study the events and history of our fatherland, and in particular the history of the city of Zurich. To this end I have made an effort to get different printed works and manuscripts and to study them. I have also consulted old men, by whom I have sought to inform myself. All this information I have written down on pieces of paper in order to list them in the correct order as soon as I was able and had the time.[31]

---

29. On Basle *HBRG* I:35f., 152; II:6f., 35-43, 81-113; on Berne *HBRG* I:110-2, 360f., 390-9, 440-6; II:1f., 13, 21-25; on Graubünden *HBRG* I:314-23; II:34f.; on Solothurn *HBRG* II:294-321.

30. *De statu religionis et rei publicae Carolo Quinto Caesare commentariorum libri XXV* (Strasbourg: 1555). On Bullinger's relationship to Sleidanus's work on the history of the Reformation, see Moser, *Studien zu Heinrich Bullingers Reformationsgeschichte*, 175-82.

31. ZB, Ms. Car C 43, 1.

This quotation makes clear that Bullinger searched systematically for his material and that from an early point his intention was to synthesise his assembled material. His position as head of the Zurich church gave him privileged access to the Zurich archives and to official documents as well as providing him with useful contacts that he exploited in gathering information. Bullinger was able to draw on his friends and acquaintances in order to obtain eyewitness accounts of events of the Reformation. His impressive circle of correspondents augmented this source base. All the while he never limited himself to documents pertaining only to the history of the Reformation; he was an avid collector of records relevant to contemporary events, older Swiss, Zurich, and church history.

Traces of Bullinger's work in collecting historical documents are evident in his extensive correspondence. For example, the Bernese reformer Berchtold Haller, who was in close contact with Bullinger, was given the task of sending to Zurich documents relating to Berne's military history in the 1520s.[32] In a letter of 29 September 1534, Haller responded rather sceptically to one of Bullinger's requests (which has not survived). According to Haller, the documents concerning Berne's conflict with Unterwalden following the unrest in the Bernese Oberland after 1528, as well as those relating to the economic blockade of the Catholic States after the First Kappel War, were possibly no longer available in Berne:

> I will attempt to obtain the documents, among which are the copies which you have requested, if they are available and if the Stadtschreiber will give them to me. They are not with Valerius [Anselm], who is writing about those things which took place in 1519. The documents relating to the Unterwalden matter, as well as those from the blockade, were available, but they were handed over to the Five States at Bremgarten under the peace treaty. I am doubtful that there are any copies here. The other documents will be sent to you as long as they are still extant and will be entrusted to me.[33]

On 16 November Haller returned to the subject of how difficult it was to provide Bullinger with the documents he wanted. He warned Bullinger that he would not only have to put up with the lacunae in the documents in the Bernese achive but also with the unwillingess of the Bernese council to grant access to sensitive material. Haller said that his hands were tied; he could only send material to Bullinger with the approval of the Bernese magistrates.[34]

---

32. On the correspondence between Bullinger and Berchtold Haller (1492-1536), see *HBBW* I:205, note 1.

33. *HBBW* IV, no. 446, 331. On the identification of those documents which Bullinger sought, see ibid., notes 6 and 8.

34. "Quod vero ad literas tuas priores attinet, quibus multa excribenda de transactis bellis petebas, nihil horum a secretario impetrare possum nisi totius senatus consensu, qui non facile patietur hec transcribi. Est item sub iuramento secretario iniunctum, ne quippiam, quod ad senatus negocia pertinuerit, cuipiam communicet. Primam reformationem impressit apud vos Froschoverus. Dess Grinderwalder kriegs handlung ist alle in dem lettsten unfriden Silvanis überantwurtet. Copy dess brieffs, so gen Capellen gschriben, ist nitt meer vorhanden; dann inn ein sunderer schriber gschriben, der sy jetz nitt wort wil han. Der Genfer und Müsser zug lit als in missifen noch hinder minen herren, ouch was imm lettsten krieg sich zütragen. Wenn es aber der

A particularly close working relationship existed between Bullinger and Johannes Stumpf, who was dean of the chapter of Wetzikon and minister in Stammheim from 1543.[35] The partnership between these two friends was extremely fruitful for both their historical endeavours.[36] This included Stumpf's major work, the historical-topographical *Gemeiner loblicher Eydgnoschafft stetten, landen und völckeren chronick wirdiger thaaten beschreybung [...]*,[37] as well as various other works on Swiss history, including the continuation of the *Swiss Chronicle* of his father-in-law, Heinrich Brennwald.[38] In the writing of this chronicle, which in many respects anticipated Bullinger's *Reformation History*, Stumpf and Bullinger worked together closely. Bullinger made useful contacts for Stumpf and organised material. An example of their partnership can be seen in an letter from 9 June 1535, when Stumpf approached Bullinger with a request that he obtain from the Wachtmeister (the official responsible for weapons in the city) Georg Ottli an account of the Zurich defeat at the battle of Gubel, which he had witnessed.[39] Two days later Bullinger was already able to report that he had received Ottli's account, adding that should he (Bullinger) not have sufficient time to write a full report of what he had heard that he would ensure that at least the raw material was sent to Stumpf:

> Georg Ottli provided me almost a month ago with a written account. I have also read several accounts from the enemy's perspective. I will attempt myself to outline for you what happened at this battle. To date I have not yet had the time.

Valerio in d'hand wurde, als es werden müß, sol er acht die cronik usschriben, da möcht es mir wol werden." *HBBW* IV, no. 475, 403f.

35. A brief biography of Stumpf and further references to literature are found in *HBBW* IV: 76, note 1.

36. On Stumpf's historical writing, see Richard Feller/Edgar Bonjour, *Geschichtsschreibung der Schweiz: Vom Spätmittelalter zur Neuzeit* vol. 1 (Basle/Stuttgart: Schwabe, 1962), 180-7; Hans Müller, *Der Geschichtschreiber Johann Stumpf: Eine Untersuchung über sein Weltbild* (Schweizer Studien zur Geschichtswissenschaft, new series 8; Zurich: Leemann, 1945) and Gustav Müller, *Die Quellen zur Beschreibung des Zürich- und Aargaus in Johannes Stumpfs Schweizerchronik* (Schriftenreihe der Stiftung von Schnyder von Wartensee 19; Zurich: Beer, 1916).

37. Manfred Vischer, *Bibliographie der Zürcher Druckschriften des 15. und 16. Jahrhunderts* (Bibliotheca bibliographica Aureliana 124; Baden-Baden: Koerner, 1990), no. C 376 and C 396.

38. The whole work is found in the volumes ZB, Ms. A 1 und A 2 divided into nine books. Ms. A 1 contains the first six books to the end of the Swabian War (essentially the Brennwald copy); Ms. A 2 is Stumpf's continuation of the history from 1499-1534. The account of the Reformation is found in books eight and nine. The volume Ms. A 2 containing the chronicle of the Reformation is edited in Ernst Gagliardi, Hans Müller and Fritz Büsser eds, *Johannes Stumpfs Schweizer- und Refomationschronik*, 2 vols (Quellen zur Schweizer Geschichte: Chroniken V und VI; Basle: Birkhäuser, 1953 and 1955). The work will be cited as Stumpf, *Reformationschronik*. Brennwald's chronicle is edited in Rudolf Luginbühl ed., *Heinrich Brennwalds Schweizerchronik*, 2 vols (Quellen zur Schweizer Geschichte: Chroniken I und II; Basle: Verlag der Basler Buch- und Antiquariatshandlung, 1908-1910). On Brennwald see *HBBW* III:26, note 1.

39. "Ich hab Görg Ottlin nechstmals im abscheidt bevolhen, mir ettliche stück des bergzügs in schrifft züverfassen, das er mir zügesagt. Were myn gar früntlich bitt, wo ir (unmüß halb) solche schrifft von im erfordren und mir züschicken köndten, wolte ich umb uch allzit früntlich verdienen." *HBBW* V, no. 590, 229. On Ottli, see ibid., note 10.

If I am not able to do this in the next while, I shall send you the documents which will help you to fill in the rest.[40]

Bullinger's heavy commitments, however, required him to answer a further, rather impatient, request from Stumpf on 19 June[41] negatively.[42] We know nothing more of Georg Ottli's account of the battle, except that on 3 January 1536 Stumpf sent to Bullinger the ninth book of his chronicle,[43] which included the account of the battle of Gubel.[44] The battle of Gubel was just one of many holes in Stumpf's *Reformation Chronicle* which Bullinger was asked to assist in filling. Bullinger, however, was not always able to help. In sending his account on 3 January 1536 Stumpf included, along with the battle of Gubel, a whole catalogue of desiderata.

Dear Lord and brother, you have requested that I send you the last three books of the chronicle. I am sending you only the last book, because the other two, namely the seventh and eigth books, are not yet finished because I lack some material for the following events: in the seventh book on the battle of Marignano [1515], the summoning of the Zurich rural communities and the military campaign of the emperor to Milan [1516]. In addition I am lacking material on the papal procession [1521], the battle of Bicocca [1522], the Ittingen affair [1524], and the alliances between the cities. Now, when you have time and it is possible for you, could you ask the Stadtschreiber whether it might be possible to get copies of the contracts between the cities and the documents relating to the Ittinger affair. At your request I will come to Zurich and copy the documents.[45]

We know nothing more about the exchange of information between Bullinger and Stumpf in this case, but what we do know is that when he completed his chronicle a little later Stumpf was able to provide full accounts of the Battle of Marignano in 1515, the summoning of the Zurich rural communities, and the Ittingen

40. "Georgeius Ottelius scriptam historiam mihi ante mensem propemodum tradidit. Perscrutatus sum etiam ipse quaedam a parte adversa. Conor ipse tibi faciem eius pugnae delineare. Negotia hactenus prohibuere. Ubi non potero brevi absolvere, fragmenta mittam, ex quibus tu sarcias omnia." *HBBW* V, no. 591, 230.

41. "Ceterum ut bellum montanum a te conscriptum transmitteres, res grata esset. Magno enim illius desiderio teneor; nam hoc perfecto mox et opus nostrum perfectum videres." *HBBW* V, no. 619, 285.

42. "Pugnam montensem nondum descripsi negotiis praepeditus." *HBBW* V, no. 620, 287.

43. *HBBW* VI, no. 710, 35. Stumpf had already on 2 December of the previous year announced that he had sent the chronicle (*HBBW* V, no. 694, 455).

44. Stumpf, *Reformationschronik*, II:220-31.

45. "Lieber herr und brüder, wie ir vergangner zyt begert habend, uch die letsten dry bücher der chronicken zuüberschicken, also schick ich uch allein das aller letst, uß der ursach, die andern zwey, namlich das 7. und 8., sind noch nit gar volkommen, sonder manglet mir noch ettwas: Im 7. an Meylander schlacht, item der ufflouf der gmeinden Zurich, item des keysers zug in Meyland. Demnach manglet mir noch des bapsts zug, item Bygogger schlacht, item Ytinger rechthandel und demnach alle foedera christianae civitatis etc. Nun wolt ich gern, das ir, sovil uch jenen müglich, ouch ettwo, so ir am müesßigsten werind, by dem stattschryber wurbind umb die copyen der burgerbriefen und umm Yttinger handel (ob es echt zethun were), so wolt ich dan hinin kommen uff uwer embieten oder schryben und die ding abschryben." *HBBW* VI, no. 710, 35f.

affair.[46] Stumpf left space in his chronicle for the information on the civic alliances that he awaited from Bullinger.[47] The correspondence between the two men, in any case, clearly reveals Bullinger's access to official documents such as acts of the council, decisions of the diets, civic agreements, and other such material. Further evidence is provided by Bullinger's reference to "the elders"[48], by which he meant those who had been eyewitnesses and had been directly involved in the events. From these people he sought to corroborate his material. In his preface to the *Eidgenössische Chronik* Bullinger spoke of this crucial source of information:

> If I heard of older, honourable, and trustworthy people, who were still alive and had been in the wars and who were informed of the past events, then I went directly to them and asked them what happened. And when I learned of other reliable accounts from the older, honourable people I wrote them down.[49]

Such eyewitness accounts are also to be found in the *Reformation History,* mostly in connection with the Kappel Wars. These parts of the history were the most dramatic and controversial. They had been constructed from a rich base of sources, and Bullinger reliably indicates in his *Reformation History* the identities of his informants. Thus the actors in the dramatic rescue of the Zurich banner at the battle of Kappel were able, for example, to provide Bullinger with an oral account of the event.[50] Other information which he was able to gain included matters such as the cost of burying the dead on the battlefield, the details of which were provided by the Seckelmeister Hans Edlibach,[51] and the material losses suffered by the city, which the Zeugmeister Hans Ulrich Stampfer gave him.[52] Hans Ulrich Stampfer held office from 1526 to 1540 and had died in 1544,[53] indicating that Bullinger had been busy collecting oral histories long before he began writing the *Reformation History.* More evidence that Bullinger had carried out specific research intended for his history comes from 1563-64, when he undertook a survey in the Thurgau in order to determine accurately the precise number of dead in the Second Kappel War.[54]

46. Stumpf, *Reformationschronik,* I:134-45 and 203-31; *HBBW* VI:35f., notes 3 and 5.
47. Stumpf, *Reformationschronik,* II:1f., 7, 15, 26, 82, 85f.; *HBBW* VI: 36, note 6.
48. See note 31.
49. "Wo ich dann von allten eeren warhafften lüthen gehört und gewüst, die noch gelápt, in den kriegen selbs gewesen, ouch aller dingen bericht warend, hab ich die selben angeströngt und gefraget, wie die sachen ergangen und wo ich sunst gloubwirdige erzellungen der allten eeren lüthen gehört, hab ichs verzeichnet." ZB, Ms. A 14, f. 27[r].
50. "Und was hie von der paner geschriben ist, hab ich verzeychnet und geschriben uß dem mund und angeben der vorgemellten eeren mannen Kleinhansen Kammlis, Hansen Hübers, Adam Näfens, und Uly Däntzlers." *HBRG* III:133.
51. "Das hab ich uß herren Seckelmeisters Edlibachs mund." *HBRG* III:142.
52. "alls mir der zůgmeister m. Hans Ulrich Stamppff selbs gesagt hat" *HBRG* III:159.
53. cf. *HBBW* VI:412, note 6.
54. "Uß den gerichten yttingen sind vil ummkummen deren namen ich nitt hab mögen erfaren. Dann imm 1563 und 1564 iar hab ich lassen in dem Turgöw flissige nachfrag hallten. Doch nitt me, dann hievor anzogen gruntlich und warlich erfaren mögen." *HBRG* III:207.

Thus long before he began writing Bullinger had assembled an extensive collection of original documents, copies, complete texts, and selected passages, some unaltered and other covered in notes, marginalia, and emendations. Much of this material has come down to us in a partially systematic order, while the rest remains fragmentary and randomly bound together. It was to this enormous collection of material that Bullinger could turn in the 1560s when he came to write his *Reformation History*. Some of the document collections concerning the Zurich Reformation are worthy of particular attention not only because they were the basis for individual pieces of information but because these collections of documents, with their notes, excerpts and references, formed a framework for the chronology. There are three important sources. The first is found in the volume Ms. F. 178 of the Zurich Zentralbibliothek, entitled *Consignatio temporum,* with notes that are dated and chronologically arranged.[55] Most of them are found again, in an expanded form, in the *Reformation History*. The *Consignatio* is flanked by longer preparatory works on the Second Kappel War, the notes for the battle of Kappel and in particular for the exchange of correspondence between the field commanders and the Zurich council. This collection proved invaluable to Bullinger's later painstaking reconstruction of the turbulent events of the war.[56] Thirdly, a further collection of documents is found in the same volume; this is the material for the period shortly after the Second Kappel War.[57] From the late 1550s there is another important collection of documents (ZB Ms. K 4) relating to the reformation in Zurich and the Swiss Confederation during the years 1522-29. In this collection Bullinger wrote down in particular his material on Zwingli's literary activity, the Baden and Berne Disputations, and the *Prophezei*.[58] Finally, there is a well-organised collection in the Zurich Zentralbibliothek (Ms. A 127) that contains material for the years 1525-28.[59] These notes were clearly the preparatory material for the later work; it was Bullinger's intention to link together these notes with quotations from the official documents. In the collection ZB Ms. A 127 Bullinger did not leave place for official documents, rather he chose simply to refer to them with a wavy line (∼∼).[60]

---

55. ZB, Ms. F 178, f. 79^r-84^r.
56. Ibid., f. 54^t-78^v.
57. Ibid., f. 85^r-88^v.
58. ZB, Ms. K 4, f. 1^v-34^v; 36^v-65^r.
59. ZB, Ms. A 127, 105-136.
60. Compare Bullinger's account of the tithe controversy in Zurich in 1525 in ZB, Ms. A 127, 109:

> Hieruff, wie man gemerckt, das der gemein mann gern were aller bschwerden ledig sin und niemands nut gåben, ließ man Zurych das mandat von zåhenden uußgon etc.: ∼∼
> Des warend ettliche oder meerteyls übel zů friden. Und ward aber gmeindet zů Gossow und Clota. Und botten geordnet von allen gmeinden gen Zürych zů keeren und ir anligen anzůzeigen. Das beschach. Und ward Zürych ein gspråch von den gleerten uff dem radthuß von zåhenden gehallten. Daruff der radt volgende erlüterung uff das land schickt: ∼∼
> Hieruff ordnet man von yeder zunfft ein man, die sóltend die puren artickel erduren und radtschlagen, was man mitt Gott und eer thůn möchte. Das beschach. Und gieng diß erckantnus uuß: ∼∼
> Diser erckantnus warend vil übel zů friden.

These collections indicate the intensive use that Bullinger made of other chronicles of the Zurich Reformation. Alongside official documents and eyewitness accounts, Bullinger was able to use a range of other, smaller, chronicle sources from the 1520s and 1530s. So we find in his notes excerpts from histories of the Reformation written by Bernhard Wyss,[61] Johannes Stumpf,[62] the Zurich councillor Fridli Bluntschli[63] and the *Historical Relation*, an account of the Second Kappel War written by Hans Edlibach.[64]

The *Reformation History* as Testament and Legacy

Bullinger's lifelong interest in the relationship between the past and present and his tireless engagement with the documents were essential characteristic of his life and his tenure as head of the Zurich church. This activity acquired an especial importance in the last decade of his life; in considering Bullinger's engagement with history we must remember that he did not begin to write his major historical works until the 1560s. These works were not only historical accounts, however, for they formed a major part of his will and testament. They were self-consciously crafted as his legacy to the Zurich and Reformed churches.

Bullinger was keenly aware of the generational change within his close circle of fellow reformers during the 1560s, and it was with a certain world-weariness that he recorded in his *Diary* the deaths of his colleagues and friends.[65] This was

These notes were used again in the *Reformation History* (*HBRG* I:280-6), complemented by the text of the mandates, see Emil Egli ed., *Actensammlung zur Geschichte der Zürcher Reformation in den Jahren 1519-1533* (Zurich: Schabelitz, 1879; reprinted Aalen: Scientia-Verlag, 1973), no. 737, 763 and 799.

61. The account is edited in Georg Finsler ed., *Die Chronik des Bernhard Wyss 1519-1530* (Quellen zur schweizerischen Reformationsgeschichte I; Basle: Verlag der Basler Buch- und Antiquariatshandlung, 1901). On the author, see XV-XIX. Excerpts from Wyss are found in the *Consignatio temporum* in ZB, Ms. F 178 and in ZB, Ms. K 4. Compare the extract in ZB, Ms. F 178, f. 80ʳ from Wyss (Finsler, *Chronik*, 15-17) on Zwingli's disputation with Franz Lambert from Avignon.

62. On Stumpf's *Reformationschronik* see above note 38. Compare Bullinger's extract from Stumpf, *Reformationschronik*, I: 292 to a report of an official appointed after the Peasants' War to investigate the conditions. The extract is found in ZB, Ms. A 127, 110. A whole chapter is dedicated to the episode in Bullinger's *Reformation History*: "Von dem proffosen Aychili" (*HBRG* I:252).

63. Bluntschli's account is found in ZB, Ms. A 70, 191-279. On the author and his report see Moser, *Studien zu Heinrich Bullingers Reformationsgeschichte*, 45-51. Excerpts from Bluntschli's notes are found in ZB, Ms. A 127, 112.

64. The *Historical Relation* is printed in Leo Weisz, "Die Geschichte der Kappelerkriege nach Hans Edlibach," *Zeitschrift für schweizerische Kirchengeschichte* 26 (1932): 81-108 and 270-87. On the work and its author, see Ernst Gagliardi, "Mitteilungen über eine neu gefundene Quelle zur zürcherschen Reformationsgeschichte (Hans Edlibach)," *Zwingliana* 2 (1905-12): 407-14 and Feller/Bonjour, *Geschichtsschreibung*, 172f. Extracts from Hans Edlibach's account are found in ZB, Ms. F 178, f. 86ʳ-88ʳ.

65. Compare his notes concerning the deaths of the following friends, acquaintances, and correspondents: Johannes a Lasco and Philipp Melanchthon 1560 (*HBD*, 64); Peter Martyr Vermigli 1562 (*HBD*, 68); Theodor Bibliander, Andreas Hyperius, Ambrosius Blarer, Christoph Froschauer the Elder and John Calvin 1564 (*HBD*, 76); Johannes Fries, Sebastian Guldibeck and Konrad Gessner 1565 (*HBD*, 80); Johannes Fabricius 1566 (*HBD*, 85); Thomas Blarer and Philip of Hesse 1567 (*HBD*, 89).

also a major theme in his letters, wherein he lamented the loss of so many reformers who had been close to him. In December 1564, on the occasion of the death of Ambrosius Blarer, he confided to his good friend Johannes Fabricius in Chur that he too expected soon to "tie up his bundle":

> Our brother Ambrosius Blarer left us on the sixth of this month in Winterthur. Now among my colleagues only Farel is still alive who has been longer than me in the service of the church. What is left for me other than that I too must soon tie up my bundle?[66]

It was not only the deaths of the reformers of the first and second generations that Bullinger had to observe helplessly, but the plagues of the 1560s took many of his own family,[67] and he himself only narrowly escaped.[68] While Bullinger was gravely ill with the plague he lost his wife Anna, and only a few weeks later his daughter Margaretha and her newborn child.[69] In a letter to Ambrosius Blarer of 10 November 1564 Bullinger gave voice to the tremendous suffering of the time and to the continuing threat of illness:

> You know that the Lord has in my old age (I am in my 61st year) taken away the staff of my age–my dearest, my chosen one, my devoted wife. The Lord is righteous and his judgement is righteous. In the last few days he has also taken my beloved daughter, [Ludwig] Lavater's wife, in whom I had great hopes. She has left behind seven children. However, the Lord is good and his will is good, without which none of this would have happened. He may also do more which is good in his eyes, if only he does not take away his mercy from me and mine. The plague continues to take many away.[70]

---

66. "D. Ambrosius Blaurerus noster 6. huius mensis Vituduri migravit ad Dominum. Iam ergo nullus superest, quem norim, nisi unus Farellus, qui me praecesserit in ministerio sacro. Quid ergo restat, nisi ut ego iam nunc maxime sarcinas colligam?" Traugott Schiess ed., *Bullingers Korrespondenz mit den Graubündnern* vol. 2 (Quellen zur Schweizer Geschichte XXIV; Basle: Verlag der Basler Buch- und Antiquariatshandlung, 1905), no. 649, 548.

67. See the death announcements in *HBD*, 76-78; 82f., among them the note for the year 1565 (*HBD*, 83): "Dises jars was ein sterbent zu Zürich, Bern, Luzern, Uri, Schwiz, Underwalden, Zug und Glarus, ouch Fryburg, und sturb vil volks."

68. See Bullinger's account in his *Diary* (*HBD*, 76-78). Bullinger's condition was so serious that he reckoned with an imminent death and had already bade farewell to his fellow ministers, see *HBD*, 77: "Am 17. tag beruft ich alle diener der kilchen, gnadet inen, vermanet si zur beständigkeit, trüw und einigkeit, und befalch inen die kilchen."

69. Bullinger's wife Anna died on 25 September and his daughter Margaretha on 30 October, *HBD*, 77.

70. "Scis dominum in hoc meo senio (ago enim nunc 61. annum) mihi surripuisse baculum senectutis meae, uxorem charissimam, foeminam lectissimam et piissimam etc. Sed iustus est dominus et iusta eius iudicia. Superioribus diebus sustulit et filiam dilectam, D. Lavateri uxorem, ex qua multum commodi speraveram; reliquit illa pupillos 7. Sed bonus est dominus et bona eius voluntas, sine qua haec facta non sunt; faciat hic porro, quod bonum est in oculis suis, modo misericordiam suam a me meisque non auferat! Pergit alioqui pestis multos abripere." *Briefwechsel der Brüder Ambrosius und Thomas Blaurer 1509-1567*, Badische Historische Kommission ed., Traugott Schiess prep, vol. 3 (Freiburg/Br.: Fehsenfeld, 1912), no. 2637, 834. On this period of Bullinger's life see Carl Pestalozzi, *Heinrich Bullinger: Leben und ausgewählte Schriften. Nach handschriftlichen und gleichzeitigen Quellen* (Leben und ausgewählte Schriften der Väter und Begründer der reformirten Kirche V; Elberfeld: Friderichs, 1858), 485-90.

It was in these perilous times and with an increasing certainty of the finiteness of human life that Bullinger, conscious that he was one of the last witnesses to the remarkable events of the Reformation, began with renewed vigour to collate the material which he had gathered over the decades and to chronicle histories of the Reformation and of the older Zurich and Swiss past. A sense of his own impending death drove him forward in his mission to record and preserve each event of the past epoch. Despite debilitating illness and the huge pressure of work he devoted the last years of his life to the writing of history.[71] The preface to the *Reformation History* brings out clearly his overriding goal: to make available what he regarded as the wondrous events of the Reformation, to keep for future generations the origins of his church alive, and to prevent their memory from vanishing in the struggles of the second half of the sixteenth century. To achieve this it was his concern to establish the chronology and details of the 1520s and early 1530s as accurately as possible in order that posterity be left with an true account of what happened:

> For the events and deeds of these years are both wonderfully cheerful and sad, but also a pleasure to read and useful, even necessary, to know. Therein are preserved the great works of God as well as good learning and the fine examples of men which otherwise would fade because of men's activity that does not allow them to think on a long-term basis and leads them to forget even excellent things. Through rigorous notetaking these events have been recorded and most usefully and in a praiseworthy manner brought to men's memory and restored to human knowledge.[72]

It is fully justified to see Bullinger's historical endeavours in the last years of his life as part of what Pamela Biel has called his "well-planned departure".[73] The *Reformation History*, as the result of his efforts at the end of his life to record a comprehensive, accurate and truthful account of the events in Zurich, must in its specific form be understood as part of Bullinger's legacy to posterity after his death in 1575. It was, he believed, the recorded truth that would engender in men and women a sense of gratitude and encourage them to preserve the essential achievements of the Reformation.

---

71. Compare Bullinger's surprise that despite numerous other tasks he was able to complete the *Tigurinerchronik*: "Und nimpt mich zwaren selbs wunder, wie ich nåben vilen andern minen predigen schryben und geschåfften, sômlich min fûrgenommen werck habe môgen, so bald (ettwas me wenig dann in einem jar) und glücklich, vollenden. Gib sômlichs alles gentzlich der gûte und hilff Gottes zû." ZB, Ms. Car C 43, 2.

72. "Dann diser iar hândel und lôûff, sind nitt nu wunderbar fast frôlich und ouch trâffenlich trurig, sunder zû låsen lustig und zû wüssen nitt wenig nutzlich, darzû ouch nodtwendig. Diewyl sunst durch arbeitselikeit der menschen, die nitt wyt dånckt, sunder ouch fürtråffenlicher sachen bald vergåssen hat, herrliche werck Gottes, gûte leeren und fürtråffenliche exempel, gar verblichend, welche aber durch flyssige verzeichnusse in geschrifft verfasset, widerumm zû gedåchtnus gebracht und dem wûssen der menschen loblich und nutzlich yngebildet werdent." ZB, Ms. A 16, 1; *HBRG* I:1.

73. Pamela Biel, "Heinrich Bullinger's Death and Testament: A Well-planned Departure," *Sixteenth Century Journal* 22 (1991): 3-14.

9

Bullinger and the Schools

Kurt Jakob Rüetschi

The subject of Bullinger's education and teaching and his influence on the schools in Zurich may seem at first glance to have little bearing on his considerable impact upon Reformed Protestantism world-wide, but it offers us an insight into his own development and into a distinctive part of his theological, political and practical work as *Antistes* (chief minister) in Zurich.[1] Bullinger regarded his own education and teaching experience as being of the utmost importance both personally and for his later work in the church. Indeed it is from Bullinger's own writings that we gain the most significant sources and information concerning: (1) his own schooling and personal studies, (2) his teaching at the school of the monastery at Kappel am Albis; and (3) his endeavours on behalf of the schools during the time when he was first preacher at Zurich. These periods differ in character and duration; each of them is well researched, but there is no synopsis. In attempting my survey, I have drawn upon Bullinger own writings and the work of modern scholars.[2]

1. Bullinger's School and Student Years (1509-22)

Bullinger was one of the sons of the priest at Bremgarten on the river Reuss in the Aargau. He was born on 18 June 1504 and seems to have been a very bright child, an early developer, especially gifted in languages. According to his own testimony, he was able, at the age of three, to speak clearly and perfectly (*clare et plene*) in German–Swiss German of course.[3] Knowing this, we can un-

---

1. I am indebted to my sister and her husband, Hildegard and Ernest Fox-Rüetschi, Seaton (Devon) for numerous linguist improvements.

2. The sources provided by Bullinger are not all primary ones. For the early years we can rely only upon two retrospectives of his life (see note 3); for later years drafts of lectures, documents given to the council, letters, books and his histories of some schools form a broader basis. Where possible, I mention the editions of sources, and when not I list the manuscripts. For sections 1-2 of my essay I can rely directly on scholarship concerning Bullinger's schooling, studies and teaching. Good research on the schools of Zurich in his time exists, but apart from essays on details and one short survey (Bächtold, see note 36) no literature has concentrated on his connections to the schools.

3. *HBD*, 2: 11-14. Around 1541 (cf. Egli's introduction to *HBD*, VIII) Bullinger began a yearly account of important matters, eg. the completion of works, the beginnings of a series of sermons (*lectio continua*), births and death within his family, the climate, the harvest's yield, and

derstand why he was able, at barely five years, on 12 March 1509, to start at the Latin school of his native town. He learnt to read, write, to do some mathematical calculations, to tackle grammar, mainly Latin, and also to sing, as the pupils helped during divine services as singers and altar boys.[4] At the age of twelve, between 11 June and 4 July 1516, he travelled *literarum discendarum gratia* on foot and by ship to Emmerich on the lower Rhine near the Dutch frontier. There he met up with his brother Johannes, who was eight years older and whom he esteemed as one of his teachers.[5]

The St. Martin's chapter at Emmerich was famous for its humanist, reformed and nevertheless very ecclesiastical Latin school. The teachers there used not only the old grammar of Donatus, but also the modern one by Aldus Manutius. They introduced basic Greek and "dialectic" (logic) and they read many texts, which was then exceptional and a key factor in the humanist school reform. There were letters by Pliny and Cicero, poems by Virgil and Horace and, as a Christian counterweight, letters of Jerome and poems by Baptista Mantuanus, a Carthusian monk. In his retrospective Bullinger emphasised that the pupils were forced to speak Latin, that they had to compose letters, that the discipline was severe, and finally that, following his father's command, he had to beg for his upkeep, so that he might experience the misfortune of beggars and would subsequently become more merciful to them.[6] For reasons of economy he lived with an honourable citizen and not in a college. In three years he received only 33 florins and two sets of clothes from his father.[7] His rector and his teachers, all laymen, took great care, along with the priests of St. Martin's church, to provide an intensive religious education, and Bullinger intended to become a Carthusian monk.[8] Later, he judged this intention to have been blinded by superstition.[9]

---

political events. At the same time he wrote about his own life up to this time; in this retrospective (*HBD*, 1:1-28, 30; esp. 2, 11-17, 26) he gave a full account of school times and his personal studies. The short sketch of another *Vita* (of 1560) added a few more details (*HBD*, 125, 1-128, 25).

4. *HBD*, 2: 15-17. Fritz Blanke, *Der junge Bullinger* (Zwingli-Bücherei 22; Zurich: Zwingli Verlag, 1942). Reprint in: Fritz Blanke/Immanuel Leuschner, *Heinrich Bullinger. Vater der reformierten Kirche* (Zurich: TVZ, 1990), 15-17; Eugen Bürgisser, *Geschichte der Stadt Bremgarten im Mittelalter* (Phil. Diss., Zurich: 1937), 174-82.

5. *HBD*, 2: 18-23; 3,23; (Blanke, *Der junge Bullinger*, 23 says 11 November instead of 11 June).

6. We know about this practice from Luther and other students of the time (see eg. Blanke, *Der junge Bullinger*, 26-27).

7. *HBD*, 2: 24-3,8; 3,12-15 and 20-21; 4,5-6. Blanke, *Der junge Bullinger*, 23-29, 32. Some of these brief school-writings survive, see Joachim Staedtke, *Die Theologie des jungen Bullinger* (Studien zur Dogmengeschichte und systematischen Theologie 16; Zurich: Zwingli Verlag, 1962), 263-5.

8. Bullinger mentions Johannes Aelius, Petrus Homphäus and Kaspar von Glogau (*HBD*, 3,23-25; 125,15-17). It is a matter of debate which of them was rector, see Hans Georg vom Berg, "Die "Brüder vom gemeinsamen Leben" und die Stiftsschule von St. Martin zu Emmerich. Zur Frage des Einflusses der Devotio Moderna auf den jungen Bullinger" in Ulrich Gäbler/Erland Herkenrath eds., *Heinrich Bullinger 1504-1575. Gesammelte Aufsätze zum 400. Todestag* vol. 1: *Leben und Werk* (ZBRG 7; Zurich: TVZ, 1975), 1-12, esp. 5-6.

9. *HBD*, 3, 8-11: "Religionis quoque, qualis tunc esse poterat, magna habetur cura. Et superstitio ita mihi praestrinxerat oculos, ut privatim apud me meditarer, post aliquot annos Carthusianorum institutum recipere."

Nowhere does he mention the "Brethren of the Common life" (*fratres communis vitae*). The St. Martin's school and he himself were not subordinated to the *fratres* because he did not reside in one of the boarding seminaries. Blanke, in his wonderfully researched booklet on the young Bullinger, refuses to acknowledge any influence from the Brethren. Staedtke, in the "theology of the young Bullinger," and especially vom Berg, in a helpful paper on the influence of the *Devotio moderna*, have shown that all the teachers then at Emmerich were as close to humanism as they were to the "Brethren"; moreover they have also stressed the strong discipline and the exercises in piety typical of the *Devotio*, which we also find in parts of Bullinger's later theology (for example, the emphasis on ethics and his way of constructing an evangelical interpretation of the Lord's Supper). Susi Hausammann, in her study of Bullinger's early lecture on Romans, may have found the solution to this debate by demonstrating both the similarities as well as the fundamental differences between the *Devotio* and the future reformer.[10] But Bullinger, while in Emmerich, remained a loyal son of the Roman Catholic Church.

After a short visit home to Bremgarten and a further three months at Emmerich, Bullinger, aged fifteen, went to Cologne in July 1519. This decision might have been taken on account of the Carthusian monastery there, which was known for its piety and good leadership. He matriculated at the faculty of arts at *Bursa Montis*. Classified as "poor," because he received only 118 florins for two years from his father, he was allowed to board privately first with his brother, then with a chaplain, instead of at the *Bursa*'s seminary.[11] At the *Bursa Montis*, Cologne's oldest and most famous college, he attended lectures and followed tutorials. On the basis of the commentaries of Thomas Aquinas he acquired a profound knowledge of Aristotle's view of the world; it was the *Via antiqua* of the medieval scholastics. He also heard Konrad Köllin's theological lectures on Aquinas's *Summa*. At the same time he attended sessions by Johannes Matthäus Phrissemius and Arnold von Wesel explaining Aristotle in a humanist manner and lecturing on Cicero, Virgil, Horace and the humanists Rudolf Agricola and Erasmus of Rotterdam. He felt particularly attracted to Phrissemius and Wesel and to his Greek teacher, Johannes Caesarius, with whom he later corresponded.[12] Just

10. Blanke, *Der junge Bullinger*, 29-30, against Carl Pestalozzi, *Heinrich Bullinger: Leben und ausgewählte Schriften. Nach handschriftlichen und gleichzeitigen Quellen* (Leben und ausgewählte Schriften der Väter und Begründer der reformirten Kirche V; Elberfeld: Friderichs, 1858), 10-11; Staedtke, *Theologie*, 20-27; vom Berg, "Die Brüder," 3-12; Susi Hausammann, *Römerbriefauslegung zwischen Humanismus und Reformation. Eine Studie zu Heinrich Bullingers Römerbriefvorlesung von 1525* (Studien zur Dogmengeschichte und systematischen Theologie 27; Zurich: Zwingli Verlag, 1970), 186-91.

11. *HBD*, 3,16-18; 4,7-9; 6,24-26; 7,10-13; Blanke, *Der junge Bullinger*, 34-37; Hermann Keussen ed., *Matrikel der Universität Köln* (Bonn: 1919; rpt Düsseldorf: Droste, 1979), II:814, no. 523.55 ("Henr. Poellinger de Breemgaerdt; art, i. e. s.," September 1519). The medieval faculty of arts corresponds to the upper classes of present-day grammar schools, but belonged then to the university.

12. *HBD*, 4,9-5,7; 7,1-4; 125,19-23; Blanke, *Der junge Bullinger*, 37-41. Concerning the friendship between Bullinger and Caesarius see Carl Krafft, *Aufzeichnungen des schweizerischen Reformators Heinrich Bullinger über sein Studium zu Emmerich und Köln (1516-1522) und dessen Briefwechsel mit Freunden in Köln, Erzbischof Hermann von Wied etc. Ein Beitrag zur*

for practice he wrote fictitious stories, speeches and dialogues, some of which still exist.[13] Through independent study he got to know other Classical writers, such as Quintilian, Macrobius, Pliny, Mela, Homer, and Iustinum, as well as further works by Erasmus.[14] By now his thoughts and reasoning had turned from scholasticism to humanism.

The preparation for and the rigours of the Baccalaureat exams during November (until 4 December) 1520 did not allow Bullinger to follow the disputes of the Cologne theologians concerning Luther.[15] Only in 1521 and 1522, but then intensively, day and night, and very systematically, did he acquaint himself first with Catholic, patristic, and finally Lutheran theology. He started on his own with the *Sentences* of Peter Lombard and the *Decretals* of Gratian. As both referred to the church fathers, he asked for patristic works. Thanks to a member of the Dominican monastery, Georg Diener (a native of Elgg/Zurich), he gained access to the library there. Against his expectation Bullinger discovered a great difference between Lombard or Gratian and Chrysostom's homilies on Matthew. Further it struck him how near Ambrose, Origen and Augustine were to the works of Luther. He compared them with the New Testament, which he studied with the help of the commentaries of Jerome and Melanchthon's *Loci communes* (in the edition of December 1521). This biblical study confirmed Bullinger in his new insights, which he had achieved at the age of only seventeen after an intense inner struggle.[16] After his exams in February 1522 and the awarding of the degree of "Master of Arts" (*Magister artium*) on 13 March 1522 he returned to Bremgarten, where his family warmly received him. Becoming a monk or studying the scholastic theology at Cologne was no longer discussed. At home he studied works of Athanasius, Lactantius, and Luther and thereby deepened his knowledge of theology.[17]

2. Bullinger as Teacher at Kappel (1523-9)

After Bullinger had spent nine months at home Abbot Wolfgang Joner summoned the young scholar (on 17 January 1523) to the position of teacher and rector in his new school at the Cistercian monastery of Kappel am Albis. The monastery lay in the territory of Zurich but close to the border with Catholic Zug. Bullinger accepted the offer on the condition that he could preserve his religious

---

niederrheinisch-westfälischen Kirchen-, Schul- und Gelehrtengeschichte (Elberfeld: Sam. Lucas, 1870), 32-36 and 123-37; *HBBW* VII:283-85, no. 1056; IX:210-11, no. 1306; and further volumes in preparation).

13. *HBD*, 5,11-12; 16,28-31 Bullinger mentions dialogues in favour of Johannes Reuchlin against Pfefferkorn and other scholastic theologians in the year 1520 which are now lost. The few surviving works are listed by Staedtke, *Theologie*, 265-6.

14. *HBD*, 5,8-10.

15. *HBD*, 4,13 mentions October 1520; November/4 December 1520 according to Krafft, *Aufzeichnungen*, 52-55 (edition of a deanery's list); *HBD*, 5,13-15; Blanke *Der junge Bullinger*, 41-45.

16. *HBD*, 5,13-6,17; 126,1-14; Blanke, *Der junge Bullinger*, 45-47; Staedtke, *Theologie*, 16-20.

17. *HBD*, 6,17-23; 7,14-18; 126,14-15; Krafft, *Aufzeichnungen*, 56, note 3; Blanke, *Der junge Bullinger*, 47, 49.

convictions and that he would not be forced to accept monastic vows, clothes or rites.[18] Abbot Joner, who was himself favourably disposed towards the Reformation, agreed. Bullinger's firmness of mind and the abbot's broad-mindedness were astonishing considering that in Zurich the Reformation had not yet been introduced. Zwingli had been preaching since 1519, but the mass was still celebrated until spring 1525.

It was a little school that Bullinger headed from 3 February 1523 as *praefectus ludi*. There were twelve monks and some young men, only one of them, Johannes Frey (Liberianus), from the city of Zurich, where parents possibly feared that the pupils might be drawn to monasticism. Bullinger was the only teacher. During the afternoons he taught the *Trivium*: Latin grammar, according to Donatus and Erasmus, rhetoric with readings from Erasmus, Cicero, Sallust and Virgil, and "dialectic" (logic), comparisons with corresponding works of Melanchthon, Rudolf Agricola, Boethius and Cicero. It took him six years to teach these various authors. His lessons, according to Blanke, were then the most modern and advanced of all Latin schools in the Swiss Confederation.[19]

Every morning for one hour he gave theological lessons to the monks and quickly these developed into public lectures. Bullinger was two years ahead of Zwingli, who had planned in autumn of the same year (1523) to hold public biblical lessons; this plan was not realised until 1525. Few of Bullinger's listeners, mainly monks, servants and farmers of the neighbourhood, understood Latin. For that reason he gave lectures (on the basis of Latin drafts) in German, which may well have been more taxing for him than Latin, the language of scholars. He started with two short presentations on Erasmus for better understanding of the Bible (*Paraclesis* and *Compendium*) and continued with Melanchthon's *Loci Communes*. Between 1523 and 1529 he interpreted several books of the New Testament: Matthew and John (1523/24), all the letters of Paul, including the letter to the Hebrews (1524/26), Luke (1527), 1 John and the letters of James and Peter (1528). In his preparations he used patristic editions and the exegetical works of Erasmus and Melanchthon.[20] Soon there arrived written help from Zurich. At the end of 1523 he had come into contact with Zwingli and Leo Jud; later he made the acquaintance of Vadianus and Oecolampadius.[21] Zwingli and Bullinger had discovered during a discussion in autumn 1524 that they held, independently of each other, close theological convictions, especially regarding the Lord's Supper.[22]

18. *HBD*, 7,19-22; 8,2-9; 126,19-22; Blanke, *Der junge Bullinger*, 49-51; cf. also note 25.

19. *HBD*, 7,22-8,2; 8,10-12; 11,2-9; Blanke, *Der junge Bullinger*, 52-54. Johannes Frey (Liberianus) was elected 1529 as teacher and Bullinger's successor at Kappel (*HBD*, 17,25-26).

20. *HBD*, 8,13-19; 10,8-12; 11,1-2 and 5; 12,25-26; 126,22-25; Blanke, *Der junge Bullinger*, 54-56, 58-60.

21. *HBD*, 8,23-26; 126,16-18 (Zwingli and his collaborator Leo Jud, preacher at St. Peter's church, Zurich, translator of the Bible); 9,1-3 (Vadianus, medical doctor, Bürgermeister and reformer of St. Gallen, passing through Kappel on his return from a diet at Zug); 10,5-7 (Johannes Oecolampadius, reformer of Basle); Blanke, *Der junge Bullinger*, 64-67.

22. *HBD*, 9,11-18–Zwingli begged Bullinger to take part in a disputation with Anabaptists (1525) as a scribe, and later to share in the important disputation of Berne (1528). See *HBD* 9,19-24; 11,23-12,4.

Bullinger's interpretation of the Bible led to the reformation of the monastery of Kappel. Following the example of Zurich, not in blind imitation but in accordance with Bullinger's new interpretation of scripture (as Blanke writes), the monks removed the statues and whitewashed the walls of the church, abolished the mass in 1525, and on 29 March 1526 celebrated for the first time the Lord's Supper according to the new order.[23] They took off their cowls, chose a trade or prepared, under Bullinger's tuition, for the ministry; some got married. In 1527, abbot and convent handed over the cloister to the town of Zurich, which decided to continue to use the cloister as a boarding seminary and entrusted the pupils to Bullinger.[24] They were sons of citizens of Zurich and other places (outsiders had to pay), as well as gifted sons of poor people who were given a full scholarship. Among those students was Rudolf Gwalther, Bullinger's later collaborator and successor.[25]

Bullinger's reforming work spread into the territory of Zug, but soon it was clear that Zug's majority would remain Catholic and were hostile to the Protestant cloister school. Significant is an episode from summer 1524, when Bullinger and his pupils bathed in the little river Lorze just across the border; only a miracle saved them from a thrashing by some young lads from Zug.[26] Henceforth it was too dangerous for him to enter the neighbouring territory. Yet he assisted priests and nuns interested in the Reformation with drafts of his lectures or with theological letters and articles, some of which are still in existence, although partly only in fragments.[27] They show an astonishing maturity and clarity in his theological and political thinking. In his teaching Bullinger could be quite political. He even wrote (1526 or 1528) a play in German, *Lucretia and Brutus*. His principal themes were the concept of liberty, how to gain and keep it, and the political renewal of the Swiss Confederation–a government which is not corruptible by mercenaries and payments, but puts itself under God's order.[28]

In about 1527-8 he wrote a manual for private study for his best friend from Zug, Werner Steiner. This *Ratio studiorum*, in the Erasmian tradition, gives full and detailed theoretical and practical instructions for the reading of secular and biblical literature, including physiological and psychological hints for working. It

---

23. Blanke, *Der junge Bullinger*, 56-58, on the basis of *HBD*, 10,1-5 and 10,16-22.

24. Hausammann, *Römerbriefauslegung*, 16-21.

25. *HBRG* I, chap. 57, 93-94.

26. *HBD*, 9,4-10; Blanke, *Der junge Bullinger,* 60-61.

27. For the small fragment of the lecture on John see Ulrich Gäbler, "Bullingers Vorlesung über das Johannesevangelium aus dem Jahre 1523" in Gäbler/Herkenrath, *Heinrich Bullinger 1504-1575*, I:13-27. Substantial fragments from the lectures on Romans (1525) and Hebrews (1526/27) have survived; and are edited Hans-Georg vom Berg and Susanna Hausammann eds, *Heinrich Bullinger Werke: Theologische Schriften*, vol. 1: *Exegetische Schriften aus den Jahren 1525-1527*, (*HBTS* I; Zurich: TVZ, 1993); see also Staedtke, *Theologie*; Hausammann, *Römerbriefauslegung*, and Susi Hausammann, "Anfragen zum Schriftverständnis des jungen Bullinger im Zusammenhang einer Interpretation von De Scripturae Negotio'" in Gäbler/Herkenrath, *Heinrich Bullinger 1504-1575*, I:29-48. For all works from these years see Bullinger's list (*HBD*, 13,1-16,27) and their description by Staedtke, *Theologie*, 266-92, nos 21-86. Nine of them are edited in Hans-Georg vom Berg et al. eds, *Heinrich Bullinger Werke: Theologische Schriften*, vol 2: *Unveröffentlichte Werke der Kappeler Zeit* (Zurich: TVZ, 1991).

28. See Emidio Campi's contribution in this volume.

also contains plenty of loci for academic study.[29] Much of the work is drawn from other sources, but it contains also many of Bullinger's own ideas on secondary education, and it can be understood as a mirror of his own systematic private studies.

During his years at Kappel Bullinger received leave to further his own education, and from 23 June till 14 November 1527 he lived in Zurich, heard Zwingli preach and lecture, improved his Hebrew with Konrad Pellikan and his Greek with Johannes Rhellikan and Rudolf Collinus/Ambühl.[30] Only during these five months was he able to study directly with Reformed-evangelical teachers. This proved an exception in Bullinger's life, for otherwise all his theological knowledge and his evangelical convictions were gained through private study.

In June 1528 Bullinger was admitted to the synod of Zurich, and at this point, in addition to his teaching at the cloister school he had to take on the pastorate of Hausen am Albis.[31] In spite of all the burdens and of the dangerous situation so near to a Catholic area Bullinger retrospectively regarded his years at Kappel as his happiest times.[32] They came to an end in spring 1529 with his election as preacher to his native town of Bremgarten.[33] We know of no connection with the school in Bremgarten that he had himself attended as a little boy.

3. Bullinger's Involvement with the Schools as *Antistes* of Zurich (1531-75)

After Zurich's defeat and Zwingli's death at the battle of Kappel (11 October 1531) Bullinger was forced to leave Bremgarten as part of the conditions of peace (20 November). He started to preach in Zurich, and on 9 December he was elected by the council as Zwingli's successor. He was twenty-seven years old when he became preacher at the Grossmünster. Zwingli's professorship of Old Testament was given to Theodor Bibliander, so Bullinger as chief minister did not belong to the teaching staff. [34] But as first preacher for the whole church of Zurich (*Antistes*) he was principally responsible for the delicate relationship be-

---

29. Critical edition: Peter Stotz ed., *Heinrich Bullinger: Werke*. Sonderband: *Studiorum Ratio–Studienanleitung*, (Zurich: TVZ, 1987) with exhaustive introduction and detailed commentary in a second volume. A short introduction is found in Fritz Büsser, "Reformierte Erziehung in Theorie und Praxis" (translation of a French paper given in 1974) in Fritz Büsser, *Wurzeln der Reformation in Zürich. Zum 500. Geburtstag des Reformators Huldrych Zwingli* (Studies in Medieval and Reformation Thought 31; Leiden: Brill, 1985), 199-216, esp. 207-12. Pamela Biel, *Doorkeepers at the House of Righteousness. Heinrich Bullinger and the Zurich Clergy 1535-1575* (ZBRG 15; Berne: Peter Lang, 1990), 170-4, describes the *Studiorum Ratio* as an educational plan for the training of a minister.

30. *HBD*, 11,8-13; Blanke, *Der junge Bullinger*, 67-68 During his stay at Zurich he became engaged to Anna Adlischwyler, a nun, whom he married on 17 August 1529 (*HBD*, 11,14-22; 18,15-21; Blanke, *Der junge Bullinger*, 73-94).

31. At Hausen (2km north of Kappel) he preached his first sermon on 21 June. (*HBD*, 12,14-25; 126,34-36; 128,24; Blanke, *Der junge Bullinger*, 69-70.)

32. According to Bullinger's biography by his son-of-law, Ludwig Lavater, (Zurich, 1576) 14; cited by Blanke, *Der junge Bullinger*, 62.

33. His preaching soon led to the reformation of Bremgarten. (*HBD*, 17,1-26; 126,36-127,7; Blanke, *Der junge Bullinger*, 95-101.)

34. *HBD*, 20,9-21,14; 127,14-16; Blanke, *Der junge Bullinger*, 101-8 and 119-28. Bremgarten was forced to return to Catholicism.

tween church and state, which often concerned the schools. As a condition of his election the council had requested that church leaders should not interfere in politics. Bullinger, after a few days consideration, had accepted this requirement in exchange for a guarantee of freedom in preaching, which included criticism of the council's politics and being allowed to give suggestions on the basis of the Bible. Bullinger had permission to attend the council, with other church leaders or in their name, and to express the views of the church. The council apparently valued such direct criticism rather then hearing it from the pulpit. Remaining free in their decisions, the council as often agreed with the opinion of the church leader as they did not. The drafts of his speeches, or the later written summaries for the council, called *Fürträge*, form a rich source for our understanding of Bullinger's ecclesiastical and political activity.[35]

His first appearance before the council (after his election) was caused by a schooling issue. Many members of the council held the church leaders responsible for the lost war and, therefore, had proposed a secularisation of the chapter of the Grossmünster in order that Zurich could pay its war debts. Bullinger felt that the schools were threatened, for the chapter's income served as the basis for the scholarships and the preachers' and teachers' salaries. On 17 February 1532 Bullinger explained to the council the significance of education by arguing that the spread of Christianity had always been secured through teaching, that no tyrannical force could ever defeat it because there had always existed learned men, that the promotion of schools was now also important because of the urgent need for 130 new preachers to replace the older generation, and that without God's Word there would not be an obedient and God-fearing people. In Zwingli's time the further education of the clergy had been at the forefront, but now Bullinger had realised that the need for a superior quality and quantity of preachers was paramount. The council was convinced by his arguments and decided to keep the chapter and even added further prebends for scholarships.[36]

The financial security for the chapter having been achieved, there followed in 1532 the internal reorganisation of the existing higher schools in Zurich: the two medieval Latin schools, one at the Grossmünster and the other at the former cloister of the Fraumünster, and the trilingual "Biblical lessons" planned for 1523 and realised in 1525 by Zwingli.[37] By the end of August both chapters elected

35. *HBRG* III, chaps 501-2, 291-6; Hans Ulrich Bächtold, *Heinrich Bullinger vor dem Rat. Zur Gestaltung und Verwaltung des Zürcher Staatswesens in den Jahren 1531 bis 1575* (ZBRG 12; Berne/Frankfurt a. Main: Peter Lang, 1982), 11, 15-18; an index of these reports (*Fürträge*) appears on 348-59.

36. Bächtold, *Heinrich Bullinger*, 18-19, 116-21, 189-92; Leo Weisz, "Quellen zur Reformationsgeschichte des Großmünsters in Zürich," 2nd part, *Zwingliana* 7/3 (1940), 172-202, esp. 189-92; a summary is given by Hans Ulrich Bächtold, "Heinrich Bullinger und die Entwicklung des Schulwesens in Zürich" in Institut für Schweizerische Reformationsgeschichte ed., *Schola Tigurina. Die Zürcher Hohe Schule und ihre Gelehrten um 1550. Katalog zur Ausstellung vom 25. Mai bis 10. Juli 1999 in der Zentralbibliothek Zürich* (Zurich/Freiburg i. Br.: Pano, 1999), 48-51, esp. 49.

37. The literature on Zurich's schools under Zwingli and Bullinger is as follows: *HBD*, 1556, 1567 and 1574; Ludwig Lavater, *De ritibus et institutis ecclesiae Tigurinae* (Zurich: 1559 and 1567), with additions by Johann Baptist Ott (Zurich 1702), translated by Gottfried Albert Keller, *Die Gebräuche und Einrichtungen der Zürcher Kirche* (Zurich: TVZ, 1987), chaps 1, 11,

Bullinger as *Schulherr* or *Scholarch* (director of educational affairs), a function which had also been performed by Zwingli. Together with a council committee Bullinger had the task of assessing teachers, students, and lessons. He and Bibliander were asked to draw up rules for the schools. The aim of their proposals was schools with God-fearing education and good discipline; Bullinger's outline regulated the prayers, the services at church, and the time table–the morning lessons were at 6 and 8 o'clock and the afternoon lessons between 12 and 4pm, with free hours in-between for memorising what had just been taught.[38] It required the more advanced pupils to speak Latin exclusively and obliged the teachers to prevent pupils falling into vices, to promote gifted students, and to remove lazy and unfit pupils after further consultation with the *Schulherr*. It also contained a rather detailed plan for the four classes. The three lower constituted an advanced Latin school based on the study of the Latin grammar of Donatus, the New Testament in Latin, and texts by of Virgil, Terence, Cato, Cicero, Erasmus and the Swiss humanist Glareanus. In the third form pupils began to study Greek. The fourth class corresponded to a faculty of arts, with "dialectic" (according to Melanchthon), "rhetoric" (according to Quintilian), poems of Ovid's *Metamorphoses* and Homer, as well as, though only on Saturdays, mathematics and geography (according to Pomponius Mela). Being connected to Zwingli's "Biblical lessons," the fourth class also formed with its lectures in biblical exegesis a kind of theological seminary, the *Lectorium* or *Schola Tigurina*, Zurich's trilingual and theological academy.[39] The pupils stayed more than one year at one level and

---

17-20 concern the schools; Ulrich Ernst, *Geschichte des zürcherischen Schulwesens bis gegen Ende des sechzehnten Jahrhunderts* (Winterthur: Bleuler-Hausheer, 1879); Hans Nabholz, "Zürichs Höhere Schulen von der Reformation bis zur Gründung der Universität, 1525-1833" in Ernst Gagliardi et al. eds., *Die Universität Zürich 1833-1933 und ihre Vorläufer* (Die Zürcherischen Schulen seit der Regeneration 3; Zurich: Verlag der Erziehungsdirektion, 1938), 3-164, esp. 3-29; Jacques Figi, *Die innere Reorganisation des Grossmünsterstifts in Zürich 1519-1531* (Affoltern am Albis: J. Weiss, 1951), chap 2: "Die Bildungsstätte," 73-93; Kurt Spillmann, "Zwingli und die Zürcher Schulverhältnisse," *Zwingliana* 11/7 (1962), 427-48; Christoph Zürcher, *Konrad Pellikans Wirken in Zürich 1526-1556* (ZBRG 4; Zurich: TVZ, 1975), 34-45, 77-82; Bächtold, *Bullinger vor dem Rat*, chap. 6: "Die Schulpolitik," 189-231, Fritz Büsser, "Reformierte Erziehung"; Pamela Biel, *Doorkeepers*, chap. 6: "When Teaching Isn't Preaching," 166-99; Fritz Büsser, *Die Prophezei. Humanismus und Reformation in Zürich* in Alfred Schindler ed., *Ausgewählte Aufsätze und Vorträge. Zu seinem 70. Geburtstag am 12. Februar 1993* (ZBRG 17; Berne: Peter Lang, 1994); Karin Maag, *Seminary or University? The Genevan Academy and Reformed Higher Education, 1560-1620* (St Andrews Studies in Reformation History; Aldershot: Ashgate, 1995); *Schola Tigurina*; Bruce Gordon, *The Swiss Reformation* (New Frontiers in History; Manchester: Manchester Univ. Press, 2002), chap. "The Prophezei in Zurich," 232-9.

38. Bächtold, *Bullinger vor dem Rat*, 193f. The "ordination und ansähen, wie man sich fürohin mit den schuoleren, letzgen und anderen dingen halten sol in der schuol zum Grossenmünster Zürich, 1532," Emil Egli, *Actensammlung zur Geschichte der Zürcher Reformation in den Jahren 1519-1533* (Zurich: 1879, rpt Aalen: Scientia, 1973), 821-4, no. 1896; a summary in modern German by Ernst (*Geschichte*, 88-91) was also valid for the Latin school at the Fraumünster "schola inferior," which was situated in the valley, near the river Limmat. The "schola superior" was situated on the hill of the Grossmünster. The schools were of an equal level.

39. The institution of the "Biblical lessons" in Zwingli's time (Zwingli with Jakob Wiesendanger/Ceporinus and, after his early death, Konrad Pellikan, Kaspar Megander, Rudolf am Bühl/Collinus and Leo Jud on the Old Testament at the Grossmünster, as well as Oswald

remained three or four years in the highest class. The aim was to train sufficient preachers for country villages; the most gifted students studied additionally at universities and it was Bullinger who, thanks to his international contacts, could give them advice and recommend them to professors abroad.

In 1532 we can recognise two of the three ways in which Bullinger could and did use his ability to influence education. (1) He had tried successfully to win the council's approval for securing the financial basis of the schools and their enlargement, always demonstrating the need to educate a sufficient number of future preachers. (2) Within the schools he and the other preachers and teachers could (almost independently of the council) shape the lessons and set standards. (3) He would also use personal connections such as his friendly contacts with the professors of the *Lectorium* and the headmasters of the Latin schools, for whom he wrote the books used in lessons, as well as discussions and private teaching of students lodging in his house. Of course, the three ways were interconnected.

During 1537 Bullinger resigned as *Schulherr* on account of his workload, and perhaps because from 1537 he taught catechism to young people on Saturday afternoons.[40] The same year some young English students (John Eliott, Nicholas Partridge, William Woodroffe, Bartholomew Traheron) and others who were lodging with him were given private instruction on Isaiah by Bullinger. Fragments of his drafts and the entire protocol written by Gwalther "ex ore Bullingeri" still exist.[41] During these five months he was once again working as a biblical teacher, as he had done at Kappel.

After his resignation as *Schulherr* Bulilnger nevertheless remained a lifelong member of the two committees responsible for the schools. The committee for discipline and scholarships (*stipendia*) included representatives of the council, the schools, and the churches. Most important was his membership, together with other preachers and professors, in the "collegium for examinations," which biannually examined all students and decided on promotion, on which pupils would repeat a class, and the removal of unfit pupils. They examined the candidates on their ability to preach; this proved decisive in determining the level of preaching in Zurich. In the examinations it was Bullinger who asked most of the questions; significant was the wish of some councillors (23 September 1573) that, to Bullinger's relief, the other members should ask more questions. This same "collegium for examinations" prepared the nominations of two or three possible candidates

---

Myconius on the New Testament at the Fraumünster until 1531) is known in literature as the "*Prophezei*." The name was derived from "prophecy," following Zwingli's interpretation of 1 Corinthians 12, 28 and 14, 26-33, but as a term for Zurich's "high school" it is only once used in a church regulation (*Christennlich ordnung und brüch der kilchen Zürich ..., 1535*). All other sixteenth-century sources use the terms "Biblisch lection in dryen sprachen" (*HBRG* I, chap. 160, 289-91; reprinted in Büsser, *Prophezei*, 7-9), "*Lectiones publicae*," "*letzgen*" (public lessons), or "*Lectorium*" (derived from the room). See Michael Baumann/Rainer Henrich, "Das Lektorium, sein Lehrkörper, seine Studenten" in *Schola Tigurina*, 24-27. The term "*Prophezei*" may distinguish between the "Biblical lessons" in Zwingli's years and the more structured "*Lectorium*" of Bullinger's time.

40. *HBD*, 25,21-22. We do not know the purpose of his catechising. Catechising belonged otherwise to the duties of the deacons (the second preachers of the churches in the town).

41. *HBD*, 26,4-27; ZB, Ms. Car III 197c and 195e (fragments of Bullinger's drafts), and Ms. D 43, 174ʳ-327ᵛ (Gwalther's complete protocol).

for preaching posts in the parishes under Zurich's rule or even in the Thurgau and other parts of eastern Switzerland. The council would then chose one from the list. The committee also prepared the nominations for scholarships. These so-called *Fürschläge* (propositions) were almost always written by Bullinger, although occasionally by Gwalther or another.[42]

Throughout his life, Bullinger devoted time to the development of the schools and the scholarships, sometimes with success and sometimes without. In his opinion, prebends of churches and monasteries should be used for the relief of poor people and for the support of schools in town and country, for this would fulfil best the will of the original founders. Reforming a monastery should not mean its abolition and its use as an estate; rather, it should mean its transformation into a school.[43] He tried to establish in the former monastery at Rüti (Zürcher Oberland) a boarding school similar to Kappel. The project was almost successful, but then the council changed its mind. In 1538 those opposed to the proposals gained a majority on the council; they wished to concentrate all higher education in Zurich. Not only did the council refuse the plan for Rüti, but it called back all scholarship students from Kappel. The *Alumnat,* a boarding school, was established in buildings of the former cloister at the Fraumünster. The council agreed to oblige Bullinger to maintain from then onwards fifteen instead of only eight full scholarship students. But in 1550 against all promises even the school at Kappel was abolished.[44] Another of Bullinger's plans was to establish two on fee-paying German schools, but in 1556 this too failed. He only succeeded in obtaining support for two women teachers for a girls' school and in having it made compulsory for boys to attend one of the private German schools for at least one year before entering a Latin school.[45]

He was more successful with scholarships. Besides the *Alumnat* at the Fraumünster and the *Studio* or *Studentenamt* at the Grossmünster the council granted subsidies to the *Almosenamt* (the office of charity), in the first place for sixteen students. By 1547 the council counted to its horror forty-five, among them four from foreign countries, and by 1573 the total had reached ninety. The council at times reduced the number while Bullinger fought for increased generosity, arguing: "sons of rich families do not want to become preachers who earn only a small income; therefore the churches depend upon gifted boys from poor families and certainly on gifted sons of the mainly poor parsons of country-parishes for training enough young preachers and teachers." By allowing more or fewer subsidies the council could control the number of future preachers. Stu-

---

42. Nabholz, "Zürichs Höhere Schulen," 16; Bächtold, "Heinrich Bullinger und die Entwicklung des Schulwesens in Zürich," 50-51. The propositions (*Fürschläge*) are inserted into records of prebends and communities (StA, E I 30. 1-158) or records of the "Alumnat" (ibid., E I 14.1, 14.3; cf. below note 44). An index is kept by the editors of Bullinger's correspondence at the Institut für Schweizerische Reformationsgeschichte, Zurich.

43. Bächtold, *Bullinger vor dem Rat,* 194-6, 207.

44. Ibid., 196-211; Heinzpeter Stucki, "Bullinger, der Zürcher Rat und die Auseinandersetzung um das Alumnat 1538-1542" in Gäbler/Herkenrath, *Heinrich Bullinger 1504-1575,* 1:291-303.

45. Bächtold, *Bullinger vor dem Rat,* 211-4.

dents with scholarships were obliged to do future service in church or school and were subjected to a stronger discipline than the paying students.[46]

Bullinger achieved more success in developing the higher schools. Both Latin schools expanded during the 1540s to five classes and Hebrew was introduced. Only after attending five classes could students gain promotion to the increasingly separately organised *Lectorium*. In 1541 Konrad Gessner, the famous medical doctor, scholar in natural sciences and in languages, and the first bibliographer, obtained a professorship at the *Lectorium* in "physics" (natural sciences) and ethics; but this was only a subsidiary subject with a small salary. Gessner often complained of his poor situation and only in 1558 did he receive a full prebend. Central to Bullinger's interest were only the subjects which served the biblical exegesis of future preachers:[47] Latin and Greek were connected with rhetoric and dialectic, but the lecturers Johann Jakob Ammann and Rudolf Collinus (am Bühl) were highly philological in their teaching. Hebrew was taught by Konrad Pellikan, who lectured in a weekly exchange with Theodor Bibliander on the Old Testament. Bullinger listened to and took notes on Bibliander's lectures over thirty years; these notes served him and others in the preparation of sermons. Often loaned to others, the lecture notes from Bullinger's hand still exist.[48]

As we can see, Bullinger was both examiner and student, providing an example of the value of lifelong learning, which he expected from all preachers. The New Testament was not regularly lectured on before 1552 and then only by learned deacons, like Josias Simler, or later the sons of Zwingli and Bullinger. After Pellikan's death *Antistes* Bullinger summoned in 1556 Peter Martyr Vermigli, a scholar of international reputation, to the professorship of the Old Testament. After Vermigli's death in 1562, Bullinger tried in vain to appoint Girolamo Zanchi.[49] Josias Simler, an outstanding scholar from Zurich in theology, history and geography, "ascended" from lecturing on the New Testament to the more highly valued Old Testament chair as Vermigli's successor, assisted by the learned preacher at the Fraumünster, Johannes Wolf. Bullinger was both friends with these teachers and connected with their families–for example, through the marriage of his daughter Elisabeth to Simler.[50] But from 1562 onwards he could no longer resist the council's (long standing) insistence on electing only citizens

46. Ibid., 215-28.
47. Ernst, *Geschichte,* 92-94, 99, 103; Nabholz, "Zürichs Höhere Schulen," 6-10, 17-21, 24-29; Maag, *Seminary*, chap. 5: "Zurich and the Genevan Academy," 129-53, esp. 133f.
48. ZB, Ms. Car I 85, 109-22, 124-49, 151.
49. *HBD*, 68,27-28; Bullinger to Zanchi, 16 December 1562, and Zanchi's refusal 23 December 1562 (StA, E II 377, 2380-1, resp. E II 356, 781-4; printed in: Zanchi, *Epistolarum libri duo,* in his *Opera theologicarum,* vol. 8 (Geneva, 1619), 126-7, 130-1. I could only consult the 2nd edition.
50. *HBD*, 128,15-21, and cf. the register of *HBD* for all the teachers mentioned. For their biographies see Nabholz, "Zürichs Höhere Schulen," 6-8, 17-22, 24-29, and the relevant articles in *Schola Tigurina,* for many of them also Hans J. Hillerbrand ed., *The Oxford Encyclopedia of the Reformation,* 4 vols (New York/Oxford: OUP, 1996). Lists of the lecturers at the *Lectorium* are to be found in Ernst, *Geschichte,* 103 and 112. Biel, *Doorkeepers,* 197 mistakenly writes that the New Testament was lectured on between 1572 and 1575 by the *Antistes* himself, rather than by his son Heinrich Bullinger junior (1534-1583).

of Zurich to the professorships, and with this began the decline of the *Schola Tigurina* to the level of a provincial institution.[51]

1559 was a decisive year for the *Schola Tigurina*, when earlier school regulations were redrafted by Bullinger.[52] In addition to his *Summa christenlicher Religion* (first printed 1556), used in the fourth class of both Latin schools, and its Latin version *Compendium Christianae religionis*, used in the fifth class, he was asked by his colleagues in 1559 to write a detailed Latin catechism (*Catechesis pro adultioribus*).[53] It was hoped to give the advanced pupils a good basic preparation for theological studies when they entered the *Lectorium* after their exams. Bullinger dedicated this catechism to the headmasters Johannes Fries of the Latin-school at the Grossmünster and to Sebastian Guldibeck of the Latin-school at the Fraumünster.[54] The same year, following a suggestion from Bullinger, the *Schulherr* started a register of students (*Matrikel, Album in Schola Tigurina Studentium*).[55] For earlier years we know only the numbers and names of full scholarship students, again mainly thanks to Bullinger's lists.[56] Of the paying students we know only a few names mentioned in Bullinger's correspondence; and have no means of finding them all. Consequently, it is impossible to say how attractive the *Schola Tigurina* was for foreigners before the foundation of the Genevan Academy in 1559.[57] This Academy, established on the example of Zurich's *Lectorium*, soon added non-theological subjects and quickly attracted many more students than Zurich.[58] Neither Geneva nor Zurich was allowed to bestow academic degrees–Bullinger himself had no interest in them. He expected a very solid foundation from his students at home, and especially from those who could study with scholarships at other universities,[59] which he examined, but Bullinger

---

51. Nabholz, "Zürichs Höhere Schulen," 28; Maag, *Seminary*, 32, 134f. In subsequent centuries some Zurich lecturers, but never as many as in the sixteenth century, gained an international reputation.

52. Bächtold, *Bullinger vor dem Rat*, 226-8. Edition in modernised German, Johann Jacob Wirz ed., *Historische Darstellung der urkundlichen Verordnungen, welche die Geschichte des Kirchen- und Schulwesens in Zürich ... betreffen*, vol. 1 (Zurich: 1793), 257-82. It summarises in a new redaction the regulations of 1532 (see above note 38) and another only for the Lectorium of 1548.

53. *HBBibl* I, nos 283, 291. The Latin translation by Josias Simler (*HBD*, 48,9-10). Concerning their use in schools see Ernst, *Geschichte*, 114.

54. *HBBibl* I, no. 377; *HBD*, 60,9. In the dedication Bullinger explains the purpose of this edition of this catechism.

55. The Album (with a modern index of names and places by Dr. Ulrich Helfenstein) is kept in StA, E II 479, E II 479a. Ernst, *Geschichte*, 108, 121, scheduled the yearly numbers of students at Zurich from 1559 onwards. In 1560 the "Acta scholastica" began (StA, E II 458).

56. Bullinger's lists for the "Studentenamt" at the Grossmünster (ZB, Ms. F 95, no. 1, f. 2r-16v; and another ibid. Ms. Car. C 44, 918-40,) contain more than 225 for the years 1527/29 until 1574. His list for Kappel and the "Alumnat" at the Fraumünster contains 98 students on full scholarship for the period up to 1572 (including some additions); their number and names can only be ascertained from the "Studentenamtsrechnungen" (StA, G II 39. 2). The total number of students was much higher.

57. Baumann/Henrich, "Das Lektorium," 26.

58. Fritz Büsser, "'Prophezei'-'Schola Tigurina'. Prototyp, Ideal und Wirklichkeit" in *Schola Tigurina*, 18-21; Maag, *Seminary*, 136-7.

59. Karin Maag, "Financing education: the Zurich approach, 1550-1620" in Beat A. Kümin ed., *Reformations Old and New. Essays on the Socio-Economic Impact of Religious Change, c.*

dissuaded them from working towards a degree.[60] He enjoyed seeing the rebuilding of the school at the Grossmünster and the inauguration of this *nova schola elegans* on 27 September 1570 with a performance of Gwalther's *comoedia sacra* of Nabal, Abigael and David, played by pupils and students.[61]

Bullinger's political discussions with the council needed a solid background and he therefore gathered documents concerning the schools. He kept lists of students with scholarships and in 1556 wrote the histories of the school at Kappel and its transformation into the *Alumnat* at the Fraumünster and of the Latin school and *Lectorium* at the Grossmünster (1574). In 1567 he wrote the *History of the Reformation* from the beginning till 1532, but he continued the chapters on the various schools until the 1550s and 60s.[62] This gives us an insight into the well-conducted schools, or, rather, theological schools. The significance of good education is also underlined in the fiftieth sermon of his *Decades* (1551) and in his last will, written as a letter to the council.[63]

1470-1630 (Aldershot: Ashgate, 1996), 203-16; 206 characterises the education scheme of Zurich as one "which provided the best possible ecclesiastical or professional training at minimal cost to the city."

60. Maag, *Seminary*, 137, 152. Bullinger to Gwalther (and similar letters to Johannes Wolf, Johann Jakob Wick and Johannes Haller, all studying with scholarships at Marburg), around 29th November 1540. The originals are lost, but the undated draft (ZB, Ms. F 37, f. 405r-v), however, is published in *HBBW* X, no. 1437: "... Quorsum enim attinet multo sumptu gradus magisterii recipere? Ubi domum redieritis et ecclesiae vices erunt rependendae, nemo rogabit num sitis magistri an famuli, sed quam docti et boni. Non negabit vobis Marpurgensis schola testimoniales literas de vestro studio et virtute ..." Bullinger's opinion was influenced by his attitude to the dispute over the new regulations of Basle University during 1539-40 (cf. *HBBW* IX-X passim).

61. *HBD*, 102,7-9; Ernst, *Geschichte*, 162. Rudolf Gwalther, *Nabal. Comoedia sacra ... desumpta ex I. Samuelis XXV. cap* ... Editions: Zürich 1549, Strassburg 1562, Antwerp 1566 (under the wrong author Paul Grebner), Sandro Giovanoli, ed. and trans. *Rudolf Gwalthers "Nabal": ein Zürcher Drama aus dem 16. Jahrhundert* (Studien zu Germanistik, Anglistik und Komparatistik 83; Bonn: Bouvier Grundmann, 1979).

62. Heinrich Bullinger, *Von der Schuol, zuo Cappel uffgericht, und hernach in die Statt Zürych zuo dem Frowenmünster geordnet.* Manuscript (of 1556): StA, E I 14. 1, Fasc. 1, 1-16. This served as basis for the descriptions in Bullinger's *Reformation History* (manuscript in ZB, Ms. A 16-17), ed. in HBRG I:90-97, chaps 56-58 and I:125f chap 75; Heinrich Bullinger, *Von der Reformation der Propsty oder Kylchen zuo dem Grossen Münster zuo Zürich 1523-1574* (annex to his chronicle *Von den Tigurinern und der Stadt Zürich sachen...*, vol. 2, manuscript of 1574: ZB, Ms. Car. C 44, 787-941) contains at the end (889-918) a detailed history of the Latin school and the *Lectorium*, and a list of scholarship students (918-40) mentioned in note 55. On its description and dating cf. Kurt Jakob Rüetschi, "Bullinger als Schulchronist" in Gäbler/Herkenrath, *Heinrich Bullinger 1504-1575*, I:305-22.

63. Bullinger, *Decas quinta*, Sermo X: "De institutis ecclesiae" gives as titles of sections: "De Scholis–Rectores scholarum–Christus et apostoli instituunt scholas–Ad conservationem ministerii pertinent scholae–Corruptio scholarum–Scholarum certus scopus–Disciplina scholarum," first printed in: *Sermonum Decas quinta, Tomus tertius* (Zurich: 1551), esp. f. 156'-158'; reprinted in all editions of the *Sermonum Decades quinque, de potissimis Christianae religionis capitibus* (Zurich: 1552f.) and in the complete translations in German, Dutch, French and English, the last under the title *Fiftie godlie and learned Sermons* (London: 1577f.), cf. *HBBibl* I, nos 182, 184f., 218f. Bullinger's last will, written in August 1572, revised and redated on 2 August 1575 (a few weeks before his death on 17 September 1575): StA, E I 1.4, (6 pages, esp. 4).

To take up again the thread of my introduction: our understanding of the manner in which Bullinger acquired his considerable theological knowledge and Reformed beliefs, principally through private study during his school and teaching years has led us to a clearer view of why he was such an efficient preacher and why he exercised such influence on Reformed Protestantism. His endeavours for the *Schola Tigurina* merit our interest because this institution was the prototype for other Protestant academies, such as those at Berne (1528), Lausanne (1537), Strasbourg (1538), Geneva (1559) and Herborn (1584), which in time overtook Zurich.[64]

64. Büsser, "'Prophezei'–'Schola Tigurina'"; Gordon, *Swiss Reformation*, esp. 236-9; Maag, *Seminary*, 137-8.

10

Bullinger's Correspondence: An International News Network

Rainer Henrich

In times of radical change the flow of information within a society increases tremendously, an observable phenomenon of the sixteenth century. The form of communication to be treated here, the dissemination of news through correspondence, took root towards the end of the middle ages. During this period the amount of news circulating throughout Europe swelled, as did the audience for the accounts of events in foreign lands. Leading figures such as princes, city councillors, and churchmen increasingly depended on reliable networks for news from across Europe. Merchants naturally had a vital interest in this kind of information and were among the first to collect and use news for their own purposes. Heinrich Bullinger, as the leader of the church of Zurich and a committed mentor of Reformed Protestantism throughout Europe, must often have anxiously awaited the latest news from France or the Netherlands. Yet, although there was a widespread thirst for information, we need to remember that newspapers in the modern sense of the word—that is, periodically printed collections of news reports for the general public—only came into being around the turn of the seventeenth century. Lacking such newspapers, Bullinger had to await the arrival of an official messenger from a city or other travellers who could report the news from Basle, Constance, or further afield. It would have been such messengers and travellers who handed over to Bullinger the letters that had been entrusted to them by the sender.[1]

The need for precision in speaking about information networks was highlighted in 1933, when Leo Weisz published a book entitled *Die Bullinger Zeitungen.*[2] To understand the problem, we have to bear in mind the meaning of the

---

1. Only a small number of publications dealing with the history of newspapers pay sufficient attention to letters as an early medium of news exchange. See in particular R. Grasshoff, *Die briefliche Zeitung des XVI. Jahrhunderts* (Diss. phil. Leipzig: 1877); Georg Steinhausen-Kassel, "Die Entstehung der Zeitung aus dem brieflichen Verkehr," *Archiv für Buchgewerbe und Gebrauchsgraphik* 65 (1928): 51-64. A rich bibliography is provided by Kristina Pfarr, *Die Neue Zeitung. Empirische Untersuchung eines Informationsmediums der frühen Neuzeit unter besonderer Berücksichtigung von Gewaltdarstellungen* (Diss. phil. Mainz: 1994), which deals with printed news reports almost exclusively.

2. Leo Weisz, *Die Bullinger Zeitungen. Zur Halbjahrhundertfeier des Vereins der schweizerischen Presse dargebracht vom Journalistischen Seminar der Universität Zürich und von der*

German word *Zeitung*. In today's language it is the equivalent of "newspaper," but in sixteenth-century German, it was a common word for "news" in a very general sense, often combined with *neu: nüwe zyttung* meaning "topical news." The Latin equivalent is *nova*.[3] Certainly, Weisz was well aware of the fact that *Zeitungen* in the sense of newspapers did not exist, but he published twenty-one documents from Bullinger's correspondence and categorised them as *Zeitungen* in the sense of "news reports." His intention was to portray Bullinger as a pioneer of news publishing. Some documents printed by Weisz are personal letters sent to or written by Bullinger, but most of them have a different, non-personal form. While Bullinger's personal letters have been collected and studied for a very long time,[4] most non-personal news reports from his correspondence are widely dispersed and have not yet been collected and listed.[5] Weisz was successful in creating the image of Bullinger as an important figure in the history of journalism, but thus far nobody has tried to deepen the research on this aspect of his correspondence.[6]

Bullinger's correspondence was immense, and fortunately a good deal of it has survived. Over the years, he systematically built a far-reaching network of correspondents, and the sheer number of surviving documents makes his an invaluable source for the history of the sixteenth century.[7] According to the card-index at the Institute of Swiss Reformation History in Zurich, about 12,000 letters still exist, most of them sent to Bullinger by about 1000 different correspondents from most parts of Europe, while only about 2000 of his own letters have survived. Nevertheless, Bullinger's correspondence comprises a greater number

---

Buchdruckerei Berichthaus in Zürich (Zurich: Berichthaus, 1933); cf. Leo Weisz, *Der Zürcher Nachrichtenverkehr vor 1780* (Zurich: Neue Zürcher Zeitung, 1955), esp. 22-26.

3. The semantics of this word were still unclear: "Novarum, ut vocant, rerum [i.e. so-called news] habeo nihil," Bullinger to Joachim Vadian, 31 May 1543; Lutherhalle Wittenberg, 191/2228.

4. For a short introduction to the collection, transmission and edition of Bullinger's correspondence, see Fritz Büsser in *HBBW* I (Zurich: 1973), 7-21; Rudolf Schnyder, "Aus der Arbeit am Bullinger-Briefwechsel. Zu Geschichte und Bedeutung der Edition," *Zwingliana* 28 (1990/1): 329-31. General overviews are also found in Traugott Schiess, "Der Briefwechsel Heinrich Bullingers," *Zwingliana* 5 (1933): 396-408; Traugott Schiess, "Ein Jahr aus Bullingers Briefwechsel [1559]," *Zwingliana* 6 (1934): 16-33, and Oskar Farner, "Die Bullinger-Briefe," *Zwingliana* 10 (1954): 103-8.

5. Many of them are found in the volumes of the former "Antistitialarchiv" (StA, E II 342. 342a. 350. 355. 357. 441 and others). The ZB also has several volumes containing news reports collected by Bullinger (esp. Ms. A 43. 44. 65. 66). cf. also note 45.

6. A recent book on news from Poland collected in the so-called "Wickiana" touches on Bullinger and his correspondence, Jan Pirożyński, *Z dziejów obiegu informacji w Europie XVI wieku. Nowiny z Polski w kollekcji Jana Jakuba Wicka w Zurychu z lat 1560-1587* (Cracow: Nakł. Uniwersytetu Jagiellońskiego, 1995). It would be particularly desirable to study the reflection of certain major events in Bullinger's correspondence, as Demandt has done for Vadian, Dieter Demandt, "Die Auseinandersetzungen des Schmalkaldischen Bundes mit Herzog Heinrich dem Jüngeren von Braunschweig-Wolfenbüttel im Briefwechsel des St. Galler Reformators Vadian," *Zwingliana* 22 (1995): 45-66.

7. It is fascinating to observe how purposefully Bullinger "sought to include Cranmer" (and many other important personalities) "in his spider's web," as Diarmaid MacCulloch remarks: Diarmaid MacCulloch, *Thomas Cranmer. A Life* (New Haven/London: Yale, University Press, 1996), 215; cf. *HBBW* VI: 200, 400/1.

of letters than the combined correspondence of Luther, Zwingli, Calvin and Vadianus. Bullinger himself was surprised when he realised that he had consumed almost a ream (1000 sheets) of paper for his correspondence in only one year (1569).[8] Among his correspondents, we find such prominent church leaders, princes, military commanders and men of learning as Luther, Melanchthon, Calvin, Bucer, Cranmer, King Edward VI, King Sigismund II August of Poland, Philip of Hesse, Ulrich and Christoph of Württemberg, Sebastian Schertlin von Burtenbach, Gaspard de Coligny, Thomas Erastus, Bonifacius Amerbach and many more, as well as little-known pastors and schoolmasters from the countryside, refugees, students, and relatives. Bullinger corresponded with at least twenty-four women, and seventy-one letters with female correspondents are extant.[9]

The critical edition of Bullinger's correspondence has now reached the year 1540, and thus far 1441 letters have been published.[10] Many of Bullinger's letters are already known through other publications such as *The Zurich Letters* published by the Parker Society,[11] the three volumes of *Bullingers Korrespondenz mit den Graubündnern,*[12] the *Correspondance de Théodore de Bèze,*[13] and the correspondence of Calvin in the volumes of the *Corpus reformatorum,*[14] but most of them await publication.

As a medium of communication, letters fulfilled many different functions. For example, Bullinger used them as an instrument for international church politics.[15] Many letters reflect contemporary debates on theology and questions of church order, while others illustrate Bullinger's pastoral care, his guidance of Zurich students at foreign universities, and his private friendship with colleagues and relatives. To a large extent, however, the letters served as the primary me-

8. See *HBD*, 97.
9. See Hans Ulrich Bächtold, "Frauen schreiben Bullinger–Bullinger schreibt Frauen. Heinrich Bullinger im Briefwechsel mit Frauen, insbesondere mit Anna Alexandria zu Rappoltstein" in Alfred Schindler/Hans Stickelberger eds, *Die Zürcher Reformation: Ausstrahlungen und Rückwirkungen. Wissenschaftliche Tagung zum hundertjährigen Bestehen des Zwinglivereins 1997* (ZBRG 18; Berne: Peter Lang, 2001), 143-60.
10. *HBBW.*
11. The Rev. Hastings Robinson, trans. and ed., *The Zurich Letters, comprising the correspondence of several English Bishops and others, with some of the Helvetian Reformers, during ... the Reign of Queen Elizabeth.* vol. 1-2 (The Parker Society; Cambridge: 1842-5; rpt New York/London: 1968); the Rev. Hastings Robinson, trans. and ed., *Original Letters relative to the English Reformation, written during the reigns of king Henry VIII., king Edward VI., and queen Mary: chiefly from the archives of Zurich*; vol. 1-2 (The Parker Society; Cambridge: 1846/7; rpt New York/London: 1968); *Epistolae Tigurinae de rebus potissimum ad ecclesiae Anglicanae reformationem pertinentibus conscriptae A. D. 1531-1558. Ex schedis manuscriptis in bibliotheca Tigurina aliisque servatis Parkerianae societatis auspiciis editae* (Cambridge: 1848; rpt New York/London: 1968).
12. Traugott Schiess ed., *Bullingers Korrespondenz mit den Graubündnern,* vols 1-3 (Quellen zur Schweizer Geschichte 23-25; Basle: 1904-6; reprinted Nieuwkoop: 1968).
13. *Correspondance.*
14. *Thesaurus epistolicus Calvinianus*, vol. 1-11 = Guilielmus Baum, Eduardus Cunitz, Eduardus Reuss eds, *Ioannis Calvini opera quae supersunt omnia* vol. 10b-20 (*CR* 38-48; Braunschweig: 1872-9; rpt New York/London/Frankfurt a. M.: 1964).
15. See Andreas Mühling, *Heinrich Bullingers europäische Kirchenpolitik* (ZBRG 19; Berne: Peter Lang, 2001).

dium for the exchange of news, a phenomenon characteristic of sixteenth-century correspondence, and the following remarks will focus on this aspect.

The above-mentioned thirst for news looms large in Bullinger's correspondence. Often, Bullinger and his correspondents urged one other to write about news,[16] or they excused themselves because reliable news was not at hand.[17] In many letters, news reports have the character of a separate rubric,[18] distinguished sometimes by switching from Latin to German. The reason for this may be that the source of the news was a German speaker or a German text, but on the other hand, this observation indicates that there was a German-speaking audience beyond the recipient of the letter,[19] as we will see later in more detail. Numerous letters consist of nothing but news. It might be significant for the social meaning of news exchange that more than once the traditional New Year's greetings were enriched by some topical news, as in the letter of the famous Catholic politician and historian Ägidius Tschudi.[20] The addition of news to the customary salutation leaves the impression that a news report could even have the value of being a little New Year's gift.

News, however, was not always integrated into the text of a letter. By the fifteenth century, news reports were often written on separate leaves and enclosed in or added to a letter as separate *cedula*. These attachments (*Zeitungen* in a more specific sense) were not always written by the same hand as the letter, because such news reports could have their own lives. They were passed from hand-to-hand and copied for further distribution without restraint. This makes things complicated. Usually it is not too difficult to identify and register personal letters, but with non-personal news reports it is a different matter. Often they were separated from the covering letter, with date and address missing, and even if we recognise the handwriting, the writer and the author might be different persons. So it is not surprising that these reports have been neglected by most collectors and editors such as Johann Jakob Simler in the eighteenth and Traugott Schiess in the twentieth century. When they both transcribed large portions of Bullinger's correspondence, they often passed over this kind of document. That is why news reports have not been included in the current edition of Bullinger's correspondence, for they do not have the form of a letter or at least of a supplement to a formal letter. Together with other documents that were exchanged with covering letters

16. Bullinger's impatient request for news even provoked an indignant reaction from Count Georg of Württemberg: "... wan wir hin und wider [again and again] schreiben soltenn, dörfftent wir wol ein eignen canczler darzuo [we would have to engage a special chancellor only for this]" (Matthias Erb to Bullinger, s.d.; StA, E II 361, 274). cf. Ambrosius Blarer to Bullinger, 24 June 1542 (StA, E II 343a, 222; cf. Traugott Schiess ed., *Briefwechsel der Brüder Ambrosius und Thomas Blaurer 1509-1548* vol. 2 (Freiburg i. B.: 1910), 129: "Der zeytungen halber darff es by mir kains bittens."

17. Cf. note 24.

18. An instructive example is: Girolamo Zanchi to Bullinger, 23 June 1567 (StA, E II 356, 825; cf. Schiess, *Graubünden*, 3:14/5): "Venio nunc ad nova: ..."

19. Sometimes this reason is clearly articulated: "Haec paucis omnia Germanice, ut et aliis communicare possis," Johannes Haller to Bullinger, 31 July 1547; StA, E II 359, 3067.

20. Ägidius Tschudi to Bullinger, 7 January 1551, StA, E II 335, 2181. Furthermore, this letter is an example of news exchange across confessional boundaries, an uncommon phenomenon in Bullinger's correspondence.

(such as transcripts of official records etc.), news reports remain a neglected and underestimated source.

Thanks to his excellent international connections, Bullinger was one of the best-informed men of his time. Day after day he received reports about the latest developments throughout both Europe and the far-flung corners of the globe, such as Madeira and Florida,[21] Persia, and the Crimea.[22] There is no doubt that Bullinger's main focus was on the situation of Protestants, wherever they lived, so he took a special interest in news from the battlefields of the religious wars, from the courts of the leading European dynasties, and from the Imperial Diets and other momentous conventions. At the same time, Bullinger shared with his contemporaries an appetite for the spectacular; events such as horrific crimes and accidents, atmospheric phenomena, and monstrosities greatly interested him. Many of the reports that reached Zurich were not reliable, being little more than rumours, and often they were qualified as such.[23] Not infrequently what came in one report was denied or corrected in a following one. It is not uncommon to hear complaints about the unreliability of news.[24]

Some people and some places were especially prominent as news providers within Bullinger's network. Certain of his most assiduous correspondents concentrated on this special type of communication. A good example of this was Ambrosius Blarer, the "Apostle of Swabia" who sent a large amount of news to Bullinger from his various sources. As a member of one of the prominent families of Constance, he was in close contact with the leading politicians (his brother Thomas was Burgermaster), but also with widely travelled merchants.[25] Augsburg, a city that lay at the intersection of well-established postal routes, was one of the most important market places for news exchange. Bullinger himself had intensive contacts with Augsburg,[26] even at a time when Zwinglians were no longer tolerated in the city. The same is true for Nuremberg. In all of these

---

21. Cf. Beza to Bullinger, 1 January 1567, *Correspondance*, 21; Weisz, *Bullinger Zeitungen*, 48/9.

22. Cf. Martin Frecht to Bullinger, 3 July 1539 (*HBBW* IX: 173/4).

23. "Quae hic legis, vera sunt; dubia ≈notavi [I noted doubtful news with the sign ⊣]" (Ambrosius Blarer to Bullinger, 22 September 1543; Schiess, *Blarer*, 2:202/3).

24. See, for example, Ambrosius Blarer to Bullinger, 30 April 1547 (StA, E II 357, 230; cf. Schiess, *Blarer*, 2:620): "Wiewol vyl zeytung umgetragen, wirt doch nichts bestendigs und gruntlichs angezögt, sonder dermassen alles grundloß, das ich warlich gantz und gar unlustig byn, ychtzit [something] in tanta mortalium vanitate ze schreiben. [...] Darum sollt irs nitt achten, ob ich fürohin langsamer und seltner von den löffen [events] schreib; es wills nitt mehr geben. Dorffend wol ausß Augspurg, Ulm und Nürenberg yeder in sonderhait auff ain stund widerwertig und strittend zytungen [i. e. contradictory news within the same hour] geschriben werden." Ambrosius Blarer to Bullinger, 31 May 1547 (Schiess, *Blarer*, 2:630): "Zytung mag ich äben gar nitt schreiben; so wunderbarlich unglich ding wirt geschriben. Wellt schier, das ich gar nichts horte."

25. For example, Ambrosius Blarer to Bullinger, 18 March 1544 (StA, E II 357, 715; cf. Schiess, *Blarer*, 2:240): "Es sind unser kouffleut von Franckfurt widerum kommen, sind ains tails zuo Spir gewesen, sagen von mancherlay zeytung."

26. See Hans Ulrich Bächtold, "Augsburg und Oberschwaben. Der Zwinglianismus der schwäbischen Reichsstädte im Bullinger-Briefwechsel von 1531 bis 1548–ein Überblick," *Zeitschrift für bayerische Kirchengeschichte* 64 (1995): 1-19.

places, lay members of patrician families were Bullinger's main news sources.[27] In most cases, however, church leaders of Protestant cities provided him with news reports. Most news from Italy reached Zurich through the ministers of Chur, Johannes Fabricius and Tobias Egli, who depended for their part on other correspondents such as Scipione Lentolo at Chiavenna.[28] Calvin and Beza reported extensively about the situation in France. Johannes Haller in Berne was an excellent news source thanks to his close contacts with the magistrates there.[29] Many news reports came to Zurich through Basle, where Johannes Gast and others never hesitated to forward news they received from Strasbourg and other Rhenish cities. Other reports came from the courts of Hesse or even Paris (through the French ambassador to the Swiss Confederation),[30] or directly from soldiers and commanders on the battlefields. Former students and returned refugees reported from England; their letters were often collected by book traders travelling to the Frankfurt book fair, another important centre of news exchange. Often, identical news reports reached Zurich from more than one source at the same time, offering a fascinating insight into variations in the accounts.[31]

Surprisingly, we often find news from cities where Bullinger had no correspondents, such as Antwerp and Rome. The reason for this is the appearance of the ordinary post providing non-personal news reports every week.[32] While news usually travelled along well-established routes, other reports reached Bullinger in a roundabout way.[33] We should not forget, too, that Bullinger had additional news sources in addition to his correspondence. Visitors came to see him, colleagues and other citizens showed him letters that were sent to them, and members of the magistracy gave him partial access to the official correspondence of the city.[34]

27. Prolific providers of news reports included Georg von Stetten in Augsburg (144 letters to Bullinger) and Gabriel Schlüsselberger in Nuremberg (66 letters to Bullinger).

28. The forthcoming doctoral dissertation by Emanuele Fiume treats thoroughly the important role of Scipione Lentolo in providing news from Italy to Chur and Zurich.

29. With 662 letters addressed to Bullinger, Haller heads the list of Bullinger's most frequent correspondents, followed by Ambrosius Blarer, Johannes Fabricius, Oswald Myconius and Theodore Beza.

30. Cf. "Ußzug der zyttungen, so dem herren ambassador ab dem hoff denn xviij. tag octobris [1567] zuogschriben worden" StA, E II 441, 214-16.

31. News about the Treaty of Longjumeau, for example, reached the council of Zurich through Geneva as well as through Bern, and Bullinger received confirming letters from Augsburg based on news from Antwerp ("se hoc ipsum habere per postam ex Antverpia.") See Bullinger to Tobias Egli, 9 April 1568 StA, E II 342a, 530. A report about a flood disaster in the Netherlands ends with the words: "Also schript man von Antorff [Antwerp], von Augspurg und Straßburg," Bullinger to Tobias Egli, 1 December 1570; StA, E II 342a, 615; Schiess, *Graubünden*, 3:229.

32. "Unnd nach dem wir alle 8 tag post und schreibenn aus Antorff habenn [...]" (Gabriel Schlüsselberger to Bullinger, Nuremberg, 10 October 1567; StA, E II 348, 29).

33. During a dinner Duke Christoph of Württemberg told Peter Schär that he had got news from Vienna about some weather anomalies. Schär informed Ambrosius Blarer who sent the news to Bullinger, Ambrosius Blarer to Bullinger, 7 February 1561; Schiess, *Blarer*, 3:579.

34. Sometimes Bullinger was allowed to copy news reports sent to the council; an example is found in StA, A 171, 30; E II 342a, 694b; E II 350, 203 and 511; Schiess, *Graubünden*, 3:44. Several correspondents expressed the conviction that news sent to the authorities was available to Bullinger: "Was yetzund die zeytung seyen und wie sich all ding schikind unnd zuotragind,

As a church leader with international ambitions, Bullinger used the continuous and increasing flow of news as a secure base for his far-reaching political goals. But he did not restrict the use of this precious resource to his own purposes. The exchange of news within the network of his correspondence was reciprocal. More and more, Bullinger became an outstanding middleman of news exchange. He forwarded incoming letters and reports to others, often requesting that the letters be returned to him after use.[35] Many reports were copied and redistributed by Bullinger himself or by helping hands. Probably, most of them are lost, together with so many letters that Bullinger sent to others. Only a few of them were sent back to Zurich after the death of a correspondent,[36] while others survived in foreign archives.[37] However, it is almost impossible to find them if they are not in the form of a letter signed by Bullinger.

The most distinctive form of Bullinger's news reports from the time of the Schmalkaldic war (1546) was a bulletin with short extracts from both incoming letters and oral reports. In common with other news editors of his time,[38] Bullinger usually mentioned the place where the news came from and the date. This form is also typical of the famous "Fugger-Zeitungen" that was collected in Augsburg more than twenty years later.[39] Often, the news reports were anonymous,[40] but in some cases, the name of a prominent correspondent such as Beza were cited explicitly to underline the credibility of the information. Some reports give testimony of letters to Bullinger that are lost, but on the other hand, it is evident that Bullinger himself was not always the addressee of the underlying source. Most of his bulletins were edited in German, even if the source was Latin.

---

schreibend hiemitt gantz fleyssig meine herren ewern gehaimen räthen; by denen wellt euch deren ding erkundigen, wie ich dann ongezwyfelt byn, sy euch des nichts verhaltind", Ambrosius Blarer to Bullinger, 16 July 1546; StA, E II 357, 181; cf. Heinrich Thomann to Bullinger, 21 October 1546 StA, E II 340, 163; Johannes Haab to Bullinger, 22 December 1548, StA, E II 340, 198.

35. See Bullinger's Latin note on a German "Nüw zytung von Nürenberg und Antorff" (StA, E II 355, 240/1): "Remitte hanc chartam, ubi usus fueris". Similar notes are found quite often (ZB, Ms. A 44, 26: "Dises schickend mir bald wider"; Ms. A 44, 125: "REMITTE oportune", etc.)

36. The most important examples of persons whose correspondence was sent back to Zurich after their deaths are Oswald Myconius, Joachim Vadian, Tobias Egli (StA, E II 342/342a) and Johannes Fabricius, StA, E II 373.

37. Several news reports sent by Bullinger to Landgrave Philip of Hessen are printed from the Marburg archive in Christian Gotthold Neudecker, *Urkunden aus der Reformationszeit* (Kassel: J. C. Krieger, 1836), nos 202, 204, 205. A report with news about England and Scotland preserved in the British Library is published in Robert Priebsch, *Deutsche Handschriften in England*, vol. 2 (Erlangen: 1901, rpt Hildesheim, New York, Olms, 1979), 110.

38. An early example from Bullinger's own papers is a collection of news written by Ambrosius Blarer (4 October 1542), beginning with the title "Auß Wien, 17. septembris", StA, E II 343a, 256.

39. See in particular Johannes Kleinpaul, *Die Fuggerzeitungen 1568-1605* (Abhandlungen aus dem Institut für Zeitungskunde an der Universität Leipzig 1, = Preisschriften, gekrönt und hg. von der Fürstlich Jablonowskischen Gesellschaft zu Leipzig, 49; Leipzig: 1921; rpt Vaduz: Sändig, 1992).

40. "Zytung eines guten fründts uss Saxen ..." (Weisz, *Bullinger Zeitungen*, 22); "Habend mine gute fründ uss Italia mir zugesandt" (Weisz, *Bullinger Zeitungen*, 16). Cf. Blarer's preliminary remark to a news report: "Dic scriptum esse ab amico; ne addideris Blaureri nomen", StA, E II 343a, 256.

This is a clear sign that they were intended for a broader audience, not exclusively for his fellow ministers at Zurich or in other Protestant cities.

Unfortunately, we know little about the distribution of these bulletins, but it seems, that they were not written at regular intervals or as ordered and paid work, and certainly they were not intended for the general public. Unlike a modern journalist, Bullinger did not intend to provide the masses with news. While at other places, spectacular news reports were often printed as *Flugschriften* (pamphlets) with more or less standardised titles such as *"Neue Zeitung"* or *"Gründliche Relation,"*[41] this branch of publishing was almost non-existent in Zurich, and Bullinger used this medium only exceptionally.[42] There is no doubt, however, that the magistrates took a keen interest in news from Bullinger's hand. Indeed, the cities and courts had their own networks of news exchange. They received reports from friendly governments,[43] from envoys, messengers and spies.[44] But Bullinger's network was much more widespread and active than that of the council. He was a connecting link between these different networks, and both sides profited from the exchange of information, especially in a city that was not a prominent trading centre and had neither university nor court. Many documents provided to the authorities by Bullinger can still be found in the records of the city.[45] It is not unreasonable to assume that similar co-operation existed in other Protestant cities, and that one of the implicit duties of the ministers was to act as an intelligence service or news agency in support of the Protestant authorities. This special aspect of the church-state relationship seems to have been mostly overlooked.

41. See Paul Roth, *Die neuen Zeitungen in Deutschland im 15. und 16. Jahrhundert* (Preisschriften, gekrönt und hg. von der Fürstlich Jablonowskischen Gesellschaft zu Leipzig 43; Leipzig: 1914; rpt Leipzig: Zentral Antiquariat der DDR, 1963); Pfarr, *Neue Zeitung*.

42. In the case of Ulrich Campell's report about signs that had been observed on the surface of the sun, Bullinger acted as a middleman between the author and the printer, Christoph Froschauer the Younger. See J. Candreia, "Ein "zeitungs"artiger Bericht Ulr. Campell's aus dem Jahre 1572," *Die Rheinquellen* 1 (1895): 209-25; cf. Schiess, *Graubünden*, 3:320/1; Manfred Vischer, *Bibliographie der Zürcher Druckschriften des 15. und 16. Jahrhunderts* (Bibliotheca bibliographica Aureliana 124; Baden-Baden: Koerner, 1990), no. C 847a. I am obliged to Franz Mauelshagen who kindly brought this interesting pamphlet to my attention and will discuss it at length in his forthcoming book (see n. 52).

43. The frequent exchange of news between Strasbourg and Basle is proved by the documents published in Hans Virck et al. eds, *Politische Correspondenz der Stadt Strassburg im Zeitalter der Reformation*, vols 1-5 (Strasbourg/Heidelberg: 1882-1933). In a similar way, Basle and Zurich shared politically relevant news.

44. During the Schmalkaldic War, a councillor in Zurich, Heinrich Thomann, acted as a "liaison officer" in the chancellery of the Schmalkaldic princes, providing Zurich and Bullinger with news; see Bullinger to Philip of Hesse, 6 September 1546 (Neudecker, *Urkunden aus der Reformationszeit*, no. 193); Philip of Hesse and Simon Binge to Bullinger, 12 September 1546 ZB, Ms. A 51, no. 22; Heinrich Thomann to Bullinger, 21 October/13 November/15 November 1546, StA, E II 340, 163/164a/165. Bullinger took note of the high costs caused by this special mission; see Bullinger to Oswald Myconius, 1 December 1546, StA, E II 342, 158. Reconnaissance activity in France is mentioned as the source of a report from Berne, 21 October 1567, StA, E II 355, 187.

45. Some of them are collected in StA, A 171 ("Zeitungsberichte an Heinrich Bullinger"), but they can be found also in A 170 ("Zeitungen") and–depending on the subject–in fascicles such as A 248 ("Graubünden") and A 225 ("Frankreich").

In the delicate relationship with the magistrates, the question of confidence was crucial, and sometimes this problem was reflected in Bullinger's correspondence. For example, Blarer was not pleased when he heard that one of his personal letters to Bullinger had been read to the Zurich council,[46] and on the other hand, Bullinger had to be cautious when he distributed documents he had received from officials such as the city's clerk, for example.[47] Some officials clearly disliked ministers corresponding about political matters.[48] Usually Bullinger's bulletins, which were copied and distributed more easily than personal letters, concentrate on news from outside the Swiss Confederation, and Zurich news is almost entirely absent. Of course, Bullinger informed his correspondents occasionally about events in Zurich, but he entrusted internal information to personal letters only. In his correspondence with Blarer, he even used a form of cryptography invented by the latter,[49] but this is a rare exception and Bullinger did not really get used to it.[50]

Bullinger did not only read and forward topical news, he also collected it and supported others who pursued a similar goal. He used news reports when he wrote his diary. As a historian, he was very keen on collecting all kinds of records. We have evidence of his effort to sort his rich documentation covering important political events,[51] but it is impossible to reconstruct the original order. We can see that for Bullinger, however, non-personal news reports were but one form of *Zeitungen*, together with letters and other testimonies of topical events. It has been well established by scholarship that Bullinger generously supported his colleague Johann Jakob Wick, who was establishing a huge collection of news reports, the famous *Wickiana*.[52] We find in the *Wickiana* a large number of reports

---

46. "Es hat mich nitt wenig beschwert, das ir minen langen brieff im rath haben lesen lassen; dann es ist ettlich darinn, das sich nitt geschickt hat, das es verlesen wurde", Ambrosius Blarer to Bullinger, 26 March 1544; StA, E II 357, 663; cf. Schiess, *Blarer*, 2:244.

47. Bullinger tried to prevent ill-considered diffusion of delicate news; see *HBBW* V:486: "Nitt meer ist mir ze wissen von disen zitungen. Wellist sy nitt gfarlich usßspreiten." In times of war, news dispatching was put under threat of severe punishment. See Ambrosius Blarer to Bullinger, 20 October 1546, StA, E II 357, 201; Schiess, *Blarer*, 2:524: "Ist zuo Augspurg yetz und by leyb und leben verpotten, das nieman zeytung hinauß darff schreiben."

48. One of them was the clerk of Constance, Jörg Vögeli, see Ambrosius Blarer to Bullinger, 16 July 1546, Schiess, *Blarer*, 2:472f.

49. Ibid. An example from Bullinger's hand: Bullinger to Ambrosius Blarer, 3 October 1546, Schiess, *Blarer*, 2:515.

50. Blarer noted that Bullinger mixed up two of the characters, see Ambrosius Blarer to Bullinger, 31 August/1 September 1546, Schiess, *Blarer*, 2:498.

51. Bullinger often noted the subject(s) of a news report on the back of the sheet, see StA, E II 342, 287a^v. Sometimes, he collected different items in a fascicle and noted the content on a separate leaf, see StA, E II 350, 275 and 273: "1. Wirtenberger frid. 2. Nüw zytung vom Türggen. 3. etc."

52. See Franz Mauelshagen, *Johann Jakob Wicks "Wunderbücher." Reformierter Wunderglaube im Wandel der Geschichtsschreibung* (Zurich: Chronos, in press). Bullinger's important contribution to the creation and growth of Wick's collection has been underlined previously by Matthias Senn, *Johann Jakob Wick (1522-1588) und seine Sammlung von Nachrichten zur Zeitgeschichte* (Mitteilungen der Antiquarischen Gesellschaft in Zürich 46/2; Zurich: Leemann, 1974), esp. 25, 38-9. 47-50.

provided by Bullinger, and after Bullinger's death, his own collection of *portenta* was handed over to Wick.[53]

By this point we have a pretty clear idea of Bullinger's role in international news exchange, but we need to return to Weisz' thesis that Bullinger was "one of the founding fathers of modern journalism."[54] There is no doubt that Bullinger's letters and papers are an outstanding source for the study of early-modern news exchange because the Zurich *Antistes* was deeply engaged in collecting and providing topical news. But as we have seen, other church leaders and learned men did a similar job: Christoph Scheurl, Joachim Camerarius, Johannes and Jakob Sturm and many others wrote innumerable news reports. The most prominent example is Philip Melanchthon, who made Wittenberg a main centre for news, and in many respects his correspondence resembles Bullinger's as far as news exchange is concerned.[55] According to Weisz, Bullinger was among the first who not only collected news to bring it to a broader audience, but tried to influence the opinion of the recipients through his reports. But similar observations can be made about other correspondence of his time, and it is not easy to verify the assertion that Bullinger was uniquely important, for the authorship of many news reports remains uncertain. To give an example: Weisz presents a detailed report about the massacre of St Bartholomew's day,[56] but it is probably not Bullinger's work. We have to assume this, because in several of his letters Bullinger mentions a report written in French that he received through Ulisse Martinengo and that was translated in Zurich.[57] Of course, Bullinger's own reports are written from a definite Protestant perspective, and he does not hide his sympathies and antipathies. While news bulletins typically reveal much less of the author's feelings than personal letters do, interwoven pious reflections are not uncommon.[58] On the other hand, sarcastic remarks occur only occasionally.[59] As far as I can see, most of Bullinger's bulletins are not merely propaganda; usually they are condensed but accurate summaries of the underlying sources.

53. Franz Mauelshagen, "'...die portenta et ostenta mines lieben Herren vnsers säligen...'". Nachlassstücke Bullingers im 13. Buch der Wickiana," *Zwingliana* 28 (2001): 73-117.

54. "Erzvater des modernen Journalismus," Weisz, *Bullinger Zeitungen*, 61.

55. The results of any research about Bullinger's news publishing have to be compared with the dissertation of Richard Grasshoff (cf. note 1), which is an old and little-known but fundamental study of Melanchthon's correspondence under the aspect of news exchange.

56. Weisz, *Bullinger Zeitungen*, 51-60; cf. Fritz Büsser, "Die Bartholomäusnacht. Eindrücke und Auswirkungen im reformierten Zürich," *Neue Zürcher Zeitung*, 27 August 1972, no. 398, 49/50.

57. Bullinger to Tobias Egli, 3 October 1574, Schiess, *Graubünden*, 3:368; Bullinger to Hans Rudolf Bullinger, 4 October 1572 (ZB, Ms. F 37, 432b).

58. ZB, Ms. A 44, 73: "Dorumb ists eewig waar: 'Nolite confidere in principibus, in filiis hominum, in quibus non est salus' [Psalm 145, 2f Vulgate]. Es kann und wirdt Christus nüt des minder sin volck erhallten. Dem sye eer und prys." Highly suggestive titles given by Bullinger occur occasionally, StA, E II 355, 196: "Grosse tyrannj des hertzogen zuo Saffoy wider ettliche siner armen christen."

59. StA, E II 355, 120r (marginal note commenting on news about a massing of Turkish troops): "Lernend den wäg [study the route], lernend, lieben Türggen, lernend!" Another example of sarcastic comment in Bullinger to Joachim Vadian, 20 June 1541, see Emil Arbenz/Hermann Wartmann eds., *Die Vadianische Briefsammlung der Stadtbibliothek St. Gallen*, vol. 7 (Mitteilungen zur vaterländischen Geschichte 30a; St. Gallen: 1913), 98-9, no. 70.

As an outstanding example of Bullinger's journalistic skills, Weisz cites a strikingly vivid and graphic account of the horrible death of several noblemen whose carnival costumes caught fire.[60] However, Weisz missed the fact that the source of this account was not a letter, but an oral report of a citizen of Zurich who had visited the stepmother of one of the victims.[61] For a critical assessment of Bullinger's journalistic qualities, we have to refer rather to documents he wrote as an eyewitness to the events. An interesting example is his accounts of a lightening induced fire that burnt one of the towers of his Grossmünster church in 1572. There are at least two different reports that were sent to colleagues at Schaffhausen and Chur.[62] Interestingly enough, they are not identical, although they agree on all the main details. Not surprisingly, Bullinger interprets the event as a visitation by the Almighty, but his reports reveal not so much bewilderment as objective observation. In his news reports, as in his historical writings, Bullinger proves himself to be a calm and reliable observer of the events of his time. In the field of news publishing, he was not as innovative as Weisz thought him to be. Much more than a news reporter, he was a collector and news editor, and thanks to the clever use of his astounding correspondence network, he definitely belongs to the notable forerunners of modern journalism.

60. Weisz, *Bullinger Zeitungen*, 63-4.

61. See Felix Burckhardt, "Die böse Fastnacht auf Schloss Waldenburg" in *Aus der Welt des Buches. Festgabe zum 70. Geburtstag von Georg Leyh* (Zentralblatt für Bibliothekswesen, Beiheft 75; Leipzig: Harrassowitz, 1950), 273-82.

62. See Bullinger's report to Johann Konrad Ulmer, 9 May 1572, Stadtbibliothek Schaffhausen, Ministerialbibliothek, Cod. 127, 591/2, no. 198; printed in Eduard Scherrer, "Der Brand des Grossmünster-Glockenturms in Zürich am 7. Mai 1572," *Neue Zürcher Zeitung*, 21 March 1937, no. 513; Wick's copy: ZB, Ms. F 21, 140r-141r, and the report sent to Tobias Egli on the same day, Schiess, *Graubünden*, 3:337/8, published previously in *Zwingliana* 2/8 (1908): 254-5. For an insightful discussion of both reports see Mauelshagen, *Wunderbücher*.

11

Heinrich Bullinger as Church Politician

Andreas Mühling

Introduction

In March 1539 attempts by Martin Bucer and Philip Melanchthon to persuade the Swiss to accept the *Wittenberg Accord*, a consensus on the disputed question of the Lord's Supper, finally came to nothing. On 8 March Heinrich Bullinger was forced to accept that the negotiations on the acceptance of the *Accord* had failed. Bullinger opined that if it were a condition of the *Accord* that no one could speak the truth any longer or raise his voice in opposition to Martin Luther, then he wanted nothing to do with it; Luther, like all other mortals was capable of error and should be made aware of these errors.[1] This assessment serves to illustrate the extent to which the relationship between the two theologians and their church politics were burdened by differences both substantial and personal. After two years of fruitless negotiations over the acceptance of the *Wittenberg Accord* by the Swiss, the trust between the two camps had been ruptured completely. Where once the two had engaged in discussion in the spirit of theological fraternity, there remained now only damaged personal relations. Neither side wished to pursue any further dialogue over the disputed question of the Lord's Supper.

In 1544 the argument over the Eucharist broke out again. After aggressive, and in part very personal attacks by Luther on the Zurich ministers in August 1543, he increased the heat further in September 1544.[2] It was in this month that Luther's *Short Confession of the Holy Sacrament* appeared, in which the reformer drew a clear line between himself and the Zurich theologians, bringing all sense of commonality to an end.[3] Luther emphasised that "I completely condemn and denounce the fanatics and the enemies of the sacrament, Karlstadt, Zwingli, Oecolampadius, Stenkefeld (sic) and your successors in Zurich and wherever they are."[4]

---

1. Letter of Bullinger to Calvin dated 8.3.1539 in *CO* 10, no. 162. On the possible causes of this breakdown and where blame should be attributed see Martin Friedrich, "Heinrich Bullinger und die Wittenberger Konkordie," *Zwingliana* 24 (1997): 59-79, in particular 59-61.

2. See also Martin Brecht, *Martin Luther* vol. 3: *Die Erhaltung der Kirche 1532-1546* (Stuttgart: Calwer, 1987), 322.

3. *D. Martin Luthers Werke* (Weimar: 1883-), 54:141-67.

4. Ibid. 141.

At the end of August and even before the text went to print, Melanchthon informed Bullinger of the content of the work, shocked by the harshness of Luther's "dreadful polemical writing." As Luther revived the war over the Lord's Supper Melanchthon believed that even he himself was in no little danger.[5] This assault from Luther placed the Zurichers in a very difficult position. Not only could this condemnation have political consequences in the Empire where it was possible, for example, that Zurich writings would be forbidden, but the consequences could be felt throughout the whole of Europe. Bullinger believed that it was now essential that he take action. In 1543 and at the urging of Bucer and Melanchthon he had remained silent in the face of Luther's accusations, but now he could no longer stand by and observe the ramifications of a one-sided polemical war for the Reformation. On 3 December 1544 Bullinger had assured Melanchthon that the Zurichers would await Luther's text and reply to it promptly. But now he continued, they could no longer remain impassive, for Luther had repeatedly attacked Zwingli and the Zurichers. The Zurich clergy would not follow Luther's pattern of excessive aggression, but would respond to him in measured tones. Above all it would be made clear that they had nothing in common with the radical sects.[6] The following day Bullinger drafted the Zurich response: it should be asserted that Luther had made common cause with the Roman church and his position on the Lord's Supper was to be refuted with reference to scripture and the apostolic fathers. Bullinger proposed drawing up distinct lists of true and false doctrine which would enable the reader to make his/her own decisions. And the reader was to be very strongly encouraged to make that decision.[7]

On 12 March 1545 Bullinger's answer was printed in the form of the official confession of the Zurich church and its preachers.[8] The text had already been accepted by a synod of the Zurich church, with both the knowledge and approval of the council.[9] Typically, Bullinger also put the occasion to the service of church politics. He sent the text of the Zurich confession, with an accompanying letter, to a number of influential figures and groupings. The accompanying letters were all identical.[10] Bullinger sought the support of men such as Duke Ulrich of Württemberg, the later Palatinate elector Ottheinrich and the most important figure in the church politics of the period, Landgrave Philip of Hesse.

---

5. Letter of Melanchthon to Bullinger dated 31.8.1544, StA, E II 347, 1400. On 31.10.1544 Bucer informed Bullinger about Luther's *Kurtzes Bekenntnis*.

6. Bullinger to Melanchthon, 3 December 1544, StA, E II 346, 143.

7. Bullinger to Joseph Macarius, 4 December 1544, StA, E II 346, 143b.

8. *HBBibl* I, no. 161. See also the edition and commentary on the Zurich confession by Andreas Mühling, "Das Zürcher Bekenntnis von 1545" in E. Busch et al. eds, *Edition Reformierter Bekenntnisschriften* vol. I/2 (forthcoming).

9. See the letter to Philip of Hesse dated 12 March 1545, StA, E II 337, 366.

10. In addition to the copy of the Confession sent to Philip of Hesse (StA, E II 337, 366), copies were received by, amongst others, the Council of Berne on 12 March (StA, E II 337, 367) and the clergy of Berne (StA, E II 337, 368), the clergy of Neuchatel (*CO* 12, Nr. 622), Martin Bucer (StA, E II 346, 145), Pfalzgraf Ottheinrich (StA, E II 337, 371), Duke Ulrich of Wurttenberg (on 15 March 1545; Stuttgart HStA, A 63, Bündel 7; see Immanuel Kammerer, *Schweizer Quellen zur württembergischen Reformationsgeschichte* (1957), 24f. and the town council of Frankfurt am Main (StA, E II 337, 370).

It pains us greatly that Doctor Luther has written so forcefully against us, who are innocent, and has published this text. We regret in particular the damage which is done to simple Christians who are infuriated by this strife and in particular that we who preach one Lord Jesus Christ from one Gospel are drawn into a lengthy quarrel with one another over his holy sacrament and symbols. We greatly regret that the attempts by your Princely Grace and other pious Christian princes, estates, and cities, who have sought in both a friendly and peaceful manner to influence Doctor Luther, have been without success, so that after some years he has chosen to renew the battle. We Zurichers would rather have had peace and would have remained silent as we have done up until now, although we have perhaps been silent for longer than has been good for us. But the silence and patience we have demonstrated has only had the effect that in his last confession Luther has damned us as heretics and has insulted the faith and honour of our faithful ancestors, who were honourable Christian men, and our churches. Now that Luther's writings have been printed honour, duty, and our office demand that we reply. We have not done this for the Zurich church alone and without reference to our magistrates and the councillors, but rather we have acted with their knowledge and blessing, for all the faithful here are outraged by Luther's appalling dishonouring of the living and the dead.... As our teaching is drawn closely from the first apostolic holy church, Dr Luther ought not to separate himself from us and provoke an unfounded split in the church.

As your princely grace is also mentioned in our reply—we wrote there of the Marburg Colloquy—we send you most humbly our answer and our confession with the earnest request that your grace kindly receive this text of your servants, and further that you read it when time allows. We beseech you further that for the sake of God and his holy word you ensure that our confession and response and indeed all our other writings are not prohibited in your lands and that we who are innocent are not condemned, unheard, as heretics. Your honourable lords and superiors permit that in your towns, lands, villages and countryside all of Luther's books, as well as those of our other opponents, are sold and can be bought. We advise others to read these works. It is only right that both sides should be heard and that no one is suppressed without first having been read. We trust God and his clear eternal truth, that all the faithful will recognise that neither our churches nor we are damned people such as Dr Luther wishes to convince the whole world. God be merciful to him.

Bullinger's political goal was that the Landgrave should ensure that neither the "Zwinglian" confession be prohibited nor "Zwinglian" writings forbidden. Above all he strove to ensure that the Landgrave put all his political weight behind ensuring that Zurich theology and writings not be declared unlawful in Electoral Saxony and the Duchy of Saxony.

One aspect is clearly evident in Bullinger's approach and method of argument: by March 1545 it was no longer his intention to engage Luther in further debate about the Eucharist. His intentions lay wholly in the realm of church politics. It was crucial to Bullinger to represent the Zurich church during these weeks to those with political influence as "orthodox"; the Zurich theology of the Eucharist must be proven to be scriptural and indeed superior to that of the Lutherans. Only if persuasive proof of the orthodoxy of the Zurichers in the controversial and politically sensitive question of the Lord's Supper could be given to the political authorities in the Empire would the Zurich church and its followers be protected from potentially disastrous political implications.

On the Concept of "Church Politics"

This brief account of the dramatic confrontation which comprised the final stage of the violent clash between Martin Luther and Heinrich Bullinger serves as an example of the close connection between theological debate and its political consequences for the church, more broadly stated between theology and its historical context. Church history without reference to its political, social, and economic context runs the risk of turning into a simple history of ideas. Conversely, church history which fails to acknowledge the theological motives of the protagonists and their impact can be little more than a poor version of very generalised historical writing.

Church politics are therefore inseparably linked to both theological debate and ecclesiastical development in equal measure.[11] In other words, theology, church, and politics are constants which vary in their relationship with each other and which combine to determine church history. Church politics are determined by these reciprocal relationships and incorporate three elements: the concept cannot be applied simply to the first of these alone–the politics of the state in relation to the church–but must also be seen in terms of, secondly, the political activities of church officials in relation to the state, and, thirdly, political activities which take place within the church itself. The political activities of church officials, whether in dealing with the state or within the church, are informed by theological debate and its practical implementation. Church history embraces this tension between politics and theology and is characterised by conflict when theological knowledge is contested and its implementation therefore challenged, as for example in the case of church discipline. The events which led to the formation of the Zurich Confession illustrate this point clearly. Bullinger, the church politician, acted politically, representing his church in the debate with the state; at the same time he was striving to achieve unanimity within the church over its teachings. As theologian Bullinger was a church politician, as a church politician he was a Christian answerable for his theology and his church.

Rather than simply describe here a number of individual issues which serve to demonstrate this concept in action, in this paper I intend first to examine the circumstances of Bullinger's, the church politician's, relationship with the authorities in Zurich and, secondly, to consider the fundamental principles which governed his decisions and actions as a church politician.

11. On this term see Joachim Mehlhausen, "Kirchenpolitik. Erwägungen zu einem undeutlichen Wort," *Zeitschrift für Theologie und Kirche* 85 (1988): 275-302.

I. On the Relationship Between the Church and the Political Authorities in Zurich after 1531

The defeat at Kappel in 1531 signalled the end of the political plan based on civic alliance which had been created by Zwingli. Zurich's vision of becoming a leading Protestant power on the European stage had vanished. The alliances were dissolved and Zurich shied away from the politics of expansion. In late 1531 it was unclear whether the Reformation in Zurich which had been successfully pursued under Zwingli would even survive.[12] In light of the highly precarious nature of this political situation for the Zurich church, the church politics which Bullinger now inherited were extremely challenging. In December 1531 and for the sake of internal stability the council promised its rural territories, in article four of the "Kappel Letter," that it would place the clergy, who were widely held to be responsible for the war, under its control; the magistrates promised that the clergy would be kept away from all political matters.[13] Having made this promise the council then sought to put it into effect in their relationship with the Zurich clergy. The principal change which the council foresaw was in limitations placed on the preaching carried out in Zurich. Their intention was not just to respond to accusations that the warmongering clergy were responsible for the outbreak of the war, but also to take this response a step further by integrating the Zurich church into the institutions of the state where it would occupy a subservient position.

The new head of the Zurich church had to act without delay. Immediately after taking up office on 13 December 1531, Bullinger, in his inaugural address, promised that the clergy would be loyal to the political authorities in order to preserve peace and calm within the Christian community. Nevertheless, he reserved the right to condemn error without respect of person or status, according to the standards set by scripture. He insisted that scripture could not be fettered and that the freedom of the sermon was a cornerstone of the church.[14] Bullinger assured the magistrates that the clergy would not involve themselves in temporal affairs, and acknowledged the right of the authorities to intervene where criticism by the clergy was excessive: "if we do too much of this, we shall gladly endure our punishment."[15] This was a shrewd political maneuver on the part of the young leader. The council, delighted by the ecclesiastical promise of restraint in political af-

---

12. *HBRG* III:250f.; see also Hans Ulrich Bächtold, "Bullinger und die Krise der Zürcher Reformation im Jahre 1532" in Ulrich Gäbler/Erland Herkenrath eds, *Heinrich Bullinger 1504-1575. Gesammelte Aufsätze zum 400. Todestag*, vol. 1: *Leben und Werk* (ZBRG 7; Zurich: TVZ, 1975), 269-89; Gottfried W. Locher, *Die Zwinglische Reformation im Rahmen der europäischen Kirchengeschichte* (Göttingen: M. Hensius, 1979), 537-9; Carl Bernhard Hundeshagen, "Die Gestaltung des Verhältnisses zwischen Staat und Kirche in Zürich unmittelbar nach Zwinglis Tod" in Carl Bernhard Hundeshagen, *Beiträge zur Kirchenverfassungsgeschichte und Kirchenpolitik insbesondere des Protestantismus*, vol. 1 (Wiesbaden: Minerva, 1864), 258-87; Rudolf Mau, *Evangelische Bewegung und frühe Reformation 1521-1532* (Kirchengeschichte in Einzeldarstellungen II/5; Leipzig: Evangelische Verlagsanstalt, 2000), 231-3.

13. See *HBRG* III: 284-91.

14. Ibid., 293-6.

15. Ibid., 294.

fairs, fundamentally accepted Bullinger's position. Thus the basis for further discussions had been created.

Further discussions were indeed necessary. The council had not grasped the theological implications of Bullinger's arguments. A central issue was impressed upon his audience by the new head of the Zurich church in his acceptance speech: the freedom of the sermon–and therefore also Bullinger's understanding, construed from such preaching, of the "office of guardianship"–formed an unassailable foundation stone of a Christian church. He would not be shifted from this belief and was prepared to stand up to the magistrates, however sharp the conflict. On 27 June 1532 he warned the council that it was greatly in error in its commands to the clergy only to treat "gentle matters." It was, according to Bullinger, the "prophetic obligation" of the preachers to point out wrongdoings which were against the command of scripture, even when the magistrates ordered them otherwise. If the magistracy continued to demand "unpolitical preaching," then the clergy would be obliged to revoke their obedience to the magistrates.[16]

In the years 1531-2 the case Bullinger presented to the council not only successfully defended the church against the encroachments of the secular authority but also ensured that the church retained the right to preach freely. This confrontation did, however, lead into a debate about the freedom and limitations of preaching which would last for decades; again and again particular events made it necessary to examine precisely what could be covered by the term "too much," as used by Bullinger in his inaugural speech in 1531.

The arguments which Bullinger set out before the council also formed an agenda which he sought to see acknowledged within the Zurich church. In March 1532 he had undertaken a robust discussion of church/state relations with Zwingli's close friend and colleague Leo Jud. It is striking that this discussion clearly anticipated the future debate between Zurich and Geneva over ecclesiology. In his dispute with Jud, Bullinger repeated the convictions he had put before the council.[17] After the defeat of Kappel Jud had lost all trust in the impact of the Word of God on the Christian magistracy and sought, therefore, a strict separation of ecclesiastical and magisterial powers.[18] Bullinger countered Jud by seeking an intertwining of the powers of the church and the council. In the course of this dispute Bullinger formulated a model for the relationship between church and state that would characterise his church politics through subsequent decades. The totality of the Christian "citizens," according to Bullinger, constituted both the community and the state. Excommunication is fundamentally a matter for the church community, but must be implemented by the secular authorities. This transfer of competency from church to lay authorities is necessary because the community lacks the necessary executive powers. Additionally, in cases of conflict with very powerful individuals the church would be at risk of division and

16. See *HBRG* III: 322-9.

17. Letter of Bullinger to Leo Jud dated 15.3.1532 *HBBW*: II, no. 74; see also Carl Pestalozzi, *Heinrich Bullinger: Leben und ausgewählte Schriften. Nach handschriftlichen und gleichzeitigen Quellen* (Leben und ausgewählte Schriften der Väter und Begründer der reformirten Kirche V; Elberfeld: Friderichs, 1858), 96-98; Locher, *Zwinglische Reformation*, 549.

18. See the letter from Jud to Bullinger from the beginning of March 1532, *HBBW* II, no. 70 after the letter of 15.3.1532, *HBBW* II, no. 75. Also Pestalozzi, *Heinrich Bullinger*, 95f. 98.

split. For Bullinger, above all the freedom of the sermon and the office of prophetic guardian must be undisputed.

Thus by mid-1532 the roles of council and *Antistes* had been clearly articulated. The council could reckon on the loyalty of the clergy and would therefore work towards the building of the Protestant state; the clergy would eschew political involvement as long as they retained their prophetic freedom.[19] Bullinger's conception of the relationship between church and council was fundamentally shaped by his view of the unity of the prophet office and the magistrates, from which the *respublica christiana* would emerge. Throughout his life Bullinger would retain this vision of close co-operation, even through it was at times marred by conflict.

II. Bullinger as Church Politician

Hans Ulrich Bächtold's 1982 work, *Heinrich Bullinger vor dem Rat. Zur Gestaltung und Verwaltung des Zürcher Staatswesens in den Jahren 1531 bis 1575*, which examined the addresses given by Bullinger before the Zurich council, marked a crucial entry into the thicket of church politics.[20] Using these addresses Bächtold was able to demonstrate how the decision-making process between the council and the church developed. This work, however, needs to be supplemented by further, archive-based studies which will pick up on the issues raised by Bächtold and develop them. We still await both an account of individual episodes which could throw additional light on Bullinger's objectives and also detailed analysis of the determinative themes of his church politics in Zurich and in the Swiss confederation.

In order to address Bullinger's activities on the wider European stage, I have developed various "models" which can be recognised within Bullinger's church politics.[21] In working through the relevant correspondence I was struck by the steadfast consistency in Bullinger's argumentation, actions and objectives over many years. Bullinger's position in church politics is typified by a recurring interaction of analysis, argumentation, action and intent; I have designated this his "behavioural model."[22] The consistency with which Bullinger maintained these principles and applied them as required to individual situations is remarkable. These principles alone were to be employed in order to achieve his political goals. This self-imposed limitation on the political tools available to Bullinger would in the long term save him much time and effort, although this was at the expense of the flexibility that would prove necessary if he were to achieve his objectives.

Research on Bullinger in the twentieth century noted with astonishment the remarkable quantity of information gathered by its subject over his lifetime; Bull-

19. Bullinger to Jud, 15.3.1532, *HBBW* II, no. 74; Pestalozzi, *Heinrich Bullinger*, 97f.

20. Hans Ulrich Bächtold, *Heinrich Bullinger vor dem Rat. Zur Gestaltung und Verwaltung des Zürcher Staatswesens in den Jahren 1531 bis 1575* (ZBRG 12; Berne/Frankfurt a. Main: Peter Lang, 1982).

21. Andreas Mühling, *Heinrich Bullingers europäische Kirchenpolitik* (ZBRG 19; Berne: Peter Lang, 2001).

22. Ibid., 271-4.

inger was one of those figures of the sixteenth century who recognised the great value of a well-functioning information network.[23] Although Bullinger rarely left the city of Zurich, which was his area of responsibility as *Antistes*, he made great efforts to obtain current and reliable information about the political, ecclesiastical, social and economic circumstances in those lands with which he was involved.[24] He was also eager for background information on the individuals with whom he dealt. If he were to be successful, Bullinger needed to know something of the lives of these men and the world in which they operated; only then would he be able to select the relevant behavioural model from his armoury and apply it to the concrete political situation. Consistently, however, one goal was at the forefront of Bullinger's intentions: to strengthen the Reformed churches throughout Europe which were founded on the model of Zurich and to support and, when possible, to extend such communities. Bullinger's first step was always to examine the political situation in the geographical area with which he was concerned. He would then select the behavioural model that seemed best suited to the realities of the situation. In examining his work over the span of his career, we can detect four principal versions of this behavioural model.

For the Protestant lands Bullinger usually based his response on an "open" model which looked to the common efforts of all evangelical communities and estates while leaving to the side divisive and disputed doctrinal questions. This framework was particularly suited to the political realities of the Empire, where the quarrel over recognition of the *Augsburg Confession* had seriously damaged relations between Lutherans and Reformed in the Protestant states. The rupture had been intensified by the legal exclusion of the Reformed in the Peace of Augsburg of 1555. In order to counter the threat of political and religious isolation for Reformed Christians and their communities, Bullinger sought to work with Lutheran authorities, as in Hesse or the Duchy of Württemberg. He argued that Reformed communities would only be tolerated in Lutheran territories when an organisational alliance of Protestant communities was in place. Bullinger's goal for these lands was therefore the creation of a political union of the Protestant churches based on evangelical freedom and reciprocal tolerance and the eschewing of sensitive doctrinal issues such as the *Augsburg Confession*. How this "open" approach to confessional relations should be implemented, whether by the magistrates or, perhaps initially, through negotiations between theologians, was for Bullinger a matter to be determined by local circumstance. The crucial issue was this: he took for granted the good will of the Lutheran authorities to work for confessional unity, believing that this attitude would be evident when the authorities no longer made their regular accusations of heresy against the Zurich congregations. The Reformed church would need to be deemed "semiofficial" or be tolerated, at least tacitly, by the authorities.[25]

23. Leo Weisz, *Die Bullinger Zeitungen. Zur Halbjahrhundertfeier des Vereins der schweizerischen Presse dargebracht vom Journalistischen Seminar der Universität Zürich und von der Buchdruckerei Berichthaus in Zürich* (Zurich: Berichthaus, 1933), 3.65; Fritz Büsser, "Die Überlieferung von Heinrich Bullingers Briefwechsel" in *HBBW* I: 7-21.

24. See the essay by Rainer Henrich in this volume.

25. There are numerous examples. See Bullinger's letters to Philip of Hesse dated 20 March 1560, StA, E II 338, 1581; to Duke Christoph of Württemberg, 28 March 1560, StA, E II 338,

Where a Protestant authority appeared receptive to the Reformed church, Bullinger applied an "internal" behavioural model, a response with a very conscious theological basis. While the application of the "open" model in Lutheran territories meant rapprochement in ecclesiastical politics which steered clear of debated dogmatic issues, in areas which favoured the Reformed church more strongly Bullinger planned that the ecclesiastical diversity of "Zwinglians" and "Calvinists" should be guaranteed within a "Reformed Church" founded on the Word of God. His political goal was therefore not the organisational alliance of Zwinglians and Calvinists but rather the creation of a Reformed church polity. This was his objective when he was drawn into political discussions about the church in territories such as Sayn-Wittgenstein, Reichenweier-Horburg and the Electoral Palatinate, and also in England. In these areas he also provided political authorities and congregations with support for the creation of a Reformed church polity. Bullinger advocated, where possible, the replication of Zurich synodal orders which would ensure that the secular authorities had power to issue directives and supervise the church on earth. As both concerned party and advisor in this process of Reformed church building, Bullinger held out the Zurich church as a model, but he did not insist that it was applied wholesale in a new setting. Recognition of variety within the Reformed church family was an integral element of the "internal" behavioural model. He accepted that individual territories had the freedom to choose between the various forms of theology, church, and political and social life contained within the Reformed tradition, but he was wary that this decision should not be linked to claims to theological exclusivity.[26]

The model which Bullinger developed for France and, in part, for Poland would have almost no political impact in the early modern period. This version was founded on toleration and was designed to be applied by Catholic authorities; the goal was the toleration of all Christian churches that were founded on the confession of the old church. An example can be found in the dedicatory address to Henry II of France in the *"Perfectio christianorum"* of 1551. Bullinger sought to generate a politically viable basis for toleration from beliefs common to both Reformed and Catholics–faith in Christ and baptism. It was his hope that the peaceful co-existence of Lutherans, Reformed and Catholics within one state and protected by the Christian authorities would secure the future of Reformed congregations in those territories where they were currently under threat.[27]

The fourth and final model was based on pastoral care. Much of Bullinger's time and effort was given to consideration, both oral and written, of pastoral care. His correspondence often addressed pastoral issues and this advice was designed to have long-term political impact. With this model Bullinger addressed a more limited audience, providing advice and pastoral care for individuals and groups,

---

1580, to Philip of Hesse dated 27 June 1546, StA, E II 337, 375 and to the Dukes Erbach, 4 November 1559, ZB, Ms S 96, 30.

26. Evidence of this can be found in Bullinger's letter of 28.10.1568 to Elector Friedrich III, StA, E II 341, 3615 (printed in *Schweizerische Stimmen aus dem Reformationszeitalter*, 1-12), the letter of 1.6.1570 to Petrus Dathenus dated 1.6.1570 (German translation, ibid., 12-20), the letter dated 4.1.1551 to Edward VI of England, Oxford BL, Ms Smith 67, 13 and in the dedicatory preface to Edward VI in *Sermonum Decas Quarta* (Zurich: 1550), *HBBibl* I, no. 181.

27. *HBBibl* I, no. 249.

often refugees, who might at some point in the future be in a position to influence political decision-making in their homeland.

The various models outlined briefly here provided the framework for Bullinger's contribution to the debate over church politics throughout Europe. Bullinger's dominance within the Zurich church also had its downside, however. The concentration of all aspects of church politics in Zurich–the creation of policy, its content, implementation and management–on one individual proved to be a severe structural weakness. Within the Zurich church there was little consideration of the course of European church politics, nor was there heated discussion of effective resolutions for individual cases. The *Antistes*, who had begun to adopt the role of Patriarch at an early age, was given a free hand on the European stage. There was little thought given to delegating aspects of church policy which would have passed individual responsibility to members of the group of willing students and colleagues who surrounded Bullinger, nor was any consideration given to the increasingly urgent issue of Bullinger's successor. As a result structural misjudgments in the models that Bullinger applied to international affairs threatened to have major implications for the status of Zurich church policy in Europe.

As early as the 1540s it was evident that by founding his church politics on reciprocal toleration by the various confessional groupings, Bullinger had seriously limited their efficacy. Whatever model Bullinger chose to apply to events, it was essential that all parties were willing to participate in discussion and to acknowledge their potential partners in any dialogue. With the onset of confessionalisation, however, "toleration" and "acknowledgment" were concepts which no longer seemed relevant to contemporary church affairs. There was therefore an unreal element to Bullinger's church politics. Remarkably untouched by the phenomenon of confessionalisation, Bullinger, his worldview formed by the dynamics of the Reformation in the 1520s, sought to realise an "evangelical" church renewed by the word of God. His fundamental ecclesiological starting point did not enable him even to begin to comprehend the attitude that regarded the "Reformed" and "Lutheran" churches as confessional "parties."[28]

This lack of comprehension, which stemmed from Bullinger's theological starting point, resulted in several decades of conflict and setbacks in his church politics. Unwilling to act outwith the inflexible boundaries of these different behavioural models, Bullinger made demands that would not be met without resistance. Yet without the "political toleration" of those congregations based on the model of Zurich which was desired by Bullinger, his political demands, whether based on the "open" model favoured in the Empire or the "tolerant" model designed for France, could not even get off the ground. Even his attempts to apply the "internal" model proved very hard to realise. In the Electoral Palatinate, Bullinger's theologically rooted conviction that diversity within the family of the Reformed church should be acknowledged and accepted was undermined by Geneva's claims to exclusivity. In England, however, political intransigence–

---

28. See Fritz Büsser, "Zürich–'Die Stadt auf dem Berg'," *Zwingliana* 25 (1998): 21-42, esp. 30-33.

although without abandoning the theological basis–alone enabled Bullinger to defend his position successfully.

On balance, however, it must be borne in mind that despite all the various set-backs he faced, Bullinger was able to achieve his principal goal–the survival and growth of the Reformed congregations created according to the Word of God and, whenever possible, in imitation of the Zurich model. Following his appointment as *Antistes* at an early age, Bullinger successfully overcame the crises of internal Zurich politics. In the same decade and as leader of the Zurich church he also become a player on the European stage, and thanks to his efforts the Zurich church was able to exercise influence over the formation of theology and church politics through difficult years for the Reformed church. Even after the death of Zwingli, the opinion of Zurich continued to be highly valued both in Reformed churches throughout Europe and by numerous Protestant politicians. Although it has been repeatedly asserted that by the early 1550s at the latest the initiative within the Reformed movement had moved from Zurich to Geneva, it is now evident that this was not the case. Although the presbyterial-synodal structure which emanated from Geneva was rapidly adopted elsewhere, this could not depose Bullinger from the position that his theological and ecclesiastical author-ity lent him, reinforced by his intricate web of informants and correspondents situated throughout Europe. Neither Calvin nor Beza could effectively challenge the status of the Zurich church as a centre for the Reformed church alongside Geneva.

What then is the legacy of Bullinger's church politics? There remains the im-age of a man who followed his goals without wavering, even if he did misjudge the realities of the political situation. It is also evident that Bullinger's intentions in church politics and ecclesiology were out of step with the times. Bullinger's demands for "improvement and the maintenance of good order," in other words for the spread of the gospel within society and within the decrees and institutions which governed, were integrally linked for Bullinger to his demands for recipro-cal acknowledgment and tolerance by the Christian churches. His church policy may have been out of step with his times, but for Bullinger it was the fundamen-tal expression of Christian *Praxis Pietatis*, whether within the institutions of the church or in determining the nature of church–state relations. By insisting that this formed a vital and unwavering element in church politics, Bullinger was well ahead of his times.

12

Bullinger's *Der Christlich Eestand*: Marriage and the Covenant

Carrie E. Euler

Heinrich Bullinger's *Der Christlich Eestand* (1540) was the most extensive vernacular treatise on marriage published by a first or second generation Protestant reformer.[1] In it, Bullinger not only discussed topics central to the Protestant reform of marriage, such as clerical marriage, parental consent, consanguinity, adultery and divorce, but he also wrote extensively on the divine origins of marriage, the love and affection that should exist between husband and wife, the division of household duties, and raising children.[2] In contrast, Luther's most important vernacular piece on marriage was much shorter than Bullinger's, and touched on only a few of these issues.[3] Johannes Brenz's more lengthy vernacular treatise on the subject treated extensively issues like the need for parental consent to marry, consanguinity, polygamy, adultery, and divorce, but Brenz did not write about the origins, virtues, or daily routines of married life.[4] Furthermore, none of Bullinger's Reformed colleagues publish vernacular sermons or treatises on marriage similar to his own.[5] Martin Bucer, Peter Martyr Vermigli, and Jean Calvin all published their opinions on marriage primarily in Latin.[6]

1.   Heinrich Bullinger, *Der Christlich Eestand* (Zurich: Christoff Froschauer, 1540). The text went through two more Zurich editions during the sixteenth century, in 1548 and 1579. *HBBibl* I, nos 129, 130, 131.

2.   These latter, less controversial issues formed the content of an earlier unpublished work by Bullinger entitled *Volkommne[r] underrichtung desz christenlichen Eestands* (1527), ZB, Ms. D 200, no. 2. For the 1540 book, Bullinger revised and expanded his commentary on these matters, and added chapters on clerical marriage, fornication, adultery, parental consent, consanguinity, and divorce. See Susanna Burghartz, "Zwischen Integration und Ausgrenzung: Zur Dialektik reformierter Ehetheologie am Beispiel Heinrich Bullingers," *L'Homme: Zeitschrift für Feministische Geschichtswissenschaft* 8, no. 1 (1997): 35.

3.   Martin Luther, "Vom ehelichen Leben*"* in Otto Clemen ed., *Luthers Werke in Auswahl,* vol. 2 (Berlin: Walter de Gruyter & Co., 1950), 335-59.

4.   Johannes Brenz, "Wie in eesachen und den fellen, so sich derhalben zutragen, nach götlichem billichem rechten christenlich zü handeln sey" in Martin Brecht et al. eds, *Werke, Eine Studienausgabe* part 2: *Frühschriften,* (Tübingen: J.C. B. Mohr, 1974), 255-96.

5.   "Reformed" designates specifically the urban Protestant tradition first dominant in Swiss and German imperial cities such as Zurich, Berne, and Strasbourg, and later in Geneva.

6.   Bucer wrote one significant vernacular treatise on marriage entitled "Von der Ehe und Ehescheidung aus göttlichem und keyserlichem rechtenn," but it was never published. cites the manuscript extensively in H. J. Selderhuis ed., John Vriend and Lyle D. Bierma trans., *Marriage*

This article offers an explanation of why Bullinger was the only reformer to write extensively on marriage in a format accessible to the laity. Through an examination of *Der Christlich Eestand* in the context of Bullinger's covenant theology and the marriage theologies of other reformers, it will be argued that Bullinger's belief that a reformation of marriage and morals was an integral part of the restoration of obedience to the covenant led him to write a more thorough treatise than any other reformer, and one that blended his theology of marriage into the traditional genre of the domestic conduct book. It will be demonstrated that the subtle distinctions between Bullinger's idea of the covenant and that of other reformers did not significantly alter or affect his opinions on specific marital issues.[7] In fact, Bucer, Vermigli, and Calvin would have agreed with nearly all the material in Bullinger's book, while writers outside the Reformed tradition, such as Luther or Erasmus, would have agreed with much of it. What Bullinger's unique conception of a unified, conditional (duopleuric) covenant *did* do, however, was cause him to stress, more than any other Continental Protestant, the reformation of religion and society along the lines of the Old Testament. This led him to emphasise not only the unity of the secular and religious spheres and importance of Old Testament law, but also the connection between theory and praxis and the need for the laity to have a better understanding of the place of marriage in society.[8] Thus, while the covenant had only a small impact on specific points of marital theology, it did influence Bullinger's motivation for discussing these issues and his way of presenting them.[9]

---

and Divorce in the Thought of Martin Bucer (Kirksville: Thomas Jefferson University Press, 1999). Vermigli confined his comments on marriage largely to a Latin text defending clerical marriage that was written in response to the Oxford cleric Richard Smith and to his commentary on I Corinthians John Patrick Donnelly, "The Social and Ethical Thought of Peter Martyr Vermigli" in Joseph C. McLelland ed., *Peter Martyr Vermigli and Italian Reform* (Ontario: Wilfrid Laurier University Press, 1980), 116. Vermigli's *Loci Communes* contains a large section on marriage, but this text was compiled after Vermigli's death from his Latin writings and not published until 1576. In a similar fashion, Calvin expounded his theology of marriage primarily in the *Institutes* and his Biblical commentaries.

7.   Scholars generally agree that Bullinger believed in a unified, conditional covenant between God and humanity that existed from Genesis through to the present day. In other words, Christ did not institute a new covenant of grace, but rather reconfirmed the old covenant in which God promised humanity life and eternal salvation in exchange for faith and obedience. Scholars disagree, however, over the extent to which Bullinger's concept of the covenant influenced his theology as a whole, especially in comparison with the theology of John Calvin. See J. W. Baker, *Heinrich Bullinger and the Covenant: The Other Reformed Tradition* (Athens: Ohio University Press, 1980); idem, "Heinrich Bullinger, the Covenant and the Reformed Tradition in Retrospect," *Sixteenth Century Journal* 29, no. 2 (1998): 359-76; Richard Muller, *Christ and the Decree: Christology and Predestination in Reformed Theology from Calvin to Perkins* (Grand Rapids: Baker Book House, 1986), 40-47.

8.   Cf. Bruce Gordon, "Translation and Spirituality of Leo Jud" (paper presented at the annual Sixteenth Century Studies Conference, San Antonio, TX, October 2002). Gordon argues that the Old Testament and the practical application of God's word in the community were central to the Zurich Reformation.

9.   My understanding of the covenant in Bullinger's theology thus falls between those of J. W. Baker and Richard A. Muller. Baker is correct in his assertion that Bullinger's notion of a unified covenant affected his opinion on the roles of the magistrate, the minister, and the Old Testament law in a Christian community. Nevertheless, as Muller points out, and as Bullinger's

In the preface to *Der Christlich Eestand,* Bullinger immediately placed marriage in the context of his theology by associating the reformation of morals with the restoration of the covenant and by using covenant language to describe marital issues. He explained that he compiled the marriage treatise:

> for the good instruction of symple maried people: to the intent also that wedloke maye well proceade and be kepte, & that nothinge be done amysse thorow ignorance or euel custome, or for fault of doctryne. To the intent also that all vertue and honestie maye preuayle, and that me[n] may walke soberly according to the co[m]maundement of the lorde.[10]

For Bullinger, the Reformation involved not only religious reforms, but also a redefinition of the political, legal, and moral structures of society, using the Old Testament as a model. In other words, it involved a restoration of obedience to the bilateral covenant between God and humanity. The analysis of the twenty-five chapters of *Der Christlich Eestand* will proceed from the general to the particular. First will be a general examination of Bullinger's positive portrayal of marriage and married life, including both theoretical definitions of marriage and practical advice for married people. Following will be a discussion of his views on specific legal and moral issues surrounding marriage and divorce.[11]

Since his goal in writing the book was to instruct people on how to live honourably in wedlock, Bullinger was primarily concerned with proving matrimony itself to be holy and honourable. He accomplished this task in three different ways. First, he wrote five chapters on the Biblical origins and honourable nature of marriage. Second, he included a chapter against mandatory clerical celibacy, in which he argued that marriage was honourable for all men and women. Lastly, he dedicated several chapters to the description of the ideal emotional, domestic, and sexual relationship that should exist between a husband and his wife. This glorification of matrimony was not unique to Bullinger. However, not all sixteenth-

---

theology of marriage will confirm, the differences that resulted were largely structural, rather than doctrinal. In this light, Baker's designation of the covenant as the "basic element" in Bullinger's entire theology and his division of the Reformed tradition into the two distinct strands of Zurich and Geneva become questionable.

10.   Heinrich Bullinger, *The Christen state of Matrimonye,* Miles Coverdale trans., (Antwerp: Matthew Crom, 1541), f. A3ᶦ. "zü gütem bericht der einfaltigen Eelüten/ vnd das die Ee recht bezogen vnd gehalten/ vnd darinn nüt vß vnwüssenheit oder böser gewonheit/ oder vß mangel der leer geirret werde/ ouch das aller zucht vnnd erbarkeit vfgange/ vn[d] das man züchtigklich nach dem gebott des herren wandle." Bullinger, *Der Christlich Eestand,* f. A3ᵛ. Except when noted otherwise, the quotations of *Der Christlich Eestand* in the text are from Miles Coverdale's translation (hereinafter *CSM*), while the original German quotations from the 1540 Zurich edition (hereinafter *DCE*) are in the footnotes.

11.   Other scholars of *Der Christlich Eestand* have divided its content differently. One example is Anette Völker-Rasor, who separates Bullinger's chapters into "theory" (chaps 1-14) and "praxis" (chaps 15-25). Anette Völker-Rasor, *Bilderpaare-Paarbilder, Die Ehe in Autobiographien des 16. Jahrhunderts* (Freiburg i. Br.: Rombach Verlag, 1993), 89-90. My twofold division does not follow the order of the text so closely. For instance, I discuss chapters 19 to 24 (dealing with the running of the household) within Bullinger's general portrayal of married life, while I place chapter 25 on divorce among the legal issues surrounding marriage.

century authors of marriage treatises used all three of these tactics to celebrate matrimony or emphasised to the same extent its honourable and good character.

Bullinger laid out the definition and origins of marriage in the first three chapters of *The Christen state of Matrimonye*. In the first chapter, he recited the story from Genesis of God's creation of Eve as a helpmeet from Adam, using the language of the covenant to describe marital union and to emphasise the holy character of marriage. According to Bullinger, God's use of Adam's rib to create Eve symbolised the fleshly bond between husband and wife, while Moses himself declared the "[connection or unity] of married folkes" when he uttered the words "For this cause shall a man leaue his father & mother, & cleue vnto his wife, & they two shalbe into one flesh."[12] Out of this story, asserted Bullinger, "we perceaue all ready, where holy wedlok was instituted, namely in the paradise and garden of pleasure: yee and whan it was ordeyned, even in the begynninge of the worlde, before the fall of man, in al prosperite."[13] The prelapsarian foundation of marriage was very important to the Zurich reformer, because it proved that marriage was wholly honourable and without sin. Later in the same chapter, he emphasised this point once more: "After the fall of Ada[m] & Eve, ther was nothing added further vnto wedlok, nether altred in those thinges that were ordeyned, sauynge that, by reason of the fall & synne, ther was sorow and payne layed vpo[n] them both, & vpon us all."[14]

The idea of a covenant or unity between spouses was also behind Bullinger's definition of marriage found in the second and third chapters of the book. In the second chapter, he succinctly defined marriage as

> a laufull knott and unto god an acceptable yokyinge together of one man and one woman with the good consent of them both, to the intent that they two maye dwell together in frendshippe & honestye, one helping and confortynge the tother, eschuynge unclennesse, & bringinge up childre[n] in the feare of god.[15]

12. *CSM*, f. A5[r-v]. "Darum[b] wirt ein man[n] sinen vatter vn[d] sin müter verlassen vnd an sinem wyb hangen/ vnd werdend sy beide ein fleisch syn. Dise wort redt noch Adam/ oder ouch Moses vß dem mu[n]d Gottes/ vnd zeigt damit die pflicht vnd verbindung o[d]er vereinigung der Eelüte[n]." The phrase "connection or unity" is mine rather than Coverdale's. Interestingly enough, Coverdale translated "verbindung oder vereinigung" as "covenant." This may not have been true to Bullinger's original intentions, however, as the Zurich reformer generally used "bund" or "pundt" to refer to the Latin word for covenant, "foedus." Thus, Coverdale's translating amplified the covenant language for his English readers. *DCE*, f. A6[r-v]. For more on Coverdale's style of translating and the reception of the book in England, see Carrie Euler, "Heinrich Bullinger, Marriage, and the English Reformation: 'The Christen state of Matrimonye' in England, 1540-53," *SCJ* 34/2 (summer 2003): 365-91.

13. *CSM*, f. A4[r]. "wir schon habe[n] wo der Eestand vfgesetzt sye/ namlich im[m] Paradyß vnd lustgarten: ouch wen[n]/ grad in angang der wält/ vor dem faal des menschen in allem wolstand." *DCE*, f. A4[v].

14. *CSM*, f. A5[v]. "Nach dem faal Adam vnd Eue wirt der Ee nützid wyters hinzü gethon/ oder im[m] geordneten geenderet/ onet das von des faals vnd der sünden wegen angst not vnnd schmertzen jnen beiden vn[d] vns allen angehenckt wirt." *DCE*, A7r.

15. *CSM*, f. A6[v]. "eins manns vnd eins wybs von Gott vfgesetzte rächtmässige vn[d] Gott wolgefellige/ mit beider güter verwilligung/ züsamenfügung/ das sy beide fründtlich vnd erberlich by einandren woning/ einandren beholffen vnd beradten syend/ vnküscheit vermydind/ vn[d] kinder ziehind." *DCE*, f. A8r.

The German word *Ehe*, Bullinger noted, was an old word, "sometime take[n] for a law or statute, sometyme for a bonde or [agreement]."[16] In the third chapter, he extended this definition by describing in more detail the things necessary for a marriage to exist: monogamy, adherence to the local public laws of marriage, living together, sharing of bodies and goods, a mutual feeling of good will between the spouses, and last but not least, adherence to God's will and his matrimonial laws as declared in scripture. If couples would follow these precepts, Bullinger concluded, they committed no sin by marrying. Marriage was sinful only if entered into recklessly or against God's word.[17] This chapter, with its reference to the importance of matrimonial law, provided Bullinger with a transition into chapters four to nine, which dealt with different legal issues surrounding marriage.

In chapters ten and eleven, Bullinger returned to the more theoretical question of the purpose of marriage and stated once again how sacred and honourable it is. In chapter ten, "The occasions of wedlok/ why and wherfore it shulde be contracted," he outlined the three reasons for marriage: procreation, avoidance of the sin of fornication, and companionship.[18] In chapter eleven, entitled "The ende frute and commendacion of holy wedlok: How blessed honourable/ and good a thinge it is," he provided more evidence for the virtue of marriage. Here, for example, he cited standard Biblical arguments, such as the fact that many Old Testament characters were married and Jesus's miracle at the wedding at Cana.[19]

Much of this material on the definition and honourable nature of marriage was not original to Bullinger or even to the Reformation. Luther, Bucer, and Calvin, for example, all portrayed matrimony as founded by God in paradise and stated repeatedly in their writings that marriage was a good and honourable institution.[20] This notion was also present in pre-Reformation humanist writings. Erasmus, in his treatise the *Praise of Matrimony*, commends marriage as a natural and excellent state of life. The Spanish humanist Juan Luis Vives also praised marriage in his *Instruction of a Christian Woman*.[21] Even Bullinger's definition of marriage was consistent with Roman law, Catholic teaching, and definitions expounded by his Reformed colleagues Bucer and Vermigli.[22] Finally, Bullinger's

---

16. *CSM*, f. A6^{r-v}. "Das wörtlin Ee ist ein vralt Tütsch wörtlin/ vnd wirt etwan gebrucht für gsatzte vnd recht/ etwan für vereinigu[n]g vn[d] verkumnuß." Once again, Coverdale made the covenant language more blatant here, translating "verkumnuß" as "covenant." *DCE*, f. A7^v.

17. *CSM*, f. A8^i. *DCE*, f. B1^v.

18. *CSM*, f. D1^v-D4^v. "Von den vrsachen der Ee/ warumb sy sölle bezogen werden." *DCE*, D7^v-E3^i.

19. *CSM*, f. D4^v-D6^i. "Der heiligen Ee end/ frucht vnnd lob/ wie heilig/ eerlich vnd güt sy sye." *DCE*, f. E3^i-E5^i.

20. Luther, *Vom ehelichen Leben*, 550-7; Heribert Schützeichel, *Katholische Calvin-Studien* (Trier: Paulinus-Verlag, 1980), 101-8; Selderhuis, *Marriage and Divorce*, 165-93.

21. Albert Hyma, "Erasmus and the Sacrament of Matrimony," *Archiv für Reformationsgeschichte* 48 (1957): 145-64; Margo Todd, *Christian Humanism and the Puritan Social Order* (Cambridge: CUP, 1987), 98-99.

22. Selderhuis, *Marriage and Divorce*, 165; Donnelly, "The Social and Ethical Thought of Peter Martyr Vermigli," 112; John Jackson, "*Reformatio legum ecclesiasticarum* and Canon Law

threefold division of the purpose of marriage–procreation, a remedy for the sin of fornication, and companionship–was a wholly traditional one, found in pre-Reformation literature and in the marriage writings of other reformers. Bucer and Calvin were the only theologians to change the order of these three. They put love and companionship first, thus distancing themselves further from the pre-Reformation emphasis on procreation.[23]

Nevertheless, Bullinger's positive portrayal of the origins and definition of marriage was not quite so traditional as it first appears. The Zurich theologian did break with Catholic tradition, and even with some of his Protestant colleagues, in three subtle ways. All three are differences in tone or emphasis, rather than major doctrinal innovations, but they are important, because they appear to stem from Bullinger's idea of the unity of the covenant. First was Bullinger's emphasis on the importance of definition in his discussion of marriage. Although the definition itself was traditional, its prominent location at the beginning of the book was a result of Bullinger's pastoral and comprehensive approach to moral and societal reform. As he established in the preface, the first step towards a reformation of marriage was to educate the people about the institution. The only other Protestant writer to place such importance on the definition of matrimony was Bucer.[24] Vermigli expounded a definition similar to Bullinger's, yet he did so not at the beginning of any general treatise on marriage, but in a discussion of polygamy in his commentary on 1 Corinthians 7.[25]

Bullinger's second deviation from tradition was his stress on the prelapsarian foundations of marriage. As noted above, he specifically mentioned in the first chapter of the book that nothing had been changed or added to marriage after its first foundation in the Garden of Eden. This ran contrary to the medieval theory that God reestablished marriage as an accommodation for humanity's concupiscence.[26] While Bullinger did include the avoidance of fornication among one of the reasons for marriage, he was adamant in arguing that marriage itself and the "worke of matrimony"–sexual intercourse between husband and wife–bore no taint of original sin.[27] Rather, men and women polluted marriage with sin only when they did not live and marry according to God's laws. The distinction Bullinger made here was a very fine one, perhaps lost on many of his readers, yet one that struck at the heart of his marital theology. The continuity of marriage from Genesis to the present was parallel to the unity of the covenant. The inability of

---

Reform under the Tudors: Society, Politics, and Religion" (D.Phil. diss., Oxford University, forthcoming), chapter on marriage and marital jurisdiction.

23. Selderhuis, *Marriage and Divorce*, 165-6, 172-3, 368.

24. "Bucer is emphatic in saying that, for a good answer to various questions regarding marriage and divorce, one must first have a clear understanding of what marriage is." Selderhuis, *Marriage and Divorce*, 165.

25. Jackson, "*Reformatio legum ecclesiasticarum* and Canon Law Reform under the Tudors," chapter on marriage and marital jurisdiction.

26. Charles William Pfeiffer, "Heinrich Bullinger and Marriage" (Ph.D. diss., St. Louis University, 1981), 65-71, 88-90. Pfeiffer is to be commended for pointing out this important aspect of Bullinger's marital theology, but he goes too far, in my opinion, when he argues that the lack of change to marriage after the fall was *the* "leitmotif" and "culmination" of that theology.

27. *CSM*, f. D3ʳ. *DCE*, f. D8ᵛ.

sin to corrupt an institution founded by God was central to the Zurich reformer's desire to demonstrate the essential goodness of marriage. Among the other Protestant writers, Bucer was the only one to place the same emphasis on the continuity of matrimony before and after the fall.[28] Brenz and Vermigli did not address the issue directly; Luther and Calvin declared that original sin had indeed altered the institution of marriage.[29]

Finally, Bullinger differed from his pre-Reformation and Protestant colleagues in his presentation of the positive definition and origins of matrimony. Not only did he put most of this material at the beginning, but he dedicated five full chapters to these issues, much more than the space allotted in published treatises by Luther or Brenz. Throughout these five chapters, moreover, Bullinger used language reminiscent of the covenant. While comparing marriage to the covenant between God and humanity was not a new concept, Bullinger did so in the context of his unified, bilateral covenant theology. Readers of *Der Christlich Eestand* had available to them vernacular texts such as Bullinger's *Der alt Gloub* (1537) and *Von dem einigen unnd ewigen Testament oder Pundt Gottes* (1534), which stated his theology of the covenant explicitly.[30] They had also Bullinger's own preface to the marriage treatise, where he explained the significance of the reformation of marriage for the larger reformation of society and for the restoration of obedience to God's commandments. Marriage as covenant was old wine, but it took on a different resonance in the new bottles of Bullinger's writings.

Bullinger expanded upon the positive origins and definition of marriage in his attack on clerical celibacy, found in chapter twelve. The fact that he dedicated only one chapter to the issue was probably the result of his intended lay audience and the fact that clerical marriage had been legal in Zurich for fifteen years at the time he was writing. Nevertheless, the chapter is significant, because the Protestant rejection of mandatory clerical celibacy was a very visible and disruptive change to the theology of marriage, and because it was related to Bullinger's contention that marriage was honourable for all men and women. Bullinger began by pointing out the hypocrisy of the Catholic clergy who claim that celibacy is a holy thing but then live unchaste lives themselves. He went on to contend that the ability to remain celibate was a noble gift of God, but granted only to a very few persons, and that mandatory celibacy had no basis in scripture. He also used Biblical and historical evidence, such as references to married bishops in the New Testament and the defence of clerical marriage at the Council of Nicaea, in order to show that mandatory celibacy was a recent invention of the Church of Rome.[31]

28. Selderhuis, *Marriage and Divorce*, 181-2.

29. Heiko Oberman, *Luther, Man Between God and the Devil*, Eileen Wallizer Schwarzbart trans., (London: Fontana Press, 1993), 273; Schützeichel, *Katholische Calvin-Studien*, 102; Selderhuis, *Marriage and Divorce*, 368.

30. Heinrich Bullinger, *Das der Christe[n] gloub vo[m] anfa[n]g der w[e]lt gew[e]ret habe der recht vnd vngezwyflet glouben sye.* (Basel: Wolfgang Friessen, 1537). Published three more times in German as *Der alt Gloub*, once in Latin, and twice in English between the years 1539 and 1547. Idem, *Von dem einigen und ewigen Testament oder Pundt Gottes* (Zurich: Christopher Froschauer, 1534]). Also published in Latin. See *HBBibl* I, nos 99-103, 54-60.

31. *CSM*, f. D6ᵛ-E2ʳ. *DCE*, f. E5ⁱ-F2ʳ. Alfred Schindler has discovered an error in Bullinger's scholarship regarding the Council of Nicaea. The Council did rule favourably on clerical

These arguments regarding celibacy were the same as those put forth by other Protestant theologians and bore little relation to Bullinger's covenant theology.[32] Some were even present in the writings of pre-Reformation humanists. Erasmus was a fierce critic of clerical immorality, and in his *Praise of Matrimony* he actually advocated marriage for monks and nuns. Erasmus never married, however, and he never carried the argument further to say that clerical celibacy was against scripture and the law of God.[33] It was reformers like Luther, Zwingli, Bucer, and Bullinger who first took the definitive step by getting married in the 1520s, and who went on to declare that mandatory celibacy was ungodly.[34] Chapter twelve of *The Christen state of Matrimonye* was significant, therefore, not only as further proof of the honourable nature of marriage, but also as confirmation of the thoroughly Protestant or evangelical orientation of the book.

The third and final argument Bullinger used to portray marriage as a virtuous institution was the description of the companionable relationship between husband and wife. His views on this subject were largely unoriginal and compatible with pre-Reformation tradition, at times hinting at true equality between the spouses, but most often supporting the ideas of mutuality and the husband's authority over his wife. What was unusual was the sheer amount of space he dedicated to the subject: nine of the book's twenty-five chapters. The contents of these chapters divide into two broad categories. First is the discussion of the love and mutual fidelity between spouses, including sexual relations. Second is the description of the domestic responsibilities of husbands and wives, including behavior towards children and servants.

In chapters seventeen and eighteen, entitled "Of the first cohabitacion and loue of maryed folkes" and "How the loue/ faithfulnesse/ & dwtie of maried folkes maye be kepte and increaced," Bullinger discussed in great detail the nature of matrimonial love.[35] He explained that the love between husband and wife comes from God; couples must pray and read the Bible together in order to maintain their love.[36] He stressed equal affection between husband and wife. "For asmuch as wedloke maketh of two persones one/ for they two are one flesh," he wrote, "therfore must they be of one hert wyll and mynde/ and none to cast an-

---

marriage, but, according to Schindler, Bullinger's citation of Eusebius for this fact is incorrect, and he must have taken his account of Nicaea from a different patristic source. Alfred Schindler, "Kirchenväter und andere alte Autoritäten in Bullingers 'Der Christlich Eestand' von 1540" in *Von Cyprian zur Walzenprägung: Streiflichter auf Zürcher Geist und Kultur der Bullingerzeit*, Hans Ulrich Bächtold ed., (Zug: Achius Verlag, 2001), 35.

32.   Luther, *Vom ehelichen Leben*, 352-5; John Patrick Donnelly, "Marriage from Renaissance to Reformation: Two Florentine Moralists" in John R. Sommerfeldt/Thomas H. Seiler eds, *Studies in Medieval Culture* vol. 11 (Western Michigan University, 1977), 168-9; idem, "The Social and Ethical Thought of Peter Martyr Vermigli," 116; Selderhuis, *Marriage and Divorce*, 327-49.

33.   Hyma, "Erasmus and the Sacrament of Matrimony," 154.

34.   Bullinger married Anna Adlischwyler, a former nun, in 1529. His letter of proposal to Anna, dated 30 September 1537, contains many of the same ideas about marriage he would later put into *Der Christlich Eestand. HBBW* I:126-41.

35.   *CSM*, f. G7^r-I1^v. "Von der ersten bywonung vnd eelicher liebe." "Wie man Eeliche liebe trüw vnd pflicht halten vnd meeren möge." *DCE*, f. I3^v-L1^v.

36.   *CSM*, f. H3^v-H4^r. *DCE*, f. K1^v-K2^r.

other in the tethe wyth hys fault/ or to pryde him of hys gyft."[37] Bullinger emphasised the need for newlyweds, both the man and the woman, to be loving and patient and to accept each other's faults. He urged them to keep no secrets from each other, to be obsequious and kind, and to refrain from criticism.[38] His positive view of sex in marriage highlighted this equal relationship. He referred twice to Paul's words in 1 Corinthians 7: "The wyfe hath not the power of hir awne body, but the husba[n]de. Likewise the husband hath not power of his awne body, but the wife."[39] Bullinger used the term "due benevolence," also taken from 1 Corinthians, to refer to the sexual duty owed by both spouses to each other as part of the marriage bond, and emphasised that this act was not sinful.[40] Finally, he included beauty and health among the "riches of the body" one should look for in choosing a spouse, and he asserted that husbands and wives should never sleep apart from each other for long periods of time.[41]

In other descriptions of love and sex, however, Bullinger's belief that the husband was superior to the wife is evident. The one allusion to the enjoyment of sexual pleasure in *Der Christlich Eestand* was a reference to the Song of Solomon, and it betrayed Bullinger's masculine point-of-view: "Be glad with thy maried wife, whom thou hast taken in thy youth, & loue her as a dear chosen hynde. Let hir breastes satisfye the at all tymes, and reioyse still in hyr loue."[42] He employed traditional metaphors to describe a husband's love: a man ought to love his wife as he loves his own body and as Christ loved the church. Just as Christ was head of the church and a minister the head of his congregation, the husband was master to his wife.[43] Bullinger wrote that in order that the man's authority over his wife not turn into tyranny, he ought not to be quick to become angry with her, and ought to permit her "to make conuenient and honest chere with honest folkes."[44] Yet, just as Christ leads and guides the church, the husband should correct his wife for her failings, "to guyde them and rule them with discretion for theyr preseruacion."[45]

Bullinger's chapters on domestic order reveal the influence of classical and humanist ideals of the household economy; this is not surprising, as he took much

---

37. *CSM*, f. H4[r]. "sidmals die Ee vß zweyen menschen einen machet: dan[n] sy zwey sind ein lyb/ spricht der Herr: so söllend sy ein hertz willen vnd sin[n] haben/ vnd keins dem anderen sinen mangel vfheben/ oder sich siner gaaben erheben." *DCE*, f. K2[r].

38. *CSM*, f. G7[r]-G8[r], H4[r]-H5[r]. *DCE*, f. I4[r]-I5[r], K1[v]-K3[r].

39. *CSM*, f. D3[r], H8[r]. "Das weyb ist jres lybs nit mächtig/ sunder der mann: Deßglych ist der mann sins lybs nit mächtig/ sunder das wyb." *DCE*, f. E1[r], K7[v].

40. *CSM*, f. D3[r]. The phrase comes from Paul's words in 1 Corinthians 7. "Due benevolence" was the translation William Tyndale and Miles Coverdale gave in the English Bible translations of the 1530s and 1540s. Bullinger used the German "pflichtige gütwilligkeit." *DCE*, f. D6[r].41. *CSM*, f. F7[r-v], D4v. "Güter des lybs." *DCE*, f. H2[r], E3[r].

42. *CSM*, f. D3[v]-D4[r]. "Fröw dich mjit dinem Eewyb die du in diner jugend genom[m]en hast/ die sol dir syn wie ein geliebte vßerwelte hynd. Ire brüst söllend dich settigen alle zyt/ in jrer liebe solt dich stäts fröwen." *DCE*, f. E2[r].

43. *CSM*, f. H1[r-v]. *DCE*, f. I6[v].

44. *CSM*, f. I1[r]. "Also solt du mann dinem wyb ouch nit zimliche vnnd eerliche fröud by eeren lüten abschlahen." *DCE*, f. K8[r].

45. *CSM*, f. H1[v]-H2[r]. "Darum[b] söllend die mann der wybern höupter glycher gstalt/ vnd in glycher güthät vnd regierung syn/ vnd sy beherschen mit vernufft zü erhaltung." *DCE*, f. I7[v].

of his material from Erasmus and Juan Luis Vives.[46] Here Bullinger described the mutual, yet unequal, duties of husband and wife. He assigned to the husband the pursuit of an occupation outside the household, bringing home goods and money from without. The wife, on the other hand, was to keep and provide for the family from within. In the description of these duties, the inequality of the marriage partnership was evident. The duties of the wife included obedience and reticence. Bullinger wrote that the wife had to be modest and quiet; she could not engage in excessive conversation or venture outside the house too often.[47] Likewise, she had to bring up her daughters to be chaste, humble, and quiet creatures.[48] Though husband and wife both had some financial responsibility, the husband was clearly in control of resources. "What so euer is to be done without the house, that belongeth to the ma[n]," Bullinger explained, "& the woma[n] to studye for thinges within to be done, and to se saued or spent conueniently whatsoeuer he bringeth in."[49] In carrying out her responsibility, however, the wife had always to report to her husband, for she was "nether to go eny where without her husbandes knowledge & leaue."[50] Bullinger's chapter on how to behave towards the poor and servants reflected this same economical hierarchy: married couples ought to give to the poor, and they should conduct themselves with kindness and justice towards servants. Servants must be always obedient and refrain from fighting and gossip.[51]

Bullinger's book contained four chapters on child-rearing.[52] Chapter twenty-one discussed the first few years of childhood, offering advice on issues such as nursing, teaching the child to speak, and choosing childhood schoolmasters. Chapter twenty-two considered the importance of further education, either in letters or in a trade, depending on the talents and inclination of the child. Bullinger's concept of the proper literary education was a humanist one: the child must learn Greek and Latin literature, logic, rhetoric, history, and scripture. Chapters twenty-three and twenty-four dealt specifically with female children. Here Bullinger offered standard advice on how to raise daughters as chaste and modest, and how to school them in handicrafts and other household responsibilities, so that they will make proper wives for their husbands.

---

46.   For evidence of Bullinger's reliance on Erasmus and Vives, see Burghartz, "Zwischen Integration und Ausgrenzung," 34; Schindler, "Kirchenväter und andere alte Autoritäten," 29-32; Alfred Weber, *Heinrich Bullingers "Christlicher Ehestand," seine zeitgenössischen Quellen und die Anfänge des Familienbuches in England* (Engelsdorf & Leipzig: C. & M. Vogel, 1929), 13-50.

47.   *CSM*, f. H8ᵛ-11ᵛ. *DCE*, f. K7ᵛ-K8ᵛ.

48.   *CSM*, f. K2ʳ-K5ʳ. *DCE*, f. N4ᵛ-O5ᵛ.

49.   *CSM*, f. 12ᵛ. "Die ordnung ist die/ das der man in allen dingen vnd zü allen zyten/ alles das thüye/ das dem man[n] züstaat: vnnd das deßglych die ding thüye/ die den wybere[n] zü verwalte[n] stond." *DCE*, f. L3ʳ. Coverdale's wording here is slightly different from Bullinger's, because the translator did not translate chapters 19-24 as accurately as he did chapters 1-18. I have written more on Coverdale's translation technique elsewhere.

50.   *CSM*, f. H8ᵛ. "one jres man[n]s vorwüssen vnd erloubnuß nienan hin gon.' *DCE*, f. K7ᵛ.

51.   *CSM*, 15ʳ⁻ᵛ. *DCE*, f. M1ʳ-M2ᵛ.

52.   *CSM*, f. 15ᵛ-K5ʳ. *DCE*, f. M2ᵛ-O5ᵛ.

Bullinger's domestic advice was largely unoriginal. His concept of the love and mutual fidelity between spouses was similar to those of Erasmus, Vives, Luther, Bucer, and Calvin.[53] His chapters on raising children were similar to those found in humanist handbooks.[54] As with his definition of marriage, however, a few differences of emphasis set Bullinger's domestic material slightly apart from the other writers. The first distinction was Bullinger's attitude towards sex. For him, sexual relations in marriage were necessary and good, even if they did not lead to procreation. Here he moved one step beyond Vives, Erasmus, and even Luther, who, though they praised marriage in positive terms, never completely rid themselves of the notion that sex was tainted with sin.[55] Among the other writers, only Bucer had a more positive view of sex.[56] Bucer was also the only other Protestant theologian to conceive of the covenant as single and bilateral and to express the view that God had not altered the institution of marriage after the fall.[57] The similarities between his and Bullinger's positive evaluation of sex within marriage seem, therefore, to be directly related to covenantal theology.

The second distinction was a difference of degree only and not one that stemmed directly from Bullinger's view of the covenant. It is that Bullinger's account of the affection and behaviour of spouses towards one another and their mutual household duties was simply more extensive and more balanced than that of any the other authors. None of them, for instance, dedicated a whole chapter of a book to the first period in which a married couple lives together, or wrote much at all about domestic duties. Bucer wrote extensively about matrimonial love, but hardly at all about bringing up children.[58] Bullinger's chapter on the first period in which a married couple lives together was also unusual in that he did not give different advice to the man and woman on how to behave towards the other, but

---

53. For Erasmus and Vives, see note 46 above and Todd, *Christian Humanism and the Puritan Social Order*, 98-102. For Bucer and Calvin, see Selderhuis, *Marriage and Divorce*, 166-80, 368, Schützeichel, *Katholische Calvin-Studien*, 101-10. For Luther, see his *Ein Sermon von dem ehelichen Stand* (Wittenberg: Johann Grünenberg, 1519), and Oberman, *Luther, Man Between God and the Devil*, 272-83.

54. Todd, *Christian Humanism and the Puritan Social Order*, 108-11. A specific example was Bullinger's advice on raising daughters, taken directly from Vives's *Instruction of a Christian Woman*. Weber, *Heinrich Bullingers "Christlicher Ehestand,"* 48.

55. For Vives: Weber, *Heinrich Bullingers "Christlicher Ehestand,"* 13-19. For Erasmus: Selderhuis, *Marriage and Divorce*, 38-39. For Luther: the final paragraph of his own *Vom ehelichen Leben*.

56. Bucer, for example, wrote more openly and extensively than Bullinger about sexual pleasure. Selderhuis, *Marriage and Divorce*, 173-80. Calvin's view of sexual relations within marriage was more positive than that of Vives, Erasmus, and Luther, but not as positive as Bullinger's or Bucer's. Calvin proclaimed sex within marriage to be without sin, but in certain cases, he permitted "bed and board" divorces, when husband and wife would be permitted to live separately. Bullinger and Bucer rejected this kind of divorce, because it severed sexual relations between spouses with no opportunity for remarraige. Selderhuis, *Marriage and Divorce*, 368-69.

57. For Bucer's view of the covenant and the prelapsarian institution of marriage, see Baker, *Heinrich Bullinger and the Covenant*, 189-91; Selderhuis, *Marriage and Divorce*, 181-2.

58. Selderhuis, *Marriage and Divorce*, 242.

rather simultaneously exhorted both husband and wife to kindness, patience, and honesty.[59]

Scholars may be tempted to view Bullinger's idea of a mutual, or bilateral covenant between God and humanity as leading to more equality in the marriage partnership, but the similarities between Bullinger and the other authors belie this argument, as does his adherence to the traditional patriarchal model of the household. The Zurich reformer's more detailed description of the reciprocal relationship between husband and wife stemmed from his humanist background, his pastoral approach to theology, and his concern with order and discipline. He admired the humanist contribution to domestic theory, which leaned towards more equality between spouses, and he recognised its usefulness in the creation of a godly, disciplined society. For Bullinger, this model of gender relations was not necessarily contradictory to Old Testament notions of patriarchy and hierarchy: the God-given rule of the man over the woman carried with it a duty for the husband to treat the wife with kindness and patience, while the subjective status of the wife implied a duty to be virtuous.[60] If the husband and wife followed these prescriptions, Bullinger believed, a happier, more stable marriage would result, and the dignity and sanctity of marriage would remain intact. In this way, Bullinger's occasional hints at equality between spouses did not stem directly from the idea of a mutual covenant, but were part of a broad attempt to promote discipline and godliness within society that grew, in part, out of Bullinger's notion of a unified and bilateral covenant. This concern for order will become even more apparent in the following discussion of the Zurich reformer's approach to the legal issues surrounding marriage and divorce.

Because of the practical, handbook nature of *Der Christlich Eestand*, Bullinger included in it little theoretical discussion of the relationship between the religious and secular spheres or the absorption of marital and legal matters into secular jurisdiction. In chapters three and four, he declared that there should be a common, public law of marriage in all communities and that it should be under the control of the secular authorities, but he offered no theological justification for this.[61] Nevertheless, because Bullinger's belief in the unity of the secular and religious spheres greatly influenced his approach to the specific legal and jurisdictional issues surrounding marriage, it deserves attention here.

In writings such as *Der alt Gloub* (1537), *Von dem einigen unnd ewigen Testament oder Pundt Gottes* (1534), and the *Decades* (1549-1551), Bullinger defended a unity of the secular and religious spheres in which the magistrates held

---

59.   Monika Gsell, "Hierarchie und Gegenseitigkeit: Überlegungen zur Geschlechterkonzeption in Heinrich Bullingers Eheschriften" in Rüdiger Schnell ed., *Geschlechterbeziehungen und Textfunkionen: Studien zu Eheschriften der Frühen Neuzeit* (Tübingen: Max Niemeyer Verlag, 1998), 110-1.

60.   This is Monika Gsell's argument in "Hierarchie und Gegenseitigkeit." Gsell notes that a few passages of *Der Christlich Eestand* do imply more symmetry between spouses than found in Erasmus's writings, and she attributes this to differences in the social status of their respective audiences. Erasmus was writing more for the aristocracy; he assumed the men in his audience would be more educated and adept at instructing the sheltered women of the upper class.

61.   *CSM* f. A7ʳ-A8ᵛ. *DCE*, f. B1ʳ-B2ᵛ.

final authority over doctrine and discipline.[62] This had been a reality in Zurich since 1525, when Zwingli and the council created the first secular marriage court or *Ehegericht*.[63] The replacement of episcopal courts with magisterial jurisdiction over marriage and morality became a common feature of the Reformation in both Switzerland and Germany; many Reformed and Lutheran cities followed Zurich's model in the 1530s and 1540s.[64] Not until Calvin established the consistory in Geneva was there a serious challenge to the concept of secular jurisdiction in Protestant cities. Yet, two crucial differences existed between Bullinger's concept of secular jurisdiction and that of his Lutheran colleagues. First, for the Zurich reformer, the argument for secular jurisdiction had a strong theological foundation: the spiritual and moral authority of the magistrate stemmed from a unity of the religious and secular spheres that followed the model of the Old Testament. The models for sixteenth-century ministers to follow were the Old Testament prophets; the models for magistrates were the Old Testament kings and Christian Roman Emperors.[65] In Lutheran territories, on the other hand, secular jurisdiction in marriage and discipline was a *de facto* result of Luther's concept of the two kingdoms, one spiritual and one earthly. Luther believed the two kingdoms should remain entirely separate and provided few guidelines for the interaction between church and state. The outcome was that the secular powers took over all powers of discipline and coercion.[66] The second difference between the Zurich and Lutheran models was that the secular authorities in Zurich actually had less control vis-à-vis the clergy than did the Lutheran princes. Bullinger's unity of the two spheres meant that the secular authorities did not have *absolute* authority, but rather had a duty to listen to the ministers of the church and to follow the laws of the Old Testament. Luther's stark separation of the two spheres left little room for this reciprocal interaction. As a result, Lutheran princes or magistrates often had more authority and jurisdictional leeway than magistrates in Reformed cities, who were constantly exhorted by the clergy as to the proper interpretation of scripture and the application of discipline.

These differences are subtle. Bullinger's approach to the legal issues discussed in *Der Christlich Eestand* agreed in many aspects with that of Luther and Brenz, and even more with that of Bucer and Vermigli. Nevertheless, the impact of the Zurich reformer's uniquely pastoral and covenantal theology is also evident. The five issues Bullinger addressed in the book are: the need for parental consent in marriage, the wedding, crimes of adultery and fornication, the degrees of consanguinity allowed between spouses, and divorce.

62. See note 29 above for publication of the first two treatises. Heinrich Bullinger, *Sermonum Decades quinque* (Zurich: Christopher Froschauer, 1552).

63. For the history of this court, see Walther Köhler, *Das Zürcher Ehegericht und Seine Auswirkung in der Deutschen Schweiz zur Zeit Zwinglis*, vol. 1 of *Zürcher Ehegericht und Genfer Konsistorium* (Leipzig: Verlag von M. Heinsius Nachfolger, 1932).

64. Joel Harrington, *Reordering Marriage and Society in Reformation Germany* (Cambridge: CUP, 1997), 137-40.

65. *The First and Second Decade*, vol. 1-2 of *The Decades of Henry Bullinger*, H. I. trans., (The Parker Society; Cambridge: 1849), 323-393.

66. W. D. J. Cargill-Thompson, *The Political Thought of Martin Luther* (Sussex: The Harvester Press, 1984).

Bullinger insisted that young couples must have the consent of their parents to marry. In chapter five, "To a right mariage/ must children also haue the consent of their parentes," he criticised Catholic canon law, which required only the exchange of vows of consent between the young man and woman themselves, with no witnesses necessary. He maintained that these secret betrothals were too often induced by flattery and drunkenness, and that they rarely led to happy marriages. He asserted the rights of parents to assist their children in making decisions and the inability of children to make vows without parental guidance. Finally, Bullinger cited the sixth commandment and laws of Rome and the Holy Roman Empire as evidence of the legal necessity of parental consent.[67]

The formation of secret marriages had been a cause of concern in the church long before the Reformation. In his desire for parental consent Bullinger was in agreement not only with all the major Protestant reformers but also with many late medieval and humanist writers, including Erasmus.[68] Where the evangelicals, both Lutheran and Reformed, broke with the Catholics was in redefining the legal steps to marriage and writing parental consent into the marriage laws.[69] The requirement of consent was critical for the reformers not only in order to invalidate secret exchanges of vows, but to assert the communal, public, and wholesome nature of marriage. Chapter five of *Der Christlich Eestand*, therefore, offered no arguments not found in the writings of Luther, Brenz, Vermigli, Bucer, or Calvin. Bullinger's only unique contribution to the issue of consent came in chapters six and nine, where he warned against parents abusing their authority by forcing children to marry unwanted partners, and reminded his readers that both the bride and the groom also needed to give their free consent to a marriage.[70] This was a difference of emphasis only; certainly none of the other writers overtly supported forced marriages. As in the chapter on the first cohabitation of married couples, Bullinger's pastoral emphasis and desire for order led him once again to accentuate more than his colleagues the will and happiness of the young people themselves.

Bullinger did not describe exactly how or when the initial exchange of consent or "handfasting" was to take place, nor did he stipulate such details as how many witnesses were required at the event.[71] These were matters to be decided by the magistrates. He did, however, separate this betrothal from the church wedding, to which he dedicated an entire chapter. In chapter sixteen, "Of the Weddinge," he insisted that the couple could not live together or engage in sexual

---

67.   *CSM*, f. B2ʳ-B5¹. "Die kinder söllend zü rechter Ee ouch jrer eltern bewilligung haben." *DCE*, f. B4ᵛ-B8ᵛ.

68.   Harrington, *Reordering Marriage and Society*, 30, 57-58, 178-80.

69.   For example, see discussion of Zurich's 1525 marriage ordinance in Köhler, *Das Zürcher Ehegericht*, 73-75.

70.   "The parentes ought not to constrayne theyr children to matrimonye; neither to mary them afore thyr tyme." *CSM*, f. B5ʳ-B6¹. "Die Eltern söllend jre kind zur Ee nit zwingen/ oder sy ee zyt vermächlen." *DCE*, f. B8ᵛ-C1ᵛ. "Of the just consent of both parties in to mariage." *CSM*, f. C7¹-D1ᵛ. "Von rechter verwilligung in die Ee beider Eemenschen/ vnd das die Ee frywillig sin sölle." *DCE*, f.D4ᵛ-D7ᵛ.

71.   Coverdale translated the German "vermächlung" as "handfasting," and "Hochzyt" as "wedding." *CSM*, G3ᵛ-G4ʳ. *DCE*, f. H7ᵛ-H8ʳ.

intercourse until after the church ceremony, which was supposed to take place soon after the betrothal.[72] In this way, he reminded his readers that marriage was a spiritual and moral institution as well as a secular one. Although marriage was no longer a sacrament of the church, the wedding had to be performed in the house of God, because it was God who "knitteth the knot of marriage," and because it must be "openly declared in the syght of all the worlde." In order for a marriage to be "honourable and pleasaunt vnto god," it had to take place in the light, not in darkness or secrecy.[73] Finally, no excessive celebrations were to occur before or after the wedding. Bullinger spent several pages roundly criticising the common customs of members of the congregation coming drunk to the church ceremony, holding excessive banquets and feasts afterwards, and dancing with the bride and other women in an unseemly fashion. Such raucous behavior was highly inappropriate for a wedding, Bullinger explained, because marriage was a holy institution meant to remind us of God and inhibit our lusts.[74]

This chapter on the wedding was characteristic of Bullinger's approach to marriage in *Der Christlich Eestand*. His hesitation to allow marriage to become a wholly civil institution exemplified his belief in the unity of the secular and religious spheres, and his concern with moral order and godliness was indicative of his desire to reform society and reestablish discipline. The only other writer who considered the wedding ceremony at any length was Bucer, but he was less adamant about its importance than Bullinger. The ceremony was necessary, in Bucer's view, to confirm the marriage in the sight of God and the congregation, but not to the formation of the marriage itself. The Strasbourg reformer spent more time in his writings discussing the betrothal or exchange of consent. Unlike Bullinger, he specified the exact number of witnesses that ought to be present, and declared that the couple was indeed already married after this exchange.[75] Bullinger left this question open in *Der Christlich Eestand*. He did not address whether or not the marriage took place at the betrothal or in the church, because it was an issue for the magistrates to decide on a case-by-case basis. This approach was consistent with his view of the role of the clergy as moral and spiritual advisors and his book as a practical guide for the laity.

Bullinger's high regard for legal and moral discipline also led him to take a very harsh stance against the crimes of fornication and adultery. Chapters thirteen and fourteen, "How shamefull/ vycious and abhominable/ the synne of whordome

---

72. *CSM*, f. G3ᵛ-G7ʳ. "Von der Hochzyt." *DCE*, f. H7ᵛ-I3ᵛ.

73. *CSM*, f. G4r-v. "Zum ersten wirt mit diser ordnu[n]g offentlich aller wält für die ougen gestellt/ dz Gott der ist der die Ee zamen gibt . . . Zum anderen wirt mit diser ordnung bezüget das die Ee eerlich vnd Gott wolgefellig/ ein heilig werck des liects/ vnnd nit ein vnrein werck der finsternus ist." *DCE*, f. H8ᵛ.

74. *CSM*, f. G5ʳ-G6ᵛ. *DCE*, f. I1ᵛ-I3ʳ. Limiting excessive eating and drinking after weddings was a real concern for Bullinger and other city reformers. See Baker, *Heinrich Bullinger and the Covenant*, 125-6; Lyndal Roper, *The Holy Household: Woman and Morals in Reformation Augsburg* (Oxford: Clarendon Press, 1989), 152-4. Susanna Burghartz views Bullinger's chapter on the wedding as part of his attempt to distinguish clearly moral from immoral behaviour, good sexual relations inside marriage from bad sexual relations outside of it. Burghartz, "Zwischen Integration und Ausgrenzung," 32, 38-39.

75. Selderhuis, *Marriage and Divorce*, 212-5.

is" and "How shamefull and wicked a thing aduoutrye is and how it hath of olde tyme bene punished hitherto," provide a sharp contrast to Bullinger's positive portrayal of sexual relations within marriage.[76] They also substantiate the connection between the restoration of the covenant and moral discipline in his theology. Fornication, Bullinger explained, "deuydeth vs fro[m] god/ breaketh the couenaunt which we haue with god/ spoyleth and robbeth god of that which is his."[77] Adultery, which breaks the covenant of marriage itself, was an even more shameful crime, and Bullinger declared that it should be punished by death. To support this view, he invoked Levitical law; the practices of various ancient peoples, including the Lepreians, Locrensians, Romans, and Tacitean Germans; and the law of the Holy Roman Empire.[78] For the latter, he cited the "lawes of Bamburgh" (for which he gave no date), which decreed that a man who had committed adultery should be put to death. He declared that this law had been renewed in the statutes of Charles V at the Diets of Augsburg and Regensburg, and he expressed dismay that it was never carried out.[79]

Closing brothels and instituting stricter punishments for adultery were common demands among Protestant reformers.[80] Nevertheless, in advocating the death penalty for adultery, Bullinger placed himself squarely in the Reformed camp. Bucer, Vermigli, and Calvin also called for the execution of adulterers, relying mainly on Old Testament law to support this practice.[81] Luther and Brenz were equivocal. In his 1522 marriage sermon, Luther did not come out directly for or against the execution of adulterers; in other writings, he asserted that the Biblical law prescribing execution was too harsh.[82] In a short sermon entitled *On the Punishment of Adultery and Fornication* (1527), Brenz also refrained from countenancing the death penalty. He cited a range of legal precedents, Biblical and imperial laws calling for execution, but also other imperial laws stipulating lighter punishments. In the end, Brenz contended, it was up to the magistrates and judges to be wise and choose which legal precedent to follow.[83] Execution for

---

76. *CSM*, f. E2ʳ-F4ʳ. "Wie schantlich wüst vn[d] lasterlich die hüry sye"; "Wie schandtlich vnd lasterhafft der Eebruch/ vnd wie er von alten zyten biß hiehar gestraafft sye." *DCE*, f. F2ʳ-G6ᵛ. Bullinger made this contrast explicit for his readers in the opening sentence of chapter thirteen: "And to the intent that the prayse honoure/ goodnesse & co[m]mendacion of holy wedlok/ may the more clearly appeare/ I will now set whordome right ouer agaynst it on the other syde." ("Vnd damit der heiligen Ee pryß eer güt vnd lob dester häller glantze/ wil ich yetzund in das gegenteil die hüry stellen.") Susanna Burghartz explores this contrast in her article "Integration and Ausgrenzung."

77. *CSM*, f. e3ʳ. "die hüry trenne vns von Gott/ zerrysse die pündtnus die wir mitt Gott habend/ entfrömbde vn[d] roube Gott das syn." *DCE*, f. F3ʳ.

78. *CSM*, f. E7ᵛ-E8ᵛ. *DCE*, f. F8ᵛ-G2ʳ.

79. *CSM*, f. E8ᵛ. "In dem Bambergischen Halßgericht," *DCE*, f. G1ᵛ.

80. Roper, *The Holy Household*, chap. 3.

81. Donnelly, "The Social and Ethical Thought of Peter Martyr Vermigli," 112; Robert M. Kingdon, *Adultery and Divorce in Calvin's Geneva* (Cambridge: Harvard University Press, 1995), 116-9; Selderhuis, *Marriage and Divorce*, 313-4.

82. Luther, *Vom ehelichen Leben*, 347; Steven Ozment, *When Fathers Ruled: Family Life in Reformation Europe* (Cambridge: Harvard University Press, 1983), 88-99.

83. Johannes Brenz, "Von der straff des eebruchs und hurerey" in Martin Brecht, et. al., eds, *Werke, Eine Studienausgabe* part 2: *Frühschriften* (Tübingen: J.C. B. Mohr, 1974), 249-53.

adulterers is, therefore, a perfect example of Reformed theologians adhering more stubbornly to Old Testament law than the Lutherans. It is also an example of how close Bullinger and Calvin came in matters of moral discipline, despite the fact that they held different conceptions of the covenant. In the end, Bullinger's belief in a unified, conditional covenant was not a necessary cause for his defense of the execution of adulterers, but he used covenant language and exhortations to order and discipline to place the crimes of fornication and adultery in the context of the reformation of society and the restoration of the covenant.

The third legal issue Bullinger addressed was the degree of consanguinity and affinity allowed in marriage. Bullinger's high regard for Old Testament law greatly influenced his views on this matter, while his pastoral and didactic concern for his audience influenced how he presented his views in *Der Christlich Eestand*. Here a detailed comparison with Luther is instructive. Since the year 1215, canon law had prohibited marriage within four degrees of affinity in direct and collateral (having a common ancestor) lines. It also forbade marriages between those related by spiritual affinity, or god-parenting.[84] Protestants objected to this because it lacked scriptural support and because they saw the selling of dispensations to marry within these degrees as a form of papal fundraising.[85] Luther confined his list of illegal relationships to the twelve relationships mentioned in Leviticus 18, forbidding marriage only within the first and second degrees of consanguinity and direct affinity, ignoring collateral and spiritual affinity.[86] In chapter seven, entitled "Such degrees of consanguynite and affinite as are forbydden and inhibited," Bullinger also forbade only relationships within the first and second degrees of consanguinity and direct affinity, but his list of illegal relationships contains twenty-four, twice as many as Luther's.[87] The main reason for this was is that Bullinger believed it necessary to state explicitly those relationships implied by the Biblical enumeration. For example, since Leviticus asserted a man could not marry his mother, then, logically, a woman could not marry her father, and a father could not marry his daughter. Bullinger not only deemed it important to provide a separate list stating whom a woman could not marry, but he added "daughter" and "son" to these lists, whereas Luther had only one list and did not include "daughter." According to this rule, Bullinger also added the female and male equivalents to "step-daughter," "grandmother," "mother-in-law," and "mother's brother's wife," bringing his total up to seventeen. He then added seven more relationships within the first and second degree that Luther had not stated explicitly.[88] In order to make this link between Old Testament law and a godly society even stronger, he followed this chapter with one entitled "Whether

84. Thomas Max Safley, *Let No Man Put Asunder. The Control of Marriage in the German Southwest: A Comparative Study, 1550-1600* (Kirksville: The Sixteenth Century Journal Publishers, Inc., 1984), 21-22.

85. Ozment, *When Fathers Ruled*, 44-46.

86. Ibid., 45-46.

87. *CSM*, f. B6ᵛ-C4ᵛ. "Von den verbottnen graden der blütfrüntschafft vnd magschafft." *DCE*, f. C1ᵛ-D1ʳ.

88. He added four nieces ("Brüders tocheter," "Schwester tochter," "Wybs brüder tochter," "Wybs schwester tochter"), step-grandmother ("Großvatters wyb"), and two step-grandchildren ("Wybs suns tochter," "Wybs tochter tochter"). *DCE*, f. C7ʳ⁻ᵛ.

these degrees were perscrybed onely vnto the Jewes, & not also vnto other," in which he repeated his standard arguments for the continuity of the covenant and of Old Testament law.[89]

These differences between Luther and Bullinger highlight once again the importance of Biblical law and order for the Zurich reformer. Luther's strict adherence to Biblical precedent in this case did not stem from a consistent belief in the relevance of Mosaic law in a Christian society, but rather from a desire to counter a Roman Catholic practice that he deemed corrupt and lacking in scriptural basis.[90] This hesitation to apply Old Testament law to society was more pronounced in Brenz's writings on the subject; he admitted that Catholic canon law proscribed too many degrees of consanguinity, but he refrained from stating what the proper number should be, leaving that decision to the magistrates.[91] Bullinger's defense of the Levitical law, on the other hand, was fully consistent with his covenant theology, and his detailed elucidation of the law for his readers was characteristic of his pastoral aims. He wrote *Der Christlich Eestand* as a practical treatise, a lesson on the Biblical foundations of marriage and their application in the life of the community. By stating explicitly all the people a man or a woman could not marry, he performed his pastoral duty of scriptural interpreter for the laity, and he once again confirmed the strong connection between Old Testament law and a godly society. Bucer and Vermigli agreed with Bullinger's proscription of marriage only within the first and second degrees, but they did not spell it out clearly and didactically in their writings.[92] In fact, in his discussion of consanguinity in *De Regno Christi,* Bucer displayed a more ambivalent attitude towards the law than Bullinger. He admitted that Christians were no longer bound to the laws of Moses, but he exhorted his readers to follow Biblical laws of consanguinity anyway, because God wrote them for the benefit of mankind.[93]

Bullinger ended his book of matrimony with a brief chapter on divorce. As did all major Protestant reformers, he permitted divorce and the remarriage of the innocent party in cases of adultery.[94] God permitted divorce "for the welth & medicyne of man and for amendment in wedlok," and not allowing the innocent party to remarry was "to cast a snare about poore peoples neckes, and to drawe them vnto vyce and synne."[95] More importantly, Bullinger implied that adultery was not the only legitimate reason for divorce and remarriage. He did this by ap-

---

89.   *CSM*, f. C5ʳ-C7ʳ. "Ob dise gradus dem Jüdischen volck allein vnd nit anderen ouch vorgeschriben syend." *DCE,* f. D1ᵛ-D4ᵛᵗ.

90.   Ozment, *When Fathers Ruled,* 45-46. For Luther's stance on the law and its relationship to Christian ethics, see Oberman, *Luther, Man between God and the Devil,* 78-80.

91.   Brenz, *Wie in eesachen,* 271-6.

92.   Donnelly, "Marriage from Renaissance to Reformation," 165; Selderhuis, *Marriage and Divorce,* 202-4.

93   Selderhuis, *Marriage and Divorce,* 204.

94.   Luther, *Vom ehelichen Leben,* 346; Brenz, *Wie in eesachen,* 290-293; Ozment, *When Fathers Ruled,* 85-90; Selderhuis, *Marriage and Divorce,* 287-90; Donnelly, "The Social and Ethical Thought of Peter Martyr Vermigli," 114.

95.   *CSM,* f. K5ᵛ, K6ᵛ. "Zum ersten ist die Eeschidung zü gütem vnd zü einer artzny dem menschen, ouch zü besserung des Eestands, von Gott nachgelassen . . . ein strick armen lüten mit gewalt an halß werffen/ vnd zü schanden vnd sünden ziehen." *DCE,* f. O5ᵛ-O6ʳ, O7ᵛ.

plying a broad interpretation to Christ's words in the fifth chapter of Matthew: "What the ryghte occasion of dyuorce is hath Christ mencyoned in the gospell/ & named whordome or aduoutrie. With the whych no doute/ he hath not excepted lyke & greater occasions/ but vnderstod & comprehended them therin."[96] He advised judges not to "separate maried folkes immedyatly and in al the haast but attempte all maner of reconciliacyon," but to "differre the dyuorce whyle ther is hope of ame[n]dment and vnyte."[97] Nevertheless, he entreated his readers to "co[n]sydre, that God dyd ordeyne wedlok for the honestie and welth of man, and not for his shame and destruction."[98] He also went on to point out that several "faythfull and vertuous" Roman Emperors permitted divorce for reasons other than adultery, such as murder or poisoning.[99]

Bullinger's views on divorce fall between the Lutherans and Vermigli on the one hand, and Bucer and Erasmus on the other. Luther, Brenz, and Vermigli only allowed it for adultery and one other ground, desertion in the case of the Lutherans and difference of faith in the case of Vermigli.[100] Bucer and Erasmus wrote more extensively than Bullinger on the subject and specified more legitimate grounds for divorce.[101] Evidence exists, however, that suggests that Bullinger agreed with the opinions of both Bucer and Erasmus; in his commentary on Paul's first letter to the Corinthians (1534), he explained that he would not write that much about divorce, because Bucer and Erasmus had already written copiously on the subject.[102] At the beginning of chapter twenty-five of *Der Christlich Eestand*, he inserted a similar passage, but he did not name Bucer and Erasmus specifically: "Here shulde I also saye some what concernyng diuorce because it lyeth vnder the titel of wedlok . . . yf other Christen lerned persones had not wrytten sufficiently therof afore."[103]

The fact that Bullinger praised Bucer and Erasmus's views on divorce while simultaneously hesitating to commit them to writing himself is significant for two reasons. First, Bullinger deemed judgement in divorce cases to be a matter for the

96. *CSM* f. K6'. "welchs aber ein rächtmässige vrsach [der] Eeschidung sye/ hat vnser Herr Jesus im[m] Euangelio gmeldet/ vnd die Hüry o[der] den Eebruch benamset. Mit welichem er vngezwyflet glychs vnd grössers nit abgestrickt/ sund[er] ouch verstande[n] vnd yngeschlossen hat." *DCE,* f. O6ᵛ-O7ʳ.

97. Bullinger, *Matrimonye,* trans. Coverdale, f. K6ʳ. "söllennd die richter ouch nit ylends vnd von stundan die Een scheiden/ sunder alle mittel der vereinigung versüche[n]/ vnd diewyl hoffnung der besserung vn[d] vereinigung ist/ die schydung vfziehen." *DCE,* f. O6ᵛ.

98. *CSM,* f. K6ᵛ. "das Gott die Ee vfgesetzt hab zü eeren vnd gütem dem mensche[n]/ vnd nit ü schande[n] vnd sinem verderben." *DCE,* f. O7ʳ.

99. *CSM,* f. K6ᵛ. *DCE,* f. O7ʳ.

100. A famous case of divorce on grounds of religious difference was that of Galeazzo Caracciolo, an Italian convert to the Reformed faith whose wife and family refused to follow him to Geneva. In May 1559, Bullinger, Vermigli, and other theologians in Zurich expressed in writing their support for the decision of the Genevan Consistory to grant Caracciolo a divorce. See ZB, Ms. S 94, no. 188, and Kingdon, *Adultery and Divorce in Calvin's Geneva,* 160-1. I thank Emidio Campi for the reference to this manuscript and Rainer Henrich for procuring me a copy.

101. Selderhuis, *Marriage and Divorce,* 40-42, 257-326.

102. Ibid., 47

103. *CSM,* f. K5ʳ. "Hie sölt ich ouch etwas von der Eeschidung sagen/ diewyl sy ouch vnder den tittel der Ee gehört . . . wo nit andere Christliche geleerte lüt vorhin gnügsam daruon geschribe[n] hettend." *DCE,* f. O5ᵛ.

magistrates. He expressed his opinion openly about divorce in the case of adultery, because there the Biblical precedent was clear, but in his role as a clergyman and author of a practical book for the laity, he left the more ambiguous cases to the judges. Bullinger reminded his readers of this in the opening sentences of chapter twenty-five. He will write only briefly about divorce, he explained, not only because others have written before him, but because the matter "belongeth rather to the office of iudges/ then to such pryuate persones as I here wrytte vnto."[104] Second, the relationship between Bullinger, Bucer, and Erasmus calls into question the importance of the idea of the covenant in the matter of divorce. One is tempted to see a direct relation between the bilateral nature of the covenant and Bullinger's and Bucer's argument that when a marriage no longer served its purpose "for the honestie and welth of man," the bilateral contract of marriage could be dissolved.[105] Yet, Bullinger did not use covenant language in chapter twenty-five, as he did in so many of the previous chapters. Furthermore, this view of marriage as a bilateral contract was an old one also employed by Erasmus, who did not share the same view of the covenant as the Reformed theologians. Erasmus argued that the essence of marriage was mutual love, and when this was lacking, a marriage no longer existed. Bullinger did not employ this justification, but Bucer did. The Strasbourg reformer was able to do so because, unlike Bullinger, he had declared love and companionship to be the *first* of the three reasons for marriage.[106] In this light, Erasmus's and Bucer's views on divorce appear to be more closely related to the New Testament ideal of love and the classical notion of *aequitas* or fairness than to the Old Testament.[107] In the end, Bullinger's desire for orderly and peaceful marriages led him to perceive that a more liberal divorce policy was necessary, but his strict biblicism and belief in the authority of the magistrate made him hesitate to express the same views as Bucer and Erasmus in writing.

Several important points can be drawn from this detailed explication of the content of Bullinger's *Der Christlich Eestand*. A comparison with other reformers has demonstrated that his theology of marriage was closest to that of Martin Bucer. This corrects, in part, the view of Bucer's contemporaries and of some modern-day scholars that Bucer's ideas on the subject were far more radical than those of any other Protestant theologian.[108] Covenant theology played a role in both the overwhelming similarities and the subtle differences between the views of Bullinger and Bucer. Significantly more than the Lutherans, and slightly more than Vermigli and Calvin, Bucer and Bullinger stressed the continuity of marriage

104. *CSM*, f. K5ʳ. "darzü die Schidung mee für die richter/ dann für besondere einspännige persone[n] (denen ich hie zü dienst schryb) horte." *DCE*, f. O5ᵛ.

105. Selderhuis argues this in his *Marriage and Divorce*, 184.

106. Ibid., 165-6.

107. The relationship between ideas of *aequitas* and Reformed covenant theology is a subject in need of further investigation. Bullinger and Bucer may have adopted the notion of *aequitas* and placed it in an Old Testament, covenant context, but as their theologies of marriage demonstrate, this could lead to confusion and inconsistency.

108. For contemporary reactions to Bucer's marriage theology and for Selderhuis's own evaluation of it vis-à-vis other reformers, see Selderhuis, *Marriage and Divorce*, 1-2, 47-48, 354-72.

from the Old to the New Testaments, the authority of the magistrate, and the need for moral discipline. Bullinger's application of Old Testament mores was even more consistent than Bucer's. The subtle differences between the two theologians on the issues of love, sex, and divorce stemmed from Bucer's concern for New Testament ideals of love and freedom from the law that ran contrary to the notion of a unified covenant.[109] In Bullinger's writings, there is no such tension between the law and freedom. It is important to step back from these minutiae, however, and to note that nearly all of the arguments Bucer and Bullinger used to portray marriage as a godly institution were also present in the writings of pre-Reformation humanists and other Protestant reformers, while most of their opinions on legal issues were shared by other Reformed theologians, if not always by the Lutherans. In comparison with Bucer, Vermigli and Calvin, then, Bullinger's added emphasis on the Old Testament resulted primarily in differences of language and structure, and does not point to the existence of a second branch or tradition of Reformed Protestantism. Rather, Bullinger's salient contribution to the reformation of marriage was to write a more thorough, pragmatic treatise than any other reformer, and one that placed a Protestant theology of marriage within the traditional genre of the domestic conduct book.

109. On the tension in Bucer's writings between the law and the freedom of a Christian, see Selderhuis, *Marriage and Divorce*, 114, 204.

Selected Bibliography of Secondary Sources

Bächtold, Hans Ulrich ed. *Von Cyprian zur Walzenprägung: Streiflichter auf Zürcher Geist und Kultur der Bullingerzeit.* Studien und Texte zur Bullingerzeit 2; Zug: Achius, 2001.

―――. "Augsburg und Oberschwaben. Der Zwinglianismus der schwäbischen Reichsstädte im Bullinger-Briefwechsel von 1531 bis 1548–ein Überblick," *Zeitschrift für bayerische Kirchengeschichte* 64 (1995): 1-19.

―――. "Bullinger und die Krise der Zürcher Reformation im Jahre 1532" in Ulrich Gäbler/Erland Herkenrath eds. *Heinrich Bullinger 1504-1575. Gesammelte Aufsätze zum 400. Todestag.* vol 1: *Leben und Werk.* ZBRG 7; Zurich: TVZ, 1975, 269-89.

―――. "'Ein fine hand zů schriben': Glanz und Elend im Leben des Schönschreibers Israël Stäheli, †1596" in Hans Ulrich Bächtold ed. *Von Cyprian zur Walzenprägung: Streiflichter auf Zürcher Geist und Kultur der Bullingerzeit.* Studien und Texte zur Bullingerzeit 2; Zug: Achius, 2001, 115-43.

―――. "Frauen schreiben Bullinger–Bullinger schreibt Frauen. Heinrich Bullinger im Briefwechsel mit Frauen, insbesondere mit Anna Alexandria zu Rappoltstein" in Alfred Schindler/Hans Stickelberger eds. *Die Zürcher Reformation: Ausstrahlungen und Rückwirkungen. Wissenschaftliche Tagung zum hundertjährigen Bestehen des Zwinglivereins 1997.* ZBRG 18; Berne: Peter Lang, 2001, 143-60.

―――. "Gegen den Hunger beten. Heinrich Bullinger, Zürich und die Einführung des Gemeinen Gebetes im Jahre 1571" in Hans Ulrich Bächtold et al. eds. *Vom Beten, vom Verketzern, vom Predigen. Beiträge zum Zeitalter Heinrich Bullingers und Rudolf Gwalthers.* Zug: Achius, 1999, 9-44.

―――. "History, Ideology and Propaganda in the Reformation: the Early Writing 'Anklag und ernstliches ermanen Gottes' (1525) of Heinrich Bullinger" in Bruce Gordon ed. *Protestant History and Identity in Sixteenth-Century Europe.* vol 1: *The Medieval Inheritance.* Aldershot: Ashgate, 1996, 46-59.

―――. "Heinrich Bullinger und die Entwicklung des Schulwesens in Zürich" in *Schola Tigurina. Die Zürcher Hohe Schule und ihre Gelehrten um 1550. Katalog zur Ausstellung vom 25. Mai bis 10. Juli 1999 in der Zentralbibliothek Zürich.* Institut für Schweizerische Reformationsgeschichte ed. Zurich/Freiburg i. Br.: Pano, 1999, 48-51.

―――. *Heinrich Bullinger vor dem Rat. Zur Gestaltung und Verwaltung des Zürcher Staatswesens in den Jahren 1531 bis 1575.* ZBRG 12; Berne/Frankfurt a. Main: Peter Lang, 1982.

Bächtold, Jakob. *Geschichte der deutschen Literatur in der Schweiz.* Frauenfeld: Huber, 1892.

————. *Schweizerische Schauspiele des sechzehnten Jahrhunderts*. Frauenfeld: J. Huber, 1890.

Baker, J. Wayne. "Christian Discipline, Church and State, and Toleration: Bullinger, Calvin and Basel 1530-1555" in Heiko A. Oberman et al. eds. *Reformiertes Erbe. Festschrift für Gottfried W. Locher zu seinem 80. Geburtstag*. 2 vols, Zurich: TVZ, 1992, I:35-48.

————. *Heinrich Bullinger and the Covenant: The Other Reformed Tradition*. Athens, Ohio: Ohio Univ. Press, 1980.

————. "Heinrich Bullinger, the Covenant and the Reformed Tradition in Retrospect," *Sixteenth Century Journal* 29/2 (1998): 359-76.

Balázs, Mihály *Early Transylvanian Antitrinitarianism (1566-1571): From Servet to Palaeologus*. Baden-Baden: Editions Valentin Koerner, 1996.

Bangerter, Olivier. *La pensée militaire de Zwingli*. ZBRG 21; Berne: Peter Lang, 2003.

Baumann, Michael/Henrich, Rainer. "Das Lektorium, sein Lehrkörper, seine Studenten" in *Schola Tigurina. Die Zürcher Hohe Schule und ihre Gelehrten um 1550. Katalog zur Ausstellung vom 25. Mai bis 10. Juli 1999 in der Zentralbibliothek Zürich*. Institut für Schweizerische Reformationsgeschichte ed. Zurich/Freiburg i. Br.: Pano, 1999, 24-27.

Berg, Hans Georg vom. "Die 'Brüder vom gemeinsamen Leben' und die Stiftsschule von St. Martin zu Emmerich. Zur Frage des Einflusses der Devotio Moderna auf den jungen Bullinger" in Ulrich Gäbler/Erland Herkenrath eds. *Heinrich Bullinger 1504-1575. Gesammelte Aufsätze zum 400. Todestag*. vol. 1: *Leben und Werk*. ZBRG 7; Zurich: TVZ, 1975, 1-12.

Biel, Pamela. *Doorkeepers at the house of Righteousness. Heinrich Bullinger and the Zurich Clergy 1535-1575*. ZBRG 15; Berne: Peter Lang, 1990.

————. "Heinrich Bullinger's Death and Testament: A Well-planned Departure," *Sixteenth Century Journal* 22 (1991): 3-14.

Bitzel, Alexander. *Anfechtung und Trost bei Sigismund Scherertz. Ein lutherischer Theologe im Dreißigjährigen Krieg*. Studien zur Kirchengeschichte Niedersachsens 38; Göttingen: Vanderhoeck & Ruprecht, 2002.

Blanke, Fritz/Leuschner, Immanuel. *Heinrich Bullinger. Vater der reformierten Kirche*. Zurich: TVZ, 1990.

————. *Der junge Bullinger*. Zwingli-Bücherei 22; Zurich: Zwingli Verlag, 1942.

————. "Die Theologie des jungen Bullinger," *Neue Zürcher Zeitung* 1962, Nr. 4467.

Blösch, Emil. "Ein Brief H. Bullingers," *Anzeiger für schweizerische Geschichte* new series 5 (1887): 108f.

Bourdieu, Pierre. "Eine Interpretation der Religion nach Max Weber" in Pierre Bourdieu. *Das religiöse Feld*. Andreas Pfeuffer trans. Stephan Egger et al. eds. édition discours 11; Constance: 2000, 11-37.

Bouwsma, William J. *Calvin. A Sixteenth-Century Portrait*. Oxford: OUP, 1988.

Brecht, Martin. *Martin Luther*. 3 vols. Stuttgart: Calwer, 1983-7.

Bryner, Erich. "Ein Brief Heinrich Bullingers an den Fürsten der Moldau aus dem Jahre 1563" in Heiko A. Oberman et al. eds. *Reformiertes Erbe. Festschrift für Gottfried W. Locher zu seinem 80. Geburtstag.* 2 vols, Zurich: TVZ, 1992, I:63-69.

Burchill, Christopher J. *The Heidelberg Antitrinitarians.* Baden-Baden: Editions Valentin Koerner, 1989.

Burckhardt, Felix. "Die böse Fastnacht auf Schloss Waldenburg" in *Aus der Welt des Buches. Festgabe zum 70. Geburtstag von Georg Leyh.* Zentralblatt für Bibliothekswesen, Beiheft 75 (1950): 273-82.

Burghartz, Susanna. "Zwischen Integration und Ausgrenzung: Zur Dialektik reformierter Ehetheologie am Beispiel Heinrich Bullingers," *L'Homme: Zeitschrift für Feministische Geschichtswissenschaft* 8/1 (1997): 30-42.

Bürgisser, Eugen. *Geschichte der Stadt Bremgarten im Mittelalter.* Phil. Diss., Zurich, 1937.

Burrows, Mark S. "'Christus intra nos Vivens': The Peculiar Genius of Bullinger's Doctrine of Sanctification," *Zeitschrift für Kirchengeschichte* 98 (1987): 48-69.

Busch, E. "Der Consensus Tigurinus (1549). Einleitung" in E. Busch et al. eds. *Calvin-Studienausgabe.* vol. 4, Neukirchen-Vluyn: Neukirchener, 2002, 1-10.

Büsser, Fritz. "Die Bartholomäusnacht. Eindrücke und Auswirkungen im reformierten Zürich," *Neue Zürcher Zeitung*, 27 August 1972, no 398, 49/50.

———. "Bullinger als Prophet. Zu seiner Frühschrift 'Anklag und Ermahnen'" in Fritz Büsser, *Wurzeln der Reformation in Zürich. Zum 500. Geburtstag des Reformators Huldrych Zwingl.* Studies in Medieval and Reformation Thought 31; Leiden: Brill, 1985, 106-24.

———. "J. H. Hottinger und der Thesaurus Hottingerianus," *Zwingliana* 22 (1995): 85-108.

———. "Der 'oekumenische Patriarch' der Reformation. Bausteine zu Bullingers Lehre von der Kirche" in W. H. Neuser/H. J. Selderhuis eds. *Ordentlich und fruchtbar. Festschrift für Willem van 't Spijker.* Leiden: 1997, J.J. Groen, 69-78.

———. "De propheta officio. Eine Gedenkrede Bullingers auf Zwingli" in Fritz Büsser, *Wurzeln der Reformation in Zürich. Zum 500. Geburtstag des Reformators Huldrych Zwingli.* Studies in Medieval and Reformation Thought 31; Leiden: Brill, 1985, 60-71.

———. *Die Prophezei. Humanismus und Reformation in Zürich. Ausgewählte Aufsätze und Vorträge. Zu seinem 70. Geburtstag am 12. Februar 1993.* Alfred Schindler ed. ZBRG 17; Berne: Peter Lang, 1994.

———. "'Prophezei'–'Schola Tigurina'. Prototyp, Ideal und Wirklichkeit" in *Schola Tigurina. Die Zürcher Hohe Schule und ihre Gelehrten um 1550. Katalog zur Ausstellung vom 25. Mai bis 10. Juli 1999 in der Zentralbibliothek Zürich.* Institut für Schweizerische Reformationsgeschichte ed. Zurich/Freiburg i. Br.: Pano, 1999, 18-21.

———. "Reformierte Erziehung in Theorie und Praxis" in Fritz Büsser, *Wurzeln der Reformation in Zürich. Zum 500. Geburtstag des Reformators Huldrych*

Zwingli. Studies in Medieval and Reformation Thought 31; Leiden: Brill, 1985, 199-216.

———. "Die Überlieferung von Heinrich Bullingers Briefwechsel" in *HBBW* I:7-21.

———. *Wurzeln der Reformation in Zürich. Zum 500. Geburtstag des Reformators Huldrych Zwingli.* Studies in Medieval and Reformation Thought 31; Leiden: Brill, 1985.

———. "Zürich–'Die Stadt auf dem Berg'. Bullingers reformatorisches Vermächtnis an der Wende zum 21. Jahrhundert," *Zwingliana* 25 (1998): 21-42.

Candreia, J. "Ein 'zeitungs'artiger Bericht Ulr. Campell's aus dem Jahre 1572," *Die Rheinquellen* 1 (1895): 209-25.

Cargill-Thompson, W. D. J. *The Political Thought of Martin Luther.* Sussex: The Harvester Press, 1984.

Cecchi, Emilio/Sapegno, Natalino eds. *Storia della letteratura italiana.* vol. 7: *Il Settecento.* Milan: Garzanti, 1988.

Charbon, Remy. "Lucretia Tigurina. Heinrich Bullingers Spiel von Lucretia und Brutus (1526)" in Verena Ehrich-Haefeli et al. eds. *Antiquitates Renatae [...]. Festschrift für Renate Böschenstein.* Würzburg: Königshausen und Neumann, 1998, 35-47.

Demandt, Dieter. "Die Auseinandersetzungen des Schmalkaldischen Bundes mit Herzog Heinrich dem Jüngeren von Braunschweig-Wolfenbüttel im Briefwechsel des St. Galler Reformators Vadian," *Zwingliana* 22 (1995):45-66.

Donnelly, John Patrick. "Marriage from Renaissance to Reformation: Two Florentine Moralists" in John R. Sommerfeldt and Thomas H. Seiler eds. *Studies in Medieval Culture,* vol. 11 Western Michigan University: Medieval Institute, 1977.

———. "The Social and Ethical Thought of Peter Martyr Vermigli" in Joseph C. McLelland ed. *Peter Martyr Vermigli and Italian Reform.* Ontario: Wilfrid Laurier Univ. Press, 1980.

Dowey, Edward A. "The Old Faith: Comments on One of Heinrich Bullinger's Most Distinctive Treatises" in Willem van 't Spijker ed. *Calvin: Erbe und Auftrag. Festschrift für Wilhelm Neuser zu seinem 65. Geburtstag.* Kampen: Kok Pharos, 1991, 270-8.

———. "Wort Gottes als Schrift und Predigt im Zweiten Helvetischen Bekenntnis" in Joachim Staedtke ed. *Glauben und Bekennen. Vierhundert Jahre Confessio Helvetica posterior. Beiträge zu ihrer Geschichte und Theologie.* Zurich: Zwingli Verlag, 1966, 235-50.

Duchrow, Ulrich. *Christenheit und Weltverantwortung. Traditionsgeschichte und systematische Struktur der Zweireichelehre.* Stuttgart: Klett, 1970.

Ernst, Ulrich. *Geschichte des zürcherischen Schulwesens bis gegen Ende des sechzehnten Jahrhunderts.* Winterthur: Bleuler-Hausheer, 1879.

Euler, Carrie. "Heinrich Bullinger, Marriage, and the English Reformation: *The Christen state of Matrimonye* in England, 1540-53," *Sixteenth Century Journal* 34/2 (2003): 365-91.

Farner, Oskar. "Die Bullinger-Briefe," *Zwingliana* 10 (1954):103-8.

―――. *Huldreich Zwingli*. 4 vols Zurich: Zwingli-Verlag, 1943-60.

Fast, Heinold. *Heinrich Bullinger und die Täufer: Ein Beitrag zur Historiographie und Theologie im 16. Jahrhundert*. Schriftenreihe des Mennonitischen Geschichtsvereins 7; Weierhof: Mennonitischer Geschichtsverein, 1959.

Feller, Richard/Bonjour, Edgar. *Geschichtsschreibung der Schweiz*. 2 vols Basle/Stuttgart: Schwabe, 1962.

Figi, Jacques. *Die innere Reorganisation des Grossmünsterstifts in Zürich 1519-1531*. Affoltern am Albis: J. Weiss, 1951.

Friedrich, Martin. "Heinrich Bullinger und die Wittenberger Konkordie," *Zwingliana* 24 (1997): 59-79.

Gäbler, Ulrich. "Bullingers Vorlesung über das Johannesevangelium aus dem Jahre 1523" in Ulrich Gäbler/Erland Herkenrath eds. *Heinrich Bullinger 1504-1575. Gesammelte Aufsätze zum 400. Todestag*, vol. 1: *Leben und Werk*. (ZBRG 7; Zurich: TVZ, 1975), 13-27.

―――. "Die Schweizer–ein 'Auserwähltes Volk'?" in Heiko A. Oberman et al. eds. *Reformiertes Erbe. Festschrift für Gottfried W. Locher zu seinem 80. Geburtstag*. 2 vols Zurich: TVZ, 1992, I:143-55.

Gagliardi, Ernst. "Mitteilungen über eine neu gefundene Quelle zur zürcherischen Reformationsgeschichte (Hans Edlibach)," *Zwingliana* 2 (1905-1912): 407-14.

Garcia Archilla, Aurelio A. *The Theology of History and Apologetic Historiography in Heinrich Bullinger: Truth in History*. San Francisco: Mellen Press, 1992.

Gerig, Georg. *Reisläufer und Pensionenherren in Zürich 1519-1532. Ein Beitrag zur Kenntnis der Kräfte, welche der Reformation widerstrebten*. Zurich: Leeman, 1947.

Gilly, Carlos. *Spanien und der Basler Buchdruck bis 1600: Ein Querschnitt durch die spanische Geistesgeschichte aus der Sicht einer europäischen Buchdruckerstadt*. Basle: Helbing und Lichtenhahn, 1985.

Giovanoli, Sandro ed. *Rudolf Gwalthers 'Nabal': ein Zürcher Drama aus dem 16. Jahrhundert*. Studien zu Germanistik, Anglistik und Komparatistik 83; Bonn: Bouvier Grundmann, 1979.

Gordon, Bruce. *Clerical discipline and the rural reformation: the synod in Zürich, 1532-1580*. ZBRG 16; Berne: Peter Lang, 1992.

―――. "'God killed Saul': Heinrich Bullinger and Jacob Ruef on the Power of the Devil" in Kathryn A. Edwards ed. *Werewolves, witches, and wandering spirits: traditional beliefs and folklore in early modern Europe*. Kirsville, MO, Trueman State University Press, 2002, 155-179.

―――. "Heinrich Bullinger" in Carter Lindberg ed. *The Reformation Theologians. An Introduction to Theology in the Early Modern Period*. Oxford/Malden, Mass.: Blackwell, 2002, 170-83.

―――. *The Swiss Reformation*. Manchester: Manchester Univ. Press, 2002.

―――. "Translation and Spirituality of Leo Jud." paper presented at the annual Sixteenth Century Studies Conference, San Antonio, TX: October 2002.

—. "Transcendence and Community in Zwinglian worship: the Liturgy of 1525 in Zurich" in R. W. Swanson ed. *Continuity and Change in Christian Worship*. Studies in Church History 35; Bury St Edmunds: Boydell and Brewer, 1999, 128-50.

———. "'welcher nit gloupt der ist schon verdampt': Heinrich Bullinger and the Spirituality of the Last Judgement," *Zwingliana* 29 (2002): 29-54.

Grasshoff, R. *Die briefliche Zeitung des XVI. Jahrhunderts*. Diss. phil. Leipzig: 1877.

Gsell, Monika. "Hierarchie und Gegenseitigkeit: Überlegungen zur Geschlechterkonzeption in Heinrich Bullingers Eheschriften" in Rüdiger Schnell ed. *Geschlechterbeziehungen und Textfunkionen: Studien zu Eheschriften der Frühen Neuzeit*. Tübingen: Niemeyer, 1998.

Haas, Martin. *Huldrych Zwingli und seine Zeit*. 3rd ed., Zurich: TVZ, 1982.

Hamm, Berndt. *Bürgertum und Glaube. Konturen der städtischen Reformation*. Göttingen: Vanderhoeck & Ruprecht, 1996.

———. *Zwinglis Reformation der Freiheit*. Neukirchen-Vluyn: Neukirchener, 1988.

Harrington, Joel. *Reordering Marriage and Society in Reformation Germany*. Cambridge: CUP. 1995.

Hartmann Horst ed. *Heinrich Bullinger–Hans Sachs: Lucretia-Dramen*. Leipzig: Bibliographisches Institut, 1973.

Hausammann, Susi. "Anfragen zum Schriftverständnis des jungen Bullinger im Zusammenhang einer Interpretation von 'De scripturae negotio'" in Ulrich Gäbler/Erland Herkenrath eds. *Heinrich Bullinger 1504-1575. Gesammelte Aufsätze zum 400. Todestag*, vol. 1: *Leben und Werk*. ZBRG 7; Zurich: TVZ, 1975, 29-48.

———. "Die Rhetorik im Dienst der reformatorischen Schiftauslegung," *Kerygma und Dogma: Zeitschrift für theologische Forschung und kirchliche Lehre* 20 (1974): 305-14.

———. *Römerbriefauslegung zwischen Humanismus und Reformation. Eine Studie zu Heinrich Bullingers Römerbriefvorlesung von 1525*. Studien zur Dogmengeschichte und systematischen Theologie 27; Zurich: Zwingli Verlag, 1970.

Hauser, Martin. *Prophet und Bischof. Huldrych Zwinglis Amtsverständnis im Rahmen der Zürcher Reformation*. Ökumenische Beihefte zur Freiburger Zeitschrift für Philosophie und Theologie 21; Freiburg: Universitätsverlag, 1994.

Hauswirth, René. "Zur politischen Ethik der Generation nach Zwingli," *Zwingliana* 13 (1971): 305-42.

Hein, Lorenz. *Italienische Protestanten und ihr Einfluß auf die Reformation in Polen während der beiden Jahrzehnte vor dem Sandomirer Konsens (1570)*. Leiden: E.J. Brill, 1974.

Himmighöfer, Traudel. *Die Zürcher Bibel bis zum Tode Zwinglis (1531). Darstellung und Bibliographie*. Veröffentlichungen des Instituts für Europäische Geschichte Mainz, Abteilung Religionsgeschichte 154; Mainz: von Zabern, 1995.

Hirth, Käthe. *Heinrich Bullingers Spiel von "Lucretia und Brutus" 1533*. Phil. Diss., Marburg, 1919.

Hollweg, Walter. *Heinrich Bullingers Hausbuch. Eine Untersuchung über die Anfänge der reformierten · Predigtliteratur.* Neukirchen: Verlag der Buchhandlung des Erziehungsverein, 1956.

Hulme, Edward M. "Lelio Sozzini's Confession of Faith" in *Persecution and Liberty: Essays in Honor of George Lincoln Burr.* New York: The Century Co., 1931, 211-25.

Hundeshagen, Carl Bernhard. "Die Gestaltung des Verhältnisses zwischen Staat und Kirche in Zürich unmittelbar nach Zwinglis Tod" in Carl Bernhard Hundeshagen. *Beiträge zur Kirchenverfassungsgeschichte und Kirchenpolitik insbesondere des Protestantismus.* vol 1 Wiesbaden: Minerva, 1864, 258-87.

Hyma, Albert. "Erasmus and the Sacrament of Matrimony," *Archiv für Reformationsgeschichte* 48 (1957): 145-64.

Jackson, John. *'Reformatio legum ecclesiasticarum' and Canon Law Reform under the Tudors: Society, Politics, and Religion.* D.Phil. Diss. Oxford University: forthcoming.

Jacob, Walter. *Politische Führungsschicht und Reformation. Untersuchungen zur Reformation in Zürich 1519-1528.* ZBRG 1; Zurich: 1970.

Kingdon, Robert M. *Adultery and Divorce in Calvin's Geneva.* Cambridge: Harvard Univ. Press, 1995.

Kleinpaul, Johannes. *Die Fuggerzeitungen 1568-1605.* Abhandlungen aus dem Institut für Zeitungskunde an der Universität Leipzig, vol. 1, no 4 Preisschriften, gekrönt und hg. von der Fürstlich Jablonowskischen Gesellschaft zu Leipzig 49; Leipzig: 1921, reprinted Vaduz: Sändig, 1992.

Klescewski, Reinhard. "Wandlungen des Lucretia-Bildes im lateinischen Mittelalter und in der italienischen Literatur der Renaissance" in Eckhard Lefèvre/Eckhard Olshausen eds. *Livius. Werke und Rezeption. Festschrift für Erich Burck zum 80. Geburtstag.* Munich: Beck, 1983, 313-35.

Kobelt, Eduard Jakob. *Die Bedeutung der Eidgenossenschaft für Huldrych Zwingli.* Zurich: Leemann, 1970.

Koch, Ernst. *Die Theologie der Confessio Helvetica Posterior.* Neukirchen: Neukirchener Verlag des Erziehungsvereins, 1968.

Köhler, Walther. *Zürcher Ehegericht und Genfer Konsistorium.* 2 vols Leipzig: Heinsius, 1932.

Kok, Joel E. "Heinrich Bullinger's Exegetical Method: The Model for Calvin?" in Richard A. Muller/John L. Thompson eds. *Biblical Interpretation in the Era of the Reformation.* Grand Rapids, Mich.: William B. Eerdmans Publishing Company, 1996, 241-54.

Kolfhaus, W. *Christusgemeinschaft bei Johannes Calvin.* Neukirchen: Buchhandlung des Erziehungsvereins, 1939.

Krafft, Carl. *Aufzeichnungen des schweizerischen Reformators Heinrich Bullinger über sein Studium zu Emmerich und Köln (1516-1522) und dessen Briefwechsel mit Freunden in Köln, Erzbischof Hermann von Wied etc. Ein Beitrag zur niederrheinisch-westfälischen Kirchen-, Schul- und Gelehrtengeschichte.* Elberfeld: Sam. Lucas, 1870.

Largadièr, Anton. "Das reformierte Zürich und die Fest- und Heiligentage," *Zwingliana* 9 (1953): 497-525.

Lilliback, P. A. *The Binding of God. Calvin's Role in the Development of Covenant Theology.* Grand Rapids: Baker Press, 2001.

Locher, Gottfried W. "Praedicatio verbi Dei est verbum dei" in G. W. Locher. *Huldrych Zwingli in neuer Sicht. Zehn Beiträge zur Theologie der Zürcher Reformation.* Zurich: 1969, Zwingli Verlag, 275-87.

———. *Die Theologie Huldrych Zwinglis im Lichte seiner Christologie.* part I: *Die Gotteslehre.* Zurich: Zwingli Verlag, 1952.

———. *Die Zwinglische Reformation im Rahmen der europäischen Kirchengeschichte.* Göttingen: Vandenhoeck, 1979.

Maag, Karin. "Financing Education: the Zurich Approach, 1550-1620" in Beat A. Kümin ed. *Reformations Old and New. Essays on the Socio-Economic Impact of Religious Change, c. 1470-1630.* Aldershot: Ashgate, 1996.

———. *Seminary or University? The Genevan Academy and Reformed Higher Education, 1560-1620.* St Andrews Studies in Reformation History; Aldershot: Ashgate, 1995.

Mau, Rudolf. *Evangelische Bewegung und frühe Reformation 1521-1532.* Kirchengeschichte in Einzeldarstellungen II/5; Leipzig: Evangelische Verlagsanstalt, 2000.

Mauelshagen, Franz. "'...die portenta et ostenta mines lieben Herren vnsers säligen...'. Nachlassstücke Bullingers im 13. Buch der Wickiana," *Zwingliana* 28 (2001): 73-117.

———. *Johann Jakob Wicks "Wunderbücher." Reformierter Wunderglaube im Wandel der Geschichtsschreibung.* Zurich: Chronos, 2003.

McCoy, Charles S./Baker, J. Wayne. *Fountainhead of Federalism: Heinrich Bullinger and the Covenantal Tradition. With a Translation of De testamento seu foedere Dei unico et aeterno (1534).* Louisville, Kentucky: Westminster/John Knox Press, 1991.

MacCulloch, Diarmaid. *Thomas Cranmer. A Life.* New Haven/London: Yale University Press, 1996.

McLelland, J. C. "Die Sakramentslehre der Confessio Helvetica posterior" in Joachim Staedtke ed. *Glauben und Bekennen. 400 Jahre Confessio Helvetica Posterior. Beiträge zu ihrer Geschichte und Theologie.* Zurich: Zwingli Verlag, 1966, 368-91.

Mehlhausen, Joachim. "Kirchenpolitik. Erwägungen zu einem undeutlichen Wort," *Zeitschrift für Theologie und Kirche* 85 (1988): 275-302.

Meyer, Andreas. *Zürich und Rom. Ordentliche Kollatur und päpstliche Provisionen am Frau- und Großmünster 1316-1523.* Bibliothek des Deutschen Historischen Instituts in Rom 64; Tübingen: Niemeyer, 1986.

Meyer, Walter E. "Soteriologie, Eschatologie und Christologie in der Confessio Helvetica Posterior," *Zwingliana* 12 (1966): 391-409.

Moser, Christian. "Ratramnus von Corbie als 'testis veritatis' in der Zürcher Reformation: Zu Heinrich Bullinger und Leo Juds Ausgabe des *Liber de corpore et sanguine Domini* (1532)" in Martin H. Graf/Christian Moser eds.

Strenarum lanx: Beiträge zur Philologie und Geschichte des Mittelalters und der Frühen Neuzeit. Zug: Achius, 2003, 235-309.

————. *"Vil der wunderwerchen Gottes wirt man hierinn såhen." Studien zu Heinrich Bullingers Reformationsgeschicht.* Diss., Univ. of Zurich: 2002.

Mühlenberg, E. "Scriptura non est autentica sine authoritate ecclesiae (Johannes Eck): Vorstellungen von der Entstehung des Kanons in der Kontroverse um das reformatorische Schriftprinzip," *Zeitschrift für Theologie und Kirche* 97 (2000): 183-209.

Mühling, Andreas. *Heinrich Bullingers europäische Kirchenpolitik.* ZBRG 19; Berne: Peter Lang, 2001.

————. "Lelio Sozzini: Bemerkungen zum Umgang Heinrich Bullingers mit 'Häretikern'" in Athina Lexutt/Vicco von Bülow eds. *Kaum zu glauben: Von der Häresie und dem Umgang mit ihr.* Rheinbach: CMZ-Verlag, 1998, 162-70.

Müller, Gustav. *Die Quellen zur Beschreibung des Zürich- und Aargaus in Johannes Stumpfs Schweizerchronik.* Schriftenreihe der Stiftung von Schnyder von Wartensee 19; Zurich: Beer, 1916.

Müller, Hans. *Der Geschichtschreiber Johann Stumpf: Eine Untersuchung über sein Weltbild.* Schweizer Studien zur Geschichtswissenschaft, new series 8; Zurich: Leemann, 1945.

Muller, Richard. *Christ and the Decree: Christology and Predestination in Reformed Theology from Calvin to Perkins.* Grand Rapids: Baker Book House, 1986.

————. *Post-Reformation Reformed Dogmatics.* vol 2: *Holy Scripture: The Cognitive Foundation of Theology.* Grand Rapids: Baker Book House, 1993.

Nabholz, Hans. "Zürichs Höhere Schulen von der Reformation bis zur Gründung der Universität, 1525-1833" in Ernst Gagliardi et al. eds. *Die Universität Zürich 1833-1933 und ihre Vorläufer.* Die Zürcherischen Schulen seit der Regeneration 3; Zurich: Verlag der Erziehungsdirektion, 1938, 3-164.

Neudecker, Christian Gotthold. *Urkunden aus der Reformationszeit.* Kassel: J. C. Krieger, 1836.

Neuser, W. H. "Dogma und Bekenntnis in der Reformation: Von Zwingli und Calvin bis zur Synode von Westminster" in Carl Andresen ed. in association with Gustav Adolf Benrath, *Handbuch der Dogmen- und Theologiegeschichte.* vol. 2, 2nd edition, Göttingen: Vandenhoeck & Ruprecht, 1998, 225-38.

Oberman, Heiko A. et al. eds. *Reformiertes Erbe. Festschrift für Gottfried W. Locher zu seinem 80. Geburtstag.* 2 vols Zurich: TVZ, 1992.

————. *Luther, Man Between God and the Devil,* Eileen Wallizer Schwarzbart trans. London: Fontana Press, 1993.

Opitz, Peter. "Hebräisch-biblische Züge im promissio-Verständnis Heinrich Bullingers" in S. Lekebusch/H.-G. Ulrichs eds. *Historische Horizonte.* Emder Beiträge zum reformierten Protestantismus 5; Wuppertal: Foedus, 2002, 105-17.

Ozment, Steven. *When Fathers Ruled: Family Life in Reformation Europe.* Cambridge: Harvard Univ. Press, 1983.

Pestalozzi, Carl. *Heinrich Bullinger: Leben und ausgewählte Schriften. Nach handschriftlichen und gleichzeitigen Quellen.* Leben und ausgewählte Schriften der Väter und Begründer der reformierten Kirche V; Elberfeld: Friderichs, 1858.

Pfarr, Kristina. *Die Neue Zeitung. Empirische Untersuchung eines Informationsmediums der frühen Neuzeit unter besonderer Berücksichtigung von Gewaltdarstellungen.* Diss. phil. Mainz: 1994.

Pfeiffer, Charles William. *Heinrich Bullinger and Marriage.* Ph.D. Diss., St. Louis University: 1981.

Pfister, Rudolf. "Zu Bullingers Beurteilung des Konzils von Trient" in Ulrich Gäbler/Erland Herkenrath eds. *Heinrich Bullinger 1504-1575. Gesammelte Aufsätze zum 400. Todestag.* vol. 1: *Leben und Werk.* ZBRG 7; Zurich: TVZ, 1975, 123-40.

Priebsch, Robert. *Deutsche Handschriften in England.* 2 vols, Erlangen: 1901, rpt Hildesheim, New York: Olms, 1979.

Rich, Arthur. "Zwingli als sozialpolitischer Denker," *Zwingliana* 13 (1969): 67-89.

Romer, Hermann. *Herrschaft, Reislauf und Verbotspolitik. Beobachtungen zum rechtlichen Alltag der Zürcher Solddienstbekämpfung im 16. Jahrhundert.* Zurich: Schulthess, 1995.

Roper, Lyndal. *The Holy Household: Woman and Morals in Reformation Augsburg.* Oxford: Clarendon Press, 1989.

Rordorf, W. "Lactanz als Vorbild Bullingers" in Ulrich Gäbler/Endre Zsindely eds. *Bullinger-Tagung 1975. Vorträge, gehalten aus Anlass von Heinrich Bullingers 400. Todestag.* Zurich: TVZ, 1977, 33-42.

Rorem, Paul, *Bullinger and Calvin on the Lord's Supper.* Nottingham: Grove Books, 1989.

Roth, Paul. *Die neuen Zeitungen in Deutschland im 15. und 16. Jahrhundert.* Preisschriften, gekrönt und hg. von der Fürstlich Jablonowskischen Gesellschaft zu Leipzig 43; Leipzig: 1914, rpt Leipzig: Zentral Antiquariat der DDR, 1963.

Rotondò, A. "Esuli italiani in Valtellina nel Cinquecento," *Rivista storica italiana* 88 (1976): 756-91.

Roussel, Bernard. "La Bible de 1530 à 1600" in Guy Bedouelle/Bernard Roussel eds. *Le temps des Réformes et la Bible.* Bible de tous les temps 5; Paris: Beauchesne, 1989, 125-289.

Rudolf, Friedrich. "Der Briefwechsel zwischen Heinrich Bullinger und vier Zürcher Studenten in der Fremde, 1540/42," *Zürcher Taschenbuch.* new series 63 (1943): 51-66.

Rüetschi, Kurt [Jakob]. "Bullinger als Schulchronist" in Ulrich Gäbler/Erland Herkenrath eds. *Heinrich Bullinger 1504-1575. Gesammelte Aufsätze zum 400. Todestag.* vol. 1: *Leben und Werk.* ZBRG 7; Zurich: TVZ, 1975, 305-22.

Rusterholz, Peter. "Fastnachtsspiel und Reformation. Die Metamorphosen des Fastnachtsspiels im Widerstreit der Disziplinen" in *Gemeinde, Reformation und Widerstand. Festschrift für Peter Blickle zum 60. Geburtstag.* Heinrich Schmidt et. al. eds. Tubingen: Bibliotheca Academica Verlag, 1998, 243-60.

Safley, Thomas Max. *Let No Man Put Asunder. The Control of Marriage in the German Southwest: A Comparative Study, 1550-1600*. Kirksville: The Sixteenth Century Journal Publishers, 1984.

Sanders, Paul, "Heinrich Bullinger et le 'zwinglianisme tardif' aux lendemains du 'Consensus Tigurinus'" in Heiko A. Oberman et al. eds. *Das Reformierte Erbe. Festschrift für Gottfried W. Locher.* 2 vols Zurich: TVZ, 1992, I:307-23.

Schelbert, Leo. "Jacob Grebel's Trial Revisited," *Archiv für Reformationsgeschichte* 60 (1969): 32-64.

Scherrer, Eduard. "Der Brand des Grossmünster-Glockenturms in Zürich am 7. Mai 1572," *Neue Zürcher Zeitung*, 21 March 1937, no 513.

Schiess, Traugott. "Der Briefwechsel Heinrich Bullingers," *Zwingliana* 5 (1933): 396-408.

―――. "Ein Jahr aus Bullingers Briefwechsel [1559]," *Zwingliana* 6 (1934): 16-33.

Schindler, Alfred. "Kirchenväter und andere alte Autoritäten in Bullingers 'Der Christlich Eestand' von 1540" in Hans Ulrich Bächtold ed. *Von Cyprian zur Walzenprägung: Streiflichter auf Zürcher Geist und Kultur der Bullingerzeit.* Studien und Texte zur Bullingerzeit 2; Zug: Achius, 2001.

Schlosser, Marianne. *Lucerna in caliginoso loco. Aspekte des Prophetie-Begriffes in der scholastischen Theologie.* Veröffentlichung des Grabmann-Institutes, new series 43; Paderborn: Schöningh, 2000.

Schnyder, Rudolf. "Aus der Arbeit am Bullinger-Briefwechsel. Zur Geschichte und Bedeutung der Edition," *Zwingliana* 18 (1990/91): 329-31.

Schola Tigurina. Die Zürcher Hohe Schule und ihre Gelehrten um 1550. Katalog zur Ausstellung vom 25. Mai bis 10. Juni 1999 in der Zentralbibliothek Zürich Institut für Schweizerische Reformationsgeschichte ed. Zurich: Pano, 1999.

Schützeichel, Heribert. *Katholische Calvin-Studien.* Trier: Paulinus-Verlag, 1980.

Selderhuis, H. J. *Marriage and Divorce in the Thought of Martin Bucer.* John Vriend and Lyle D. Bierma trans., Kirksville: Thomas Jefferson Univ. Press, 1999.

Senn, Matthias. *Johann Jakob Wick (1522-1588) und seine Sammlung von Nachrichten zur Zeitgeschichte.* Mitteilungen der Antiquarischen Gesellschaft in Zürich 46/2; Zurich: Leemann, 1974.

Spillmann, Kurt. "Zwingli und die Zürcher Schulverhältnisse," *Zwingliana* 11/7 (1962): 427-48.

Staedtke, Joachim ed. *Glauben und Bekennen. 400 Jahre Confessio Helvetica Posterior. Beiträge zu ihrer Geschichte und Theologie.* Zurich: Zwingli Verlag, 1966.

―――. "Die Geschichtsauffassung des jungen Bullinger" in Ulrich Gäbler/Erland Herkenrath eds. *Heinrich Bullinger 1504-1575. Gesammelte Aufsätze zum 400. Todestag.* vol. 1: *Leben und Werk.* ZBRG 7; Zurich: TVZ, 1975, 65-74.

―――. *Die Theologie des jungen Bullinger.* Studien zur Dogmengeschichte und systematischen Theologie 16; Zurich: Zwingli Verlag, 1962.

Steinhausen-Kassel, Georg. "Die Entstehung der Zeitung aus dem brieflichen Verkehr," *Archiv für Buchgewerbe und Gebrauchsgraphik* 65 (1928): 51-64.

Stephens, W. P. "Bullinger's Sermons on the Apocalypse" in Alfred Schindler/Hans Stickelberger eds. *Die Zürcher Reformation: Ausstrahlungen und Rückwirkungen. Wissenschaftliche Tagung zum hundertjährigen Bestehen des Zwinglivereins 1997.* ZBRG 18; Berne: Peter Lang, 2001, 261-80.

Strasser, O. E. "Der Consensus Tigurinus," *Zwingliana* 9 (1949): 1-16.

Strübind, Andrea. *Eifriger als Zwingli. Die frühe Täuferbewegung in der Schweiz.* Berlin: Duncker und Humblot, 2003.

Stucki, Heinzpeter. "Bullinger, der Zürcher Rat und die Auseinandersetzung um das Alumnat 1538-1542" in Ulrich Gäbler/Erland Herkenrath eds. *Heinrich Bullinger 1504-1575. Gesammelte Aufsätze zum 400. Todestag.* vol. 1: *Leben und Werk.* ZBRG 7; Zurich: TVZ, 1975, 291-303.

Taplin, Mark. *The Italian Reformers and the Zurich Church c. 1540-1620.* Aldershot: Ashgate, 2003.

Todd, Margo. *Christian Humanism and the Puritan Social Order.* Cambridge: CUP, 1987.

Trechsel, F. *Die Protestantischen Antitrinitarier vor Faustus Socin.* 2 vols Heidelberg: Universitätsbuchhandlung von Karl Winter, 1839/44.

Tylenda, J. N. "The Warning that went unheeded: John Calvin on Giorgio Biandrata," *Calvin Theological Journal* 12 (1977): 24-62.

Venema, C. P. *Heinrich Bullinger and the Doctrine of Predestination.* Grand Rapids, Mich.: Baker Press, 2002.

Völker-Rasor, Anette. *Bilderpaare-Paarbilder, Die Ehe in Autobiographien des 16. Jahrhunderts.* Freiburg i. Br.: Rombach Verlag, 1993.

Walser, Peter. *Die Prädestination bei Heinrich Bullinger im Zusammenhang mit seiner Gotteslehre.* Zurich: Zwingli Verlag, 1957.

Walton, Robert. "Heinrich Bullinger, Repräsentant der reichen Bauern und seine Beziehungen zur städtischen Obrigkeit" in Siegfried Hoyer ed. *Reform, Reformation, Revolution.* Leipzig: Karl-Marx-Universität, 1980, 132-42.

Weber, Alfred. *Heinrich Bullingers "Christlicher Ehestand," seine zeitgenössischen Quellen und die Anfänge des Familienbuches in England.* Engelsdorf/Leipzig: Vogel, 1929.

Weir, David. *The Origins of Federal Theology in Sixteenth Century Reformation Thought.* New York: OUP, 1990.

Weisz, Leo. *Die Bullinger Zeitungen. Zur Halbjahrhundertfeier des Vereins der schweizerischen Presse dargebracht vom Journalistischen Seminar der Universität Zürich und von der Buchdruckerei Berichthaus in Zürich.* Zurich: Berichthaus, 1933.

―――. "Quellen zur Reformationsgeschichte des Großmünsters in Zürich, 2nd part," *Zwingliana* 7/3 (1940): 172-202.

―――. *Der Zürcher Nachrichtenverkehr vor 1780.* Neue Zürcher Zeitung, Zurich: 1955.

Williams, G. H. *The Radical Reformation.* 3rd ed., Kirksville, Mo.: Sixteenth Century Journal Publishers, 1992.

―――. "Strains in the Christology of the Emerging Polish Brethren" in Samuel Fiszman ed. *The Polish Reformation in its European Context.* Bloomington: Indiana U.P. 1984, 61-95.

Wirz, Hans Georg. "Familienschicksale im Zeitalter Zwinglis," *Zwingliana* 6 (1934-8): 194-222, 242-71, 470-99.

———. "Heinrich Bullingers erste Schweizerchronik" in: *Nova Turicensia: Beiträge zur schweizerischen und zürcherischen Geschichte*. Zurich: Höhr, 1911, 235-90.

Zsindely, Endre. "Bullinger und Ungarn" in Ulrich Gäbler/Erland Herkenrath eds. *Heinrich Bullinger 1504-1575: Gesammelte Aufsätze zum 400. Todestag.* vol. 2: *Beziehungen und Wirkungen.* ZBRG 8; Zurich: TVZ, 1975, 361-82.

Zürcher, Christoph. *Konrad Pellikans Wirken in Zürich 1526-1556.* ZBRG 4; Zurich: TVZ, 1975.

Index